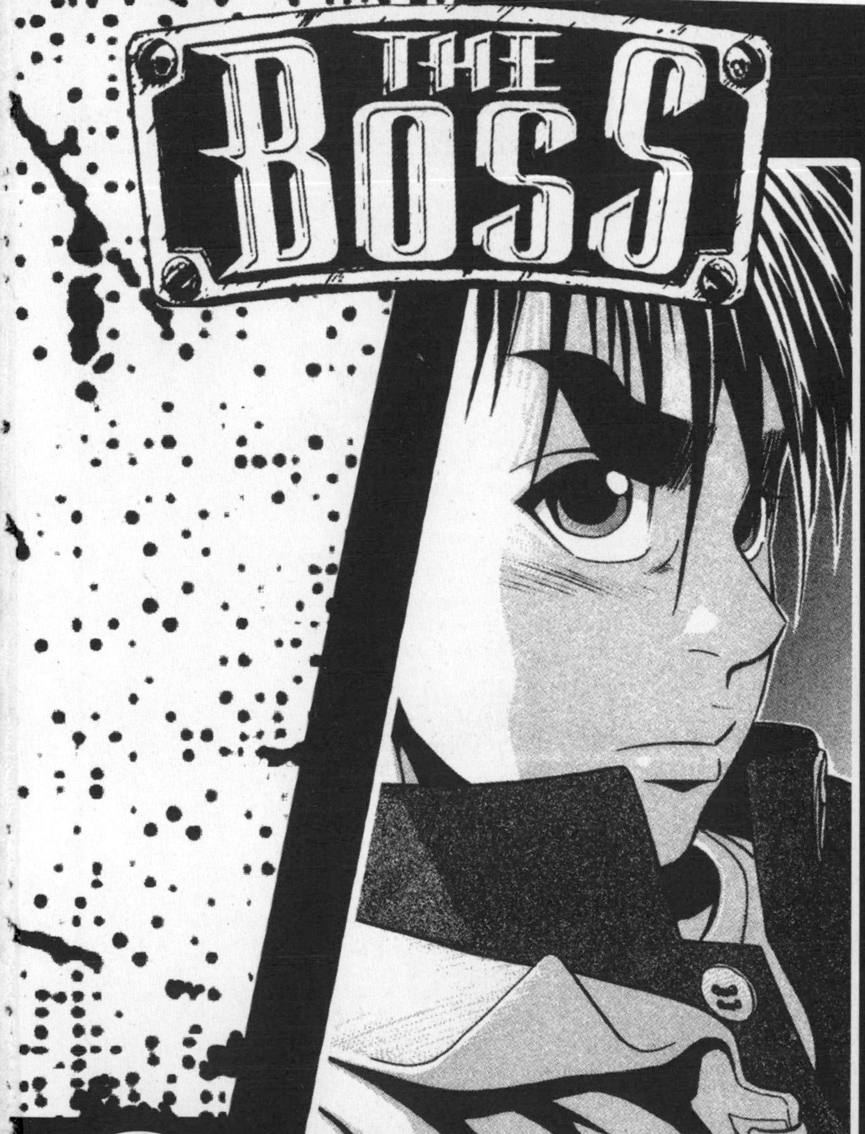
THE BOSS

www.adv-manga.com

The Boss Volume Two

© 1996 Lim Jae-Won, DAIWON C.I., Inc.
All Rights Reserved.
First published in Korea in 1996 by DAIWON C.I. Inc.
English translation rights in USA, Canada, UK, IRIE, NZ and Australia
arranged by DAIWON C.I., Inc.

Translator **TRISHA EGGLESTON**
Lead Translator/Translation Supervisor **JAVIER LOPEZ**
ADV Manga Translation Staff **JASON AN AND SIMON JUNG**

Print Production/ Art Studio Manager **LISA PUCKETT**
Pre-press Manager **KLYS REEDYK**
Art Production Manager **RYAN MASON**
Sr. Designer/Creative Manager **JORGE ALVARADO**
Graphic Designer/Group Leader **SHANNON RASBERRY**
Graphic Designer **HEATHER GARY**
Graphic Artists **SHANNA JENSCHKE, KERRI KALINEC,
WINDI MARTIN AND GEORGE REYNOLDS**
Graphic Intern **MARK MEZA**

Publishing Editor **SUSAN ITIN**
Assistant Editor **MARGARET SCHAROLD**
Editorial Assistant **VARSHA BHUCHAR**
Proofreaders **SHERIDAN JACOBS AND STEVEN REED**

Research/ Traffic Coordinator **MARSHA ARNOLD**

Executive VP, CFO, COO **KEVIN CORCORAN**

President, CEO & Publisher **JOHN LEDFORD**

Email: editor@adv-manga.com
www.adv-manga.com
www.advfilms.com

For sales and distribution inquiries please call 1.800.282.7202

™ is a division of A.D. Vision, Inc.

10114 W. Sam Houston Parkway, Suite 200, Houston, Texas 77099

English text © 2004 published by A.D. Vision, Inc. under exclusive license.
ADV MANGA is a trademark of A.D. Vision, Inc.

ISBN: 1-4139-0075-5
First printing, August 2004
10 9 8 7 6 5 4 3 2 1
Printed in Canada

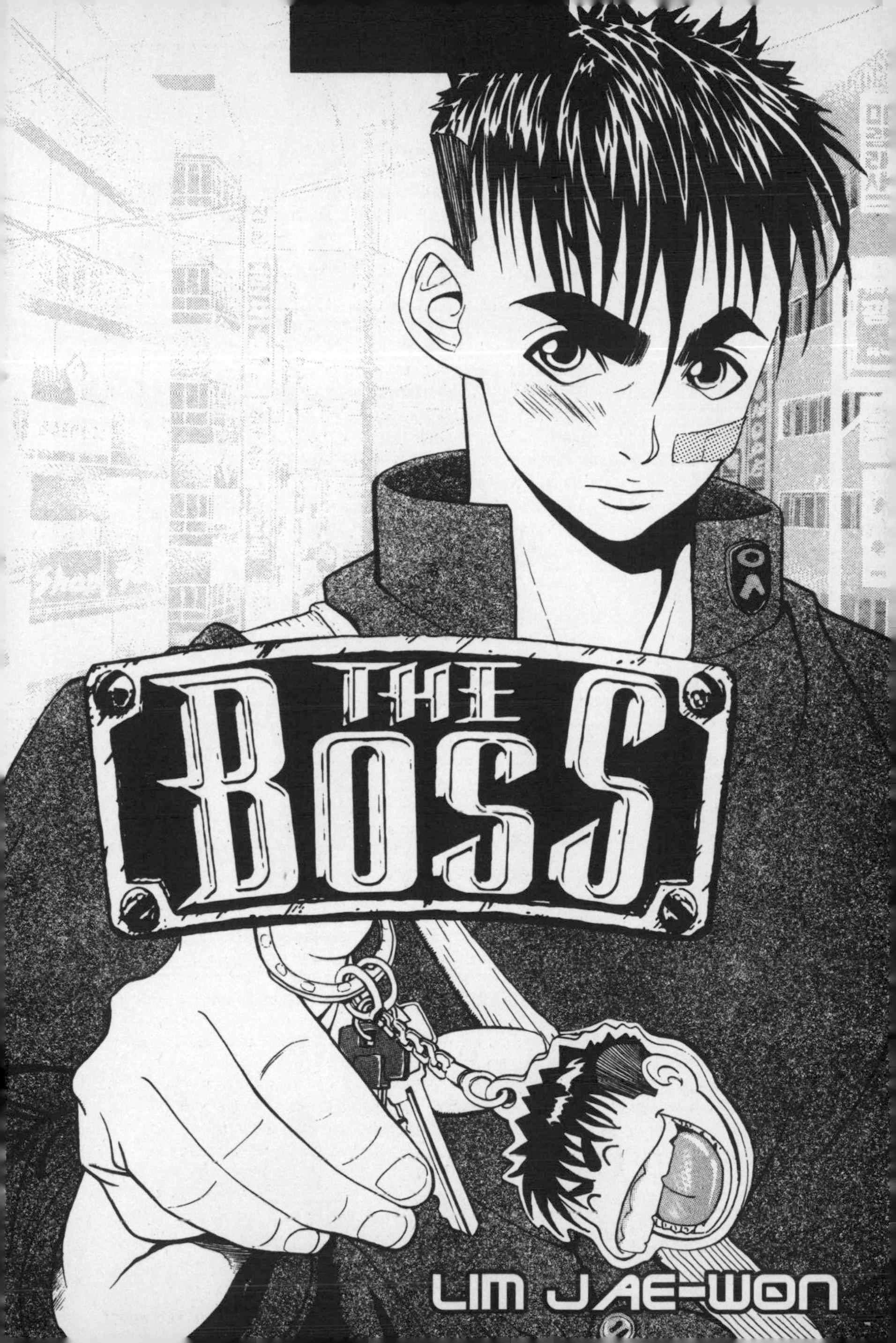
THE BOSS
LIM JAE-WON

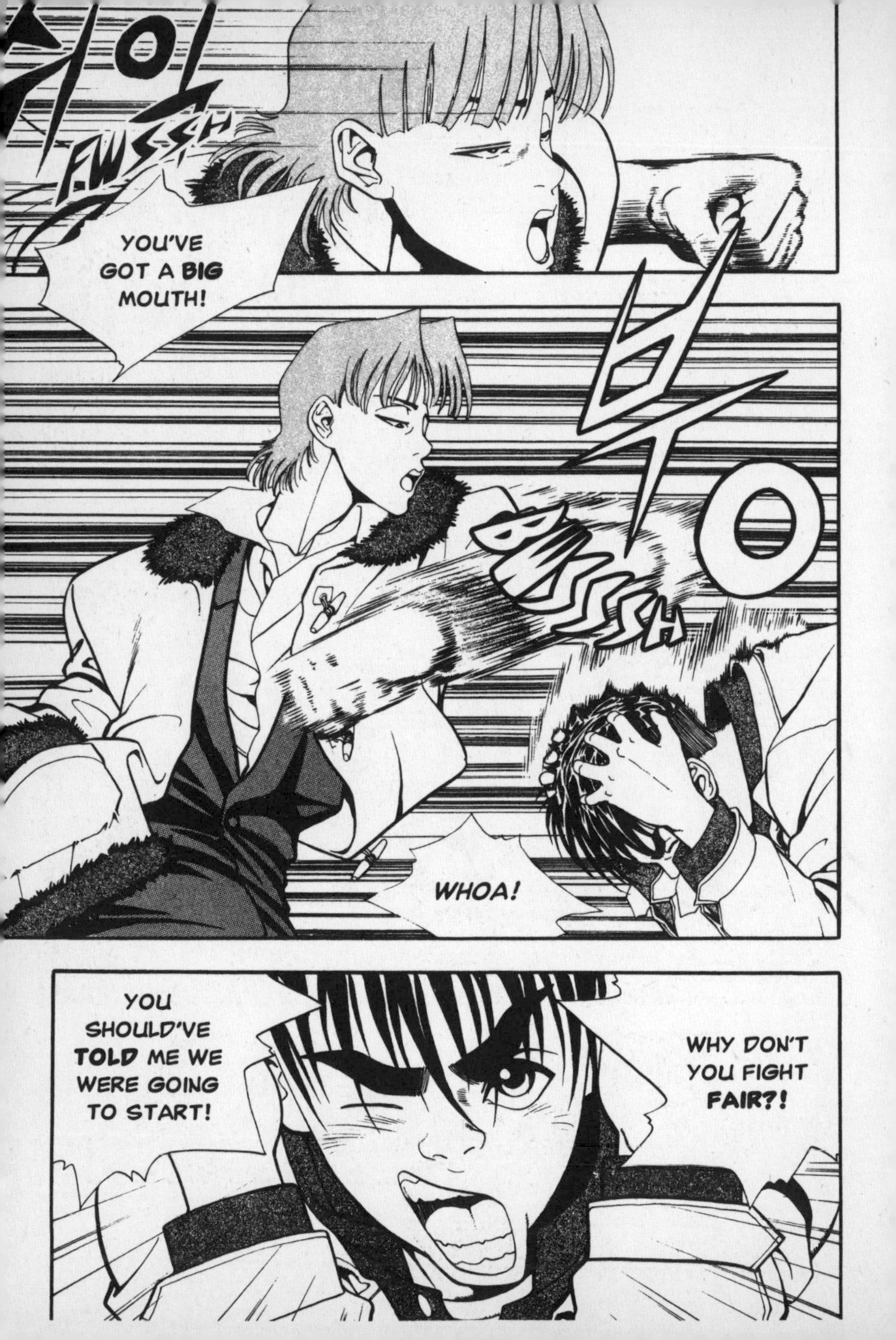
FWUSSH
YOU'VE GOT A BIG MOUTH!
BASH
WHOA!
YOU SHOULD'VE TOLD ME WE WERE GOING TO START!
WHY DON'T YOU FIGHT FAIR?!

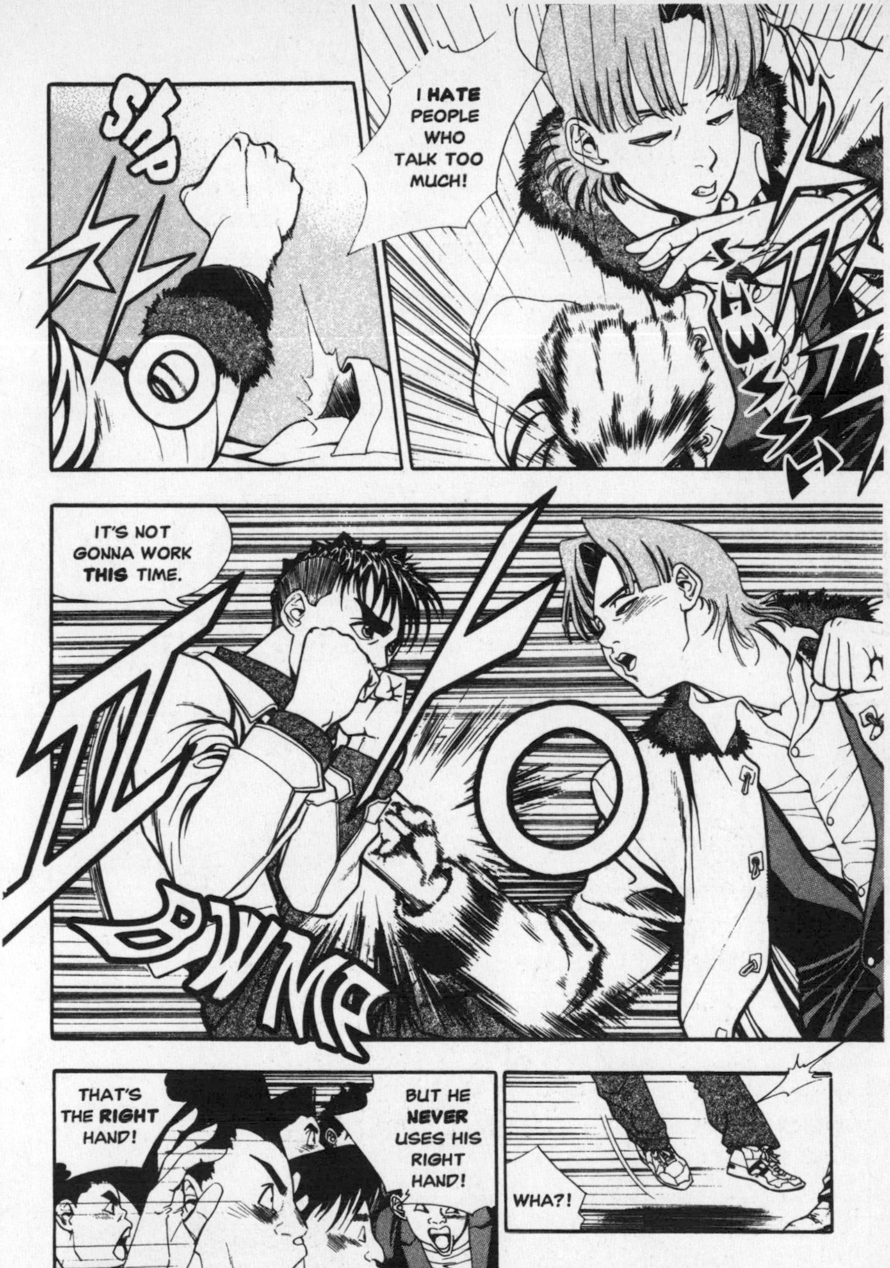
I HATE PEOPLE WHO TALK TOO MUCH!
IT'S NOT GONNA WORK THIS TIME.
THAT'S THE RIGHT HAND!
BUT HE NEVER USES HIS RIGHT HAND!
WHA?!

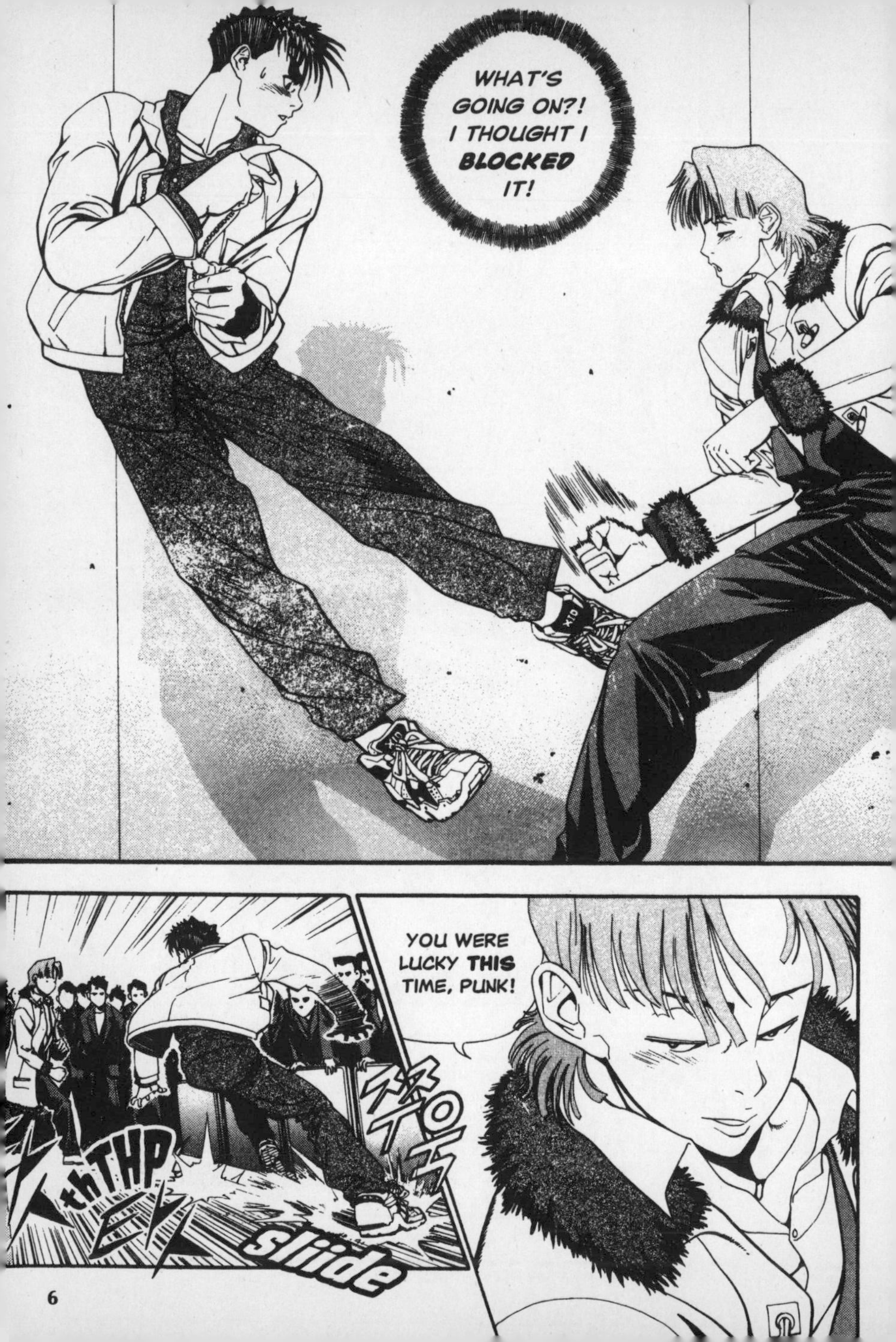
WHAT'S GOING ON?! I THOUGHT I **BLOCKED** IT!
YOU WERE LUCKY **THIS** TIME, PUNK!
thTHP
slide

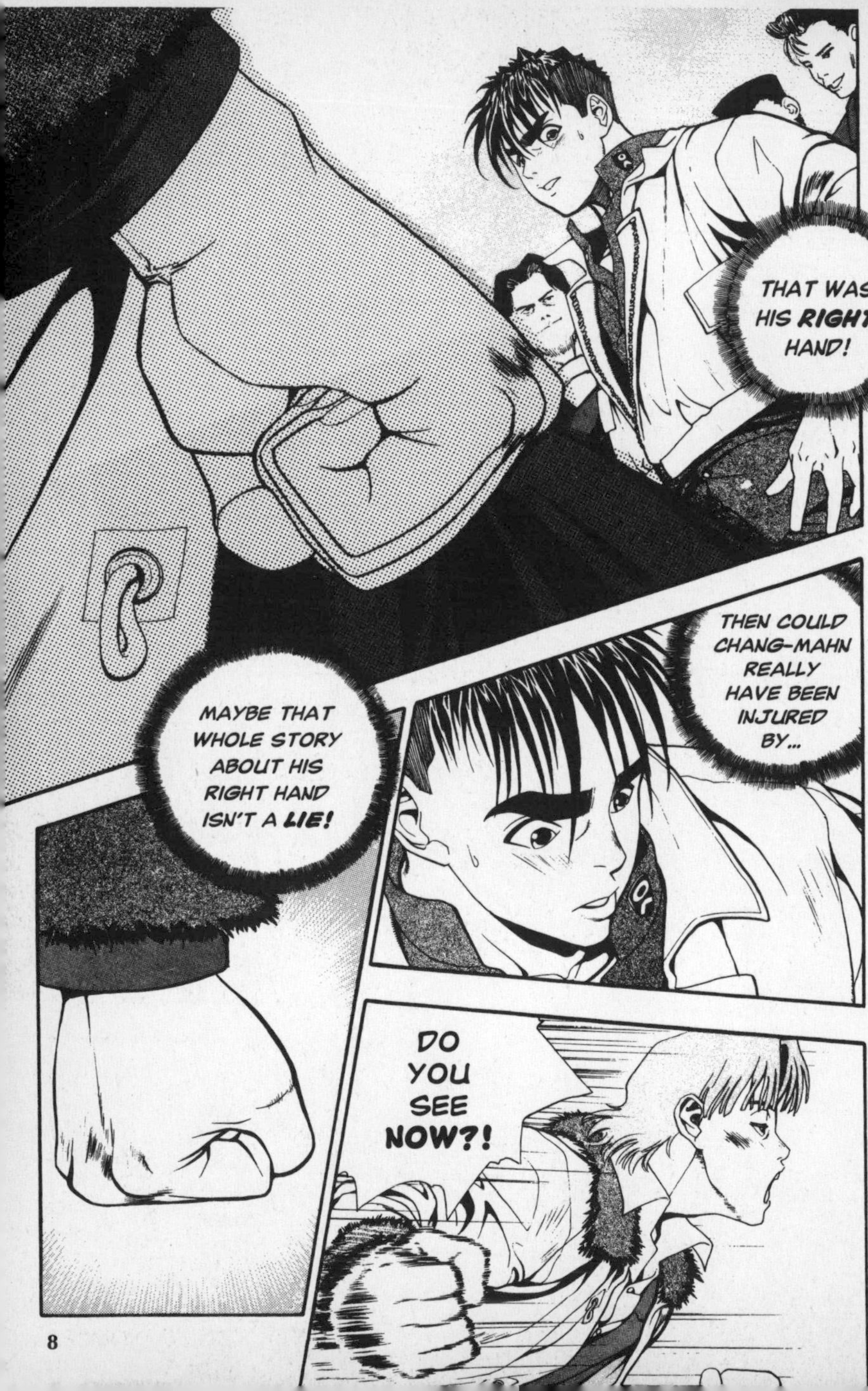
THAT WAS HIS RIGHT HAND!
THEN COULD CHANG-MAHN REALLY HAVE BEEN INJURED BY...
MAYBE THAT WHOLE STORY ABOUT HIS RIGHT HAND ISN'T A LIE!
DO YOU SEE NOW?!

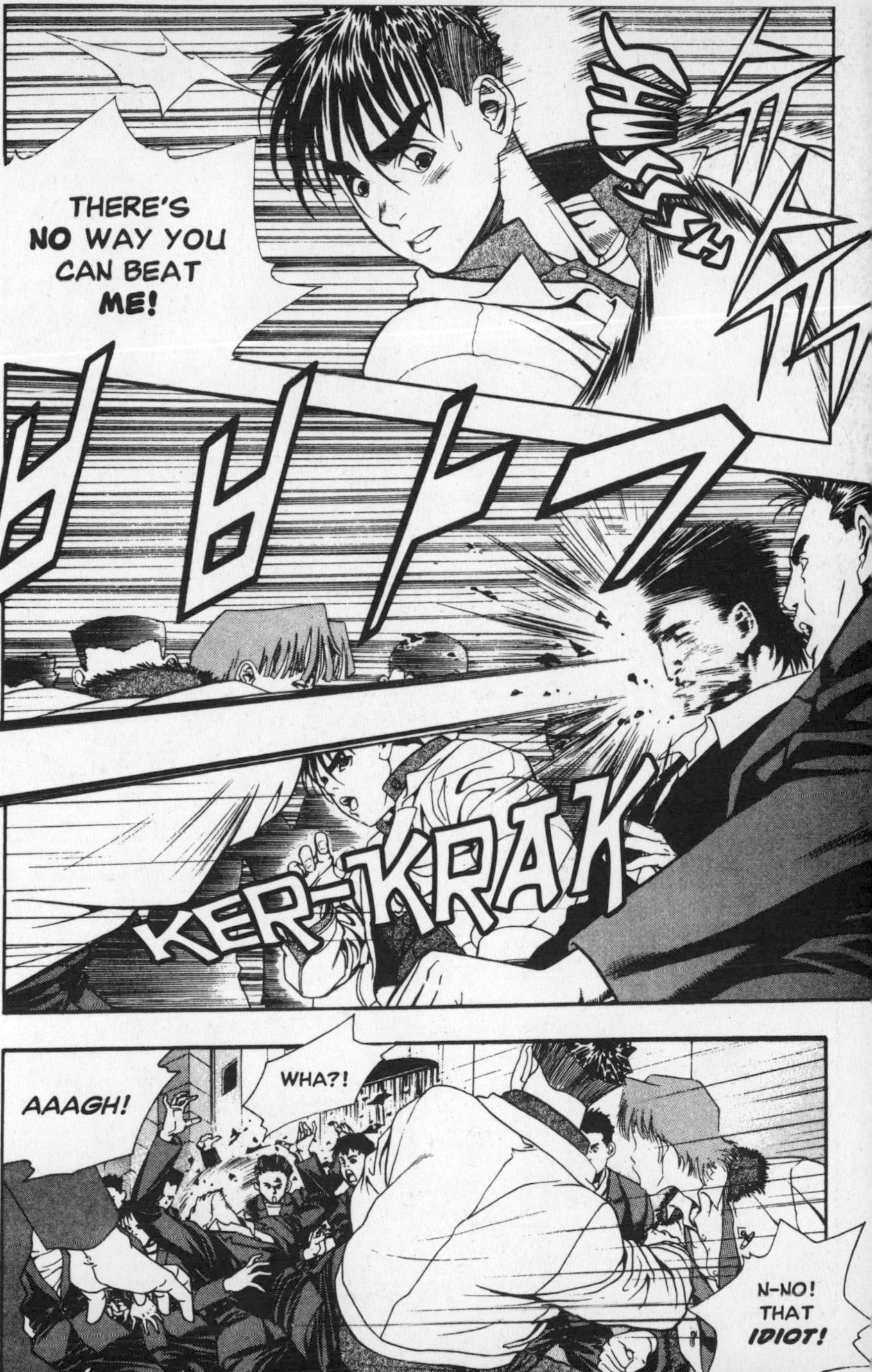
THERE'S NO WAY YOU CAN BEAT ME!
FWISSHH
KER-KRAK
WHA?!
AAAGH!
N-NO! THAT IDIOT!

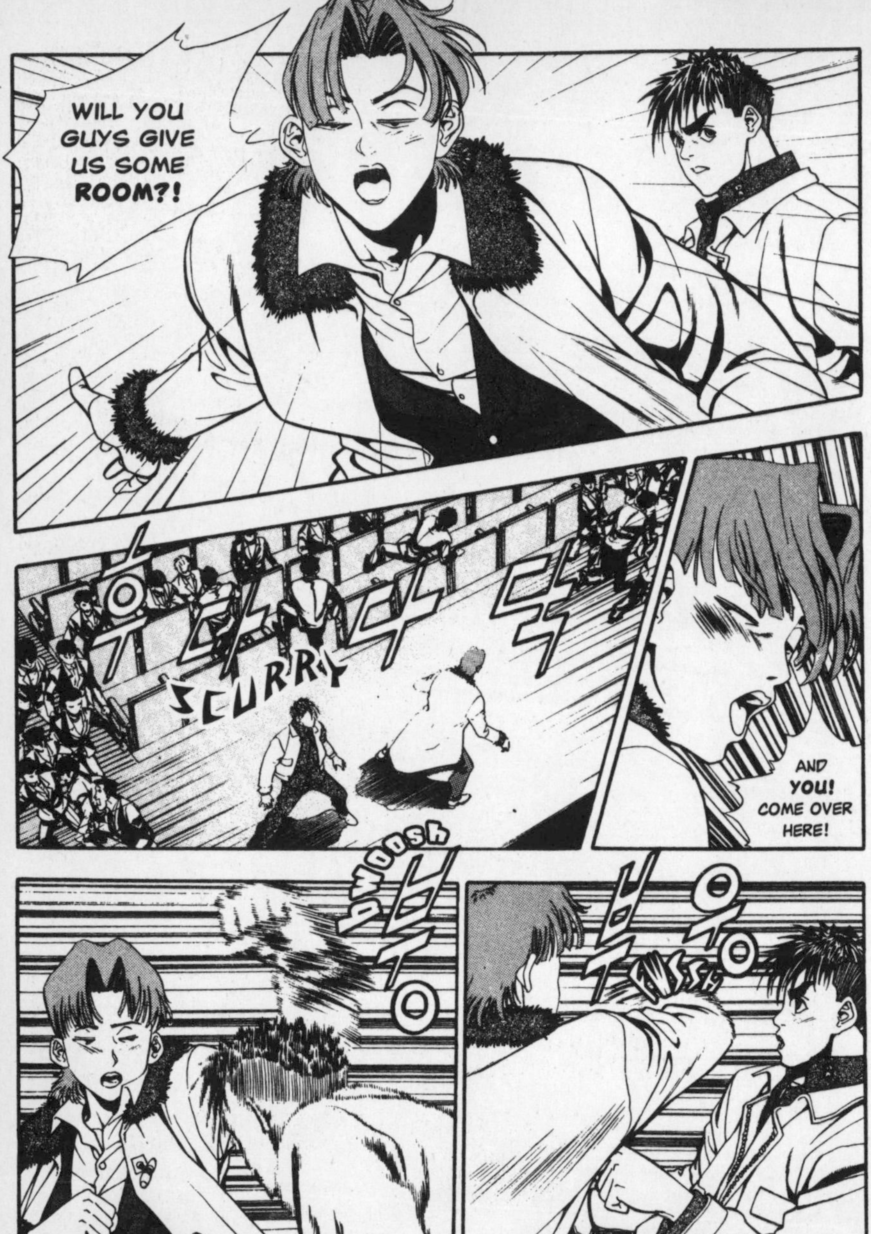
WILL YOU GUYS GIVE US SOME ROOM?!
SCURRY
AND YOU! COME OVER HERE!
bwoosh

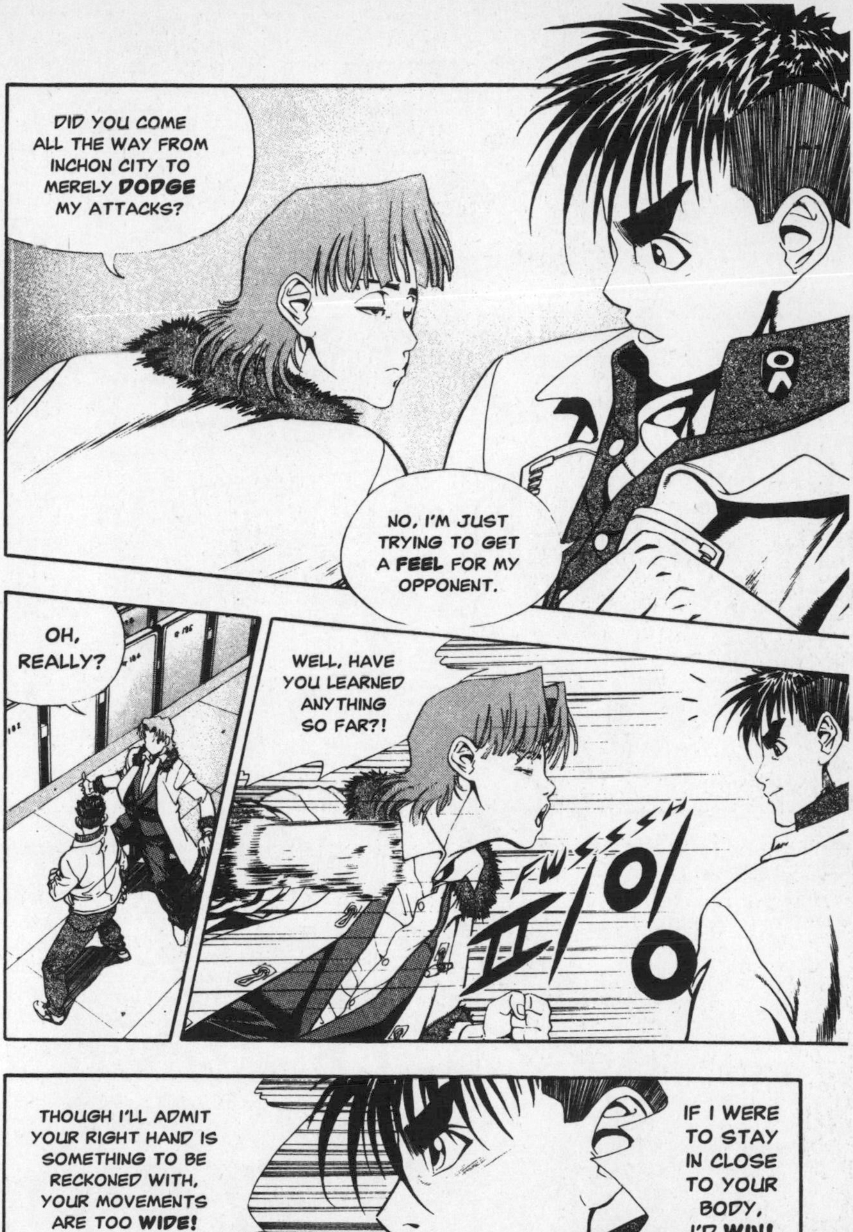
DID YOU COME ALL THE WAY FROM INCHON CITY TO MERELY DODGE MY ATTACKS?
NO, I'M JUST TRYING TO GET A FEEL FOR MY OPPONENT.
OH, REALLY?
WELL, HAVE YOU LEARNED ANYTHING SO FAR?!
FWSSSSH
THOUGH I'LL ADMIT YOUR RIGHT HAND IS SOMETHING TO BE RECKONED WITH, YOUR MOVEMENTS ARE TOO WIDE!
IF I WERE TO STAY IN CLOSE TO YOUR BODY, I'D WIN!

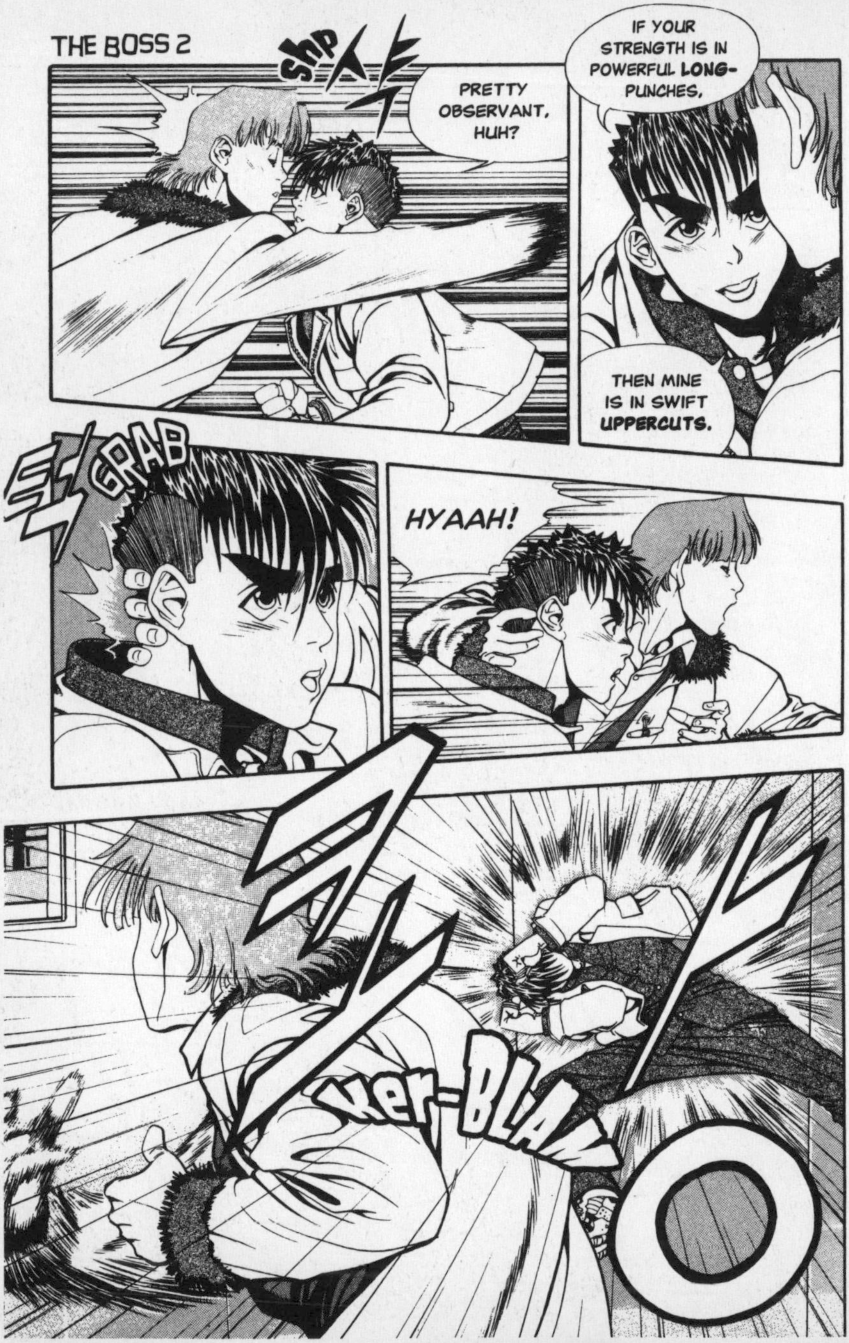
shp
PRETTY OBSERVANT, HUH?
IF YOUR STRENGTH IS IN POWERFUL **LONG-PUNCHES,**
THEN MINE IS IN SWIFT **UPPERCUTS.**
GRAB
HYAAH!
ker-BLA

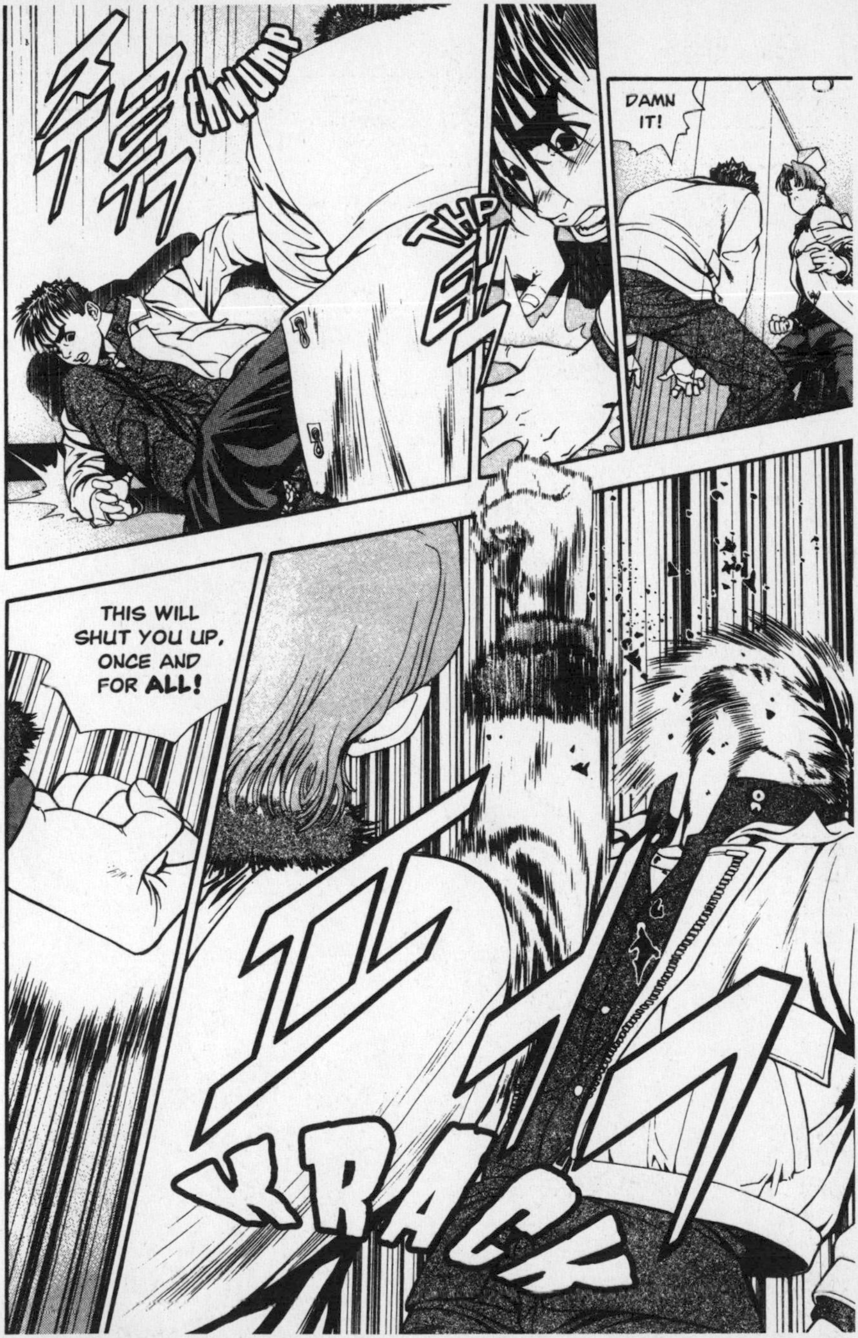
DAMN IT!
THP
thWUMP
THIS WILL SHUT YOU UP, ONCE AND FOR ALL!
KRACK

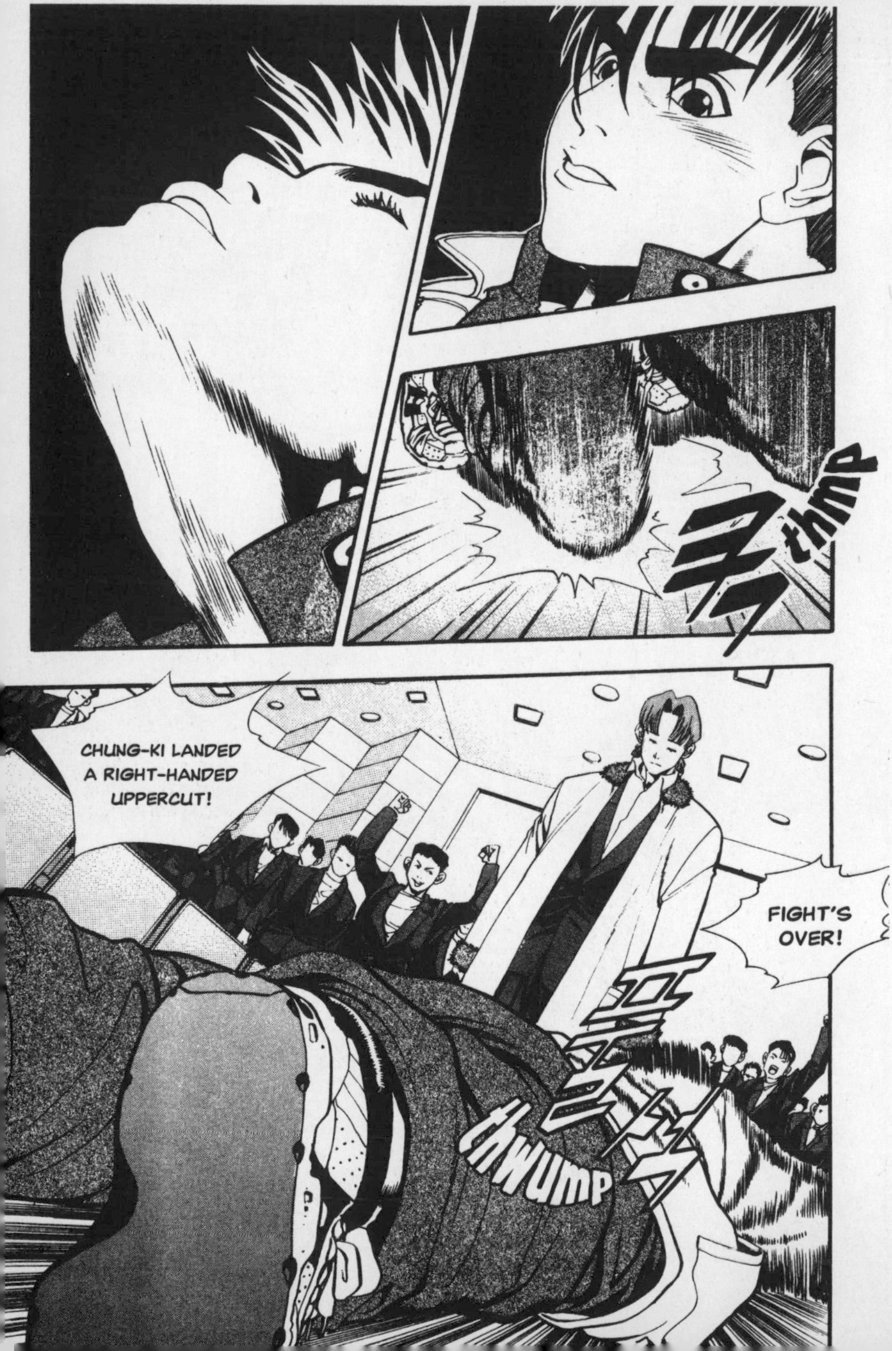
thmp
CHUNG-KI LANDED A RIGHT-HANDED UPPERCUT!
FIGHT'S OVER!
thwump

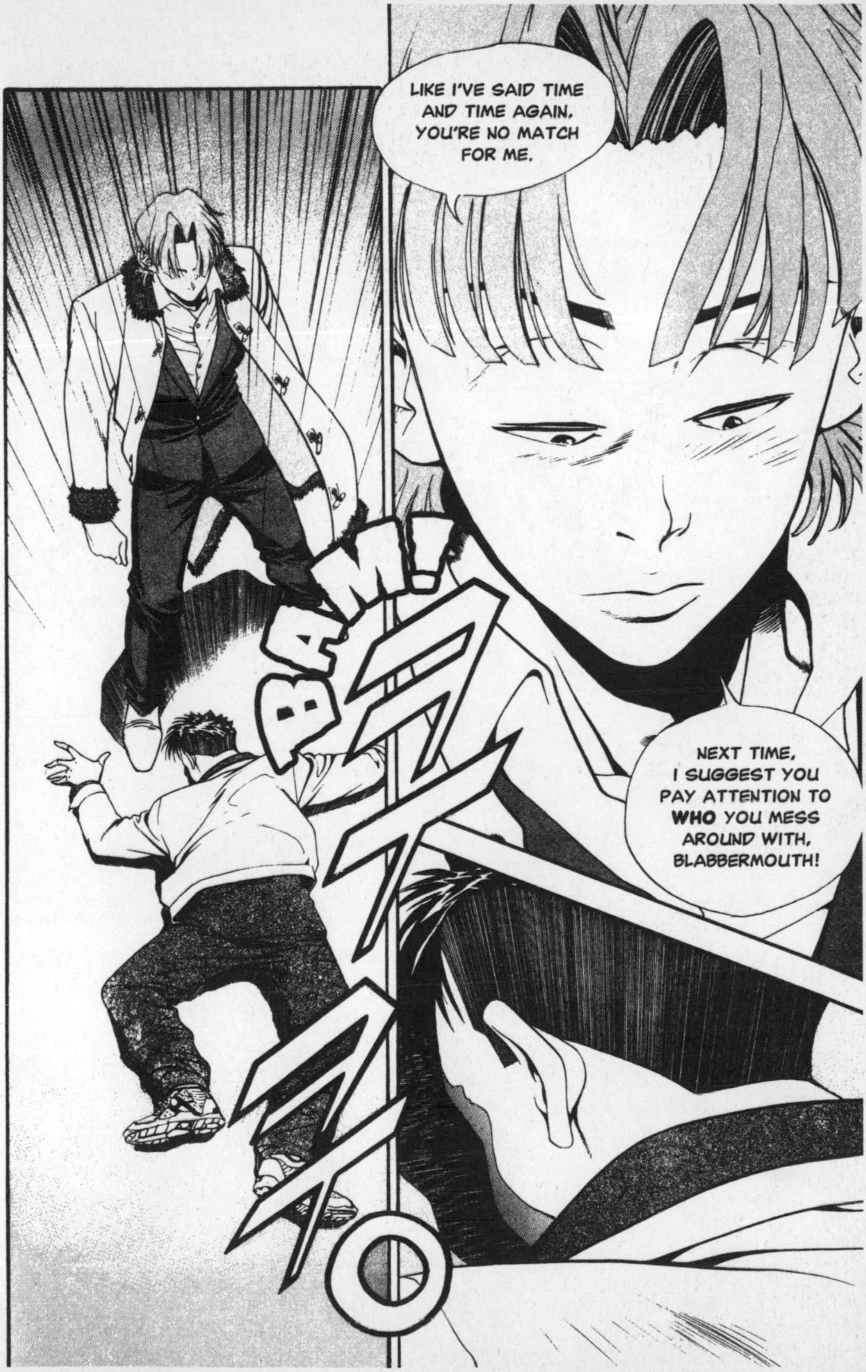
LIKE I'VE SAID TIME AND TIME AGAIN, YOU'RE NO MATCH FOR ME.
BAM!
NEXT TIME, I SUGGEST YOU PAY ATTENTION TO WHO YOU MESS AROUND WITH, BLABBERMOUTH!

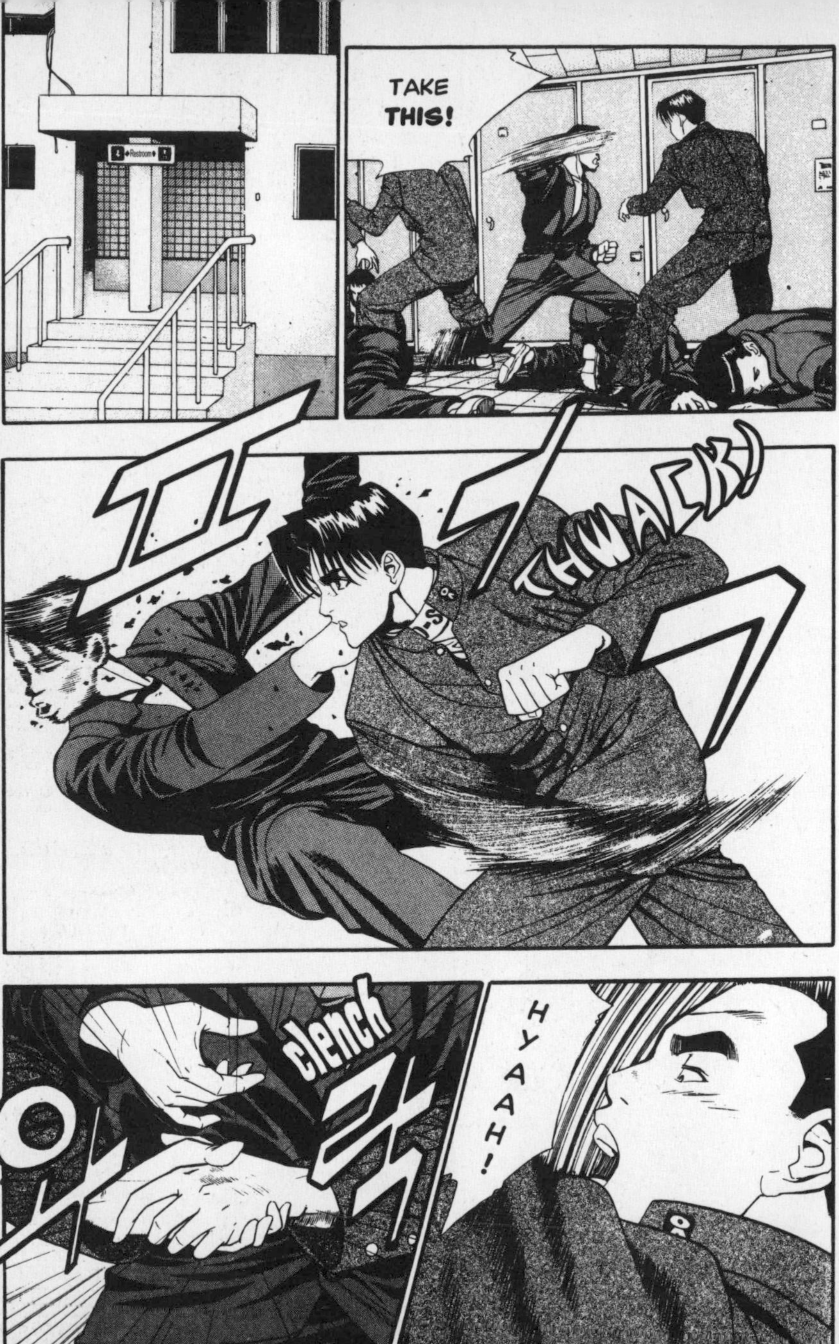
TAKE THIS!
Restroom
THWACK!
HYAAH!
clench

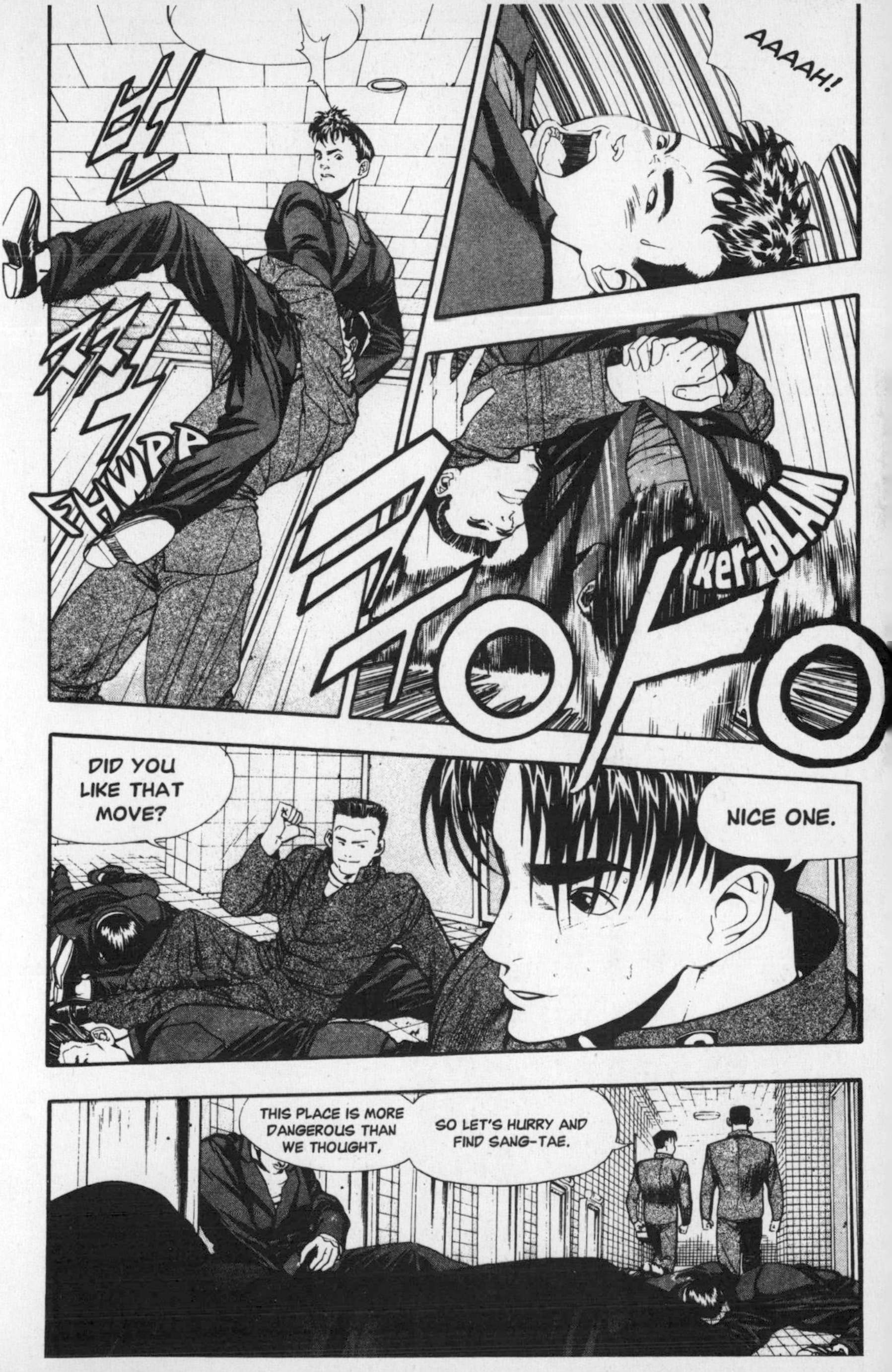
AAAAH!
FHWPP
ker-BLAM
DID YOU LIKE THAT MOVE?
NICE ONE.
THIS PLACE IS MORE DANGEROUS THAN WE THOUGHT,
SO LET'S HURRY AND FIND SANG-TAE.

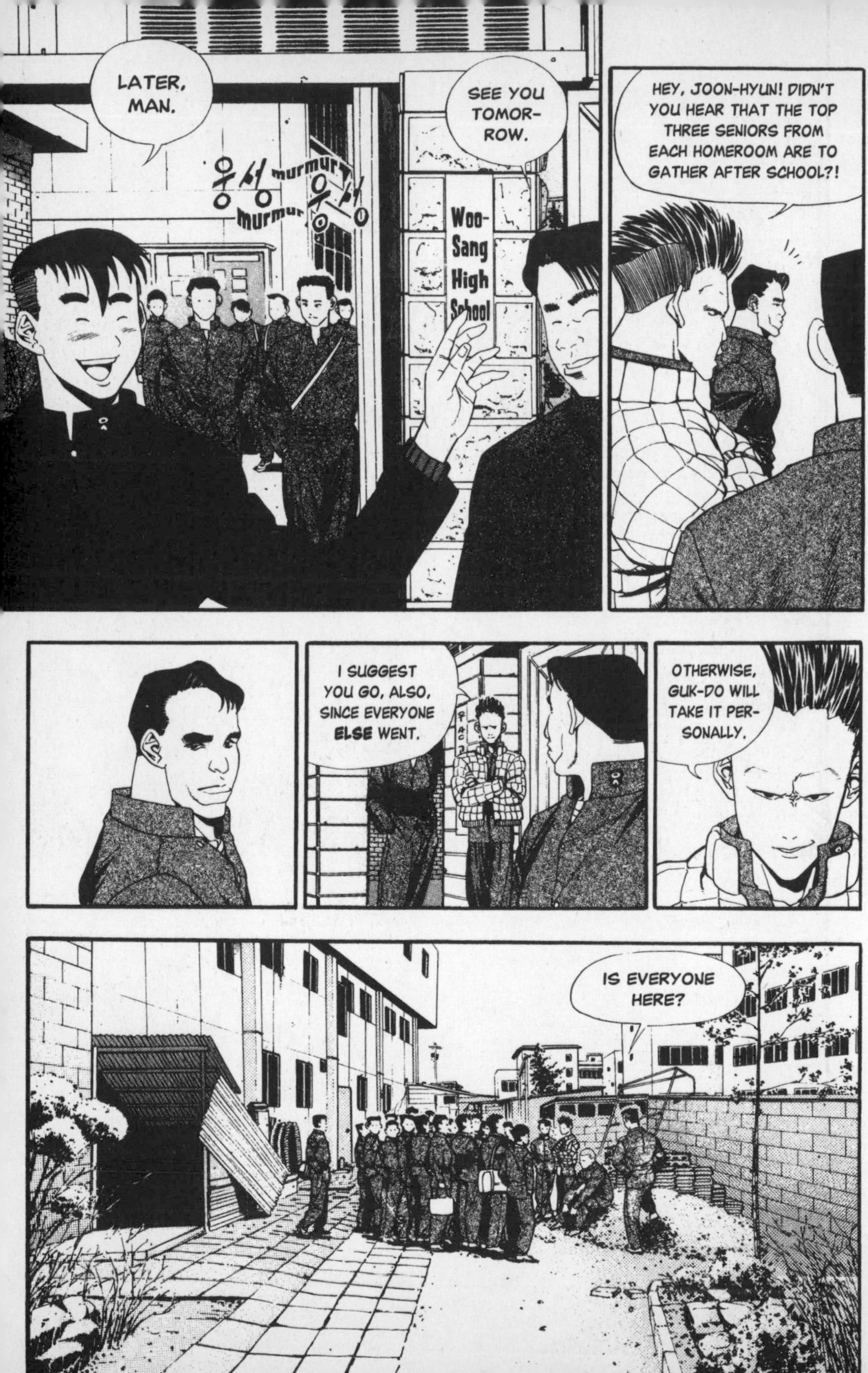
LATER, MAN.
웅성 웅성
murmur murmur
SEE YOU TOMOR-ROW.
Woo-Sang High School
HEY, JOON-HYUN! DIDN'T YOU HEAR THAT THE TOP THREE SENIORS FROM EACH HOMEROOM ARE TO GATHER AFTER SCHOOL?!
I SUGGEST YOU GO, ALSO, SINCE EVERYONE ELSE WENT.
OTHERWISE, GUK-DO WILL TAKE IT PER-SONALLY.
IS EVERYONE HERE?

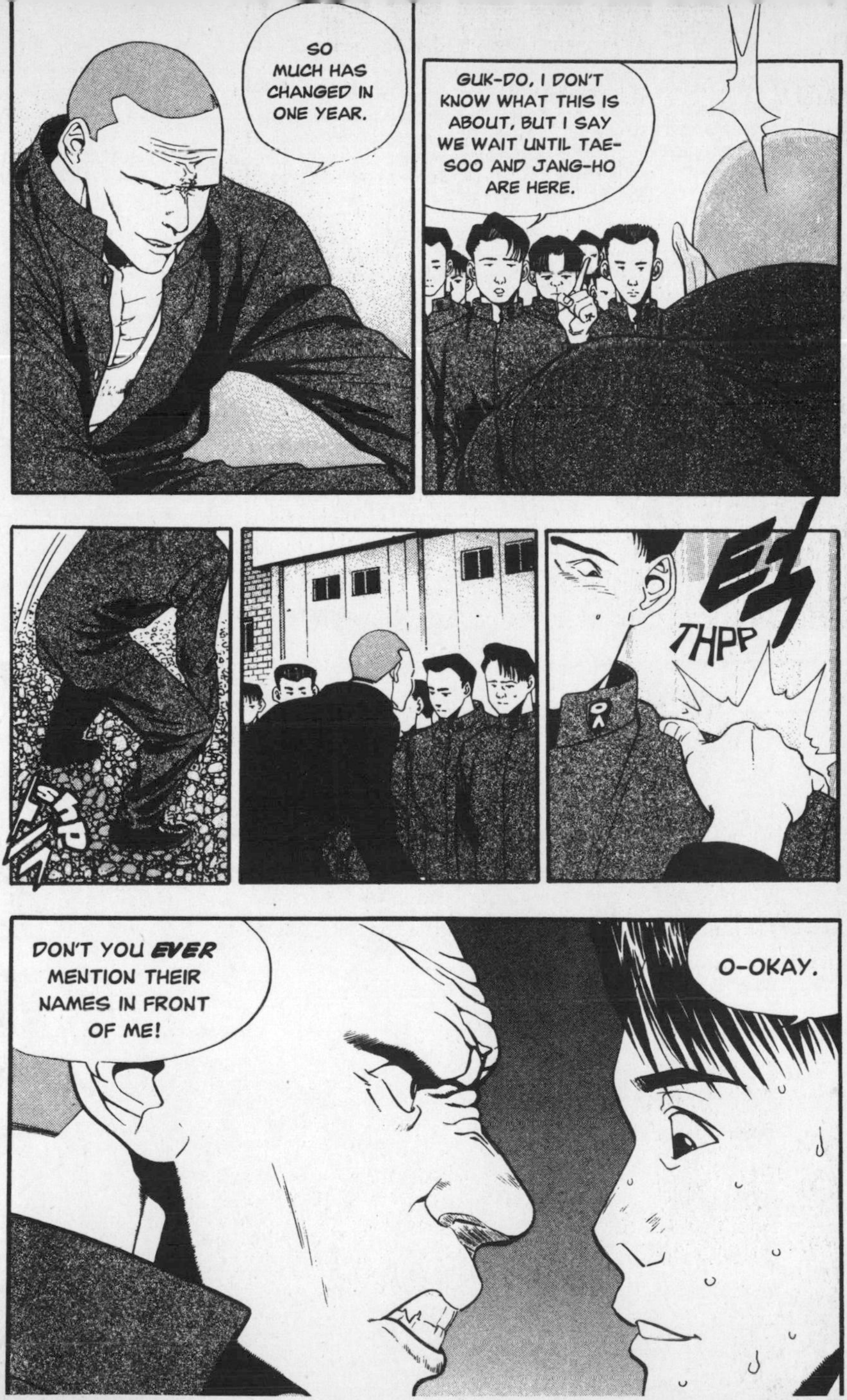
SO MUCH HAS CHANGED IN ONE YEAR.
GUK-DO, I DON'T KNOW WHAT THIS IS ABOUT, BUT I SAY WE WAIT UNTIL TAE-SOO AND JANG-HO ARE HERE.
SHP
THPP
DON'T YOU EVER MENTION THEIR NAMES IN FRONT OF ME!
O-OKAY.

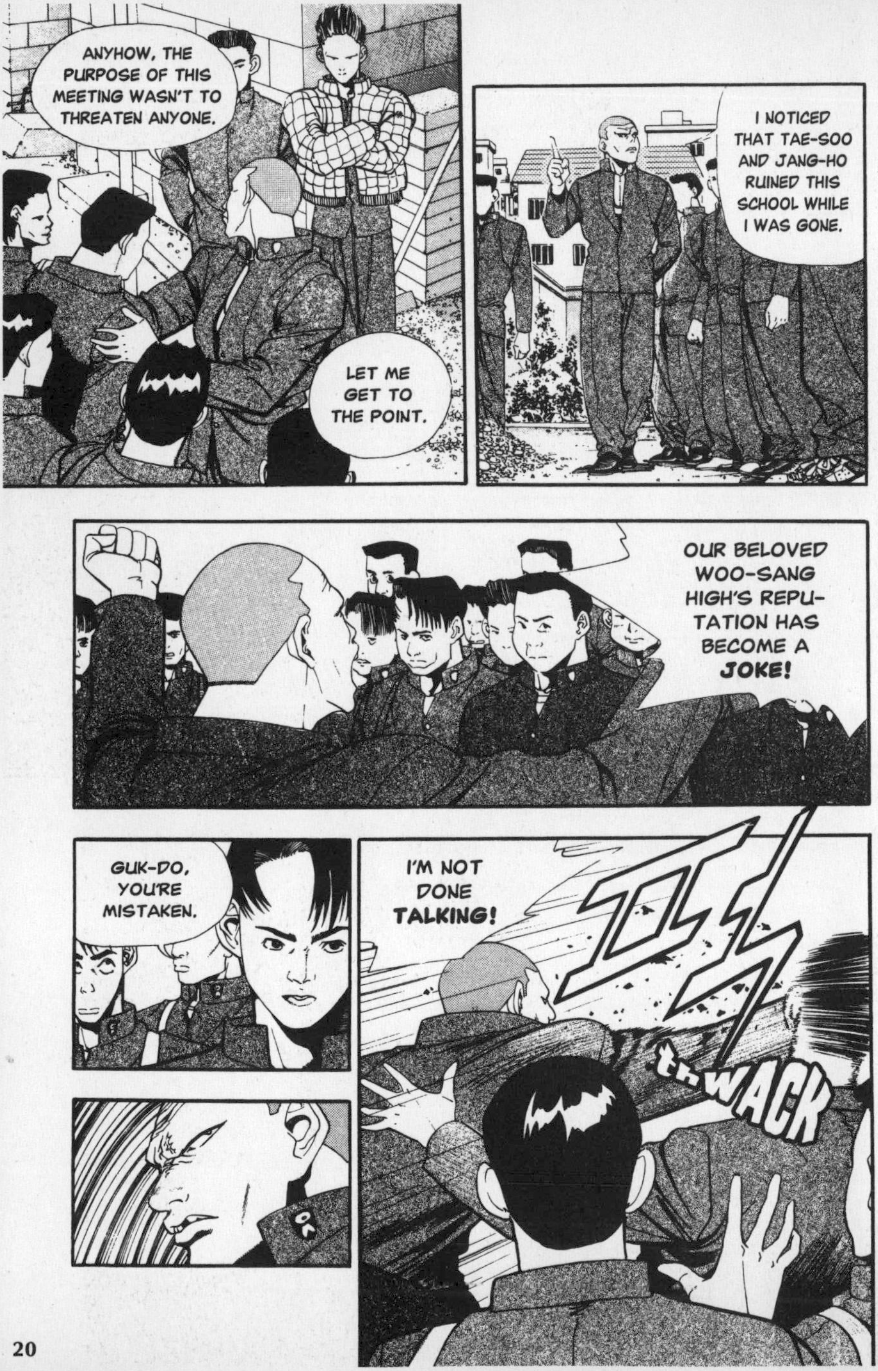
ANYHOW, THE PURPOSE OF THIS MEETING WASN'T TO THREATEN ANYONE.
LET ME GET TO THE POINT.
I NOTICED THAT TAE-SOO AND JANG-HO RUINED THIS SCHOOL WHILE I WAS GONE.
OUR BELOVED WOO-SANG HIGH'S REPUTATION HAS BECOME A JOKE!
GUK-DO, YOU'RE MISTAKEN.
I'M NOT DONE TALKING!
thWACK

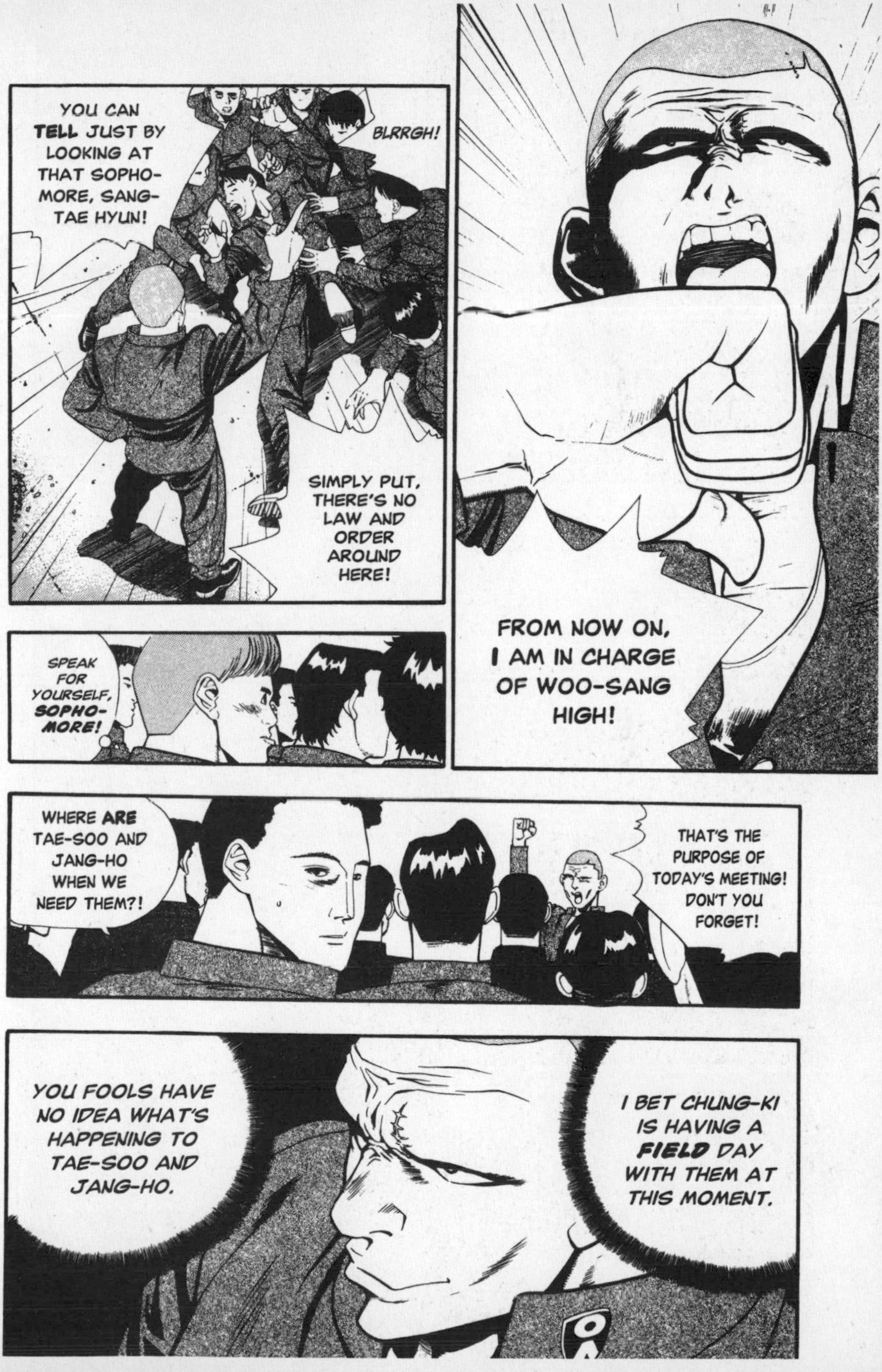
YOU CAN TELL JUST BY LOOKING AT THAT SOPHOMORE, SANG-TAE HYUN!
BLRRGH!
SIMPLY PUT, THERE'S NO LAW AND ORDER AROUND HERE!
FROM NOW ON, I AM IN CHARGE OF WOO-SANG HIGH!
SPEAK FOR YOURSELF, SOPHOMORE!
WHERE ARE TAE-SOO AND JANG-HO WHEN WE NEED THEM?!
THAT'S THE PURPOSE OF TODAY'S MEETING! DON'T YOU FORGET!
YOU FOOLS HAVE NO IDEA WHAT'S HAPPENING TO TAE-SOO AND JANG-HO.
I BET CHUNG-KI IS HAVING A FIELD DAY WITH THEM AT THIS MOMENT.

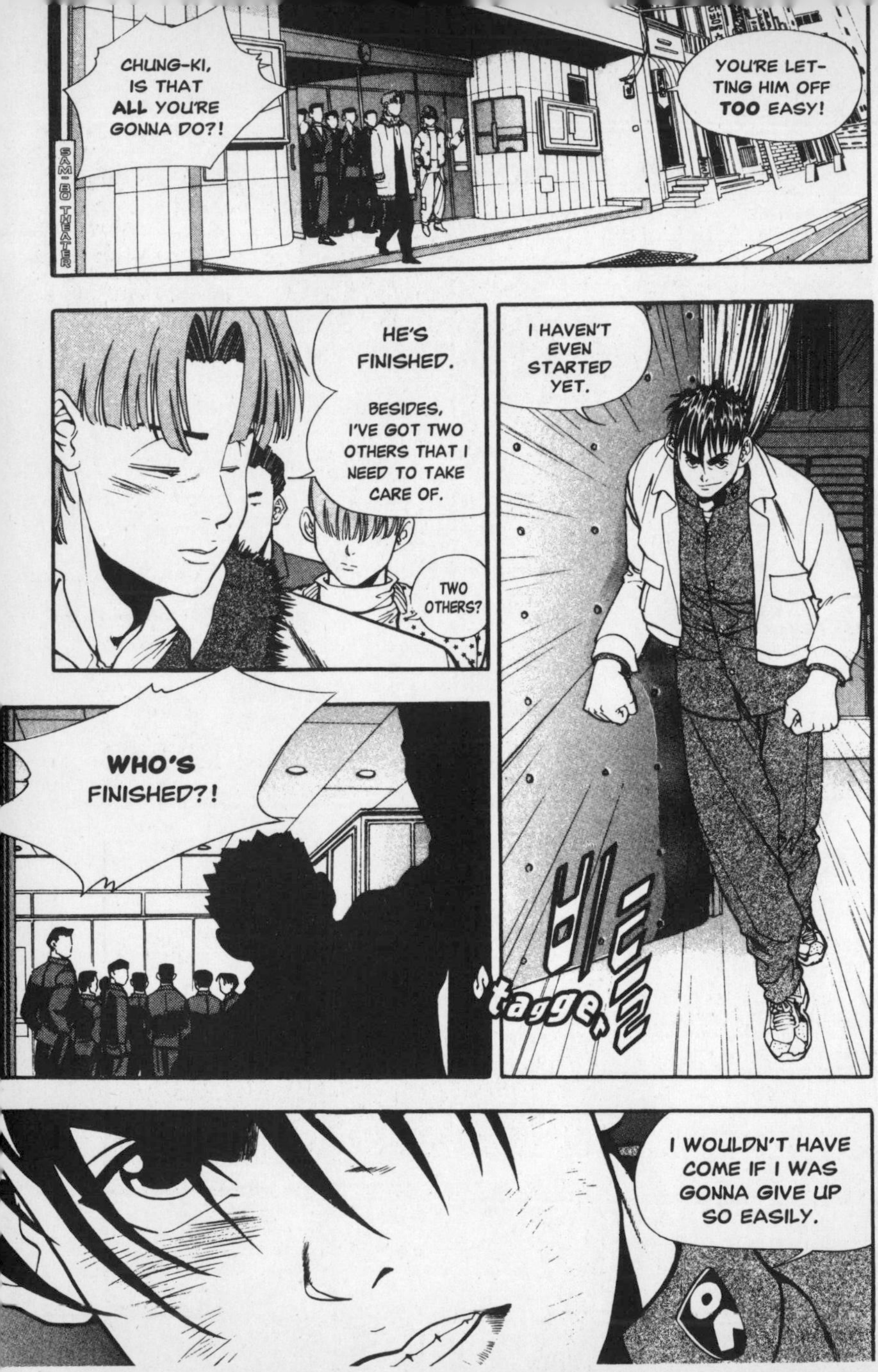
CHUNG-KI, IS THAT ALL YOU'RE GONNA DO?!
SAM-BO THEATER
YOU'RE LETTING HIM OFF TOO EASY!
HE'S FINISHED.
BESIDES, I'VE GOT TWO OTHERS THAT I NEED TO TAKE CARE OF.
TWO OTHERS?
I HAVEN'T EVEN STARTED YET.
WHO'S FINISHED?!
stagger
I WOULDN'T HAVE COME IF I WAS GONNA GIVE UP SO EASILY.

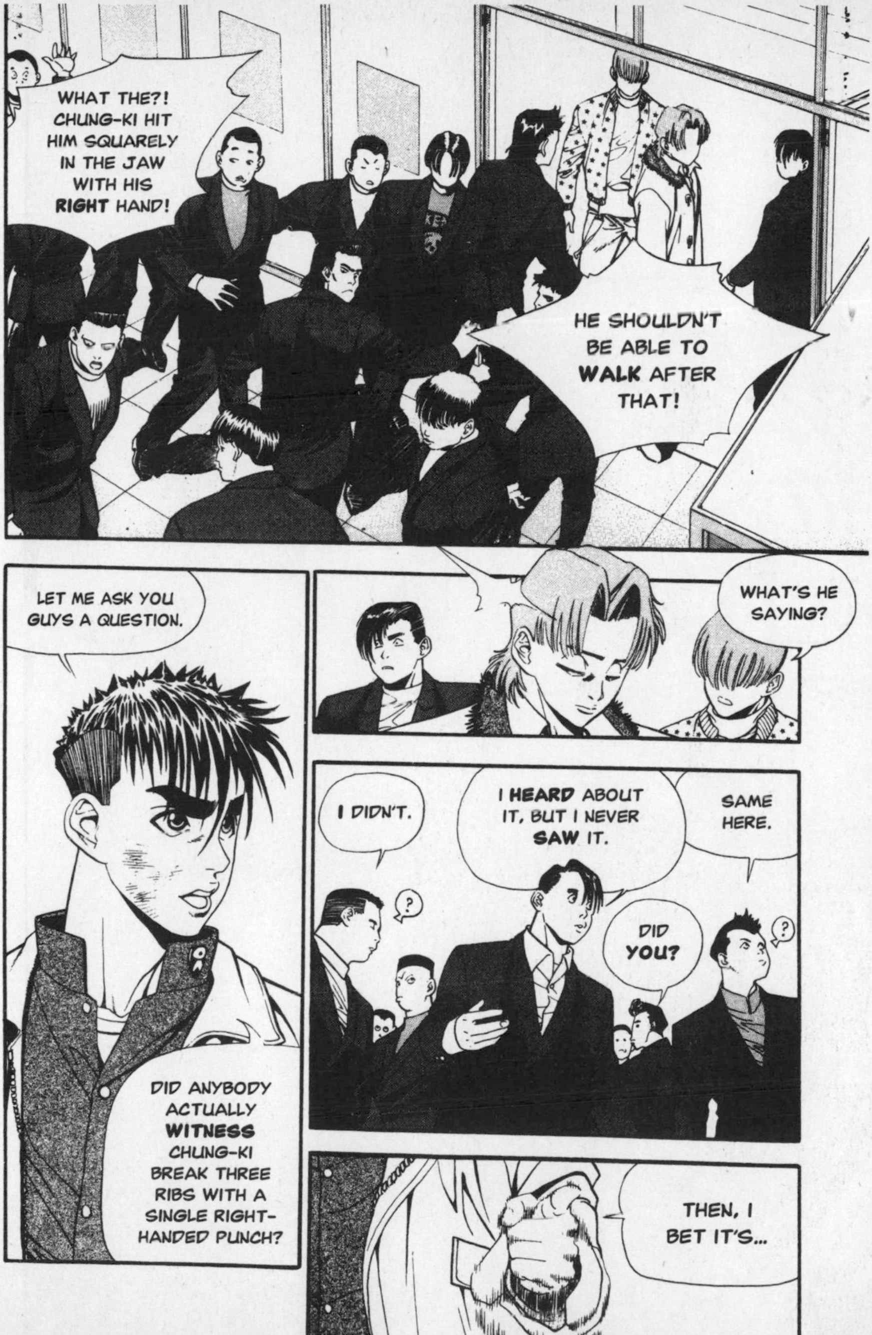
WHAT THE?! CHUNG-KI HIT HIM SQUARELY IN THE JAW WITH HIS RIGHT HAND!
HE SHOULDN'T BE ABLE TO WALK AFTER THAT!
LET ME ASK YOU GUYS A QUESTION.
DID ANYBODY ACTUALLY WITNESS CHUNG-KI BREAK THREE RIBS WITH A SINGLE RIGHT-HANDED PUNCH?
WHAT'S HE SAYING?
I DIDN'T.
I HEARD ABOUT IT, BUT I NEVER SAW IT.
SAME HERE.
DID YOU?
THEN, I BET IT'S...

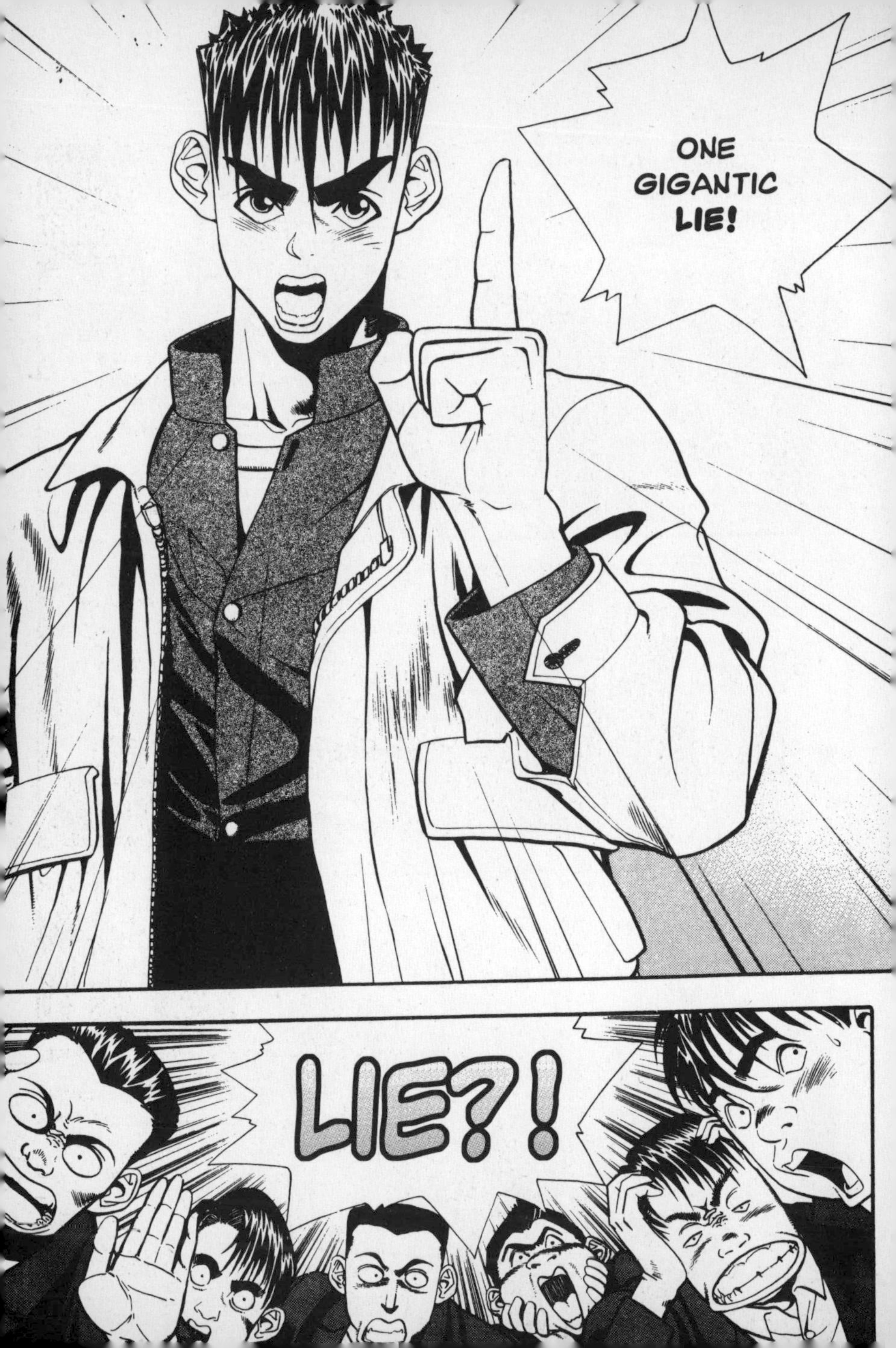
ONE GIGANTIC LIE!
LIE?!

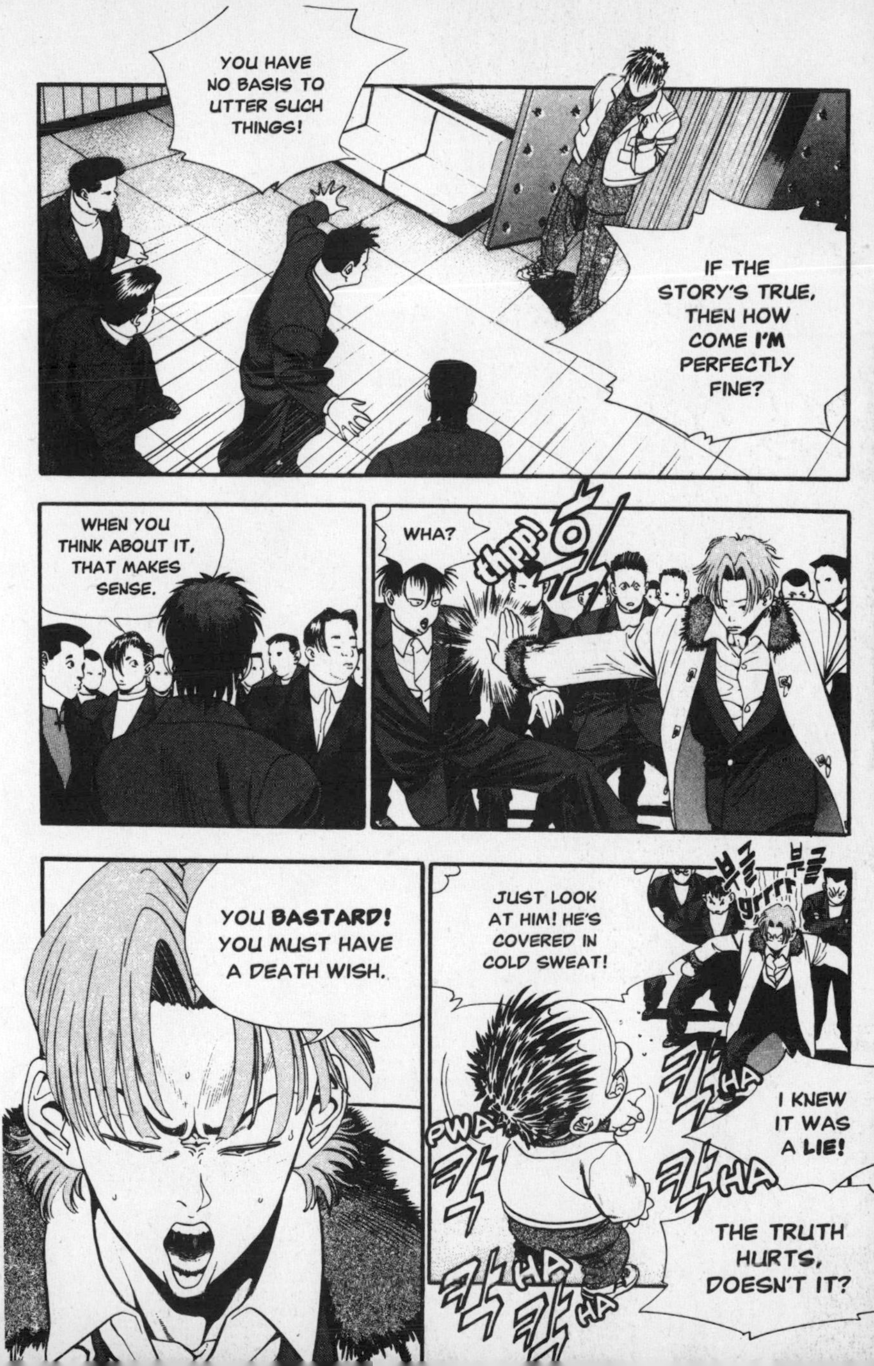
YOU HAVE NO BASIS TO UTTER SUCH THINGS!
IF THE STORY'S TRUE, THEN HOW COME **I'M** PERFECTLY FINE?
WHEN YOU THINK ABOUT IT, THAT MAKES SENSE.
WHA?
thpp!
YOU **BASTARD!** YOU MUST HAVE A DEATH WISH.
JUST LOOK AT HIM! HE'S COVERED IN COLD SWEAT!
부글 부글
grrrr
HA
I KNEW IT WAS A **LIE!**
PWA
HA
THE TRUTH HURTS, DOESN'T IT?
HA
HA

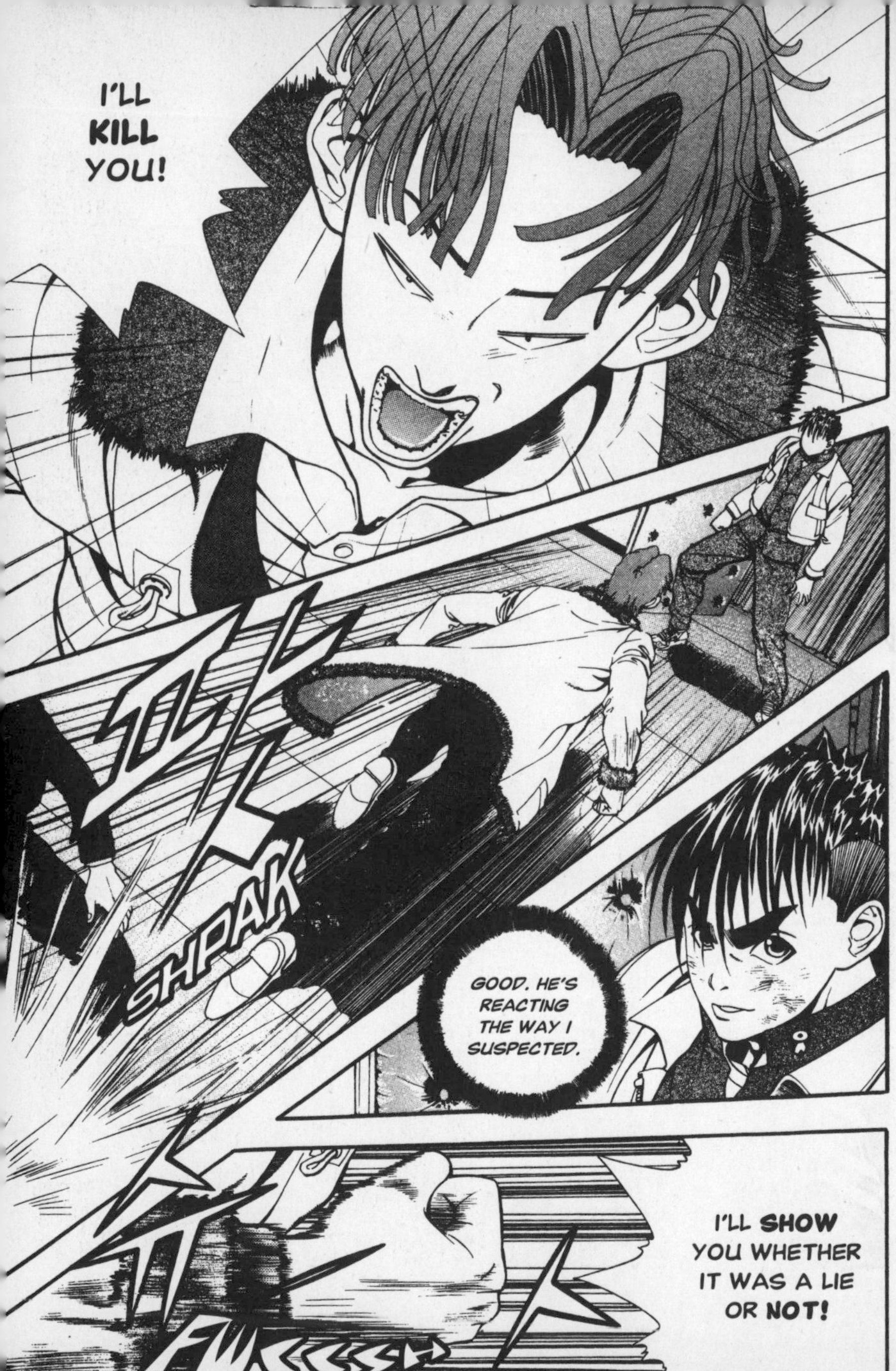
I'LL KILL YOU!
SHPAK
GOOD. HE'S REACTING THE WAY I SUSPECTED.
I'LL SHOW YOU WHETHER IT WAS A LIE OR NOT!
FWSSSSH

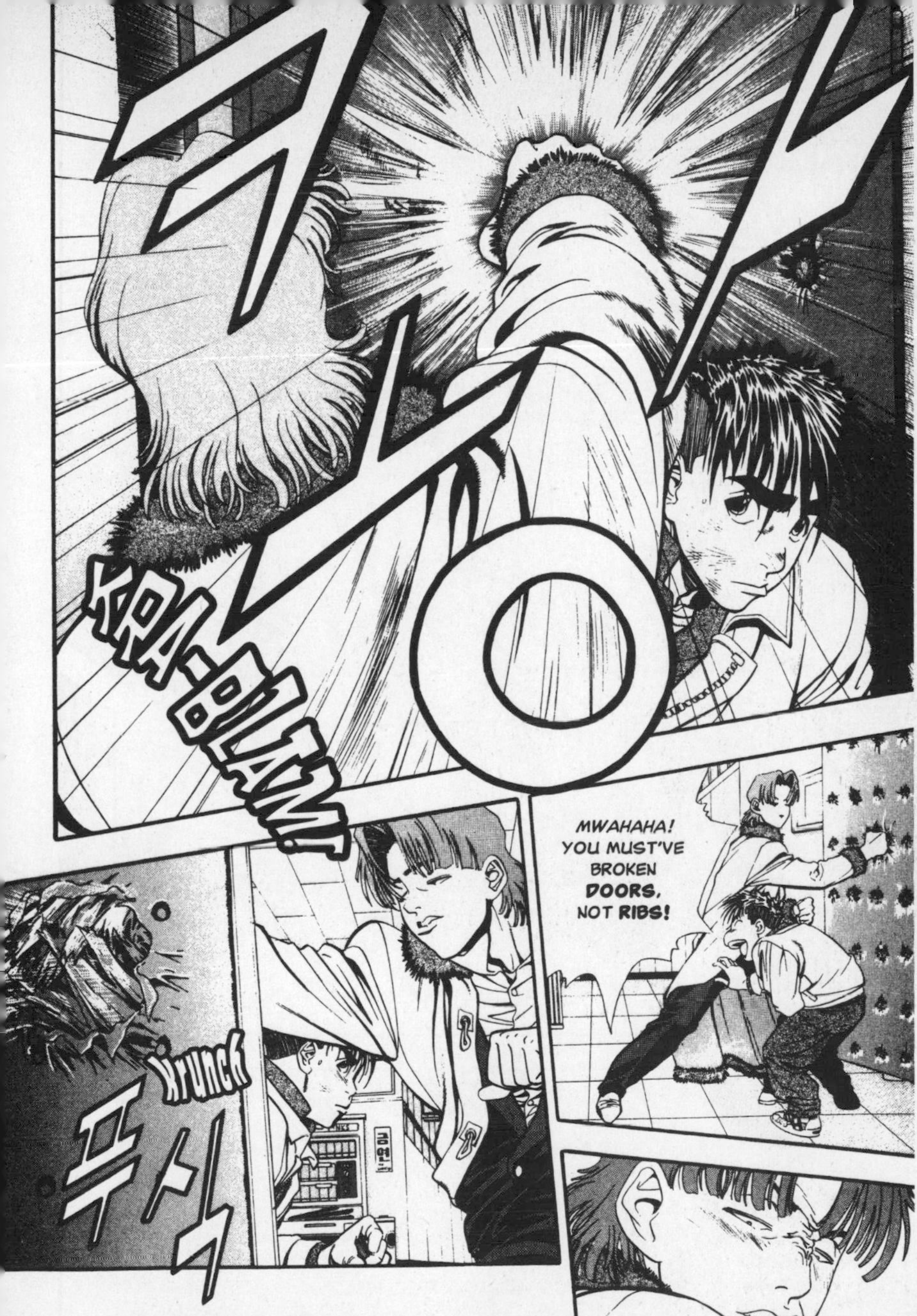
KRA-BLAM!
krunch
MWAHAHA! YOU MUST'VE BROKEN DOORS, NOT RIBS!

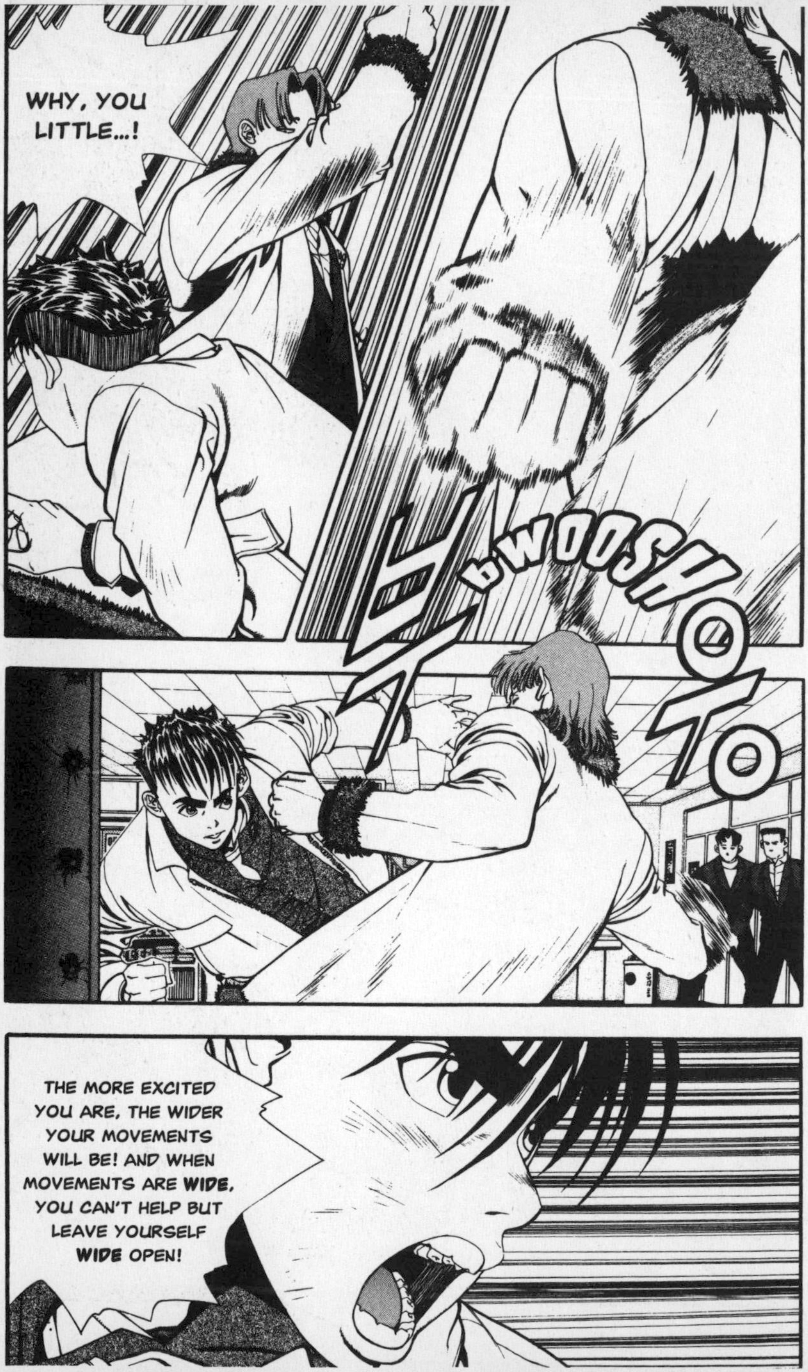
WHY, YOU LITTLE...!
WOOSH
THE MORE EXCITED YOU ARE, THE WIDER YOUR MOVEMENTS WILL BE! AND WHEN MOVEMENTS ARE **WIDE**, YOU CAN'T HELP BUT LEAVE YOURSELF **WIDE** OPEN!

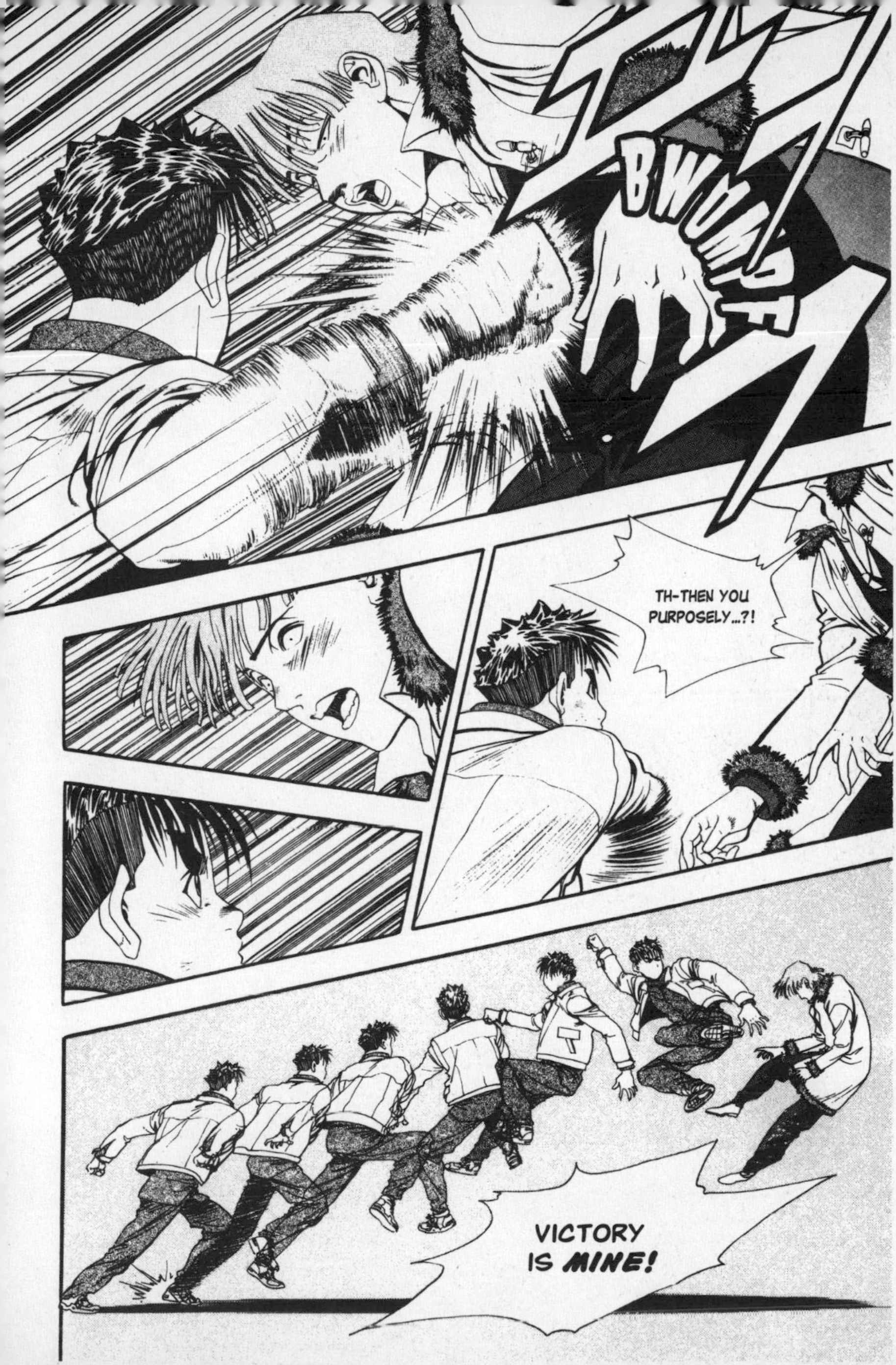
BWUMPF
TH-THEN YOU PURPOSELY...?!
VICTORY IS MINE!

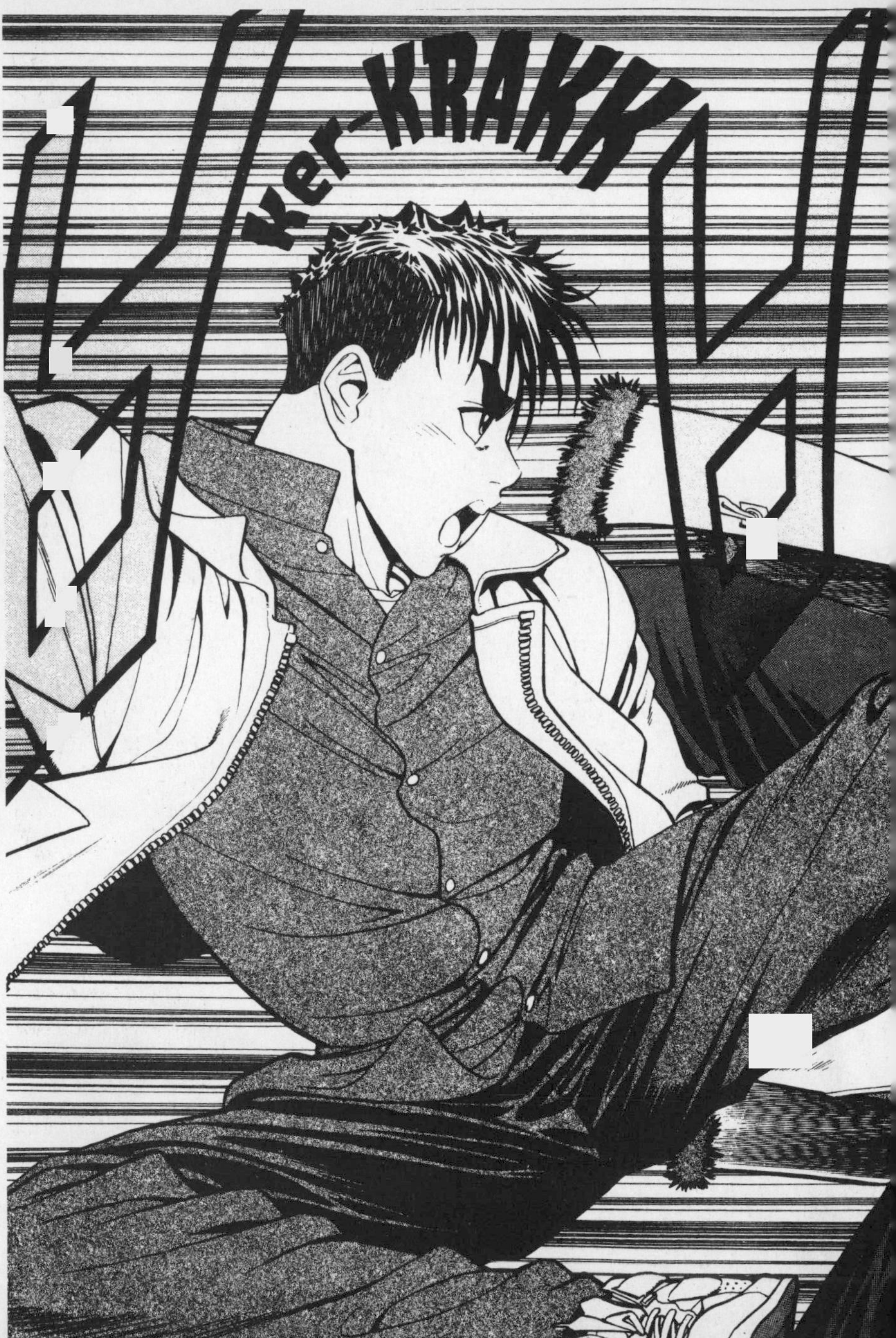
Ker-KRAKK

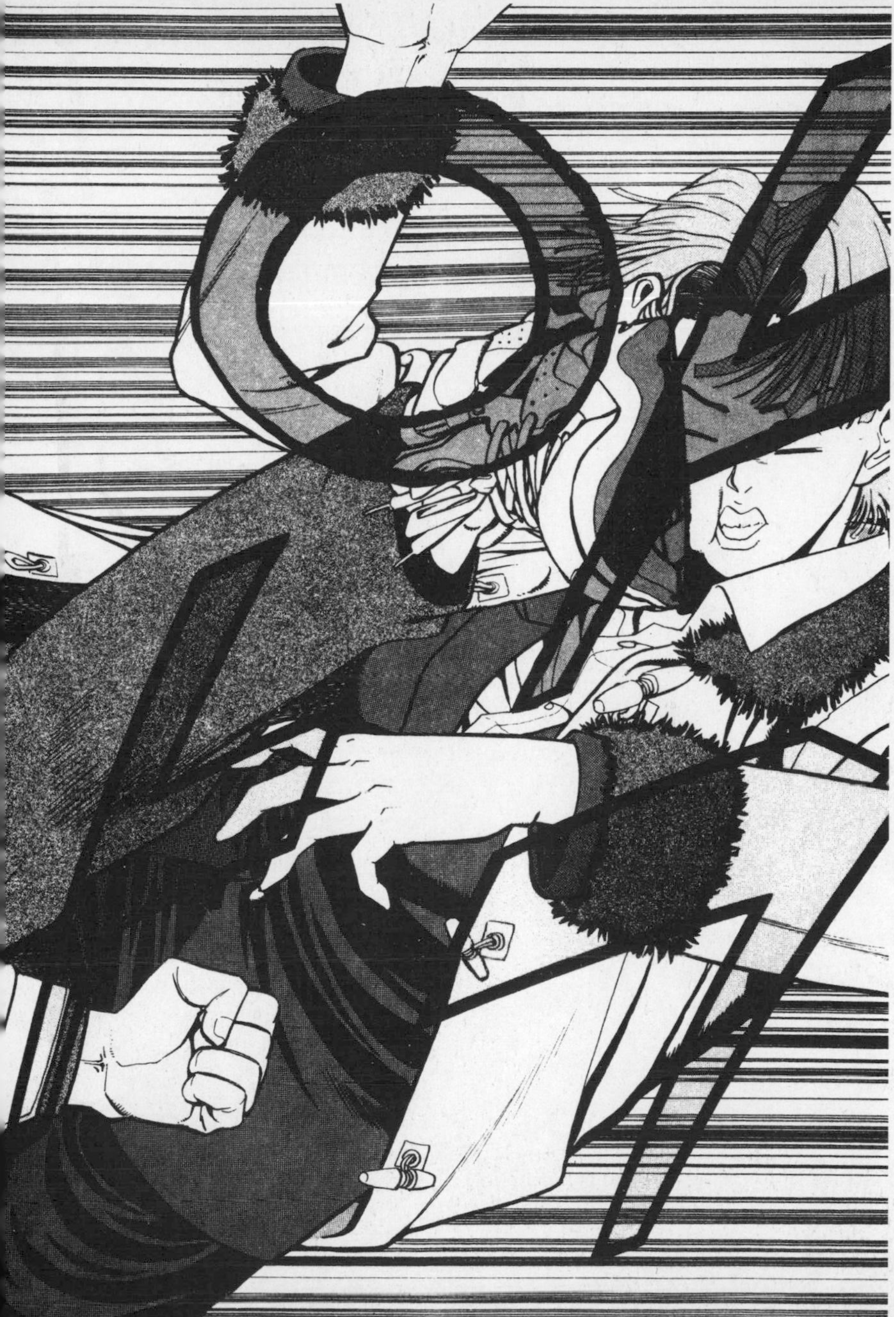

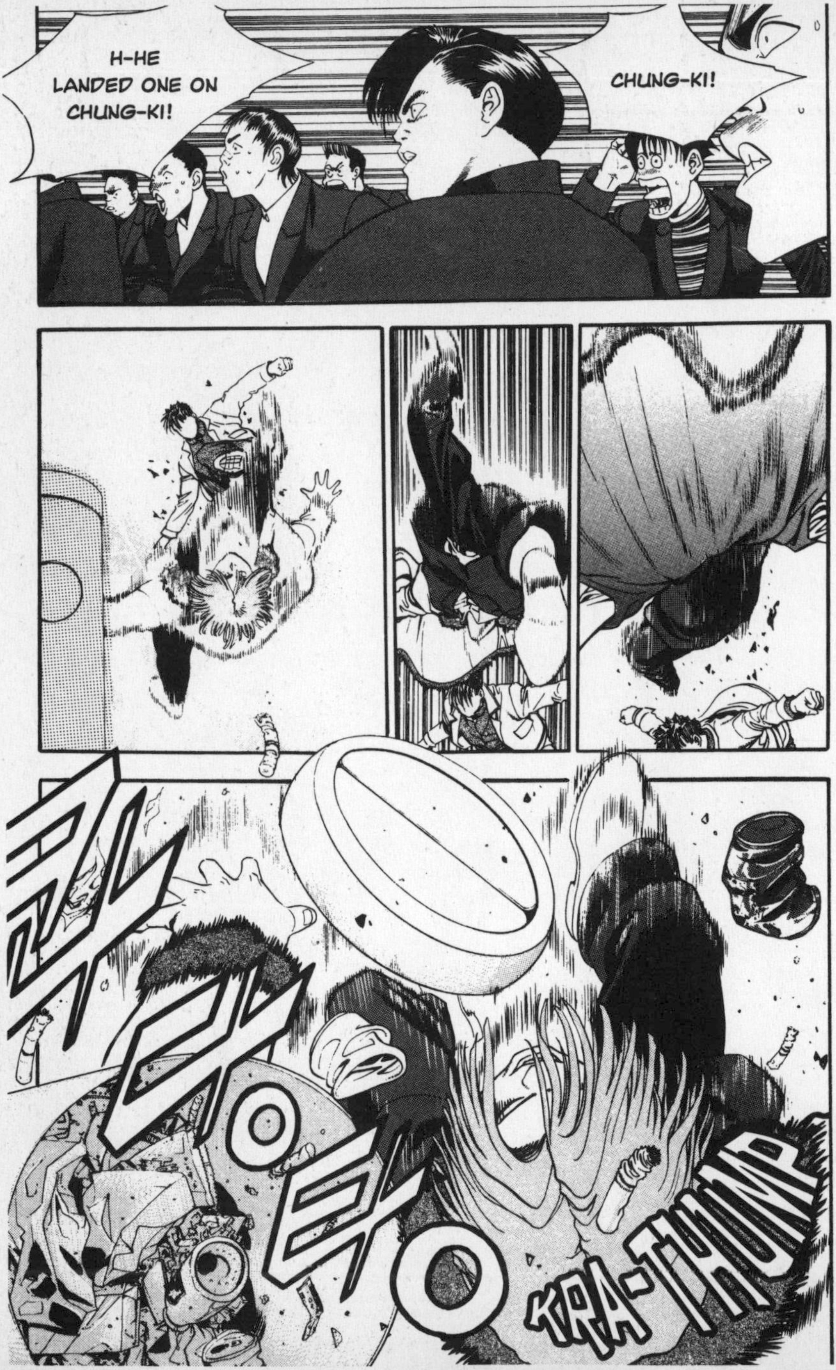
CHUNG-KI!
H-HE
LANDED ONE ON
CHUNG-KI!
KRA-THUMP

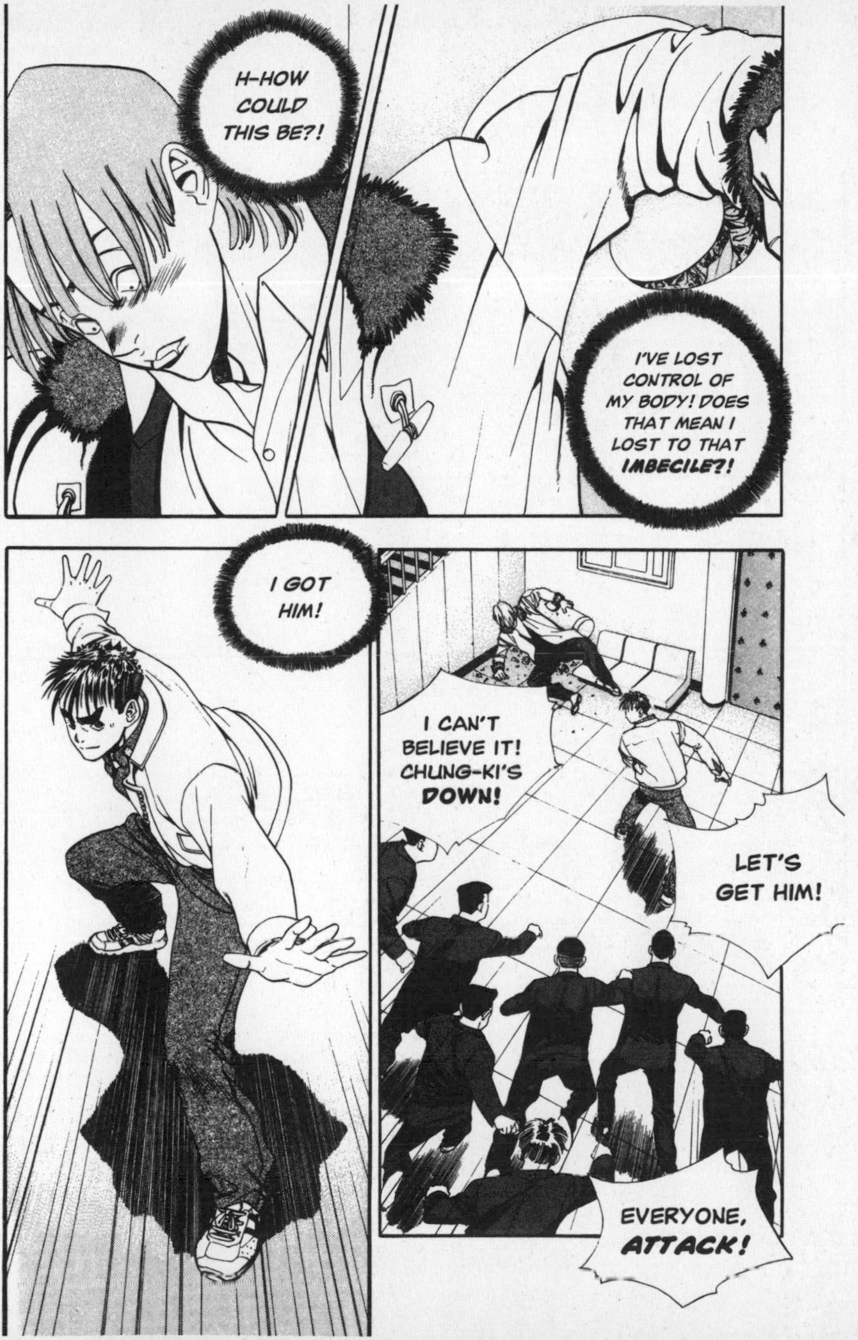
H-HOW COULD THIS BE?!
I'VE LOST CONTROL OF MY BODY! DOES THAT MEAN I LOST TO THAT *IMBECILE?!*
I GOT HIM!
I CAN'T BELIEVE IT! CHUNG-KI'S **DOWN!**
LET'S GET HIM!
EVERYONE, ***ATTACK!***

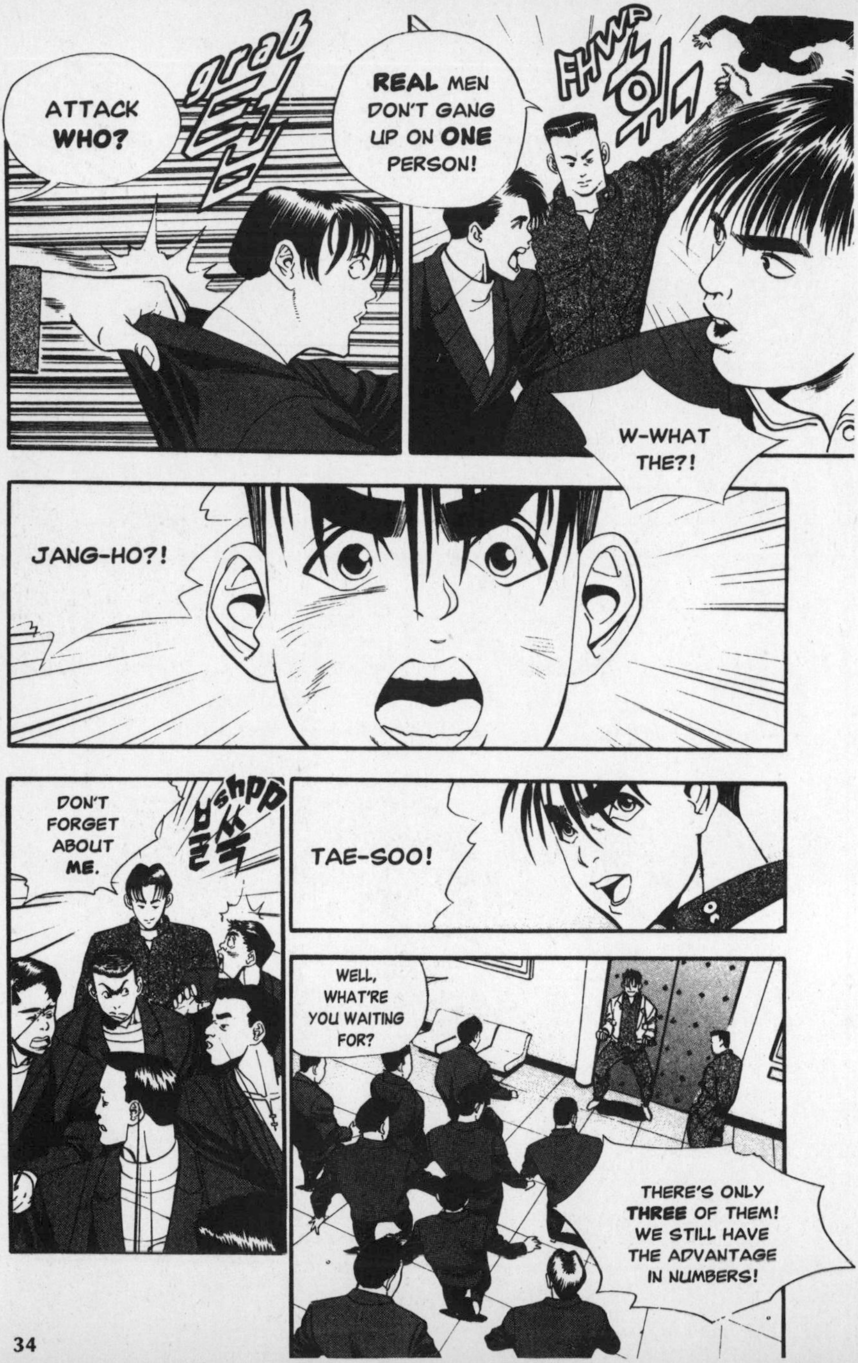
ATTACK WHO?
grab
REAL MEN DON'T GANG UP ON ONE PERSON!
FHWP
W-WHAT THE?!
JANG-HO?!
DON'T FORGET ABOUT ME.
shpp
TAE-SOO!
WELL, WHAT'RE YOU WAITING FOR?
THERE'S ONLY THREE OF THEM! WE STILL HAVE THE ADVANTAGE IN NUMBERS!

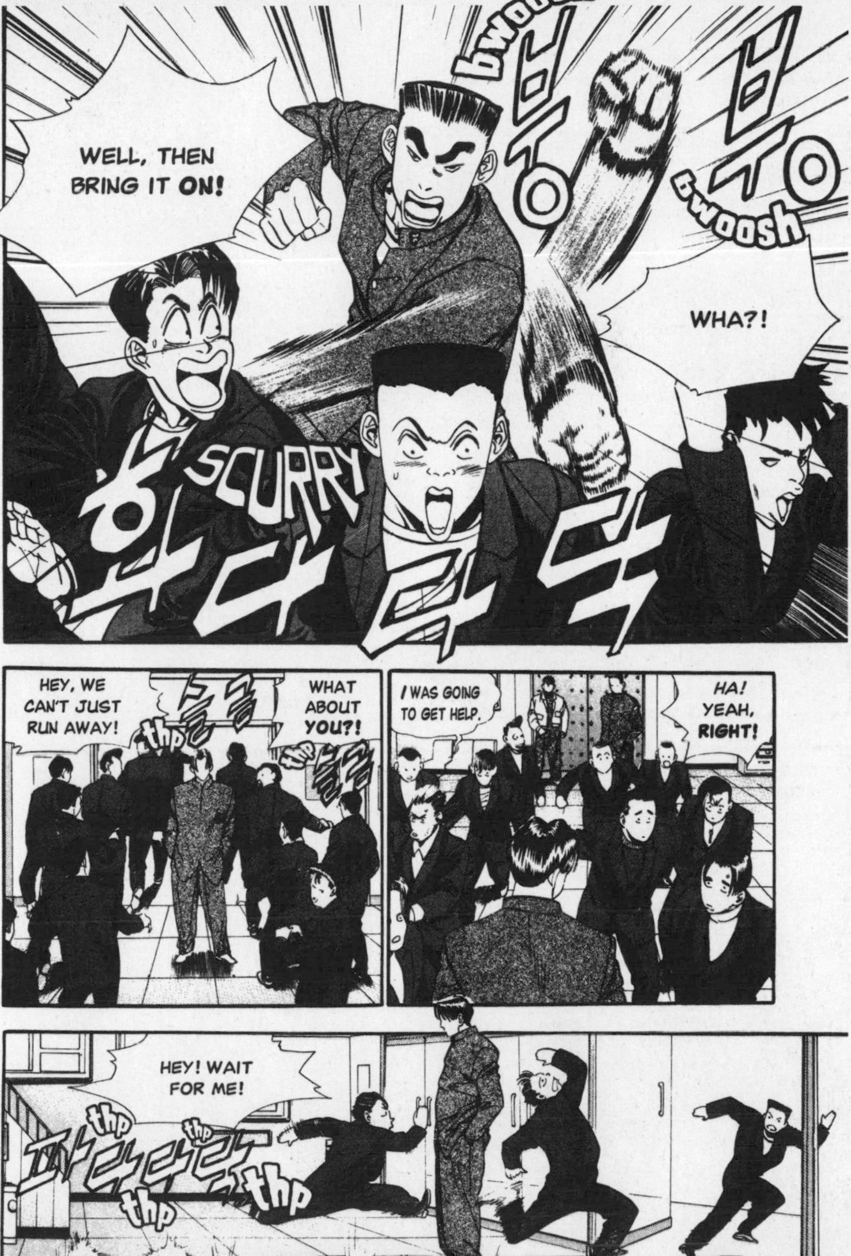
bwoosh
WELL, THEN BRING IT ON!
bwoosh
WHA?!
SCURRY
HEY, WE CAN'T JUST RUN AWAY!
thp
WHAT ABOUT YOU?!
thp
I WAS GOING TO GET HELP.
HA! YEAH, RIGHT!
HEY! WAIT FOR ME!
thp
thp
thp
thp

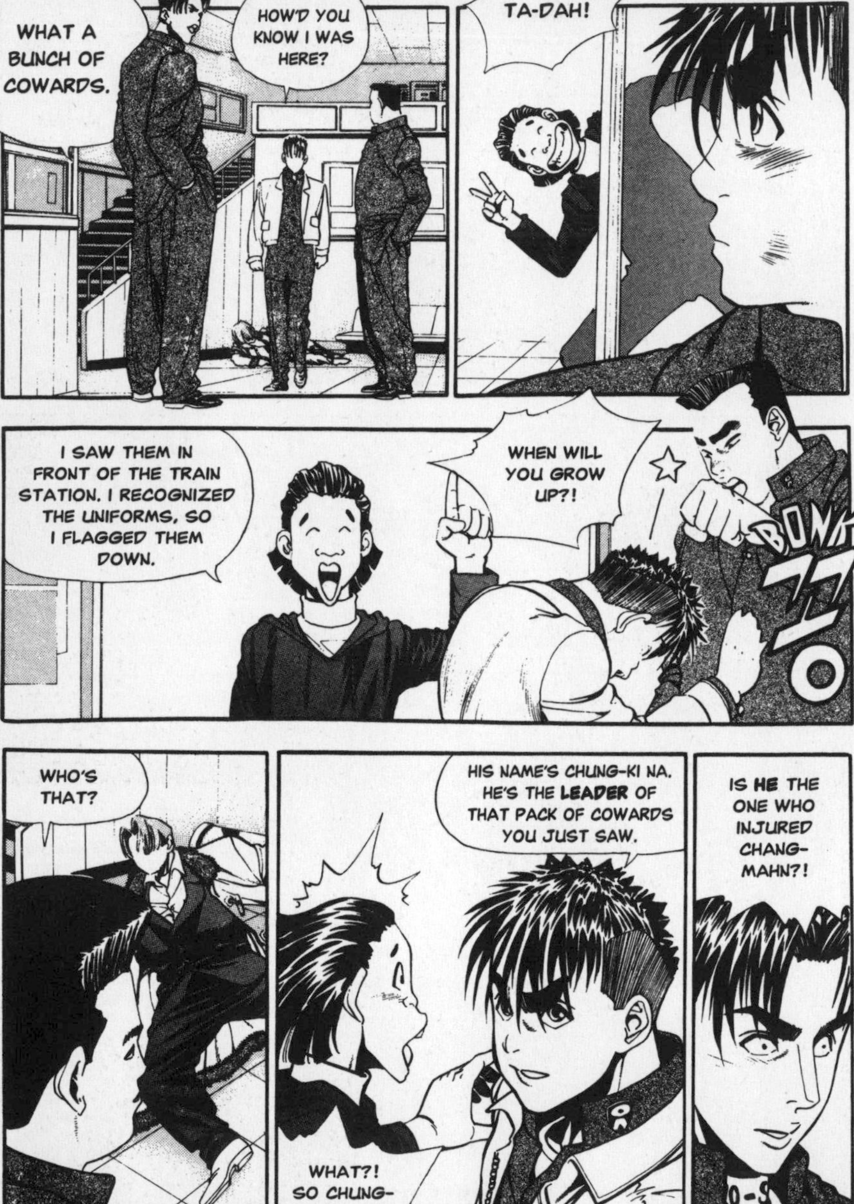
WHAT A BUNCH OF COWARDS.
HOW'D YOU KNOW I WAS HERE?
TA-DAH!
I SAW THEM IN FRONT OF THE TRAIN STATION. I RECOGNIZED THE UNIFORMS, SO I FLAGGED THEM DOWN.
WHEN WILL YOU GROW UP?!
BONK
WHO'S THAT?
WHAT?! SO CHUNG-KI HAS FINALLY...
HIS NAME'S CHUNG-KI NA. HE'S THE **LEADER** OF THAT PACK OF COWARDS YOU JUST SAW.
IS **HE** THE ONE WHO INJURED CHANG-MAHN?!

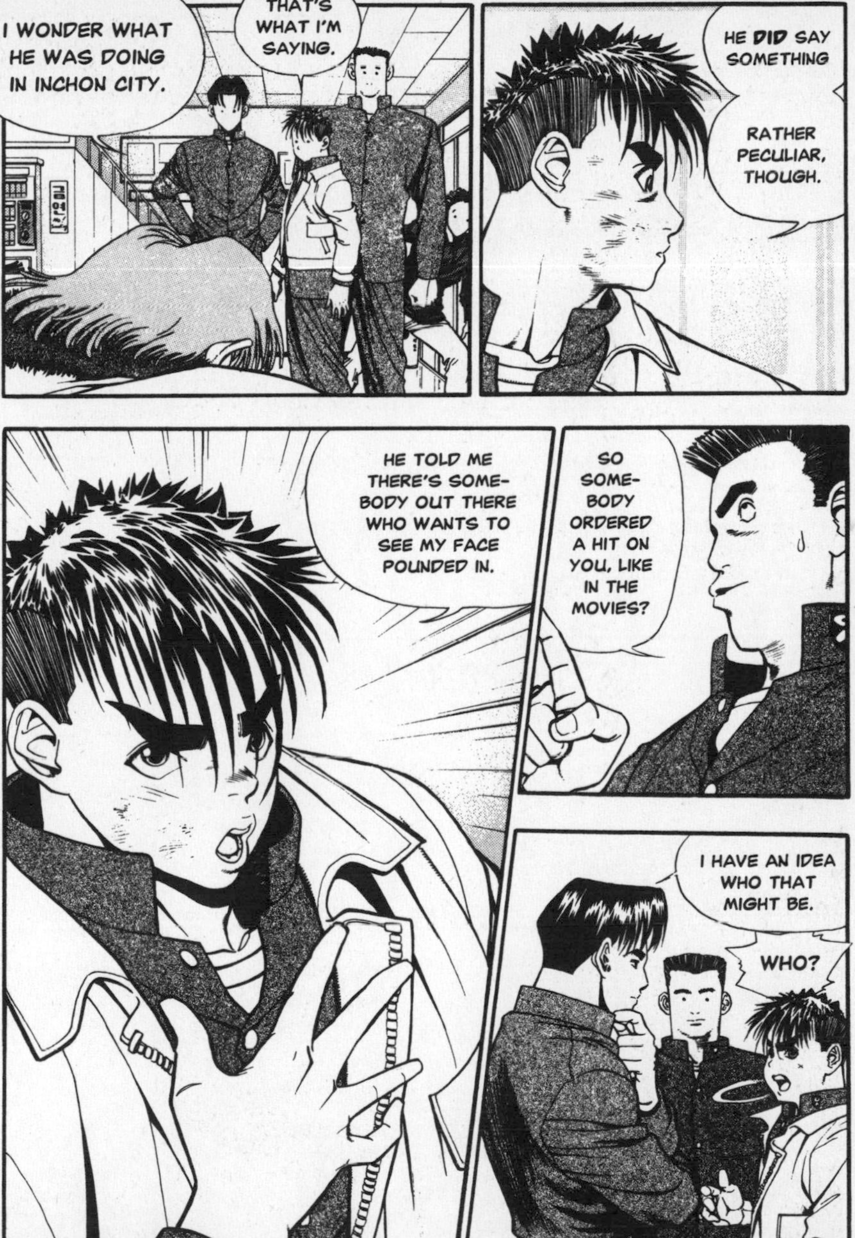
I WONDER WHAT HE WAS DOING IN INCHON CITY.
THAT'S WHAT I'M SAYING.
HE DID SAY SOMETHING
RATHER PECULIAR, THOUGH.
HE TOLD ME THERE'S SOME-BODY OUT THERE WHO WANTS TO SEE MY FACE POUNDED IN.
SO SOME-BODY ORDERED A HIT ON YOU, LIKE IN THE MOVIES?
I HAVE AN IDEA WHO THAT MIGHT BE.
WHO?

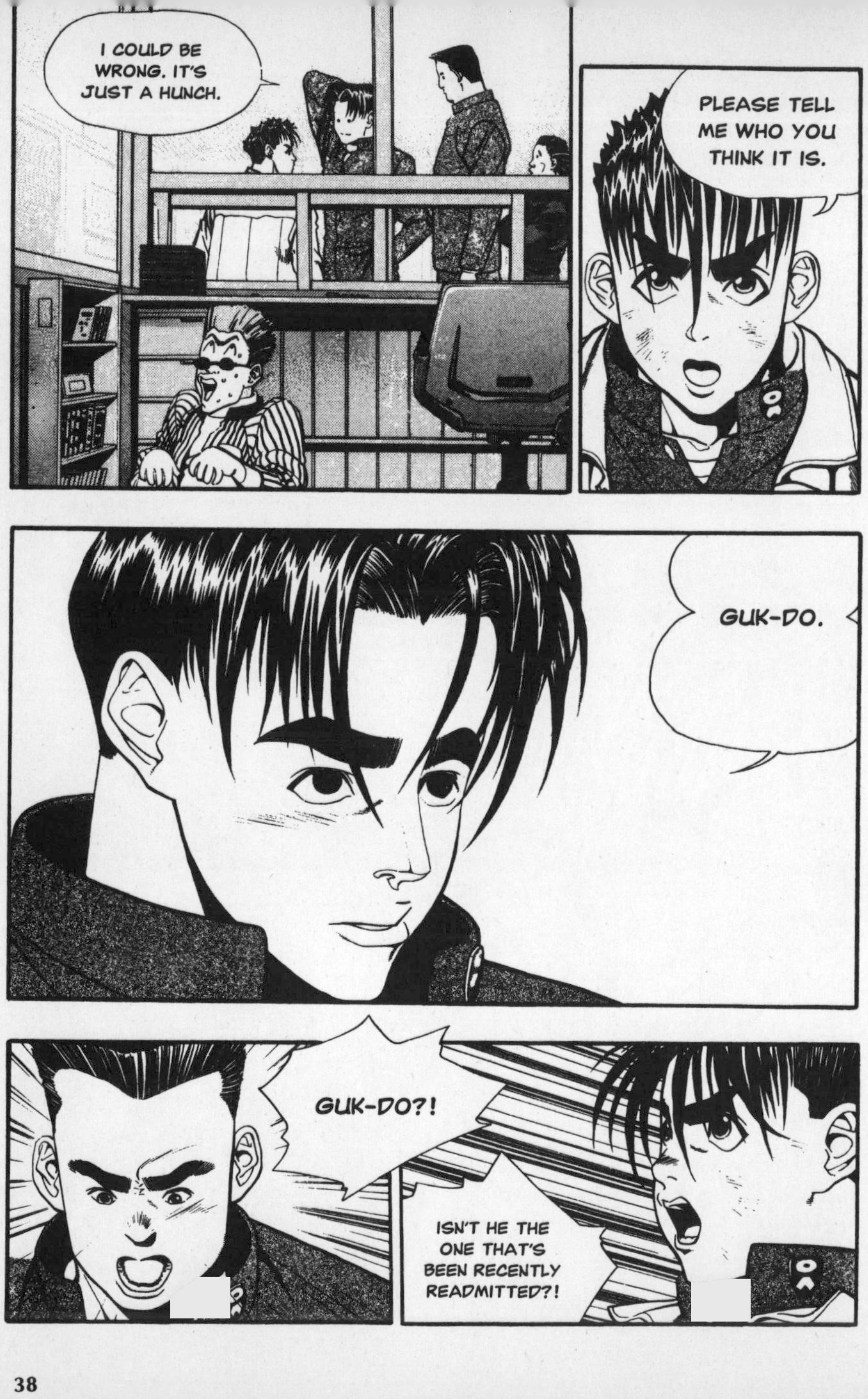
I COULD BE WRONG. IT'S JUST A HUNCH.
PLEASE TELL ME WHO YOU THINK IT IS.
GUK-DO.
GUK-DO?!
ISN'T HE THE ONE THAT'S BEEN RECENTLY READMITTED?!

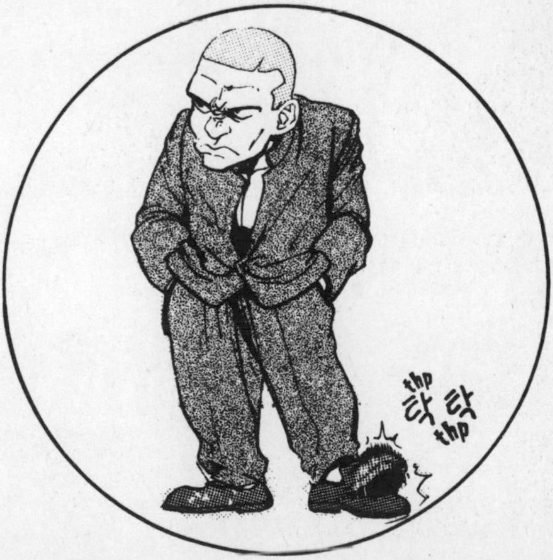
thp
탁
탁
thp

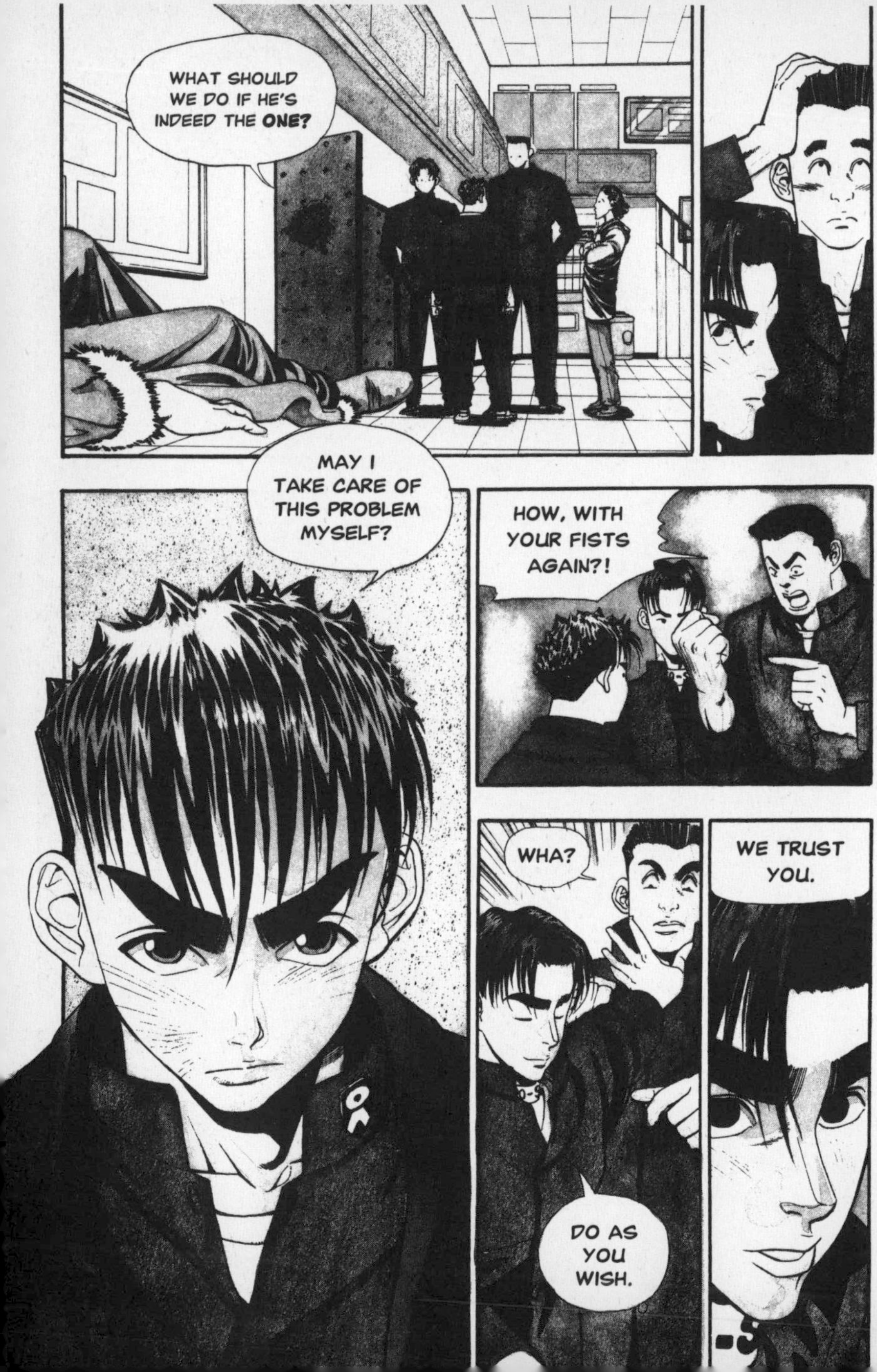
WHAT SHOULD WE DO IF HE'S INDEED THE ONE?
MAY I TAKE CARE OF THIS PROBLEM MYSELF?
HOW, WITH YOUR FISTS AGAIN?!
WHA?
WE TRUST YOU.
DO AS YOU WISH.

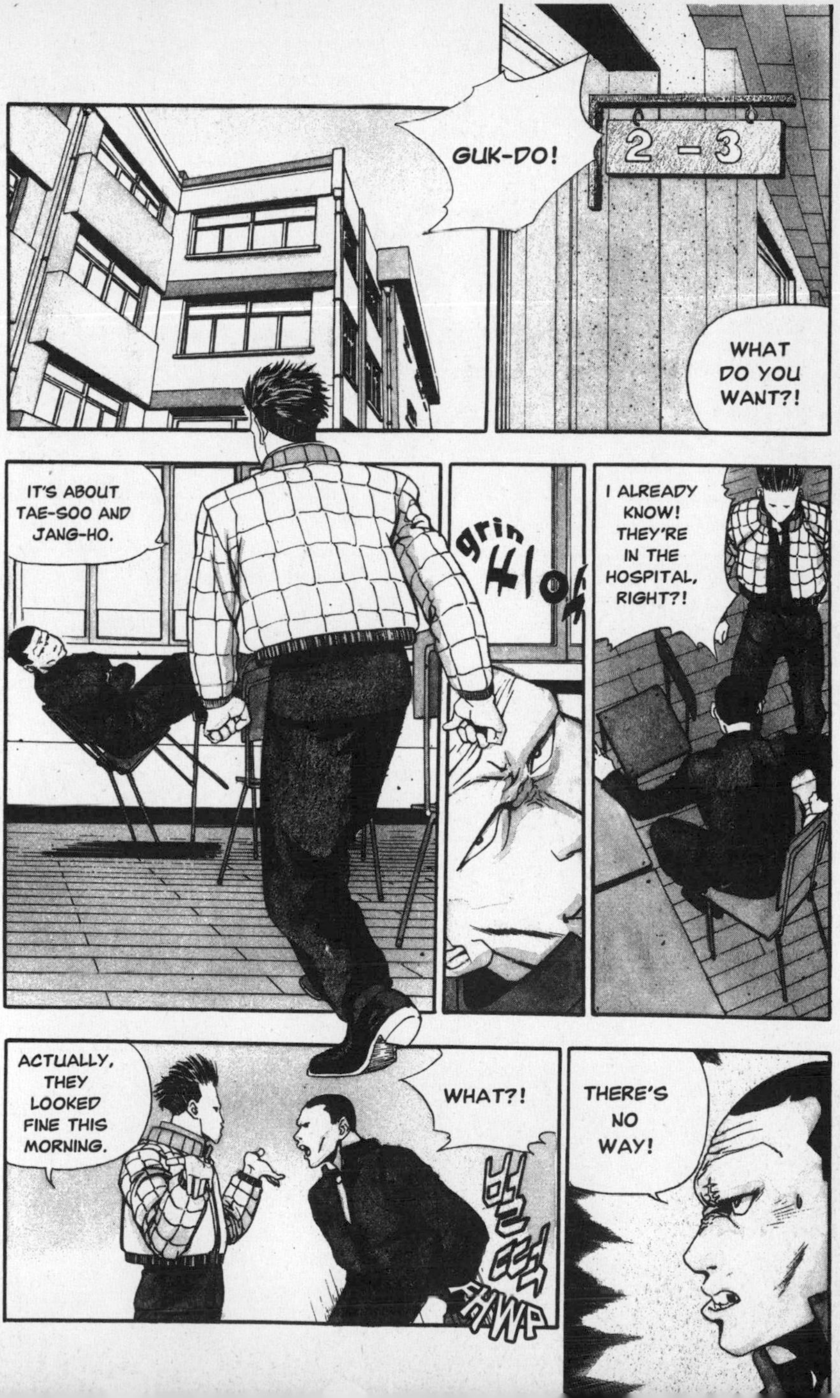
GUK-DO!
2-3
WHAT DO YOU WANT?!
IT'S ABOUT TAE-SOO AND JANG-HO.
grin
I ALREADY KNOW! THEY'RE IN THE HOSPITAL, RIGHT?!
ACTUALLY, THEY LOOKED FINE THIS MORNING.
WHAT?!
FHWAP
THERE'S NO WAY!

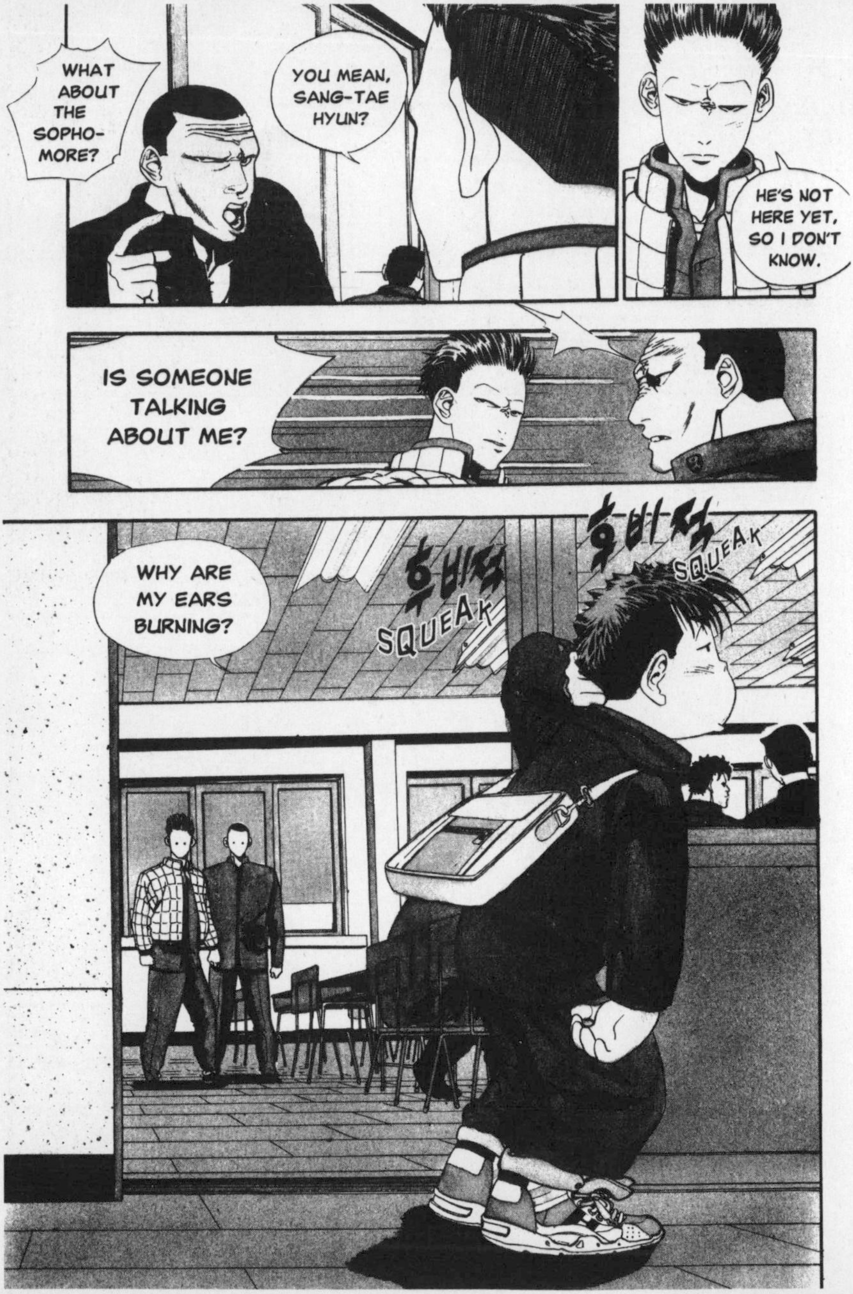
WHAT ABOUT THE SOPHO-MORE?
YOU MEAN, SANG-TAE HYUN?
HE'S NOT HERE YET, SO I DON'T KNOW.
IS SOMEONE TALKING ABOUT ME?
WHY ARE MY EARS BURNING?
후비적
SQUEAK
후비적
SQUEAK

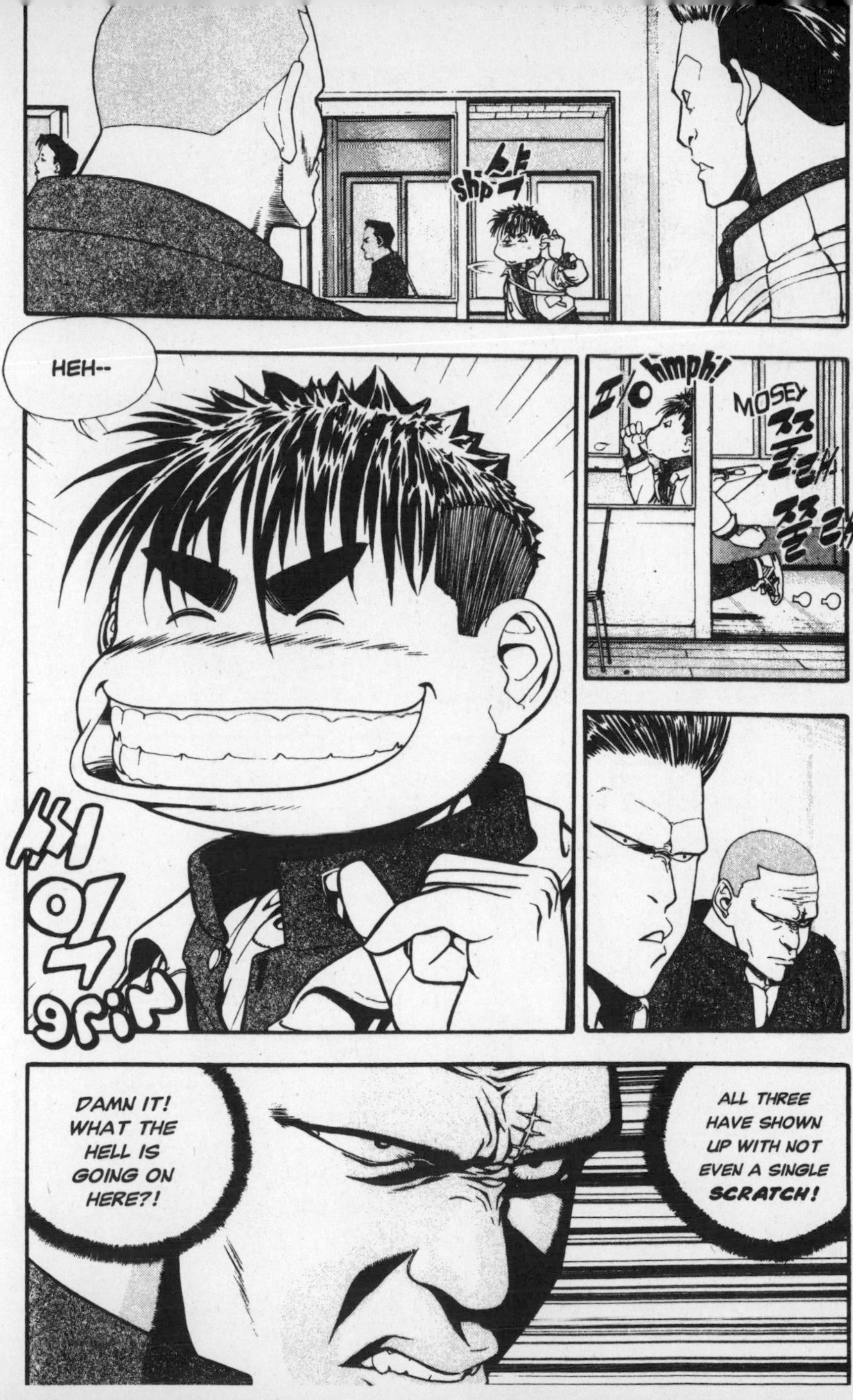
shp
HEH--
grin
hmph!
MOSEY
DAMN IT! WHAT THE HELL IS GOING ON HERE?!
ALL THREE HAVE SHOWN UP WITH NOT EVEN A SINGLE SCRATCH!

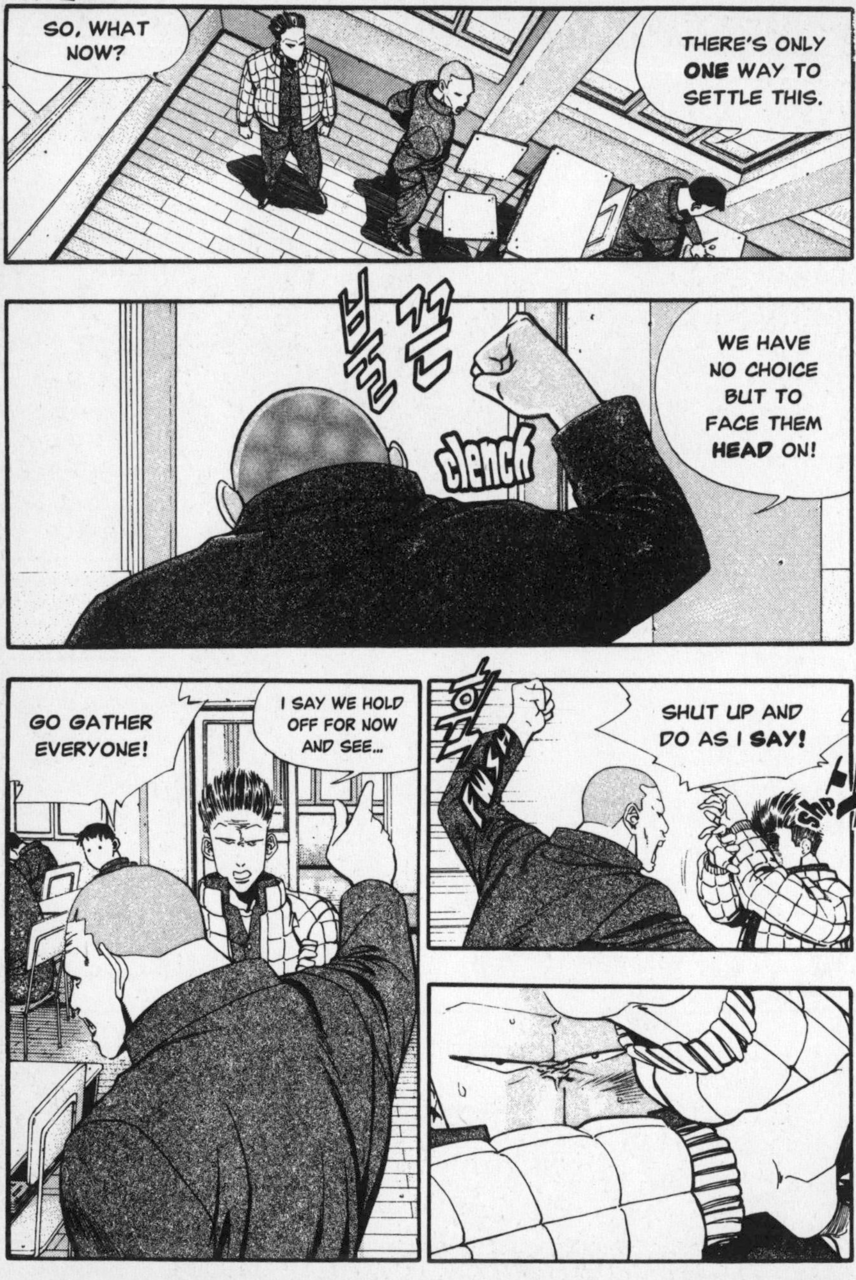
SO, WHAT NOW?
THERE'S ONLY ONE WAY TO SETTLE THIS.
불끈
clench
WE HAVE NO CHOICE BUT TO FACE THEM HEAD ON!
I SAY WE HOLD OFF FOR NOW AND SEE...
GO GATHER EVERYONE!
SHUT UP AND DO AS I SAY!

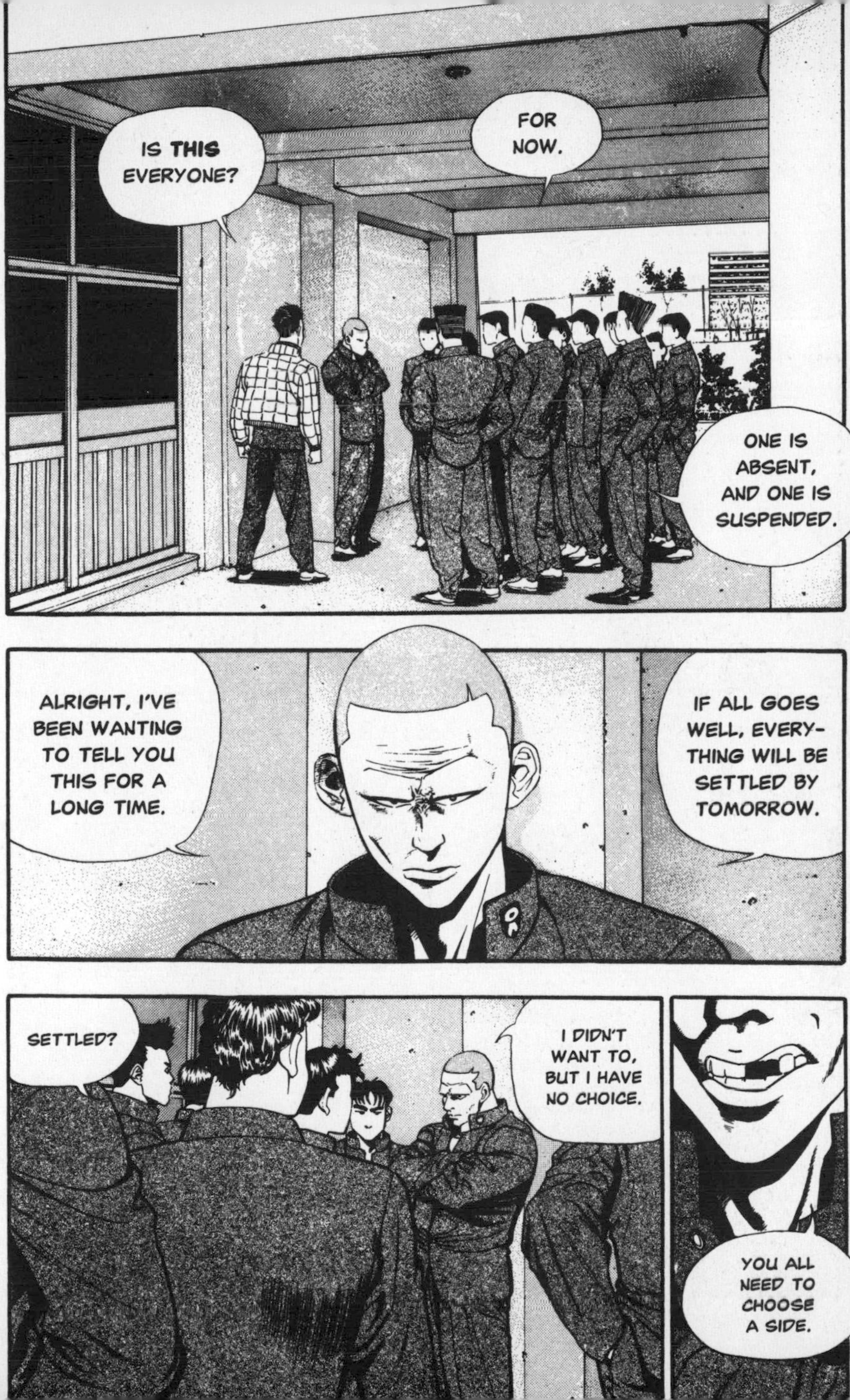
IS THIS EVERYONE?
FOR NOW.
ONE IS ABSENT, AND ONE IS SUSPENDED.
ALRIGHT, I'VE BEEN WANTING TO TELL YOU THIS FOR A LONG TIME.
IF ALL GOES WELL, EVERY-THING WILL BE SETTLED BY TOMORROW.
SETTLED?
I DIDN'T WANT TO, BUT I HAVE NO CHOICE.
YOU ALL NEED TO CHOOSE A SIDE.

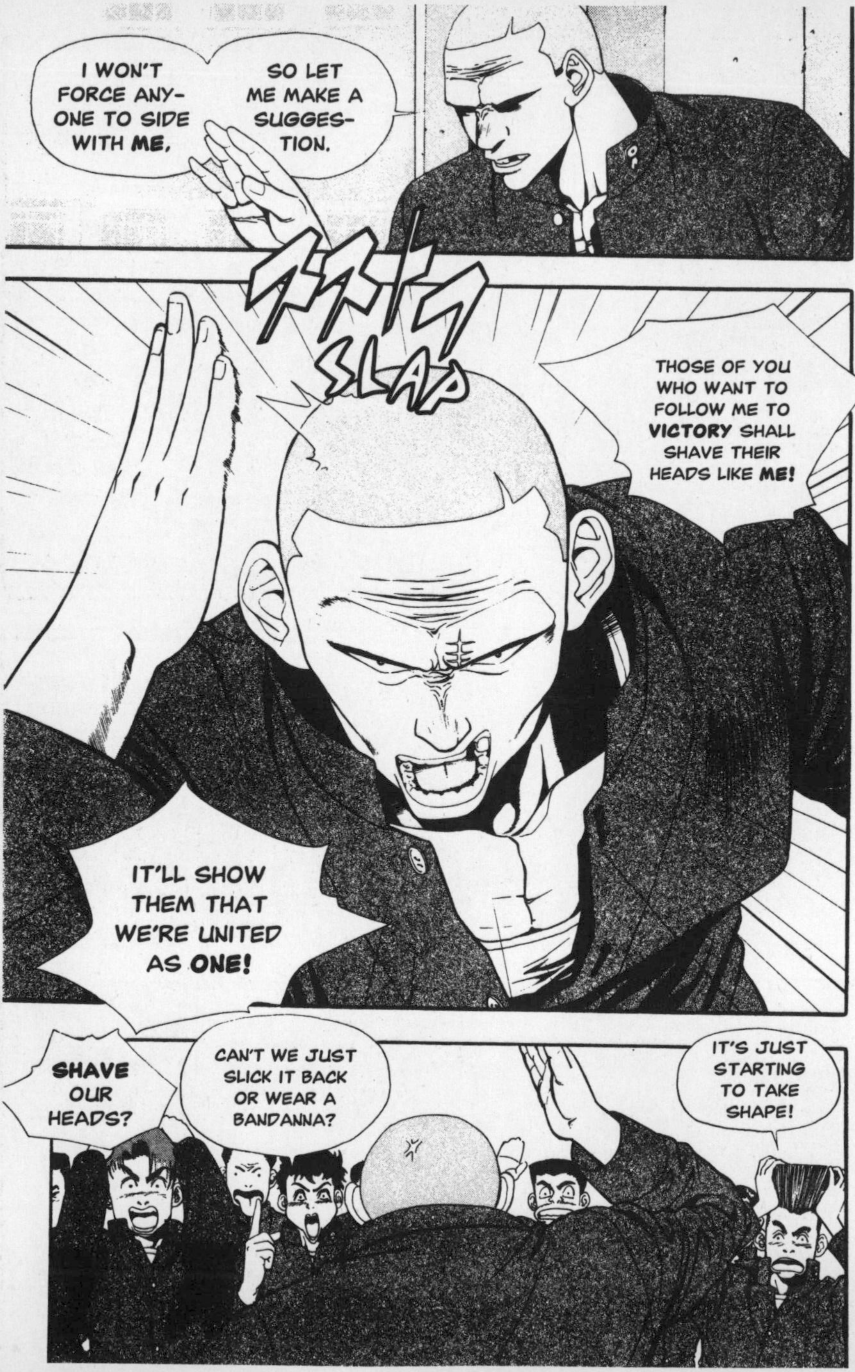
I WON'T FORCE ANY-ONE TO SIDE WITH ME,
SO LET ME MAKE A SUGGES-TION.
SLAP
THOSE OF YOU WHO WANT TO FOLLOW ME TO VICTORY SHALL SHAVE THEIR HEADS LIKE ME!
IT'LL SHOW THEM THAT WE'RE UNITED AS ONE!
IT'S JUST STARTING TO TAKE SHAPE!
CAN'T WE JUST SLICK IT BACK OR WEAR A BANDANNA?
SHAVE OUR HEADS?

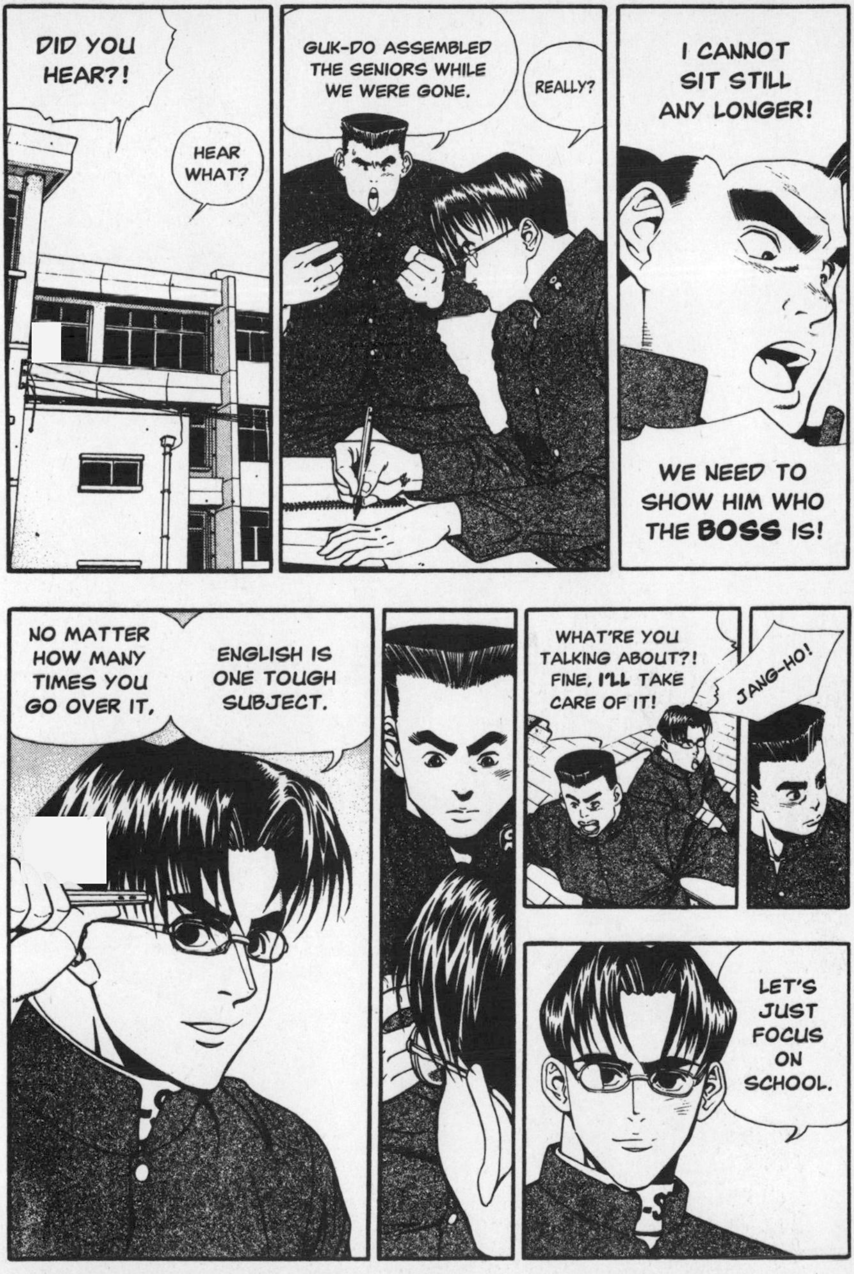
DID YOU HEAR?!
HEAR WHAT?
GUK-DO ASSEMBLED THE SENIORS WHILE WE WERE GONE.
REALLY?
I CANNOT SIT STILL ANY LONGER!
WE NEED TO SHOW HIM WHO THE **BOSS** IS!
NO MATTER HOW MANY TIMES YOU GO OVER IT,
ENGLISH IS ONE TOUGH SUBJECT.
WHAT'RE YOU TALKING ABOUT?! FINE, **I'LL** TAKE CARE OF IT!
JANG-HO!
LET'S JUST FOCUS ON SCHOOL.

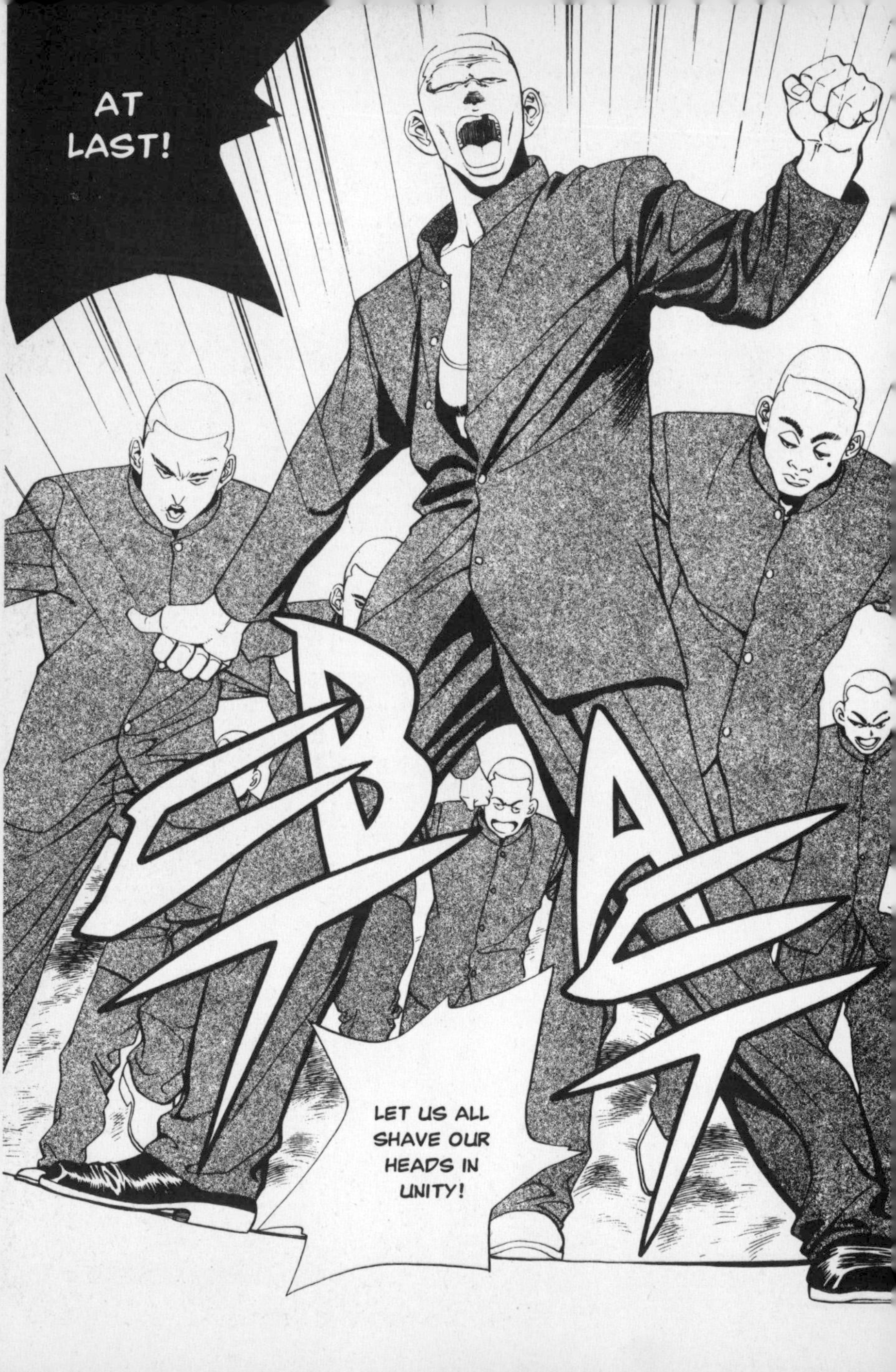
AT LAST!
LET US ALL SHAVE OUR HEADS IN UNITY!
BAT

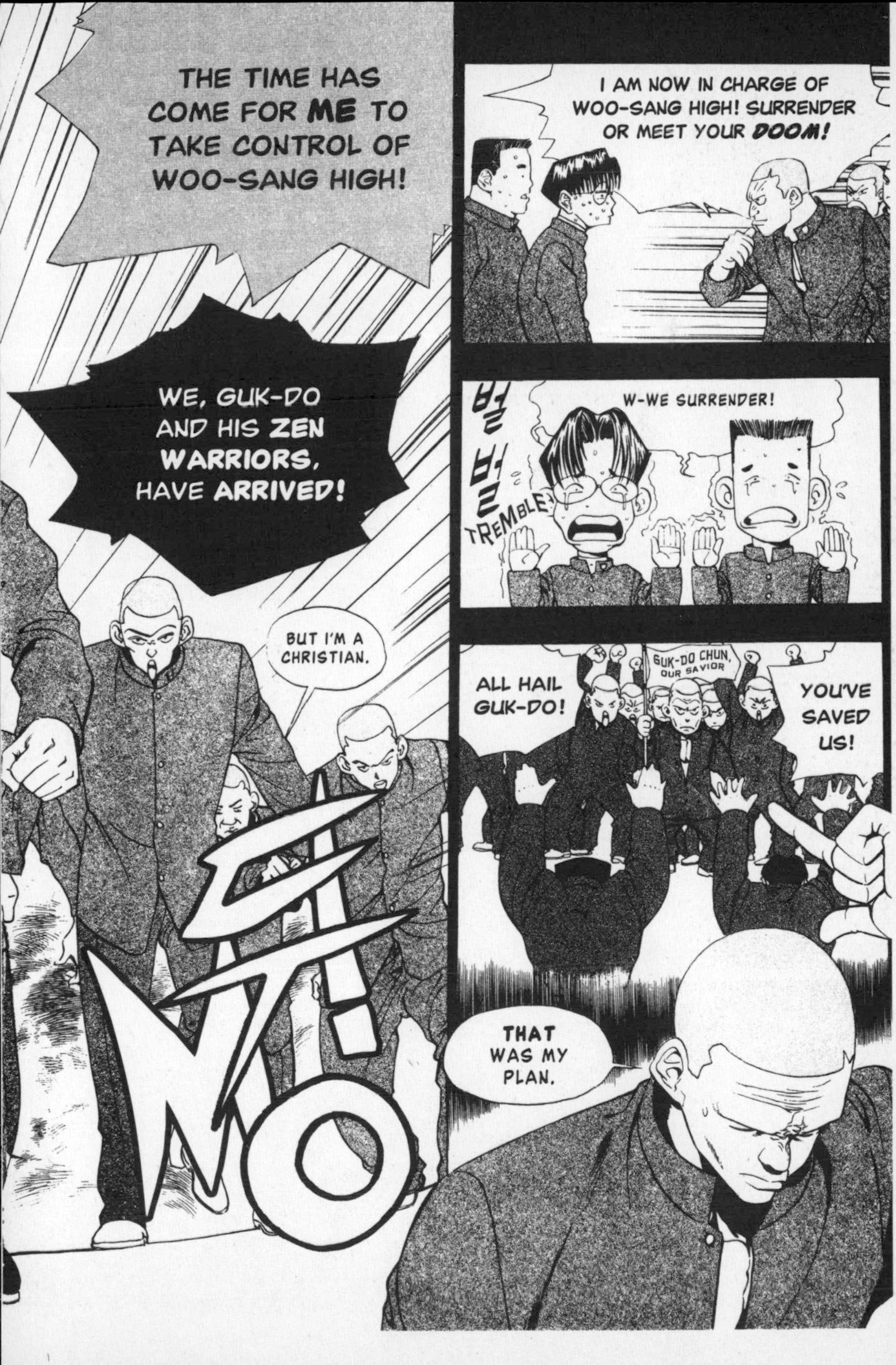
THE TIME HAS COME FOR ME TO TAKE CONTROL OF WOO-SANG HIGH!
WE, GUK-DO AND HIS ZEN WARRIORS, HAVE ARRIVED!
BUT I'M A CHRISTIAN.
I AM NOW IN CHARGE OF WOO-SANG HIGH! SURRENDER OR MEET YOUR DOOM!
벌 벌
TREMBLE
W-WE SURRENDER!
GUK-DO CHUN, OUR SAVIOR
ALL HAIL GUK-DO!
YOU'VE SAVED US!
THAT WAS MY PLAN.

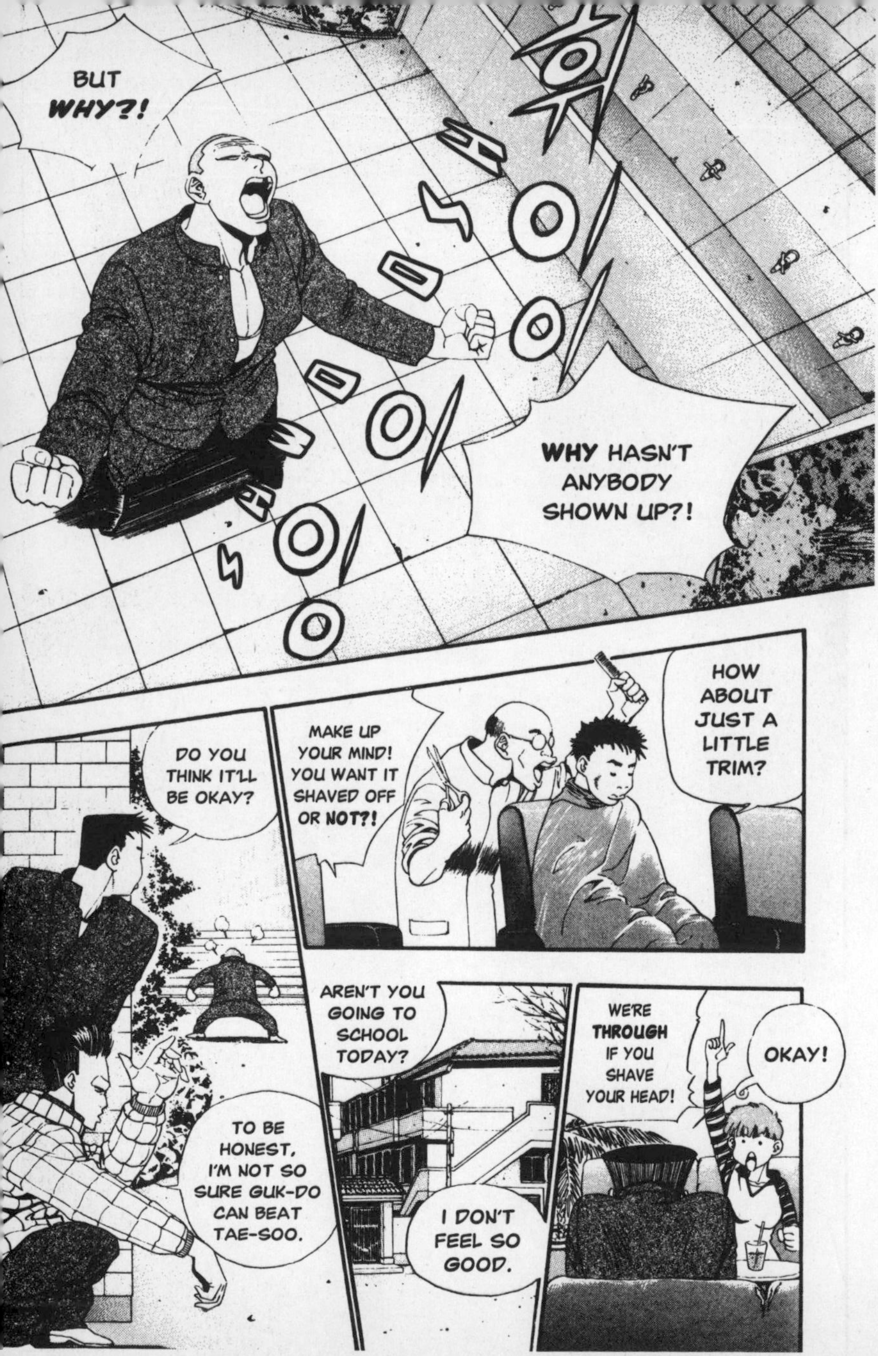

BUT WHY?!
WHY HASN'T ANYBODY SHOWN UP?!
DO YOU THINK IT'LL BE OKAY?
TO BE HONEST, I'M NOT SO SURE GUK-DO CAN BEAT TAE-SOO.
HOW ABOUT JUST A LITTLE TRIM?
MAKE UP YOUR MIND! YOU WANT IT SHAVED OFF OR NOT?!
AREN'T YOU GOING TO SCHOOL TODAY?
I DON'T FEEL SO GOOD.
WE'RE THROUGH IF YOU SHAVE YOUR HEAD!
OKAY!

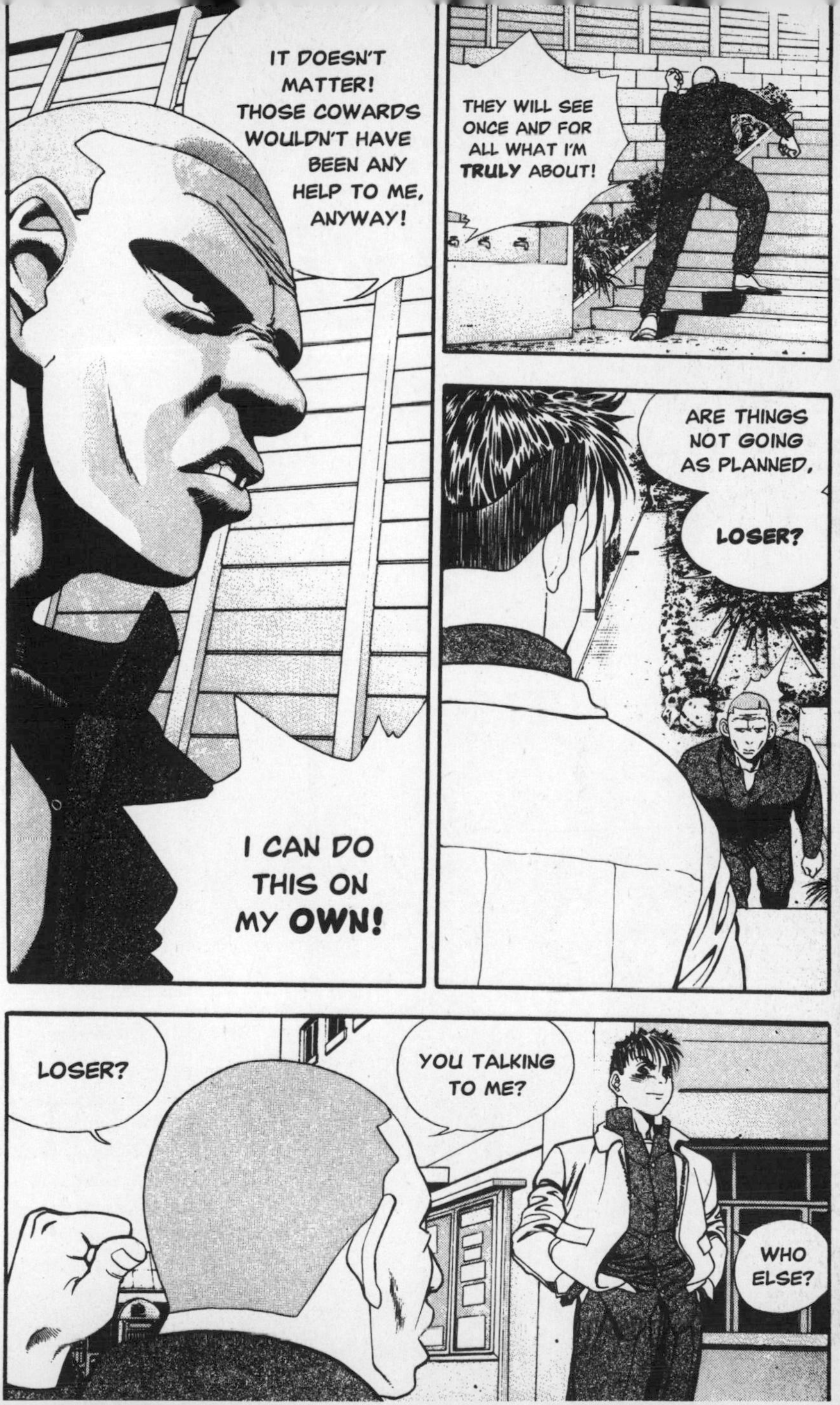

IT DOESN'T MATTER! THOSE COWARDS WOULDN'T HAVE BEEN ANY HELP TO ME, ANYWAY!
I CAN DO THIS ON MY **OWN!**
THEY WILL SEE ONCE AND FOR ALL WHAT I'M **TRULY** ABOUT!
ARE THINGS NOT GOING AS PLANNED,
LOSER?
LOSER?
YOU TALKING TO ME?
WHO ELSE?

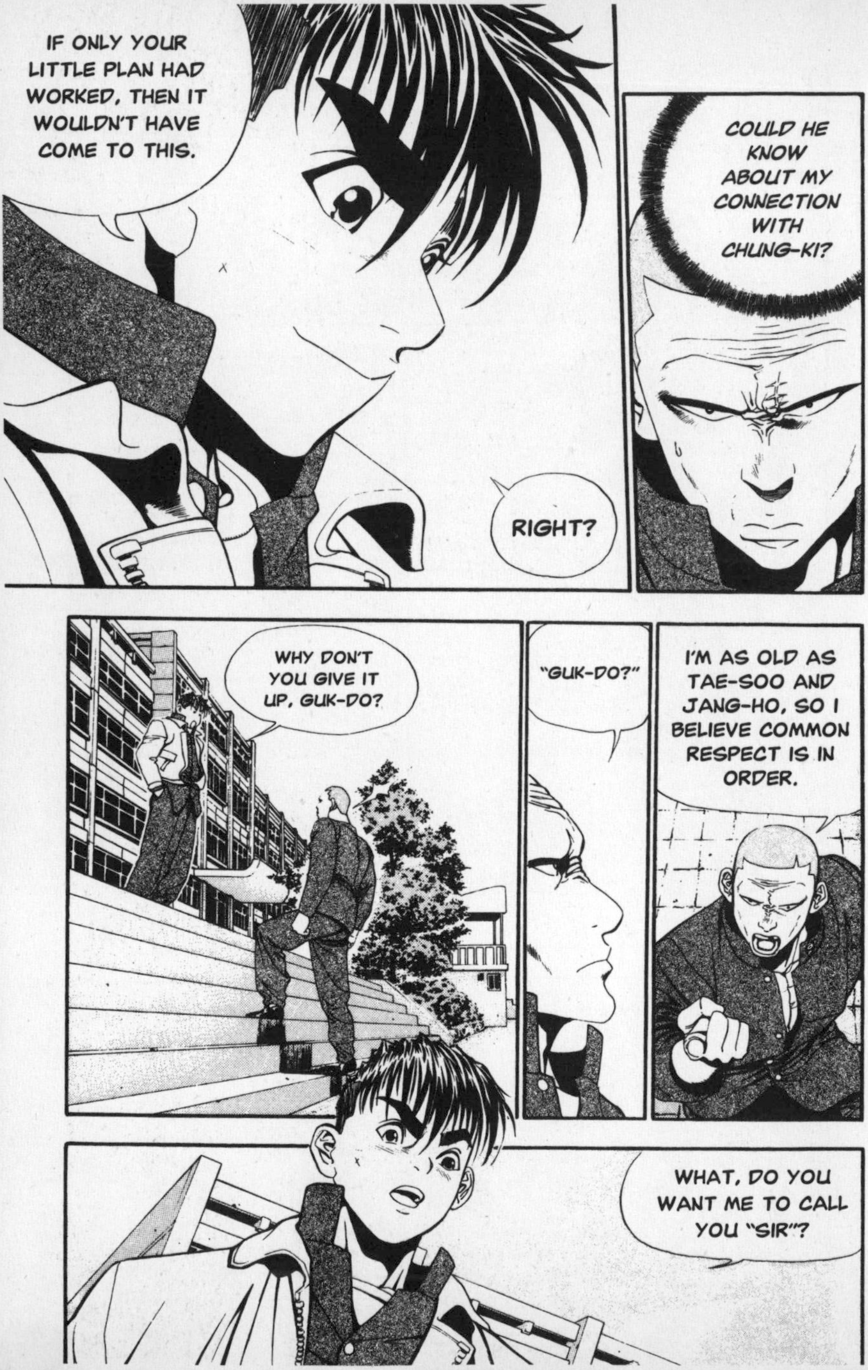
IF ONLY YOUR LITTLE PLAN HAD WORKED, THEN IT WOULDN'T HAVE COME TO THIS.
RIGHT?
COULD HE KNOW ABOUT MY CONNECTION WITH CHUNG-KI?
WHY DON'T YOU GIVE IT UP, GUK-DO?
"GUK-DO?"
I'M AS OLD AS TAE-SOO AND JANG-HO, SO I BELIEVE COMMON RESPECT IS IN ORDER.
WHAT, DO YOU WANT ME TO CALL YOU "SIR"?

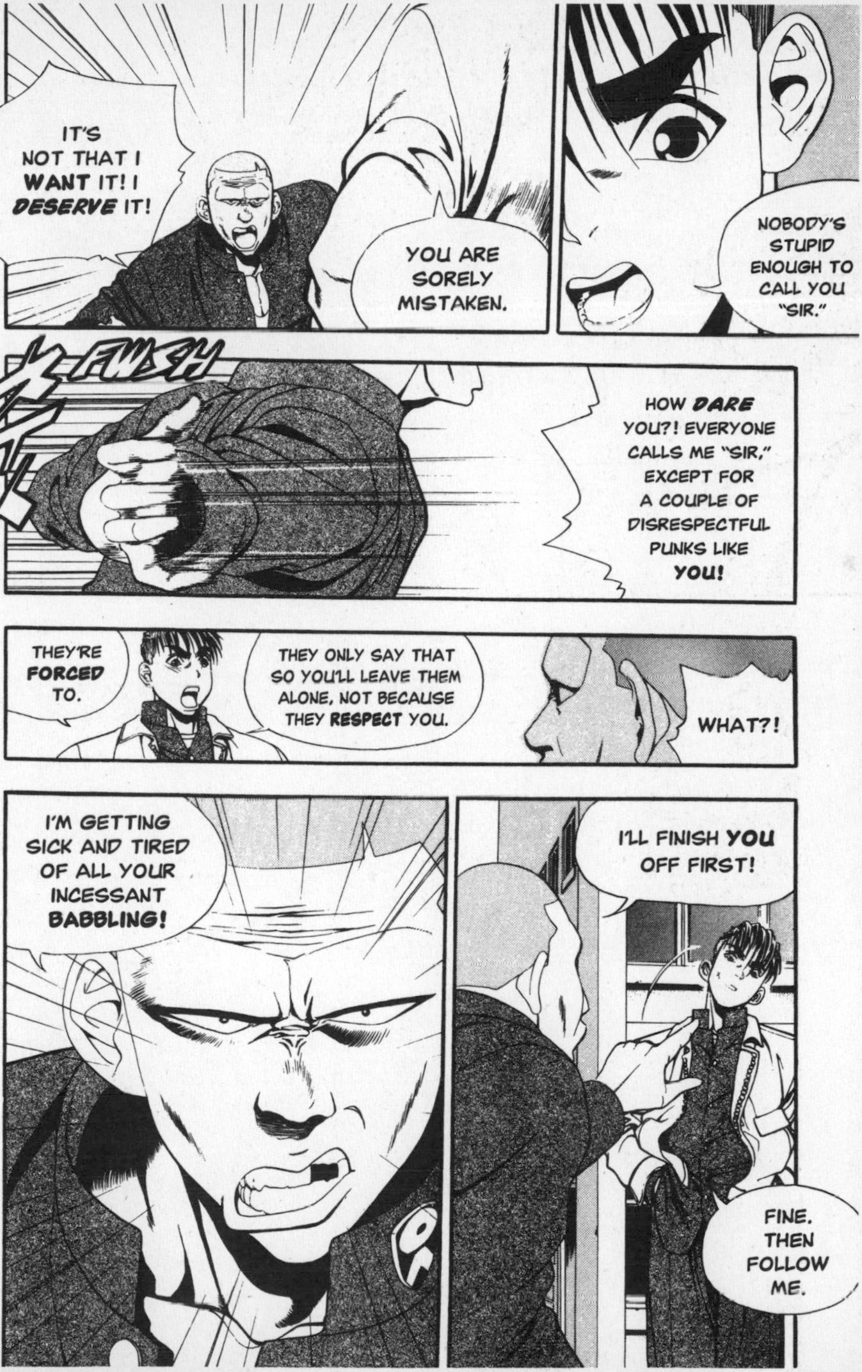
IT'S NOT THAT I WANT IT! I DESERVE IT!
YOU ARE SORELY MISTAKEN.
NOBODY'S STUPID ENOUGH TO CALL YOU "SIR."
FWISH
HOW DARE YOU?! EVERYONE CALLS ME "SIR," EXCEPT FOR A COUPLE OF DISRESPECTFUL PUNKS LIKE YOU!
THEY'RE FORCED TO.
THEY ONLY SAY THAT SO YOU'LL LEAVE THEM ALONE, NOT BECAUSE THEY RESPECT YOU.
WHAT?!
I'M GETTING SICK AND TIRED OF ALL YOUR INCESSANT BABBLING!
I'LL FINISH YOU OFF FIRST!
FINE. THEN FOLLOW ME.

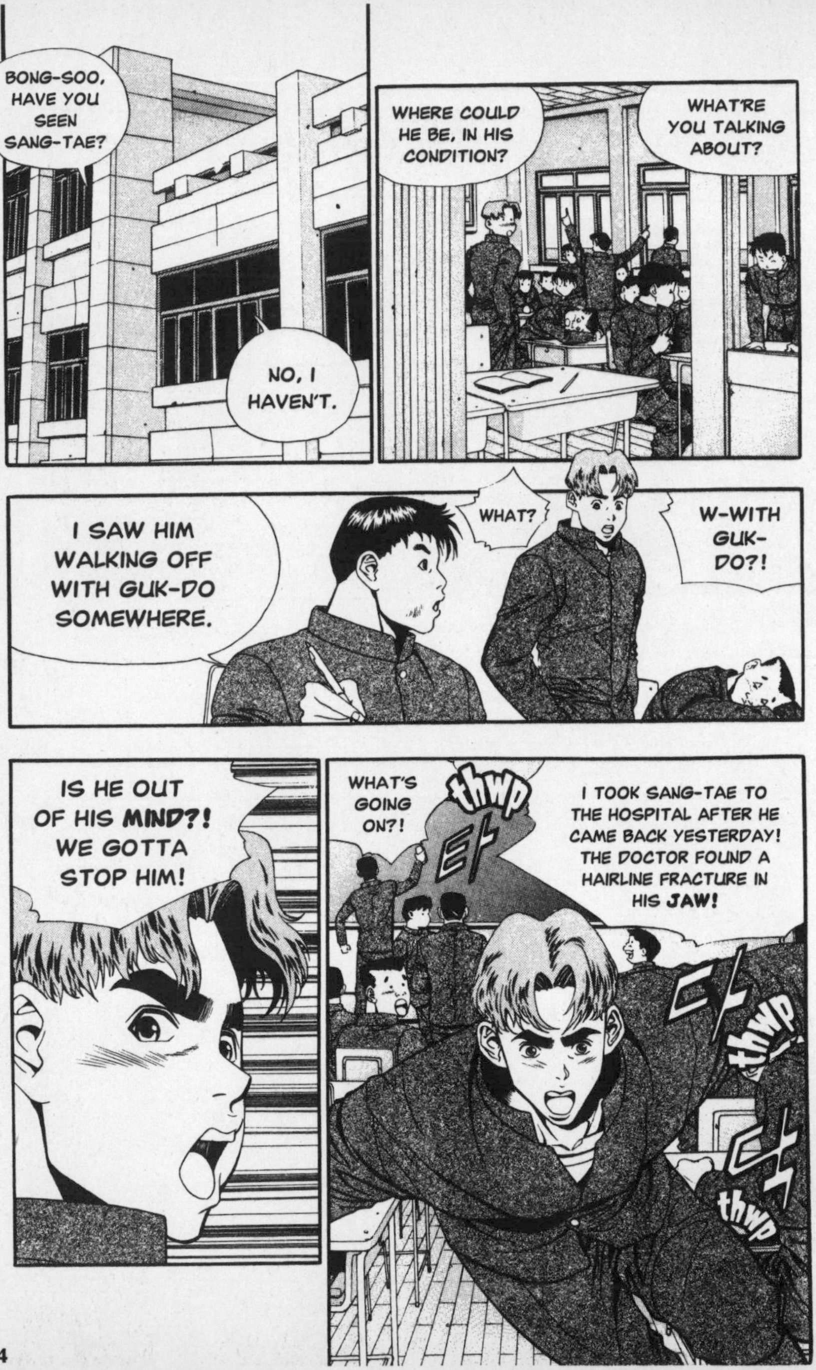
BONG-SOO, HAVE YOU SEEN SANG-TAE?
NO, I HAVEN'T.
WHERE COULD HE BE, IN HIS CONDITION?
WHAT'RE YOU TALKING ABOUT?
I SAW HIM WALKING OFF WITH GUK-DO SOMEWHERE.
WHAT?
W-WITH GUK-DO?!
IS HE OUT OF HIS MIND?! WE GOTTA STOP HIM!
WHAT'S GOING ON?!
thwp
I TOOK SANG-TAE TO THE HOSPITAL AFTER HE CAME BACK YESTERDAY! THE DOCTOR FOUND A HAIRLINE FRACTURE IN HIS JAW!
thwp
thwp

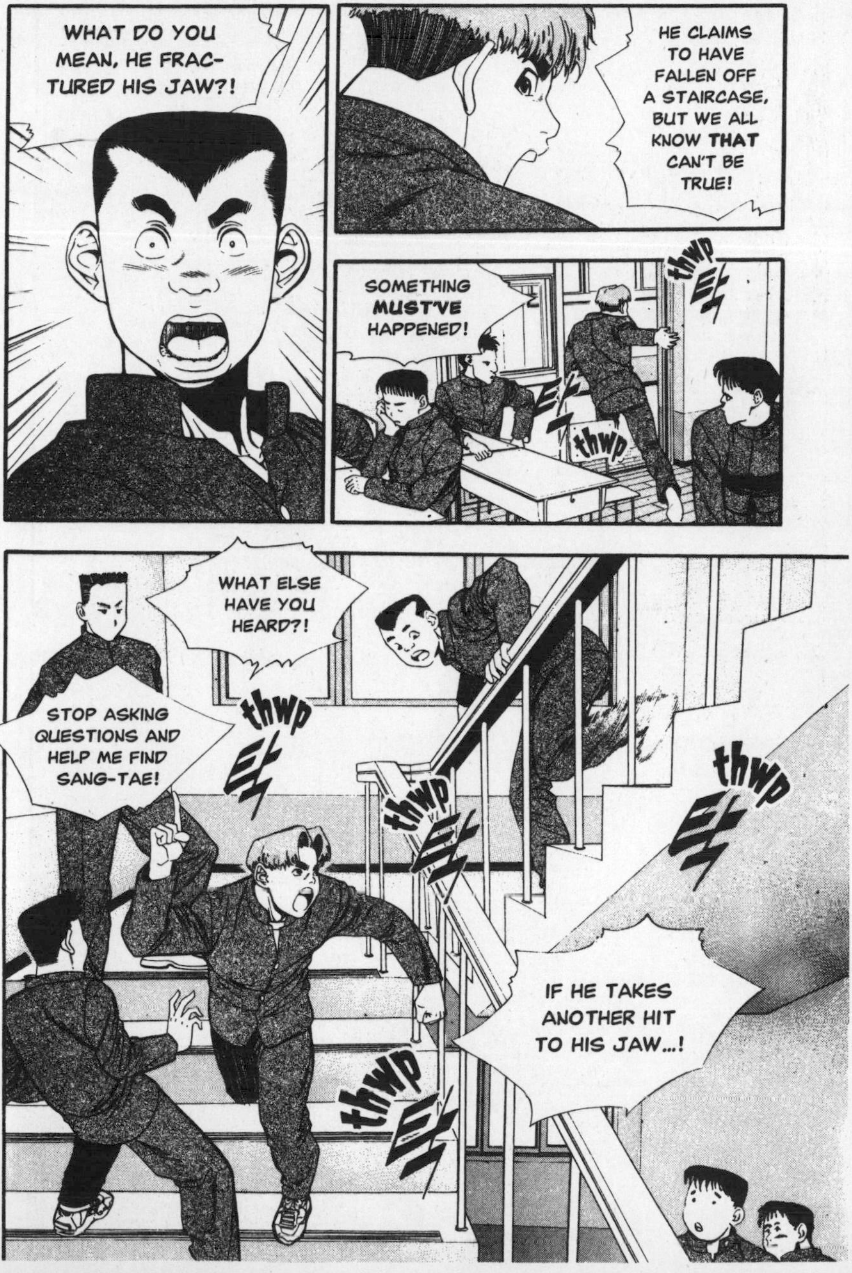
WHAT DO YOU MEAN, HE FRACTURED HIS JAW?!
HE CLAIMS TO HAVE FALLEN OFF A STAIRCASE, BUT WE ALL KNOW **THAT** CAN'T BE TRUE!
SOMETHING **MUST'VE** HAPPENED!
thwp
thwp
WHAT ELSE HAVE YOU HEARD?!
STOP ASKING QUESTIONS AND HELP ME FIND SANG-TAE!
thwp
thwp
thwp
IF HE TAKES ANOTHER HIT TO HIS JAW...!
thwp

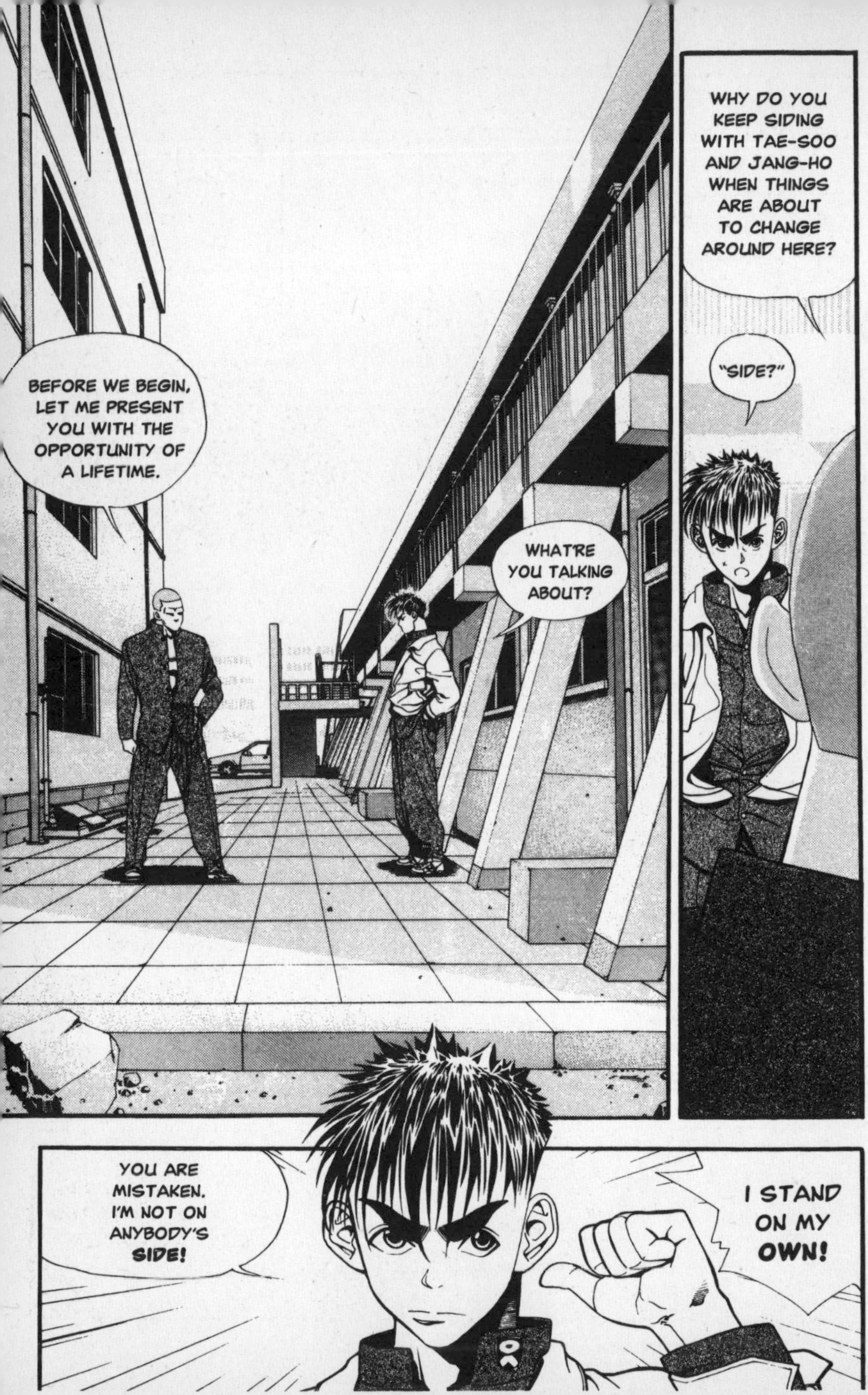

BEFORE WE BEGIN, LET ME PRESENT YOU WITH THE OPPORTUNITY OF A LIFETIME.
WHAT'RE YOU TALKING ABOUT?
WHY DO YOU KEEP SIDING WITH TAE-SOO AND JANG-HO WHEN THINGS ARE ABOUT TO CHANGE AROUND HERE?
"SIDE?"
YOU ARE MISTAKEN. I'M NOT ON ANYBODY'S SIDE!
I STAND ON MY OWN!

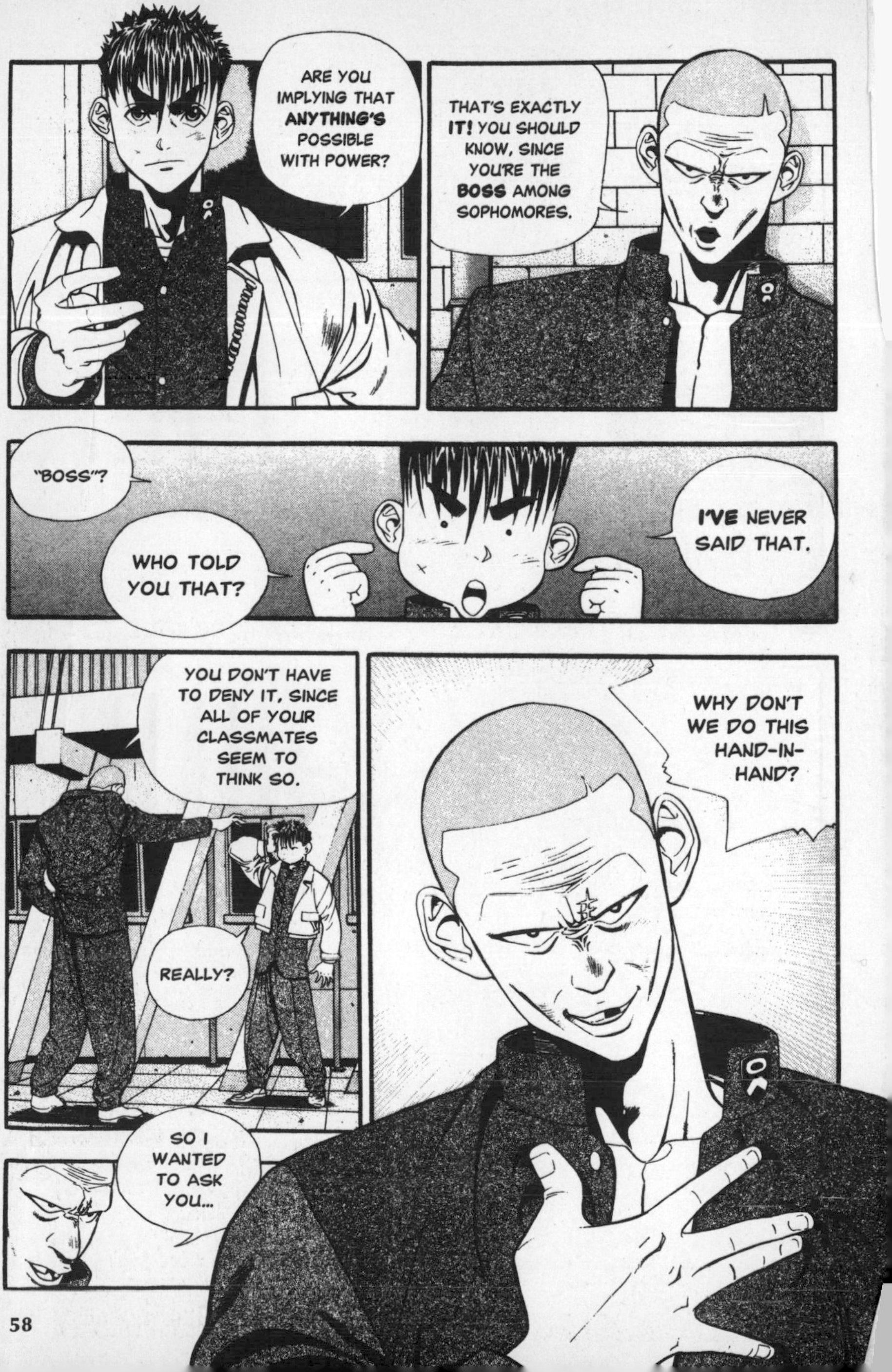
ARE YOU IMPLYING THAT ANYTHING'S POSSIBLE WITH POWER?
THAT'S EXACTLY IT! YOU SHOULD KNOW, SINCE YOU'RE THE BOSS AMONG SOPHOMORES.
"BOSS"?
WHO TOLD YOU THAT?
I'VE NEVER SAID THAT.
YOU DON'T HAVE TO DENY IT, SINCE ALL OF YOUR CLASSMATES SEEM TO THINK SO.
REALLY?
SO I WANTED TO ASK YOU...
WHY DON'T WE DO THIS HAND-IN-HAND?

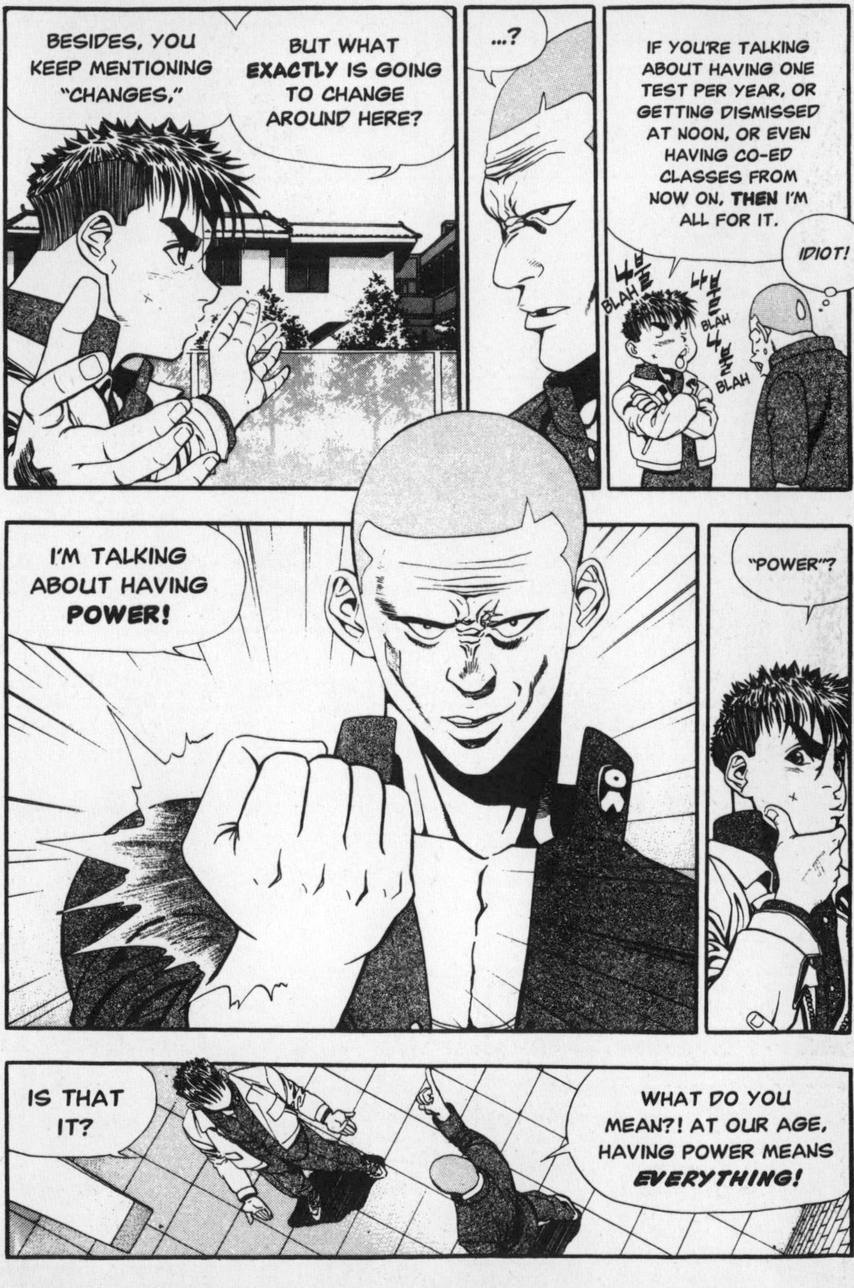
BESIDES, YOU KEEP MENTIONING "CHANGES,"
BUT WHAT EXACTLY IS GOING TO CHANGE AROUND HERE?
...?
IF YOU'RE TALKING ABOUT HAVING ONE TEST PER YEAR, OR GETTING DISMISSED AT NOON, OR EVEN HAVING CO-ED CLASSES FROM NOW ON, THEN I'M ALL FOR IT.
BLAH BLAH BLAH
IDIOT!
I'M TALKING ABOUT HAVING POWER!
"POWER"?
IS THAT IT?
WHAT DO YOU MEAN?! AT OUR AGE, HAVING POWER MEANS EVERYTHING!

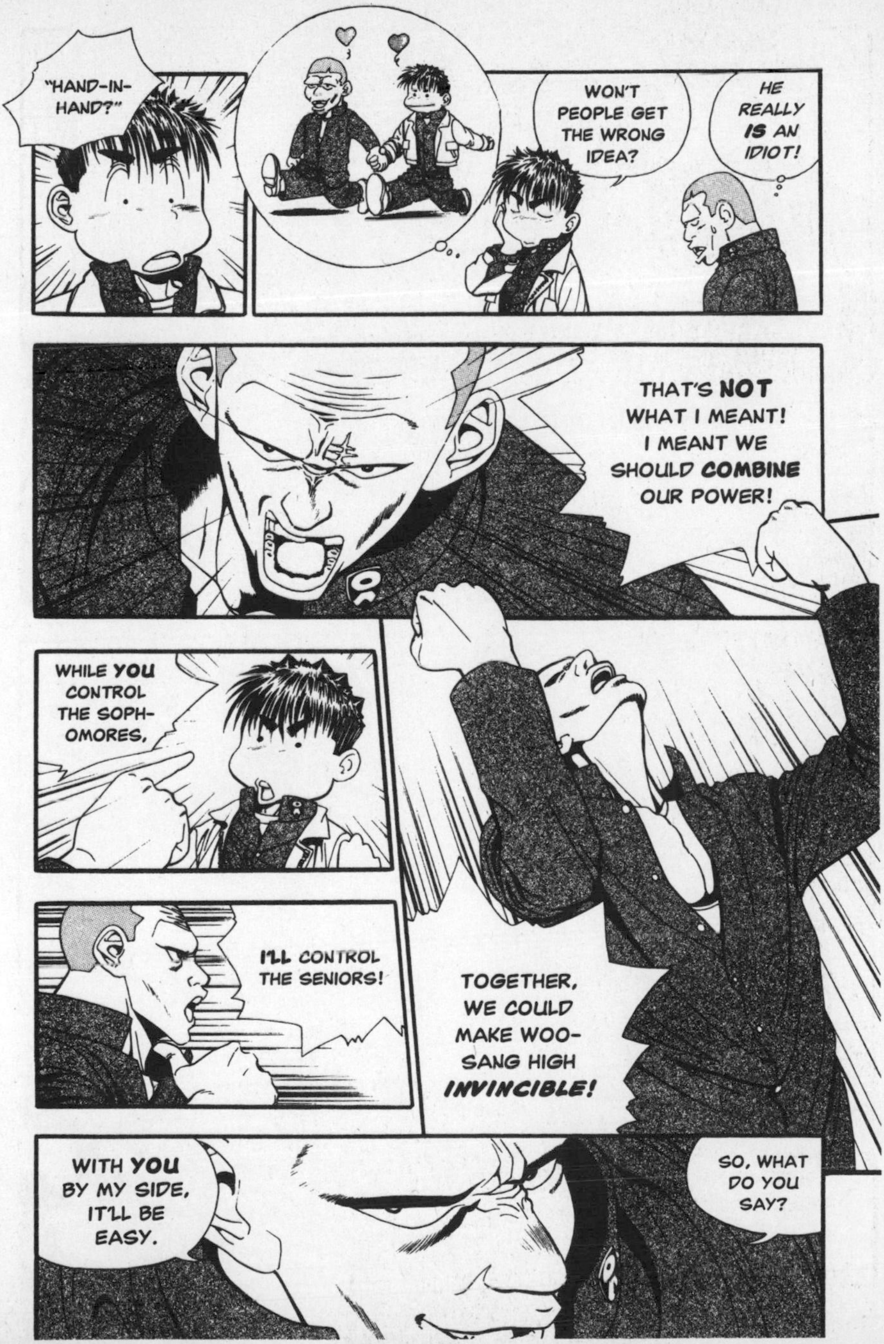
"HAND-IN-HAND?"
WON'T PEOPLE GET THE WRONG IDEA?
HE REALLY IS AN IDIOT!
THAT'S NOT WHAT I MEANT! I MEANT WE SHOULD COMBINE OUR POWER!
WHILE YOU CONTROL THE SOPH-OMORES,
I'LL CONTROL THE SENIORS!
TOGETHER, WE COULD MAKE WOO-SANG HIGH INVINCIBLE!
WITH YOU BY MY SIDE, IT'LL BE EASY.
SO, WHAT DO YOU SAY?

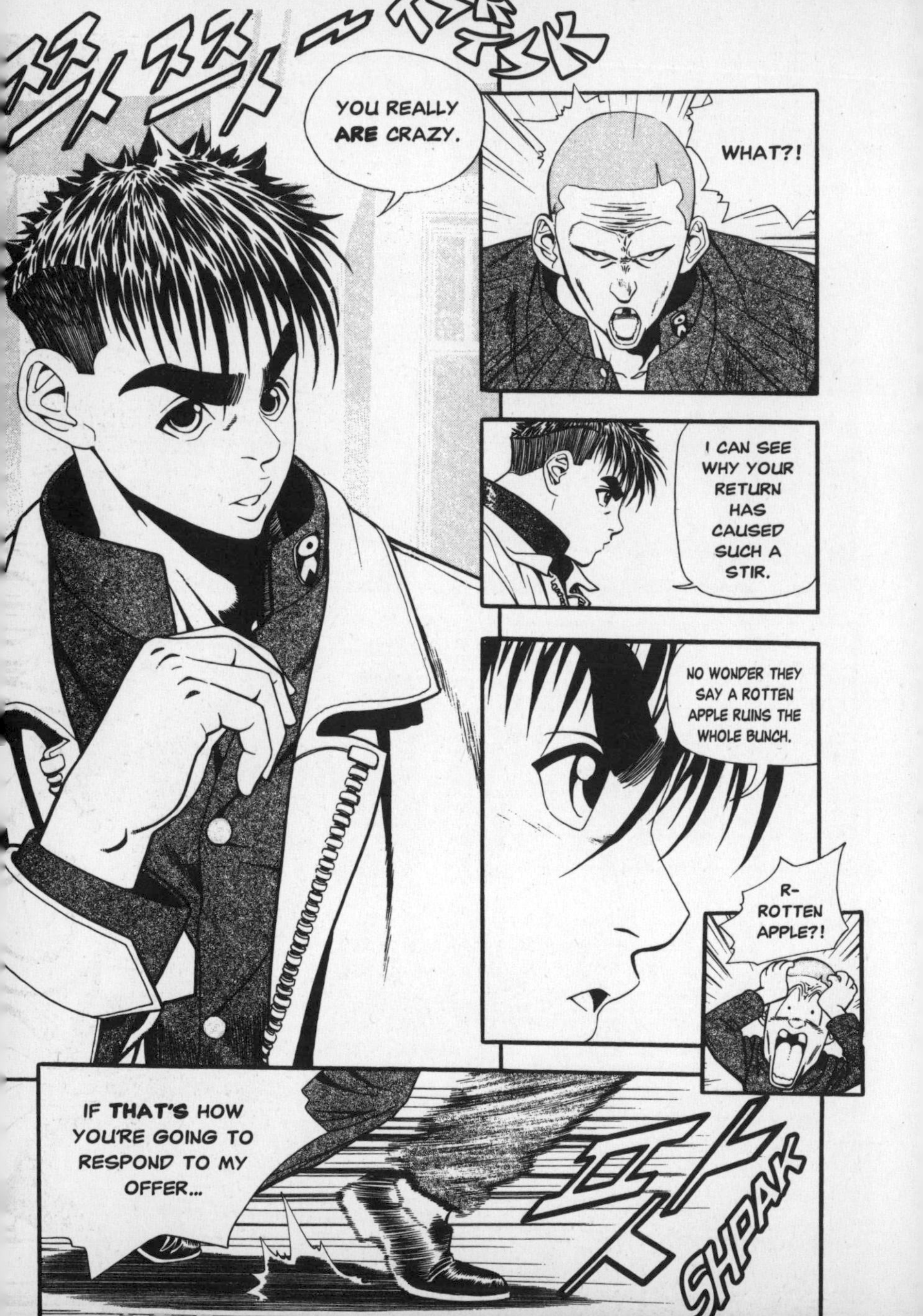
YOU REALLY **ARE** CRAZY.
WHAT?!
I CAN SEE WHY YOUR RETURN HAS CAUSED SUCH A STIR.
NO WONDER THEY SAY A ROTTEN APPLE RUINS THE WHOLE BUNCH.
R- ROTTEN APPLE?!
IF **THAT'S** HOW YOU'RE GOING TO RESPOND TO MY OFFER...
SHPAK

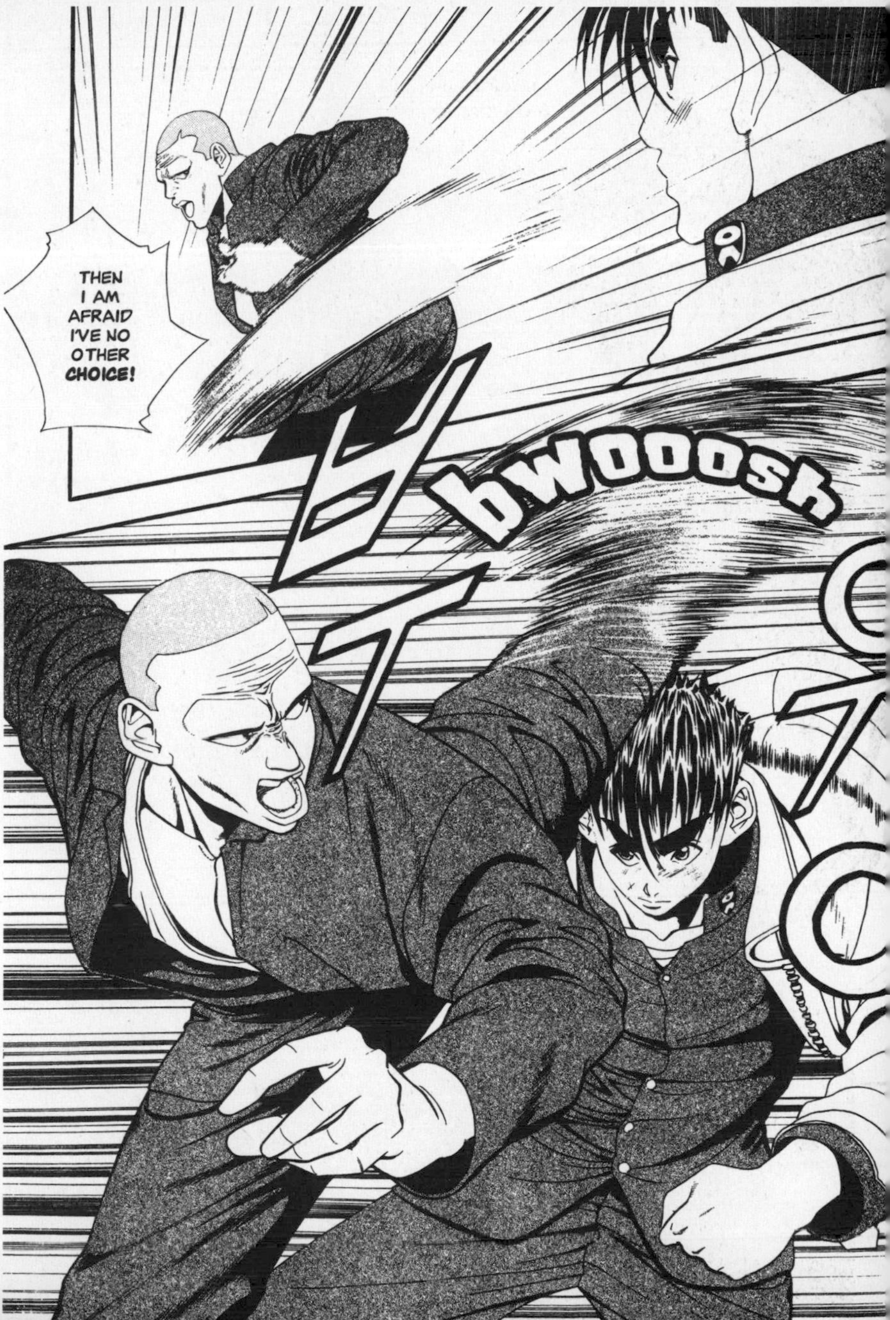
THEN I AM AFRAID I'VE NO OTHER CHOICE!
bwooosh

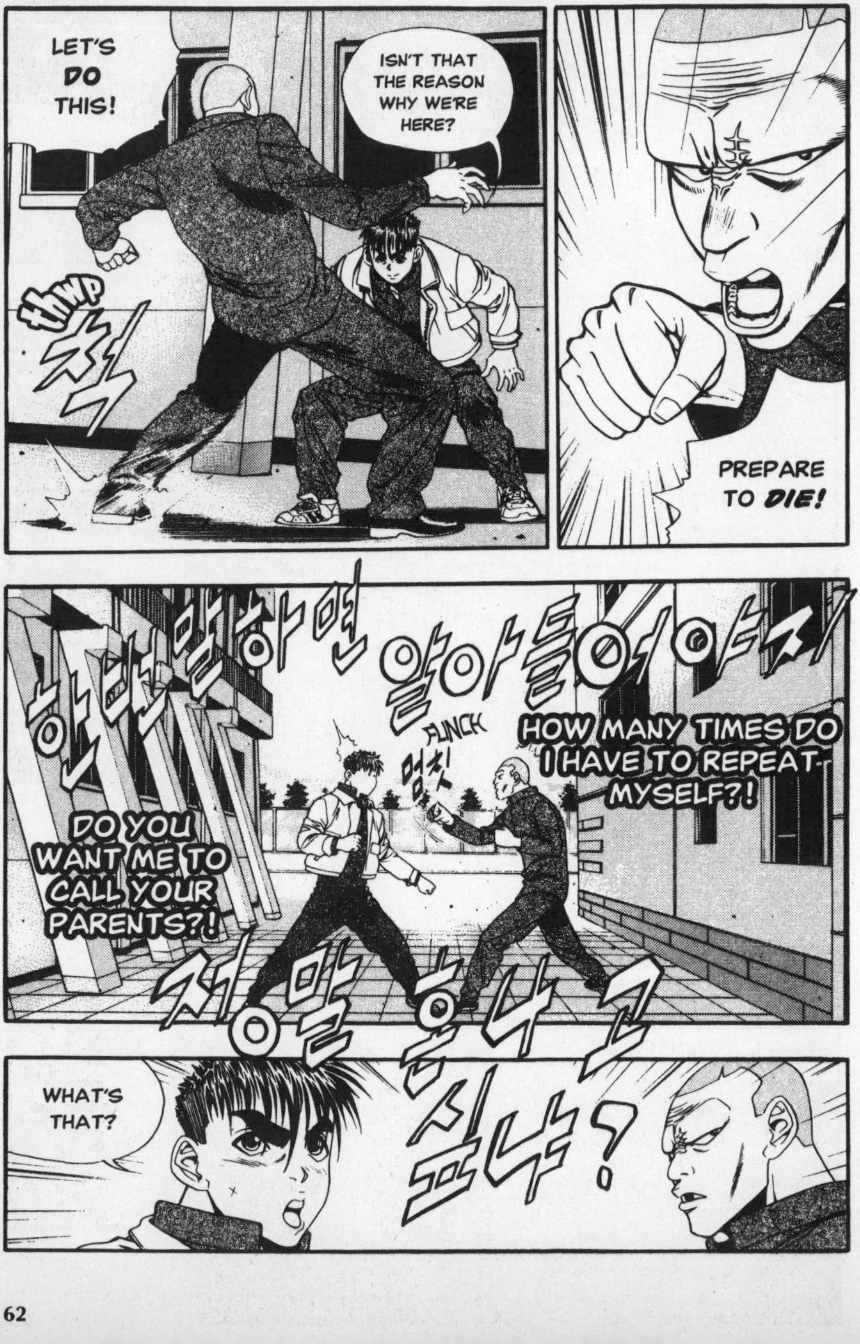
LET'S DO THIS!
ISN'T THAT THE REASON WHY WE'RE HERE?
thwp
PREPARE TO DIE!
HOW MANY TIMES DO I HAVE TO REPEAT-MYSELF?!
PUNCH
DO YOU WANT ME TO CALL YOUR PARENTS?!
WHAT'S THAT?

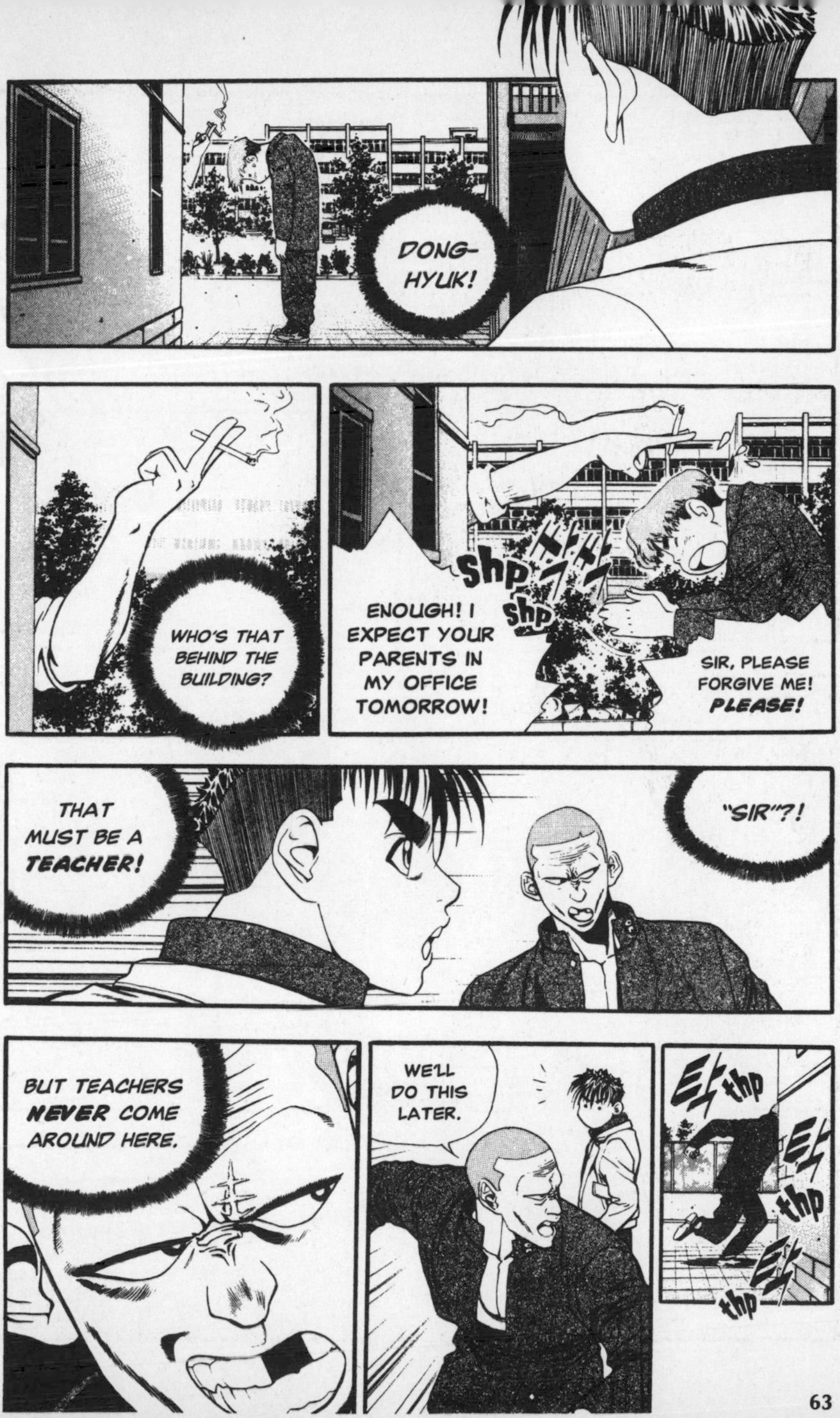
DONG-
HYUK!
WHO'S THAT BEHIND THE BUILDING?
shp
shp
ENOUGH! I EXPECT YOUR PARENTS IN MY OFFICE TOMORROW!
SIR, PLEASE FORGIVE ME! PLEASE!
THAT MUST BE A TEACHER!
"SIR"?!
BUT TEACHERS NEVER COME AROUND HERE.
WE'LL DO THIS LATER.
thp
thp
thp

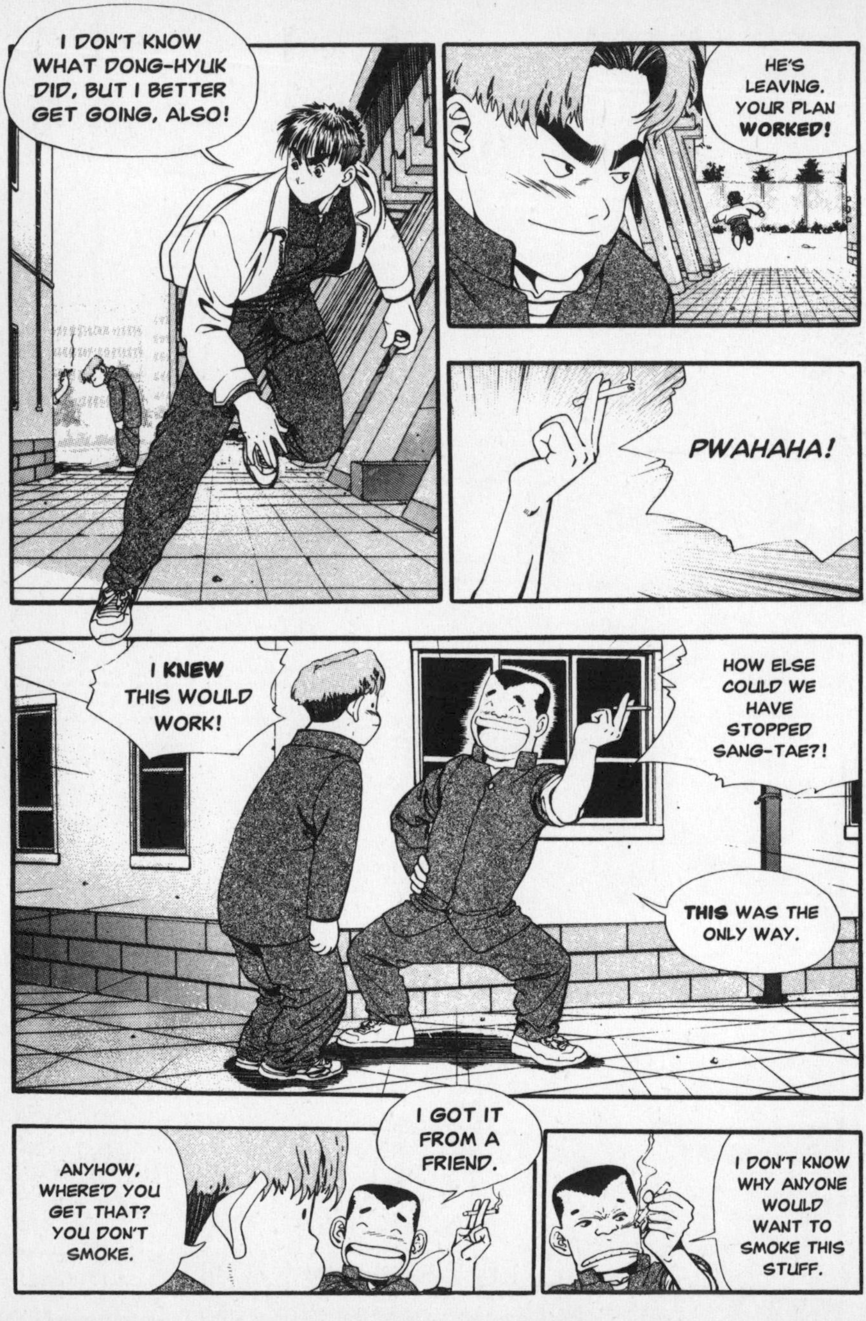
I DON'T KNOW WHAT DONG-HYUK DID, BUT I BETTER GET GOING, ALSO!
HE'S LEAVING. YOUR PLAN WORKED!
PWAHAHA!
I KNEW THIS WOULD WORK!
HOW ELSE COULD WE HAVE STOPPED SANG-TAE?!
THIS WAS THE ONLY WAY.
ANYHOW, WHERE'D YOU GET THAT? YOU DON'T SMOKE.
I GOT IT FROM A FRIEND.
I DON'T KNOW WHY ANYONE WOULD WANT TO SMOKE THIS STUFF.

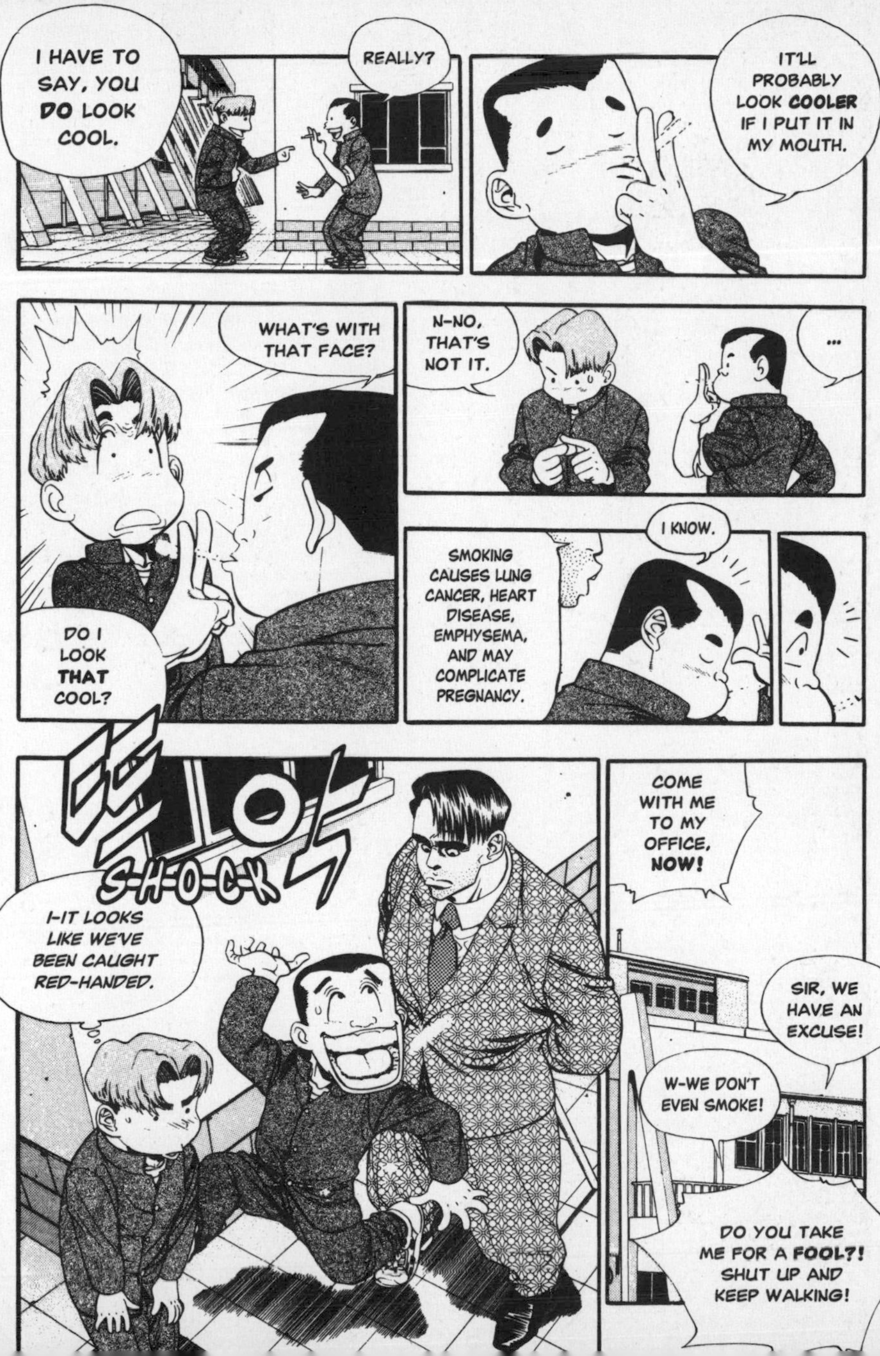
I HAVE TO SAY, YOU DO LOOK COOL.
REALLY?
IT'LL PROBABLY LOOK COOLER IF I PUT IT IN MY MOUTH.
WHAT'S WITH THAT FACE?
DO I LOOK THAT COOL?
N-NO, THAT'S NOT IT.
...
SMOKING CAUSES LUNG CANCER, HEART DISEASE, EMPHYSEMA, AND MAY COMPLICATE PREGNANCY.
I KNOW.
S-H-O-C-K
COME WITH ME TO MY OFFICE, NOW!
I-IT LOOKS LIKE WE'VE BEEN CAUGHT RED-HANDED.
SIR, WE HAVE AN EXCUSE!
W-WE DON'T EVEN SMOKE!
DO YOU TAKE ME FOR A FOOL?! SHUT UP AND KEEP WALKING!

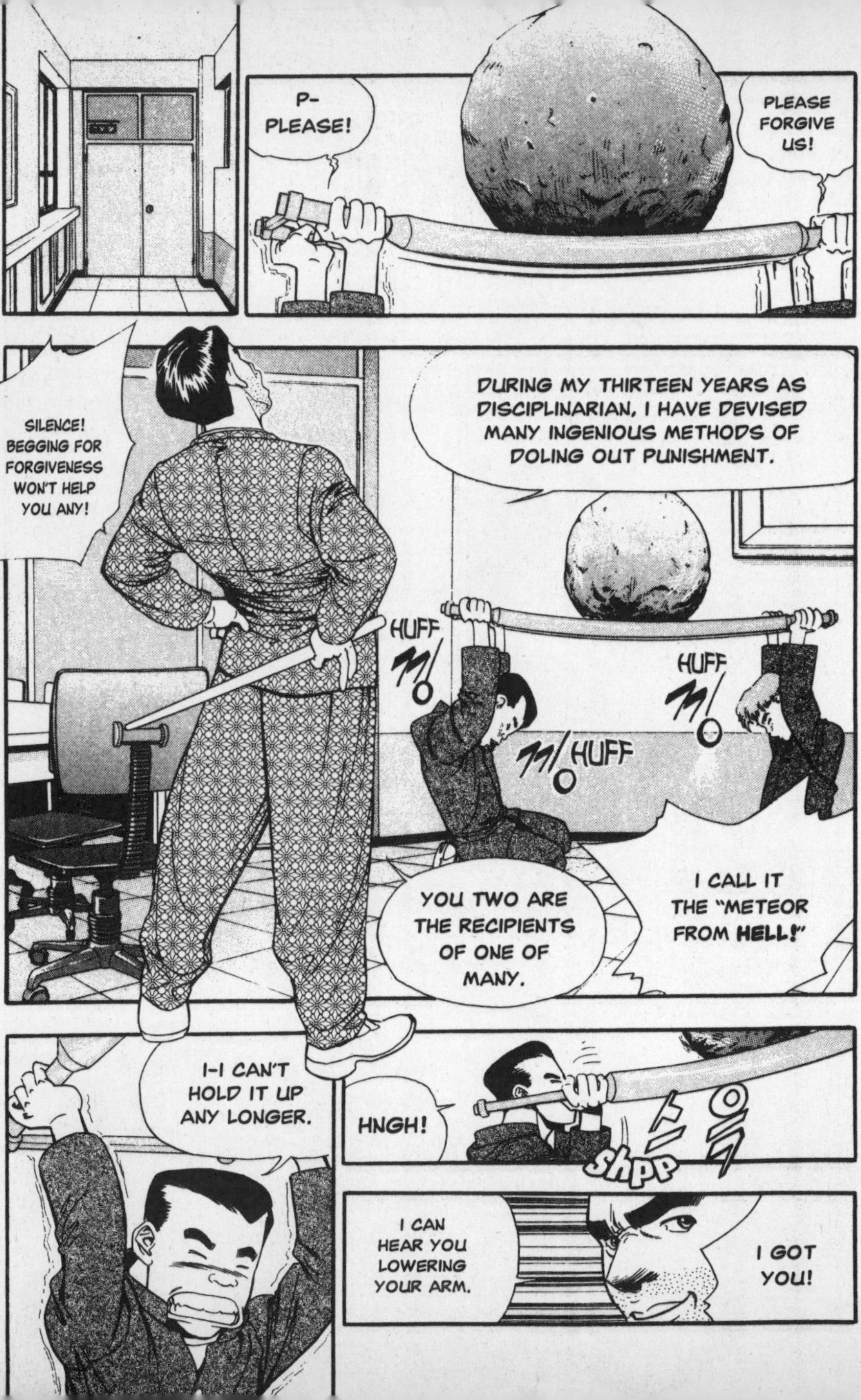
P-
PLEASE!
PLEASE FORGIVE US!
SILENCE! BEGGING FOR FORGIVENESS WON'T HELP YOU ANY!
DURING MY THIRTEEN YEARS AS DISCIPLINARIAN, I HAVE DEVISED MANY INGENIOUS METHODS OF DOLING OUT PUNISHMENT.
HUFF
HUFF
HUFF
YOU TWO ARE THE RECIPIENTS OF ONE OF MANY.
I CALL IT THE "METEOR FROM HELL!"
I-I CAN'T HOLD IT UP ANY LONGER.
HNGH!
SHPP
I CAN HEAR YOU LOWERING YOUR ARM.
I GOT YOU!

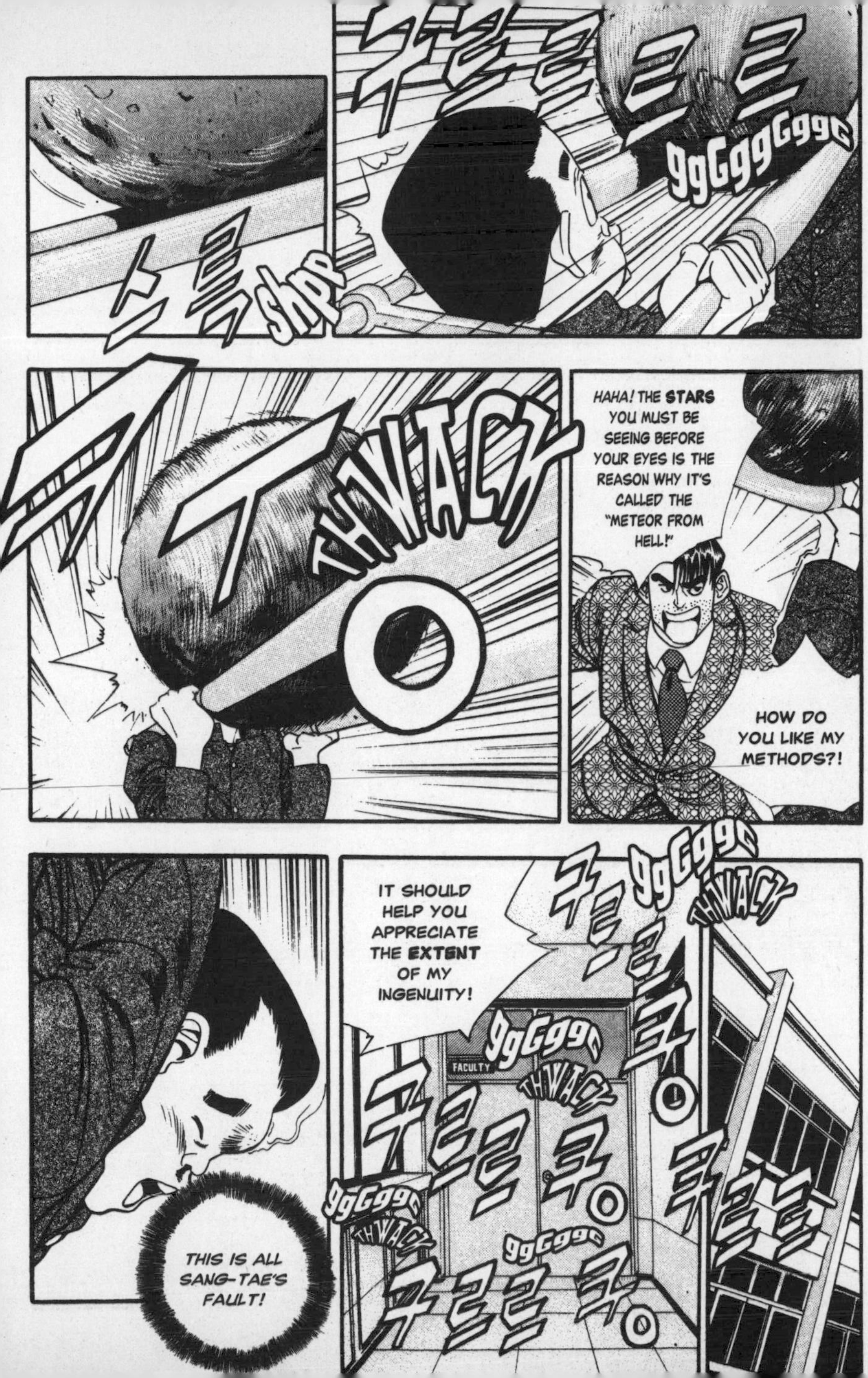
shp
ggGggGggG
THWACK
HAHA! THE STARS YOU MUST BE SEEING BEFORE YOUR EYES IS THE REASON WHY IT'S CALLED THE "METEOR FROM HELL!"
HOW DO YOU LIKE MY METHODS?!
THIS IS ALL SANG-TAE'S FAULT!
IT SHOULD HELP YOU APPRECIATE THE EXTENT OF MY INGENUITY!
ggGggG
THWACK
FACULTY
ggGggG
THWACK
ggGggG
THWACK
ggGggG

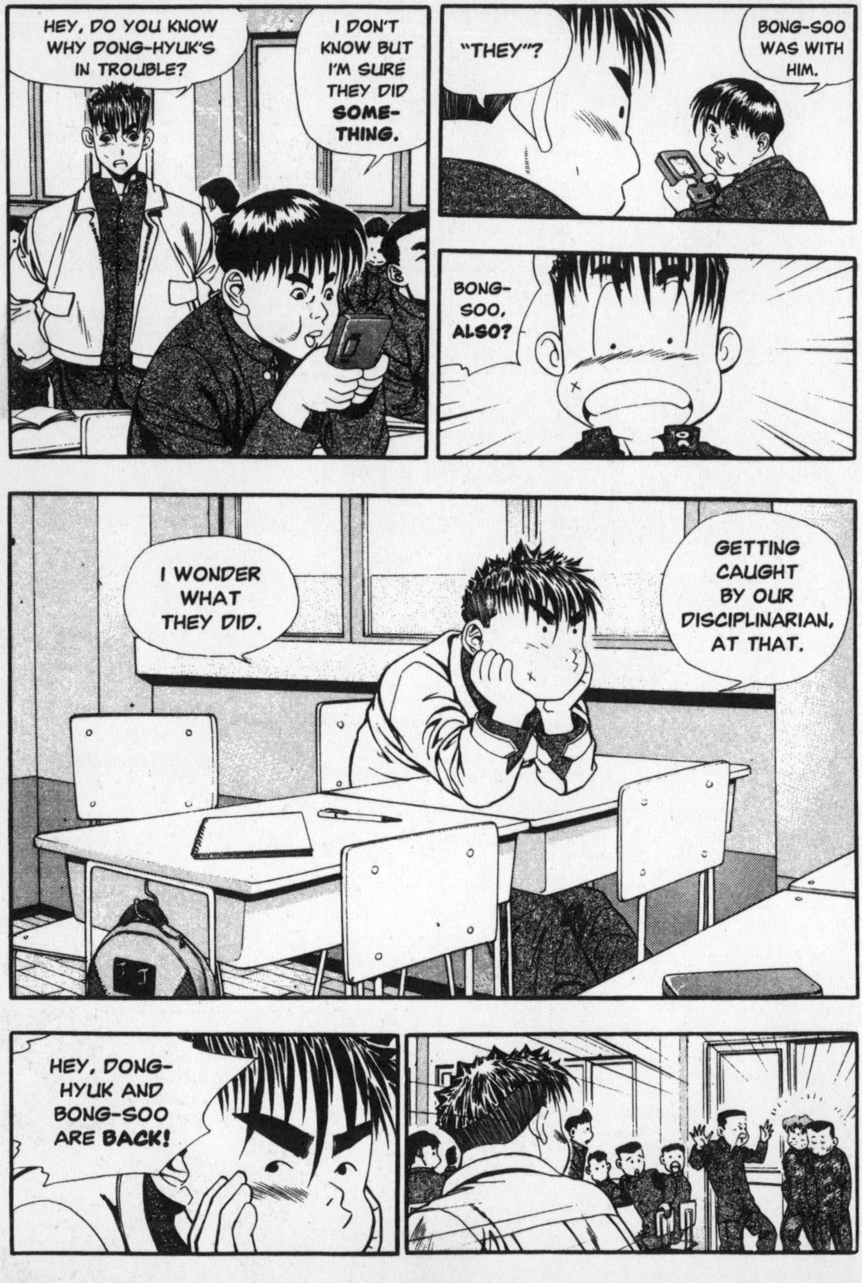
HEY, DO YOU KNOW WHY DONG-HYUK'S IN TROUBLE?
I DON'T KNOW BUT I'M SURE THEY DID SOMETHING.
"THEY"?
BONG-SOO WAS WITH HIM.
BONG-SOO, ALSO?
I WONDER WHAT THEY DID.
GETTING CAUGHT BY OUR DISCIPLINARIAN, AT THAT.
HEY, DONG-HYUK AND BONG-SOO ARE BACK!

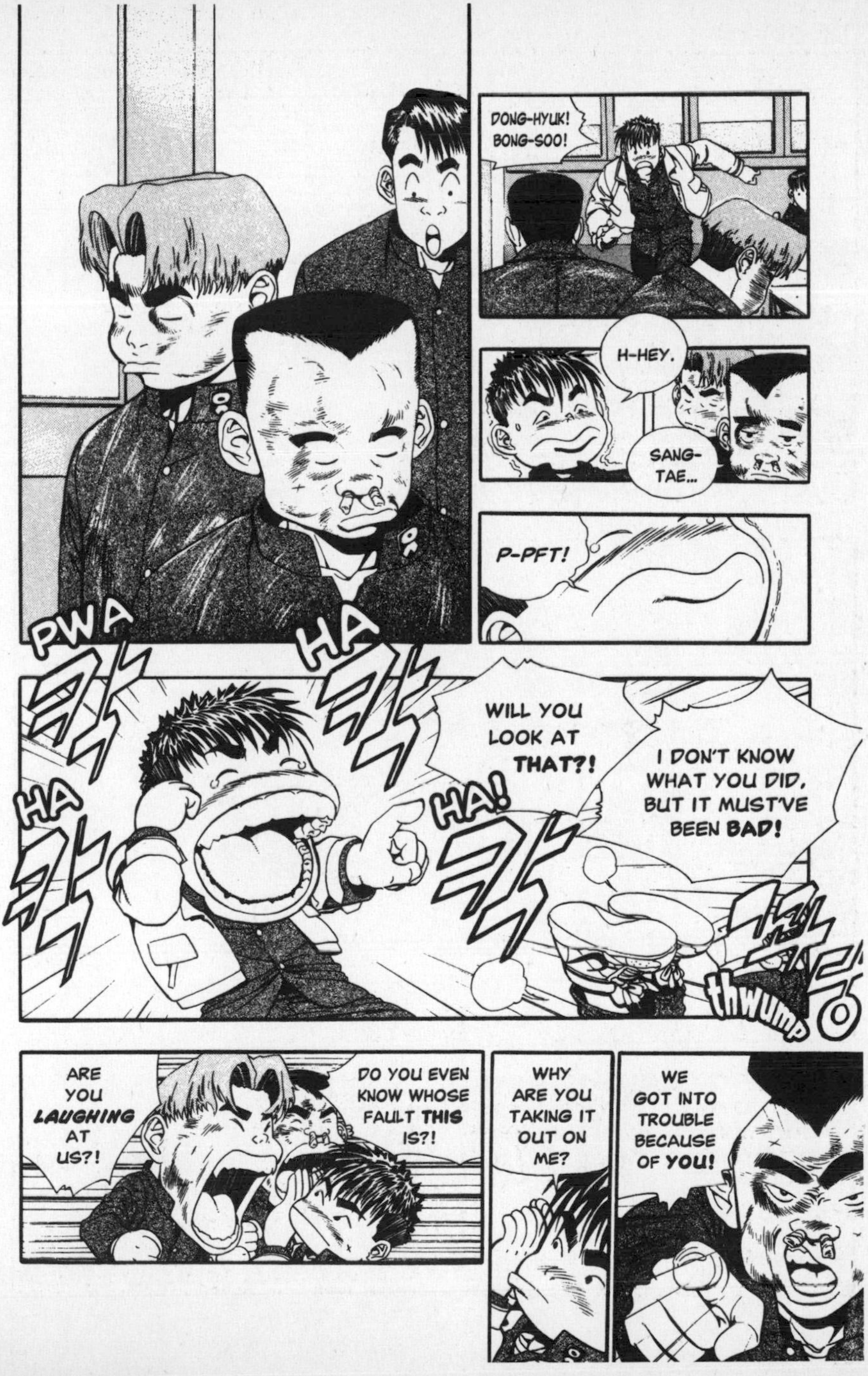
DONG-HYUK! BONG-SOO!
H-HEY.
SANG-TAE...
P-PFT!
PWA
HA
HA
HA!
WILL YOU LOOK AT THAT?!
I DON'T KNOW WHAT YOU DID, BUT IT MUST'VE BEEN BAD!
thwump
ARE YOU LAUGHING AT US?!
DO YOU EVEN KNOW WHOSE FAULT THIS IS?!
WHY ARE YOU TAKING IT OUT ON ME?
WE GOT INTO TROUBLE BECAUSE OF YOU!

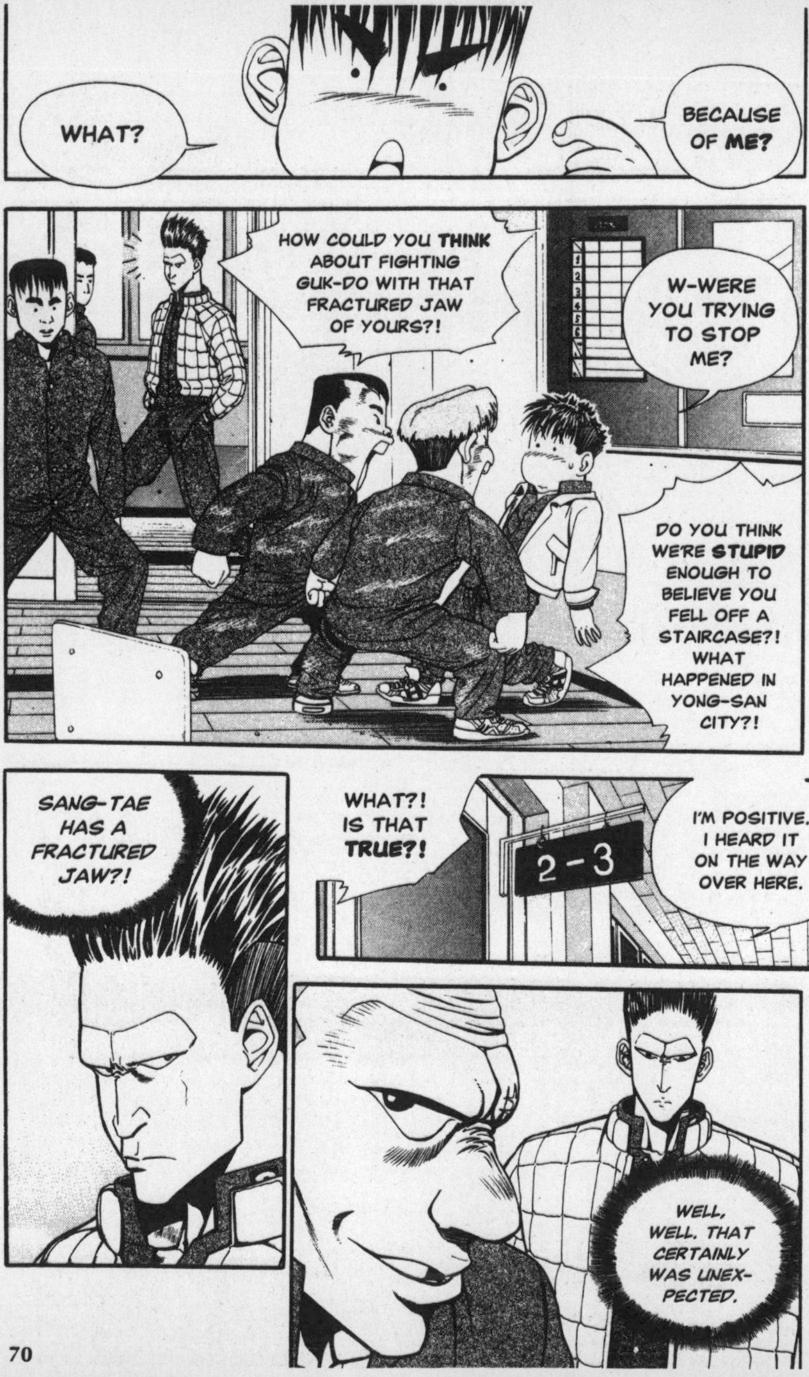
WHAT?
BECAUSE OF ME?
HOW COULD YOU THINK ABOUT FIGHTING GUK-DO WITH THAT FRACTURED JAW OF YOURS?!
W-WERE YOU TRYING TO STOP ME?
DO YOU THINK WE'RE STUPID ENOUGH TO BELIEVE YOU FELL OFF A STAIRCASE?! WHAT HAPPENED IN YONG-SAN CITY?!
SANG-TAE HAS A FRACTURED JAW?!
WHAT?! IS THAT TRUE?!
2-3
I'M POSITIVE. I HEARD IT ON THE WAY OVER HERE.
WELL, WELL. THAT CERTAINLY WAS UNEXPECTED.

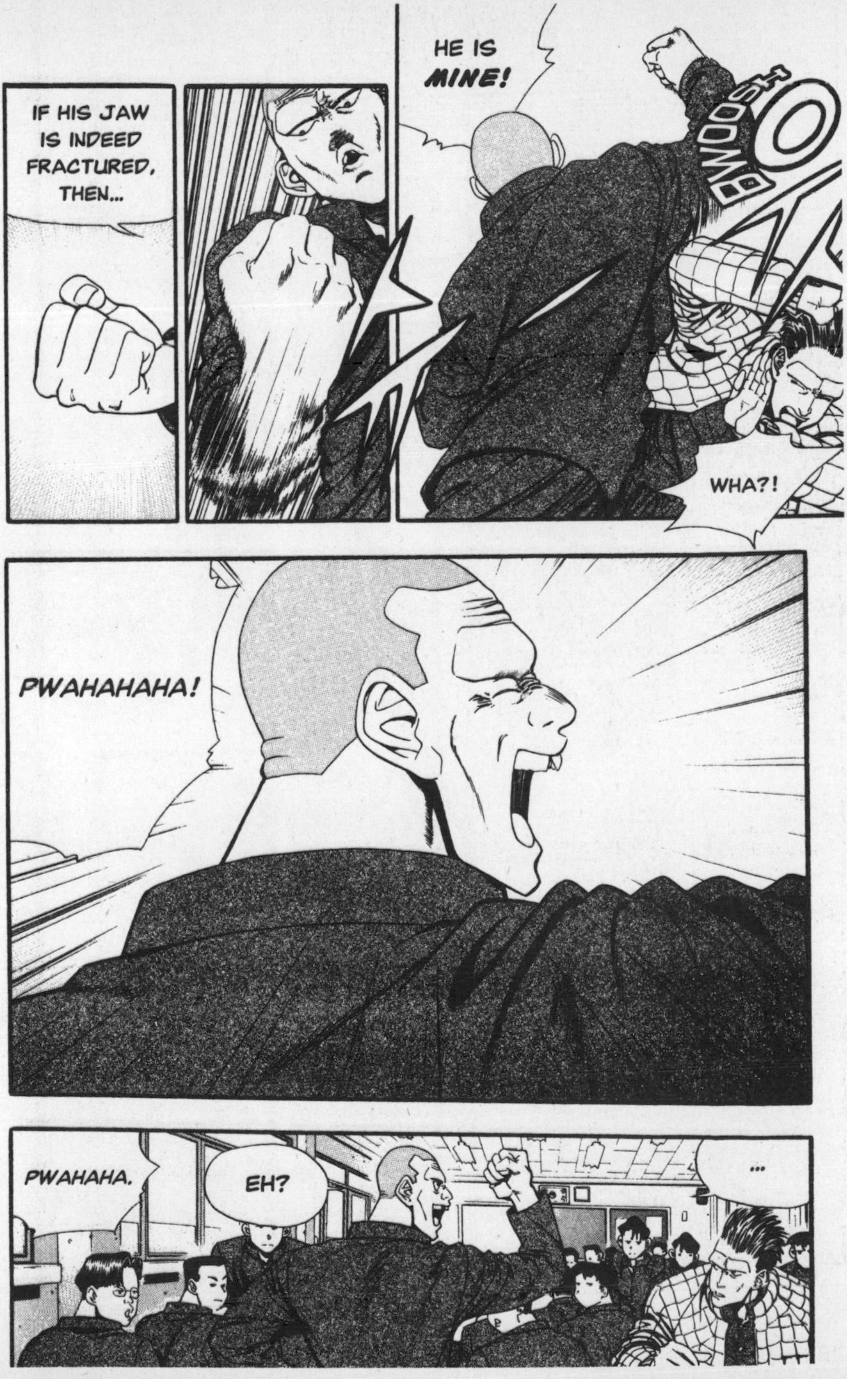
IF HIS JAW IS INDEED FRACTURED, THEN...
HE IS MINE!
BWOOSH
WHA?!
PWAHAHAHA!
PWAHAHA.
EH?
...

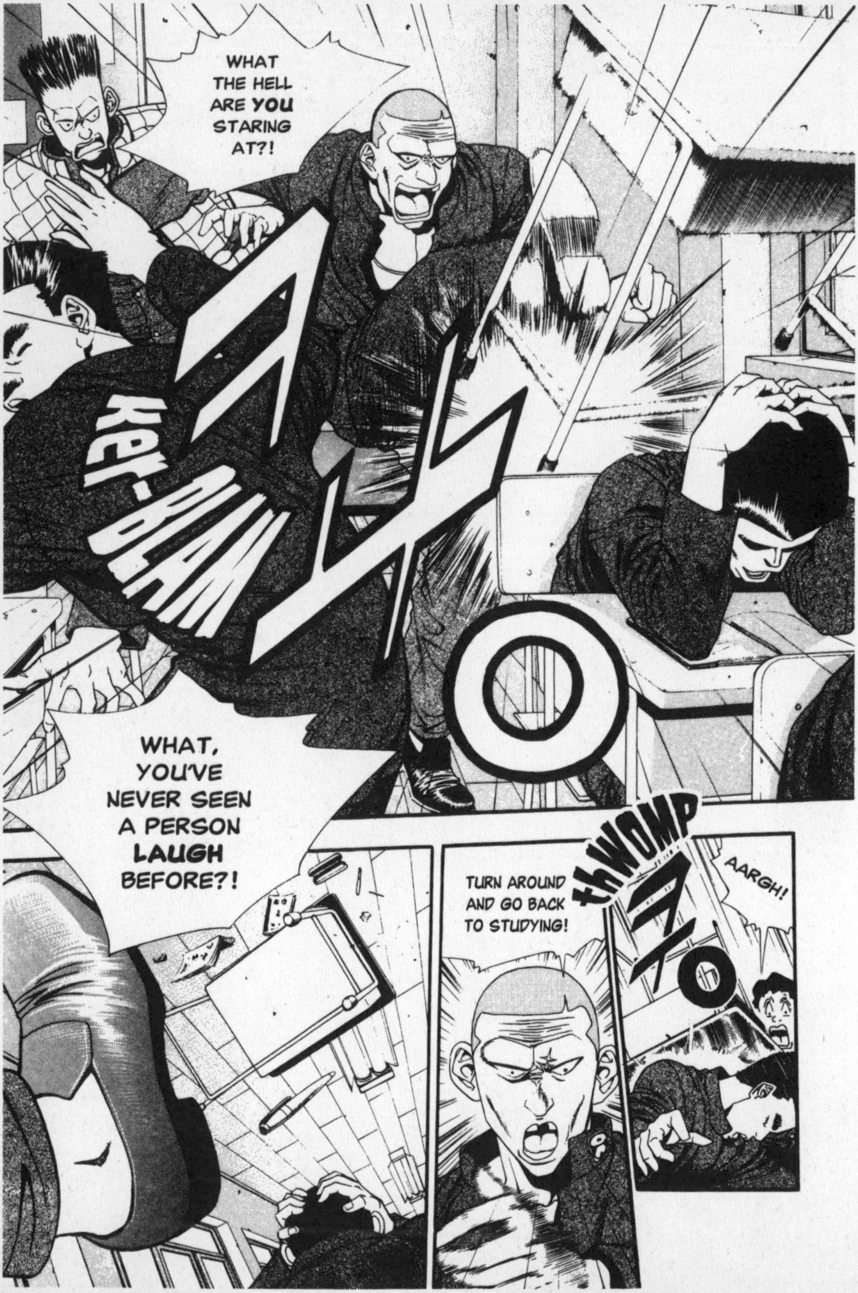
WHAT THE HELL ARE YOU STARING AT?!
Ker-BLAM
WHAT, YOU'VE NEVER SEEN A PERSON LAUGH BEFORE?!
thWOMP
AARGH!
TURN AROUND AND GO BACK TO STUDYING!

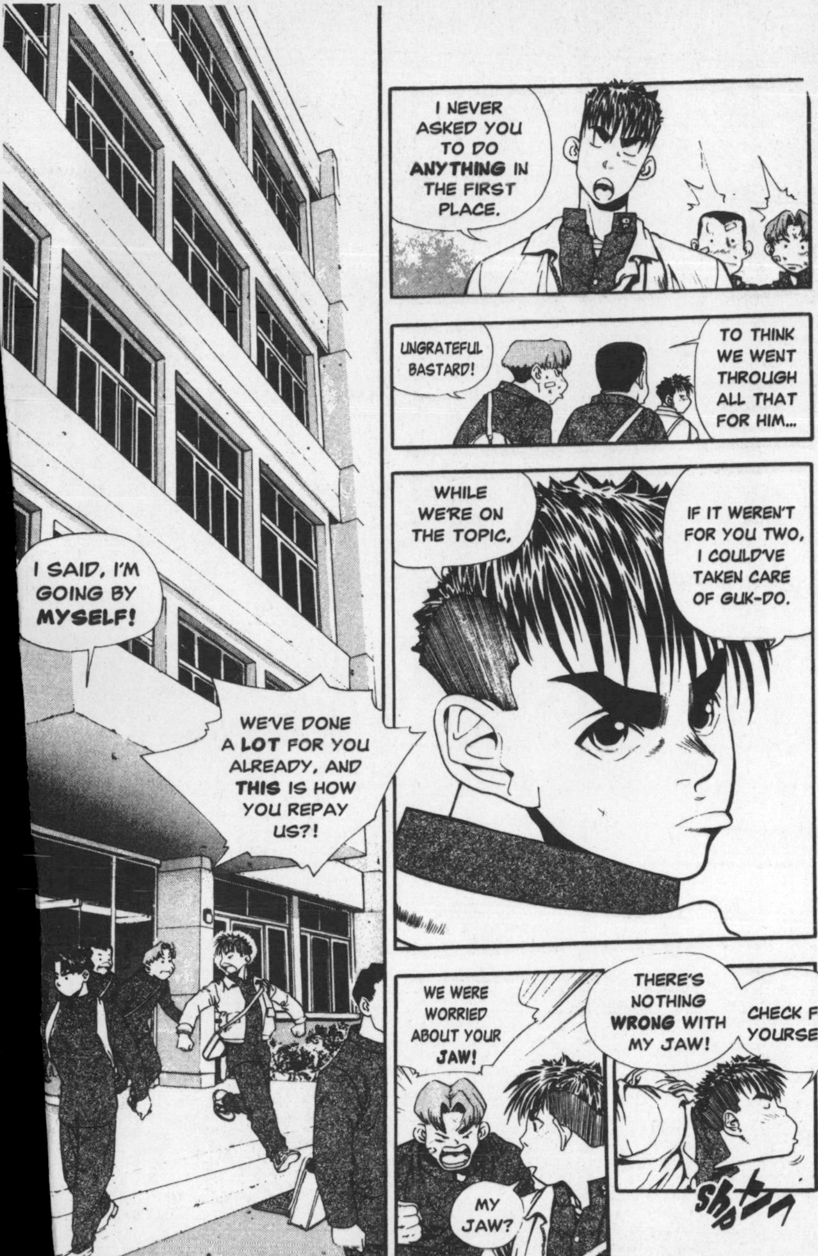
I SAID, I'M GOING BY MYSELF!
WE'VE DONE A LOT FOR YOU ALREADY, AND THIS IS HOW YOU REPAY US?!
I NEVER ASKED YOU TO DO ANYTHING IN THE FIRST PLACE.
UNGRATEFUL BASTARD!
TO THINK WE WENT THROUGH ALL THAT FOR HIM...
WHILE WE'RE ON THE TOPIC,
IF IT WEREN'T FOR YOU TWO, I COULD'VE TAKEN CARE OF GUK-DO.
WE WERE WORRIED ABOUT YOUR JAW!
MY JAW?
THERE'S NOTHING WRONG WITH MY JAW!
CHECK FOR YOURSELF!
SHP

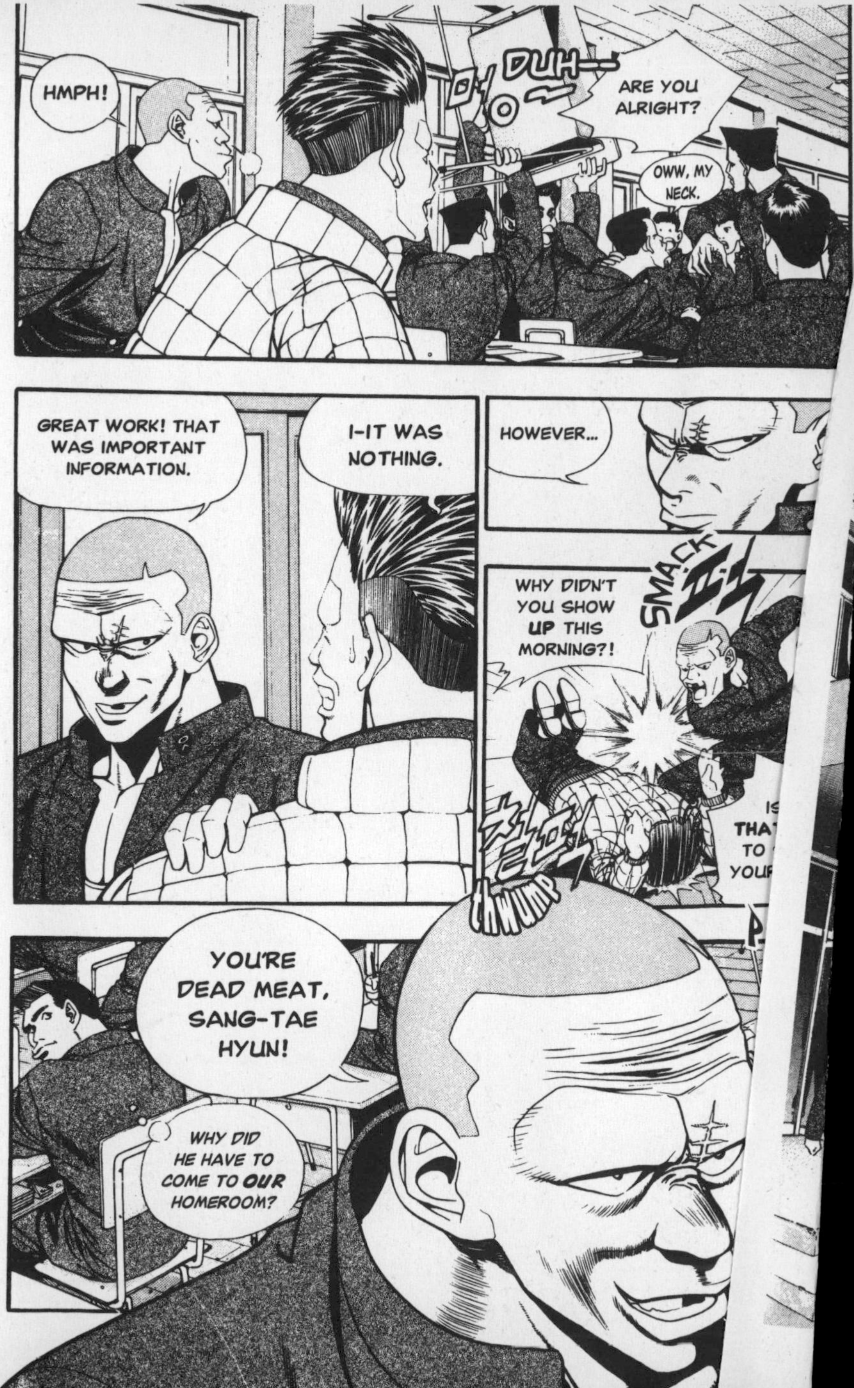
HMPH!
DUH--
ARE YOU ALRIGHT?
OWW, MY NECK.
GREAT WORK! THAT WAS IMPORTANT INFORMATION.
I-IT WAS NOTHING.
HOWEVER...
WHY DIDN'T YOU SHOW UP THIS MORNING?!
SMACK
thwump
YOU'RE DEAD MEAT, SANG-TAE HYUN!
WHY DID HE HAVE TO COME TO OUR HOMEROOM?

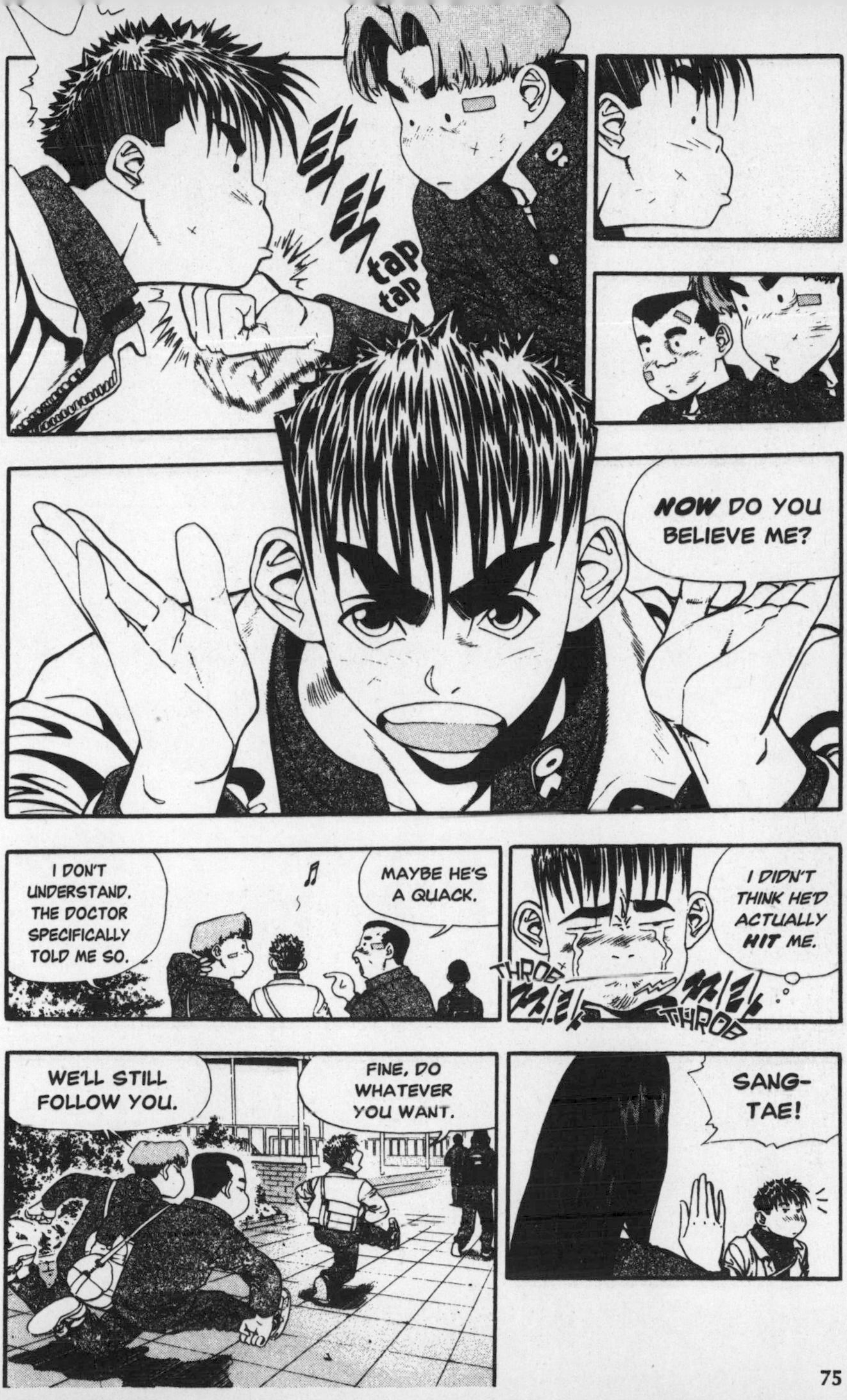
tap tap
NOW DO YOU BELIEVE ME?
I DON'T UNDERSTAND. THE DOCTOR SPECIFICALLY TOLD ME SO.
MAYBE HE'S A QUACK.
I DIDN'T THINK HE'D ACTUALLY HIT ME.
THROB
THROB
WE'LL STILL FOLLOW YOU.
FINE, DO WHATEVER YOU WANT.
SANG-TAE!

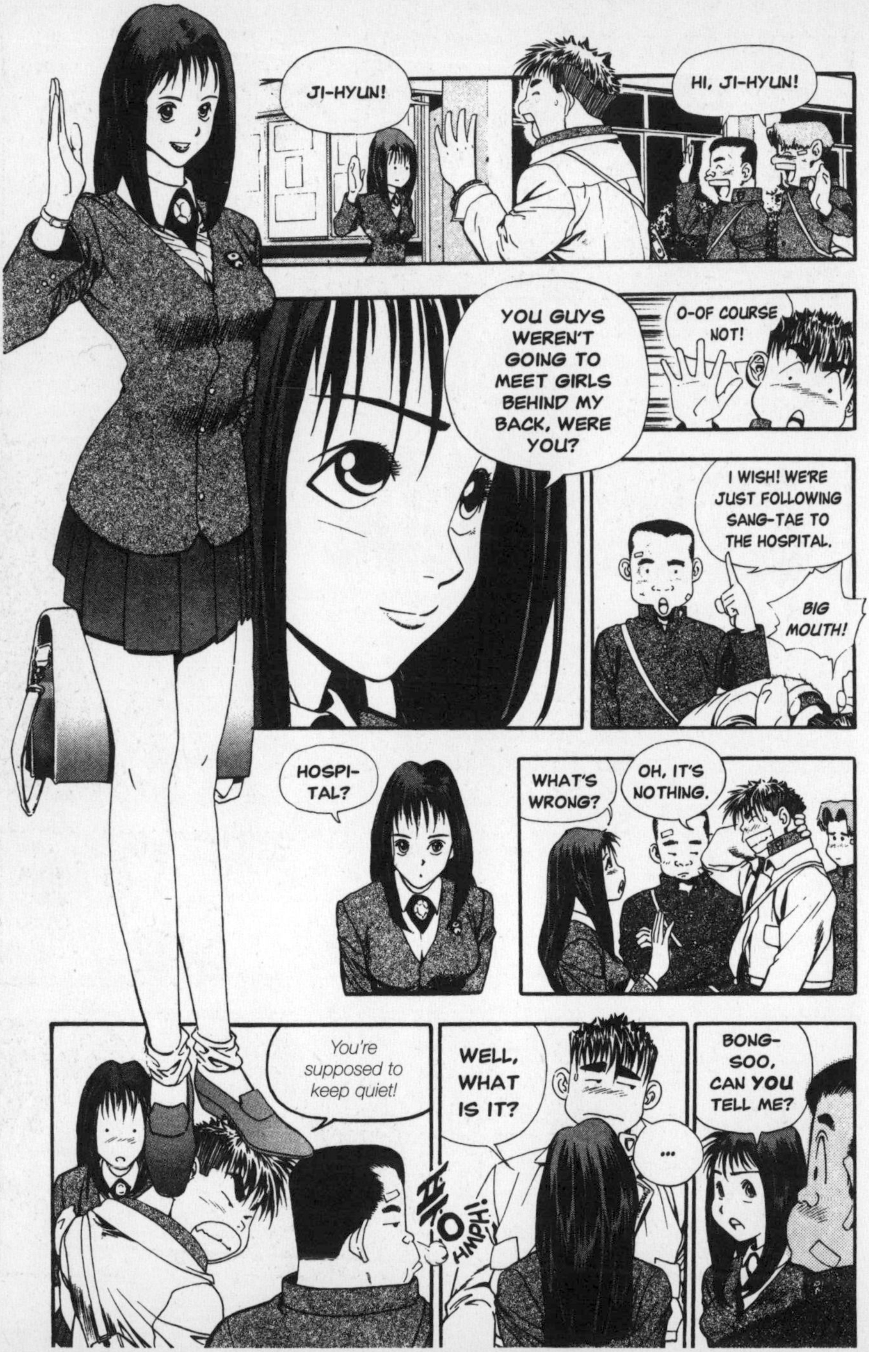
JI-HYUN!
HI, JI-HYUN!
YOU GUYS WEREN'T GOING TO MEET GIRLS BEHIND MY BACK, WERE YOU?
O-OF COURSE NOT!
I WISH! WE'RE JUST FOLLOWING SANG-TAE TO THE HOSPITAL.
BIG MOUTH!
HOSPI-TAL?
WHAT'S WRONG?
OH, IT'S NOTHING.
You're supposed to keep quiet!
HMPH!
WELL, WHAT IS IT?
...
BONG-SOO, CAN YOU TELL ME?

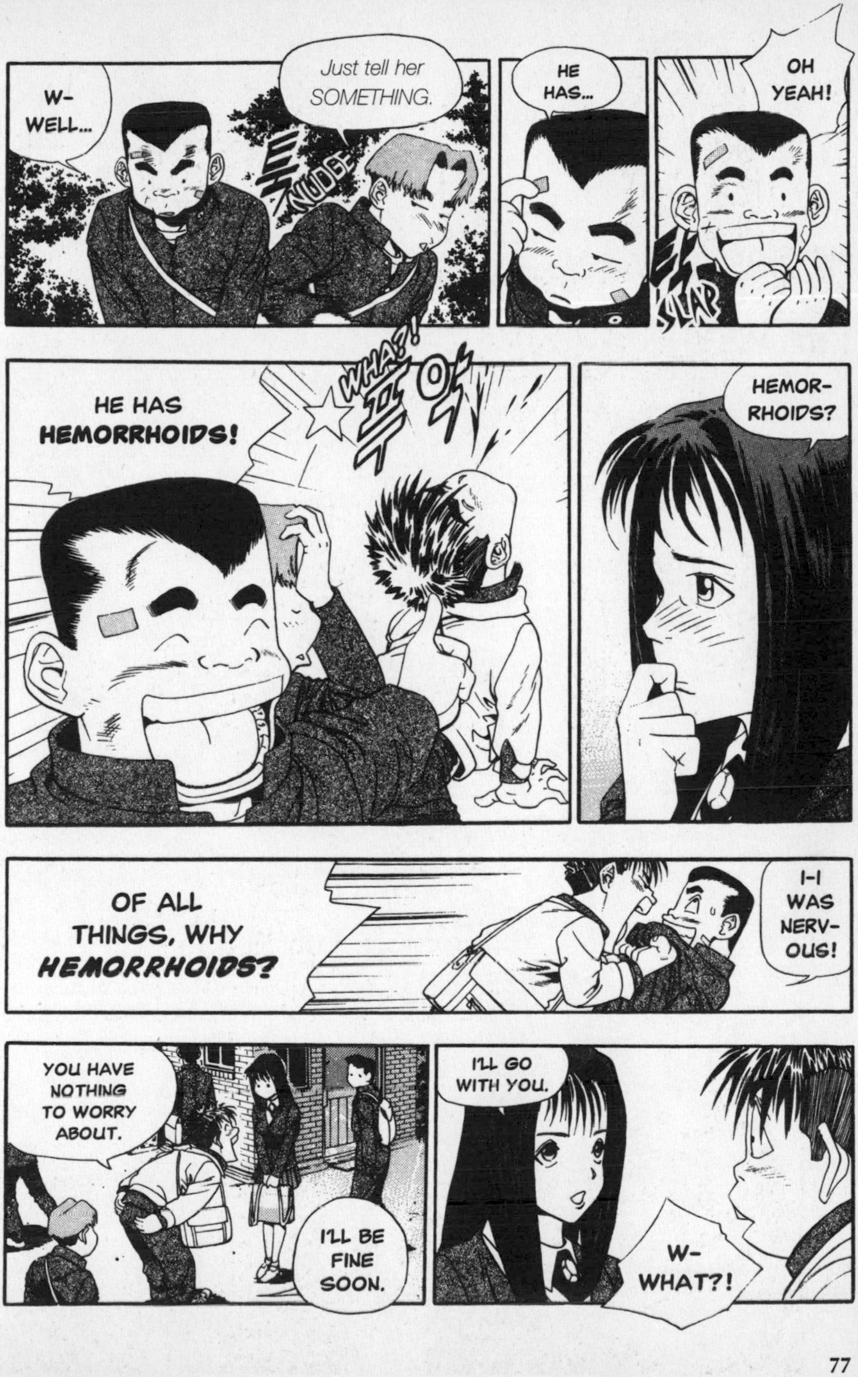
W-WELL...
Just tell her SOMETHING.
NUDGE
HE HAS...
OH YEAH!
SLAP
HE HAS HEMORRHOIDS!
WHA?!
HEMORRHOIDS?
OF ALL THINGS, WHY HEMORRHOIDS?
I-I WAS NERVOUS!
YOU HAVE NOTHING TO WORRY ABOUT.
I'LL BE FINE SOON.
I'LL GO WITH YOU.
W-WHAT?!

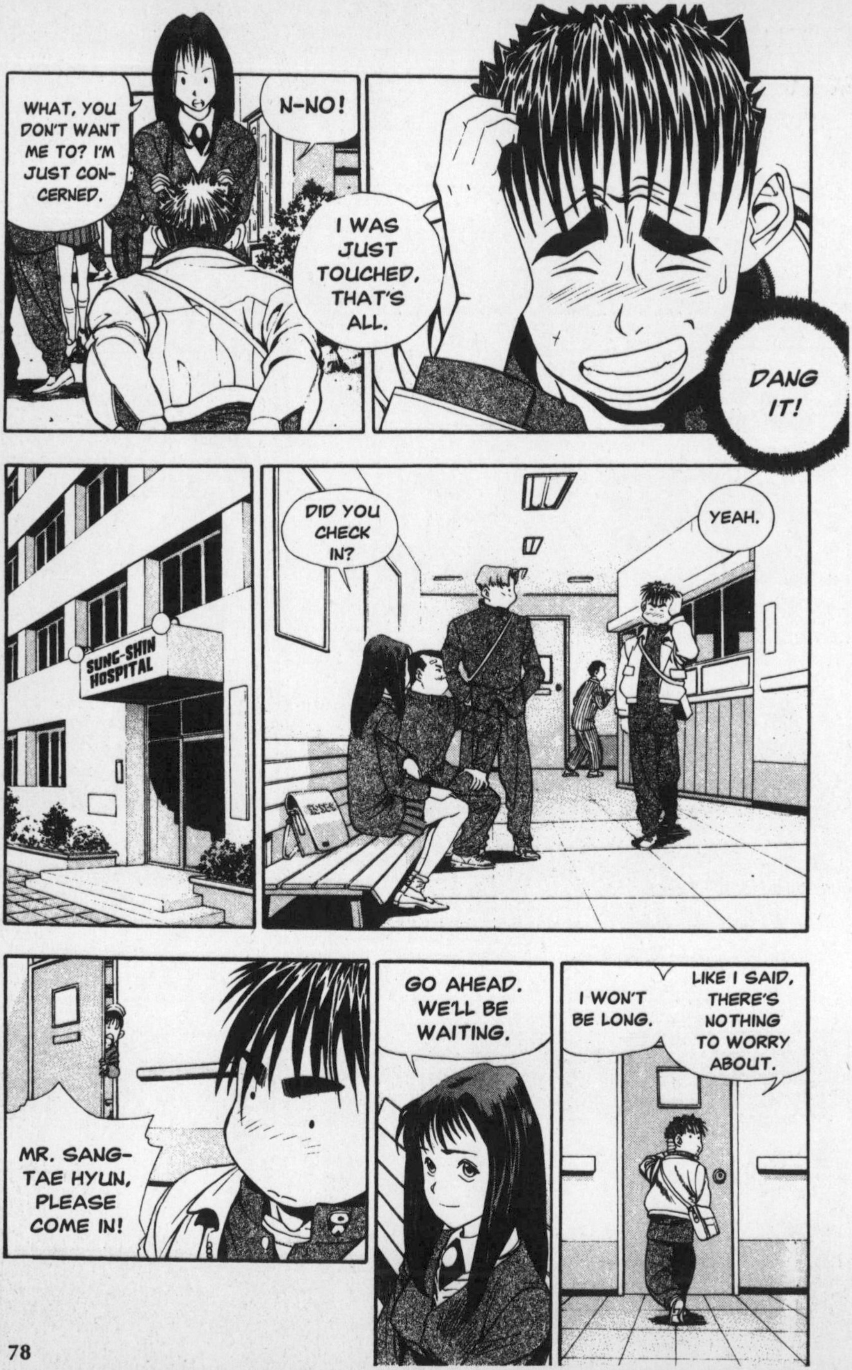
WHAT, YOU DON'T WANT ME TO? I'M JUST CONCERNED.
N-NO!
I WAS JUST TOUCHED, THAT'S ALL.
DANG IT!
SUNG-SHIN HOSPITAL
DID YOU CHECK IN?
YEAH.
MR. SANG-TAE HYUN, PLEASE COME IN!
GO AHEAD. WE'LL BE WAITING.
I WON'T BE LONG.
LIKE I SAID, THERE'S NOTHING TO WORRY ABOUT.

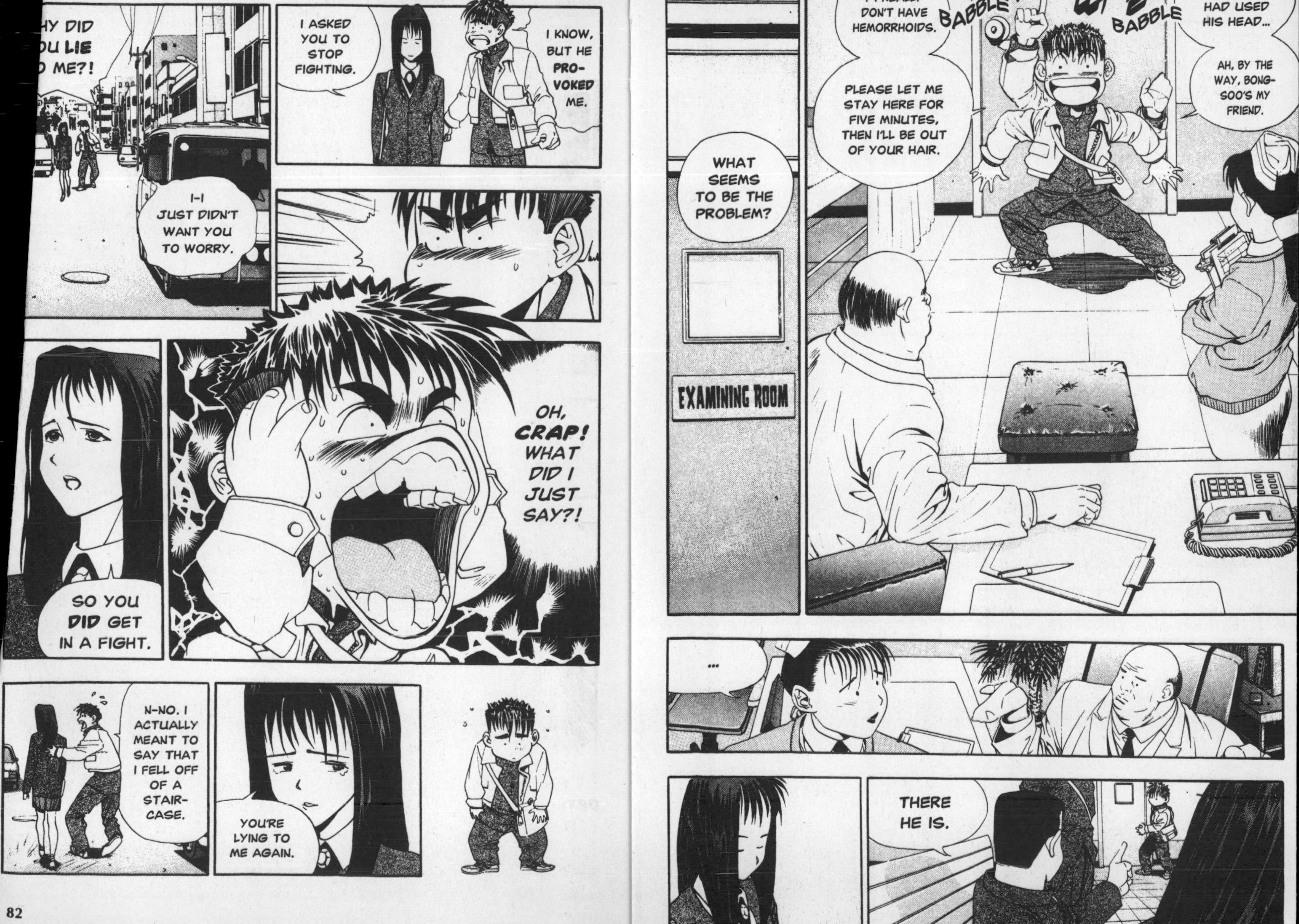
HY DID
OU LIE
O ME?!
I ASKED YOU TO STOP FIGHTING.
I KNOW, BUT HE PRO-VOKED ME.
I-I JUST DIDN'T WANT YOU TO WORRY.
OH, CRAP! WHAT DID I JUST SAY?!
SO YOU DID GET IN A FIGHT.
N-NO. I ACTUALLY MEANT TO SAY THAT I FELL OFF OF A STAIR-CASE.
YOU'RE LYING TO ME AGAIN.
WHAT SEEMS TO BE THE PROBLEM?
I-I REALLY DON'T HAVE HEMORRHOIDS.
PLEASE LET ME STAY HERE FOR FIVE MINUTES, THEN I'LL BE OUT OF YOUR HAIR.
BABBLE
BABBLE
ONLY IF BONG-SOO HAD USED HIS HEAD...
AH, BY THE WAY, BONG-SOO'S MY FRIEND.
EXAMINING ROOM
...
THERE HE IS.

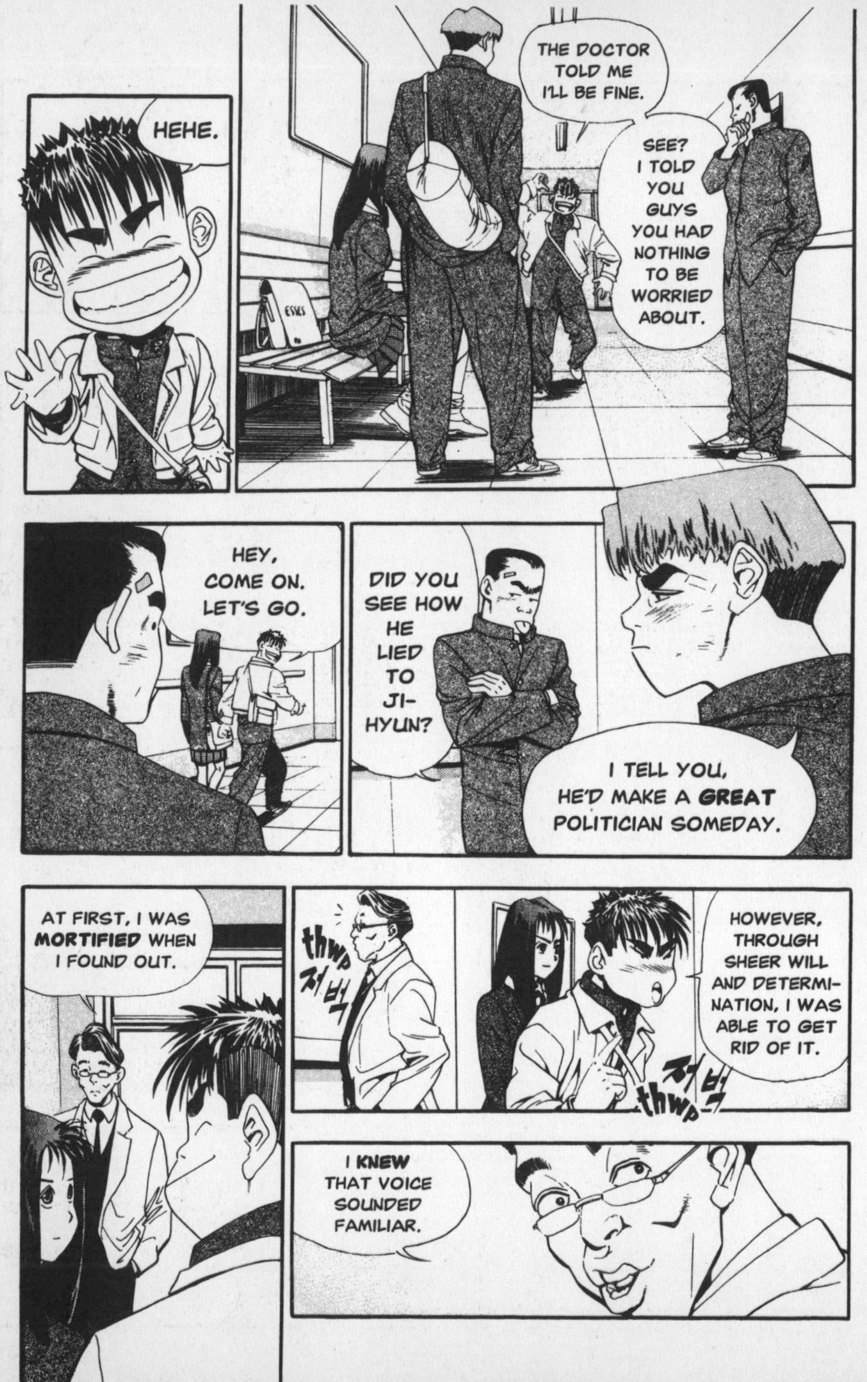

HEHE.
THE DOCTOR TOLD ME I'LL BE FINE.
SEE? I TOLD YOU GUYS YOU HAD NOTHING TO BE WORRIED ABOUT.
HEY, COME ON. LET'S GO.
DID YOU SEE HOW HE LIED TO JI-HYUN?
I TELL YOU, HE'D MAKE A **GREAT** POLITICIAN SOMEDAY.
AT FIRST, I WAS **MORTIFIED** WHEN I FOUND OUT.
thwp
HOWEVER, THROUGH SHEER WILL AND DETERMI-NATION, I WAS ABLE TO GET RID OF IT.
thwp
I **KNEW** THAT VOICE SOUNDED FAMILIAR.

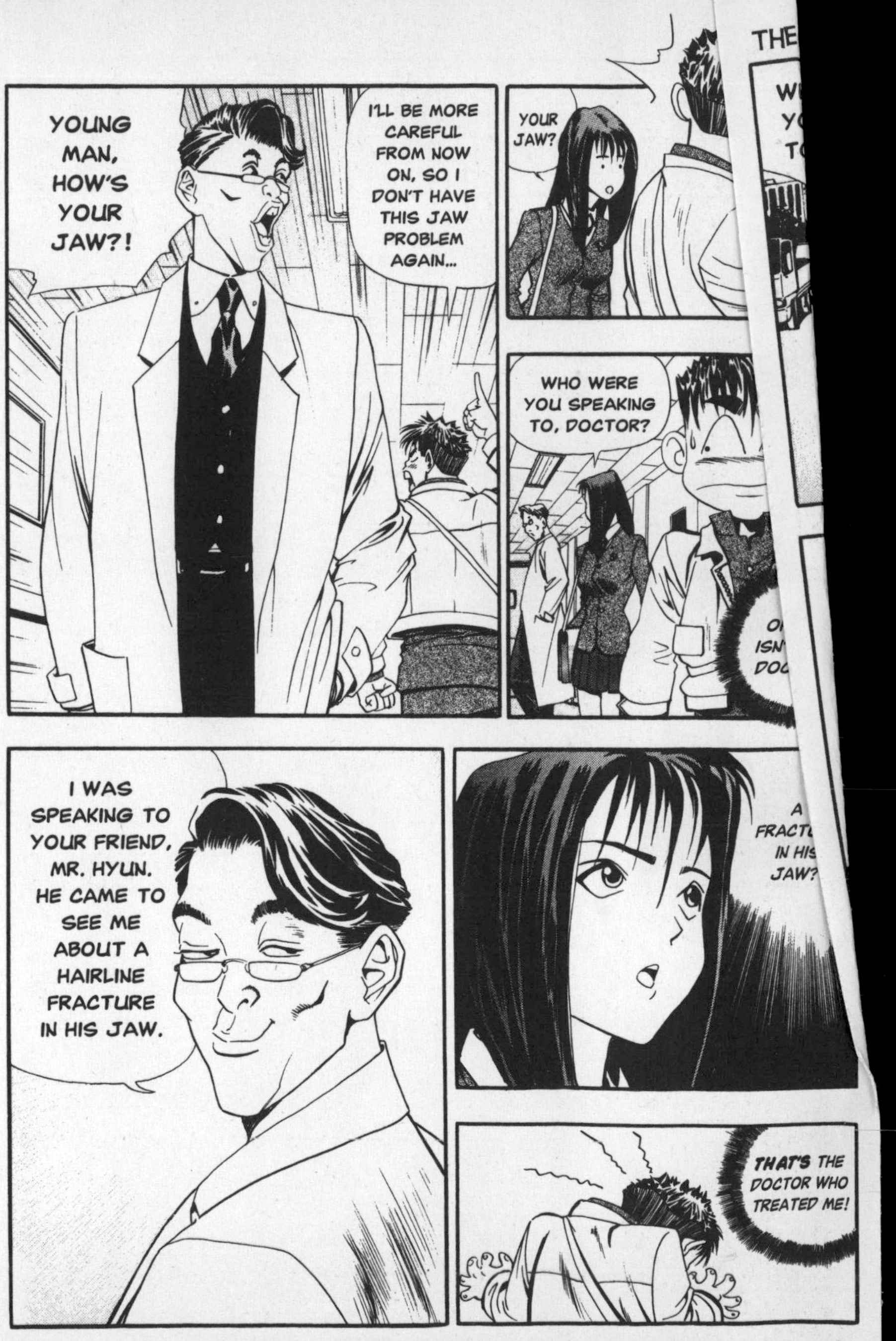

YOUNG MAN, HOW'S YOUR JAW?!
I'LL BE MORE CAREFUL FROM NOW ON, SO I DON'T HAVE THIS JAW PROBLEM AGAIN...
YOUR JAW?
WHO WERE YOU SPEAKING TO, DOCTOR?
I WAS SPEAKING TO YOUR FRIEND, MR. HYUN. HE CAME TO SEE ME ABOUT A HAIRLINE FRACTURE IN HIS JAW.
THAT'S THE DOCTOR WHO TREATED ME!

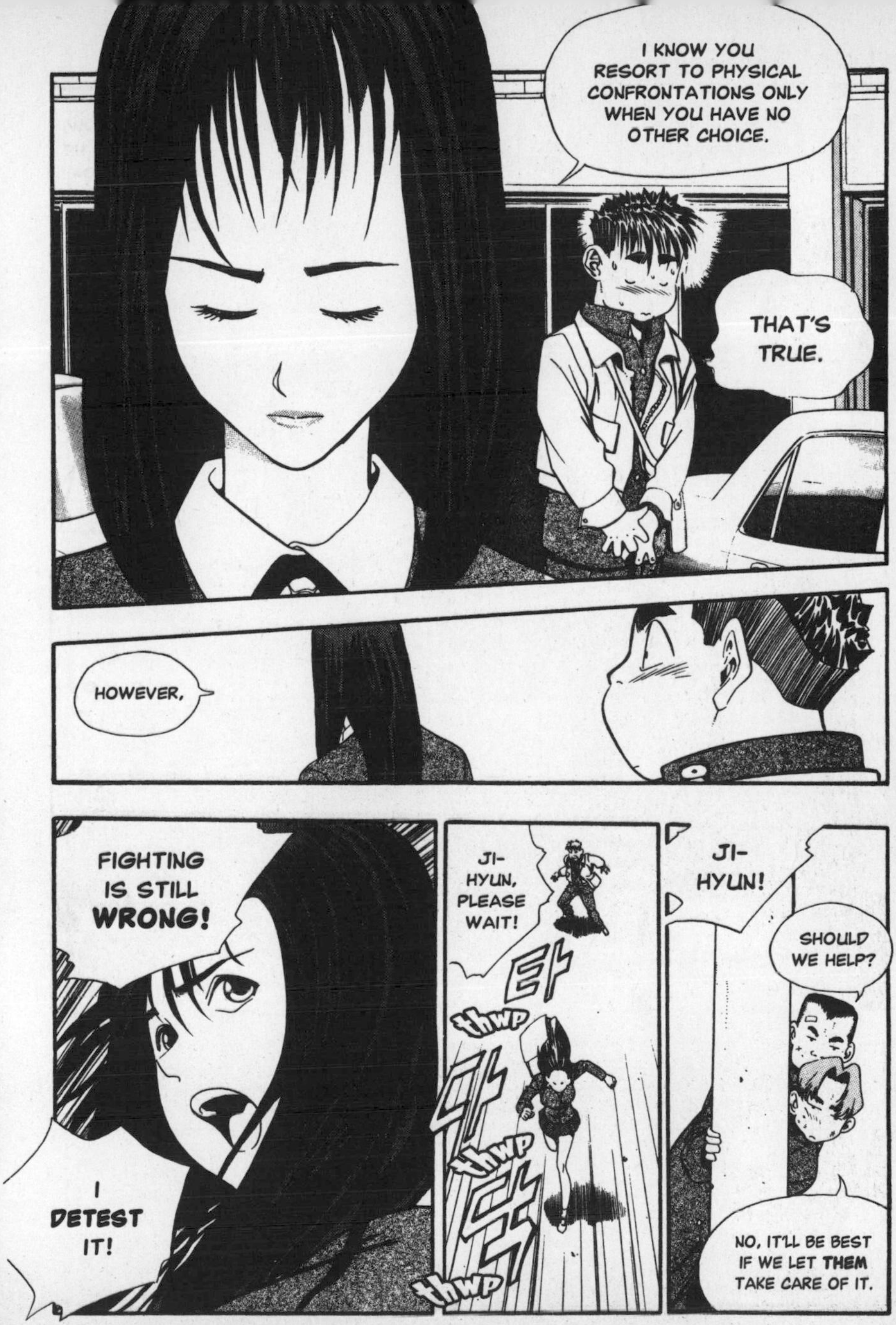
I KNOW YOU RESORT TO PHYSICAL CONFRONTATIONS ONLY WHEN YOU HAVE NO OTHER CHOICE.
THAT'S TRUE.
HOWEVER,
FIGHTING IS STILL WRONG!
I DETEST IT!
JI-HYUN, PLEASE WAIT!
thwp
thwp
thwp
JI-HYUN!
SHOULD WE HELP?
NO, IT'LL BE BEST IF WE LET THEM TAKE CARE OF IT.

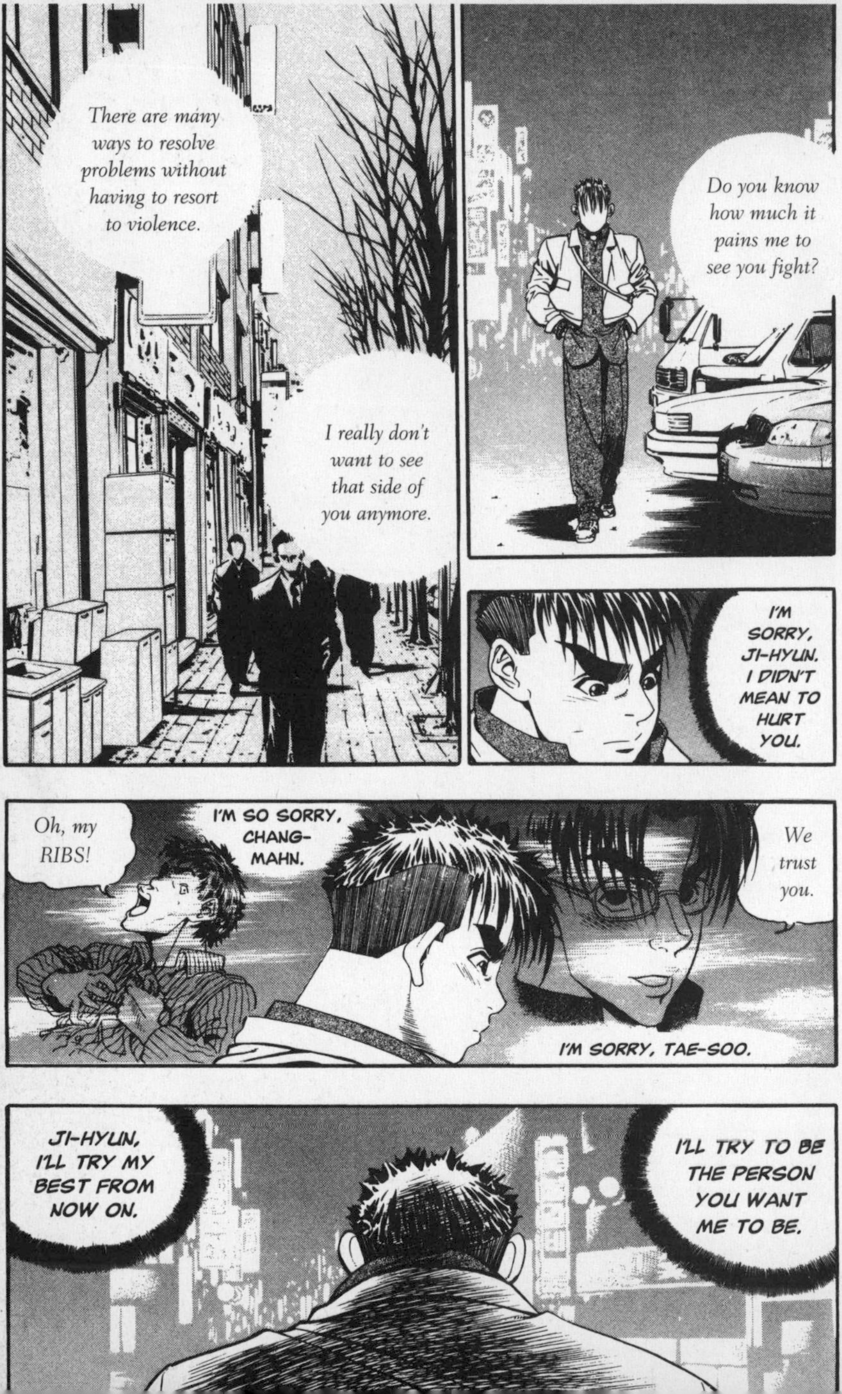
There are many ways to resolve problems without having to resort to violence.
I really don't want to see that side of you anymore.
Do you know how much it pains me to see you fight?
I'M SORRY, JI-HYUN. I DIDN'T MEAN TO HURT YOU.
Oh, my RIBS!
I'M SO SORRY, CHANG-MAHN.
We trust you.
I'M SORRY, TAE-SOO.
JI-HYUN, I'LL TRY MY BEST FROM NOW ON.
I'LL TRY TO BE THE PERSON YOU WANT ME TO BE.

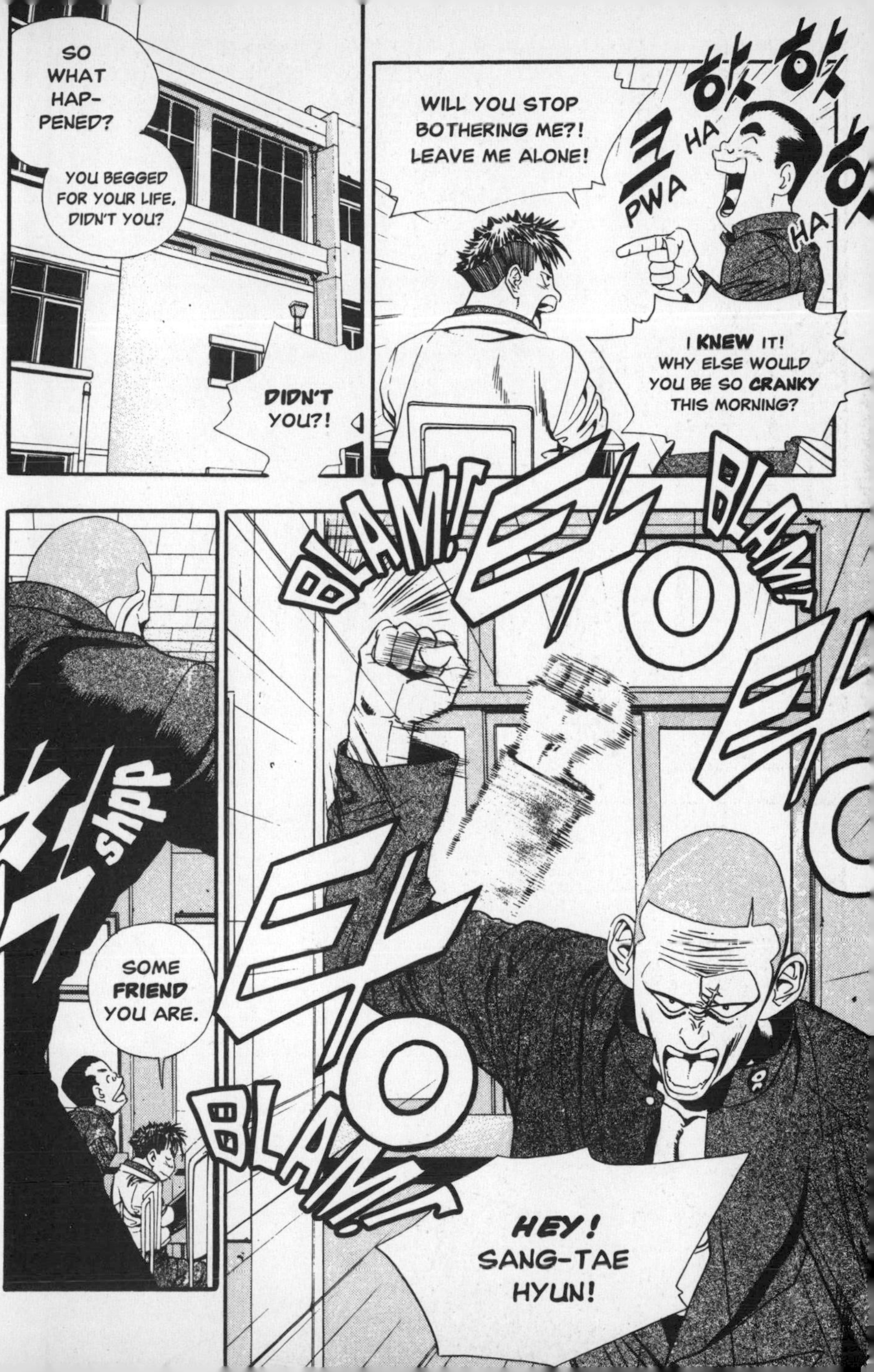
SO WHAT HAP-PENED?
YOU BEGGED FOR YOUR LIFE, DIDN'T YOU?
DIDN'T YOU?!
WILL YOU STOP BOTHERING ME?! LEAVE ME ALONE!
크
PWA HA HA
I KNEW IT! WHY ELSE WOULD YOU BE SO CRANKY THIS MORNING?
BLAM!
BLAM!
BLAM!
shpp
SOME FRIEND YOU ARE.
HEY! SANG-TAE HYUN!

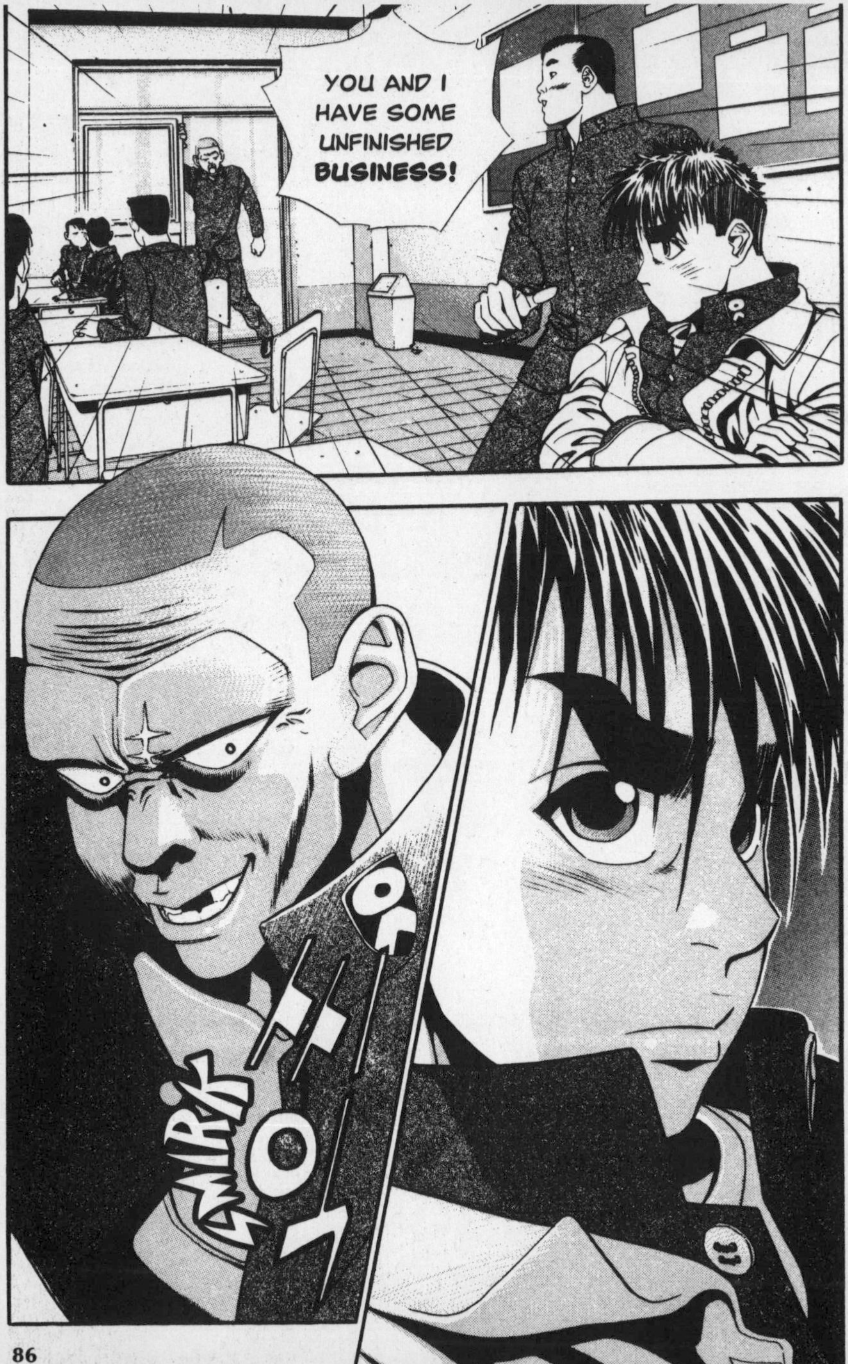
YOU AND I HAVE SOME UNFINISHED **BUSINESS!**
SMIRK

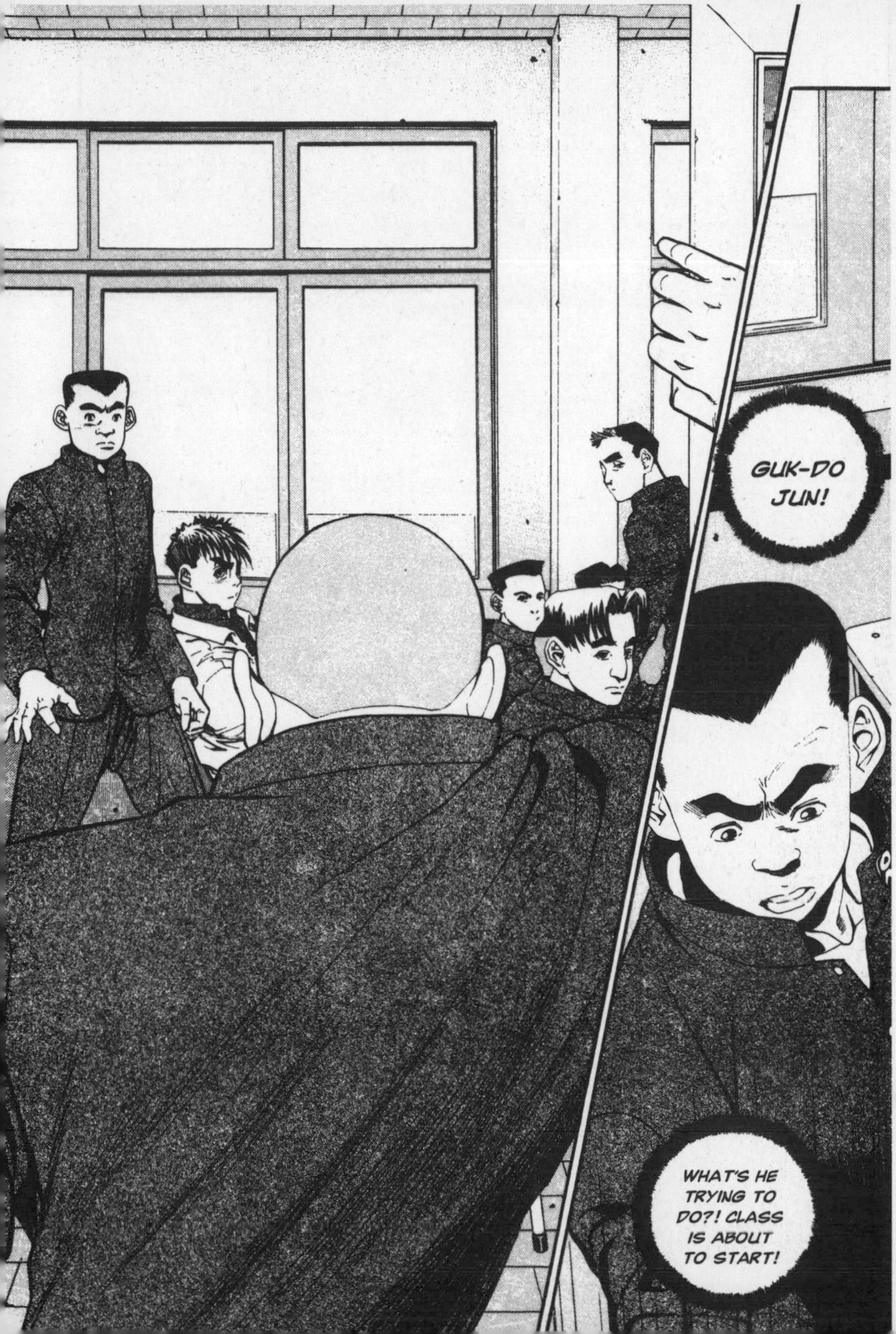
GUK-DO JUN!
WHAT'S HE TRYING TO DO?! CLASS IS ABOUT TO START!

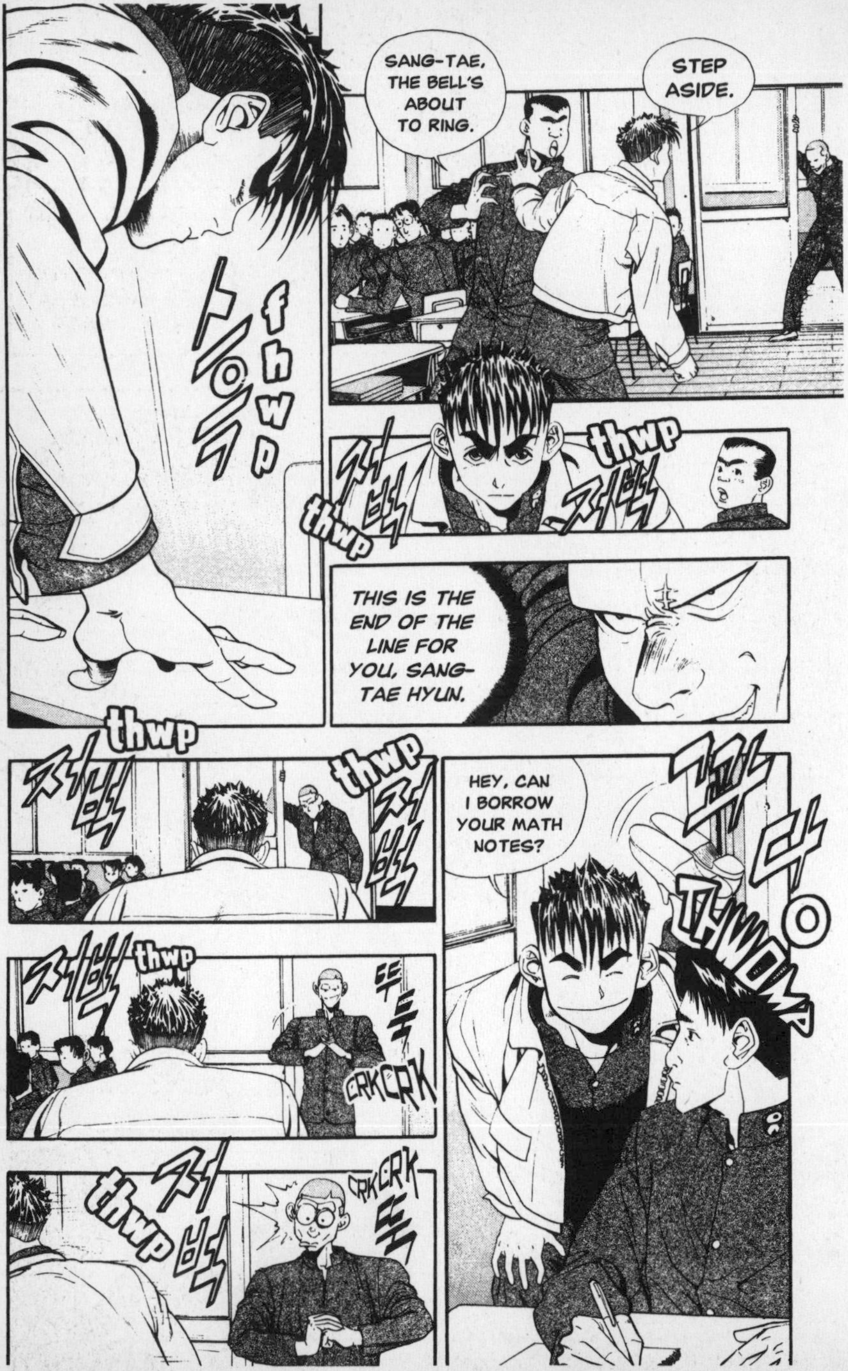
fhwp
SANG-TAE, THE BELL'S ABOUT TO RING.
STEP ASIDE.
thwp
thwp
THIS IS THE END OF THE LINE FOR YOU, SANG-TAE HYUN.
thwp
thwp
thwp
CRKCRK
thwp
CRKCRK
HEY, CAN I BORROW YOUR MATH NOTES?
THWOMP

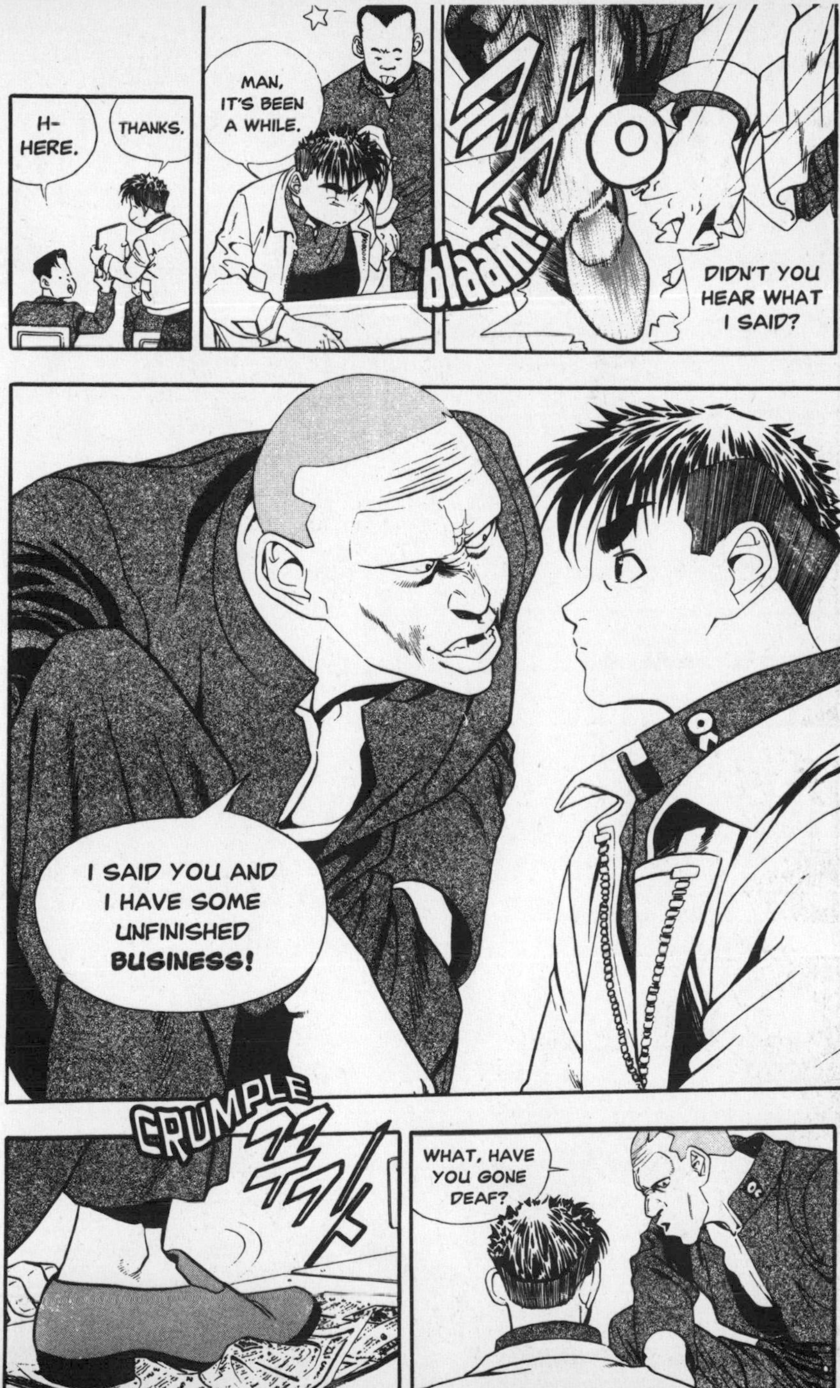

H-
HERE.
THANKS.
MAN, IT'S BEEN A WHILE.
blaam!
DIDN'T YOU HEAR WHAT I SAID?
I SAID YOU AND I HAVE SOME UNFINISHED BUSINESS!
CRUMPLE
WHAT, HAVE YOU GONE DEAF?

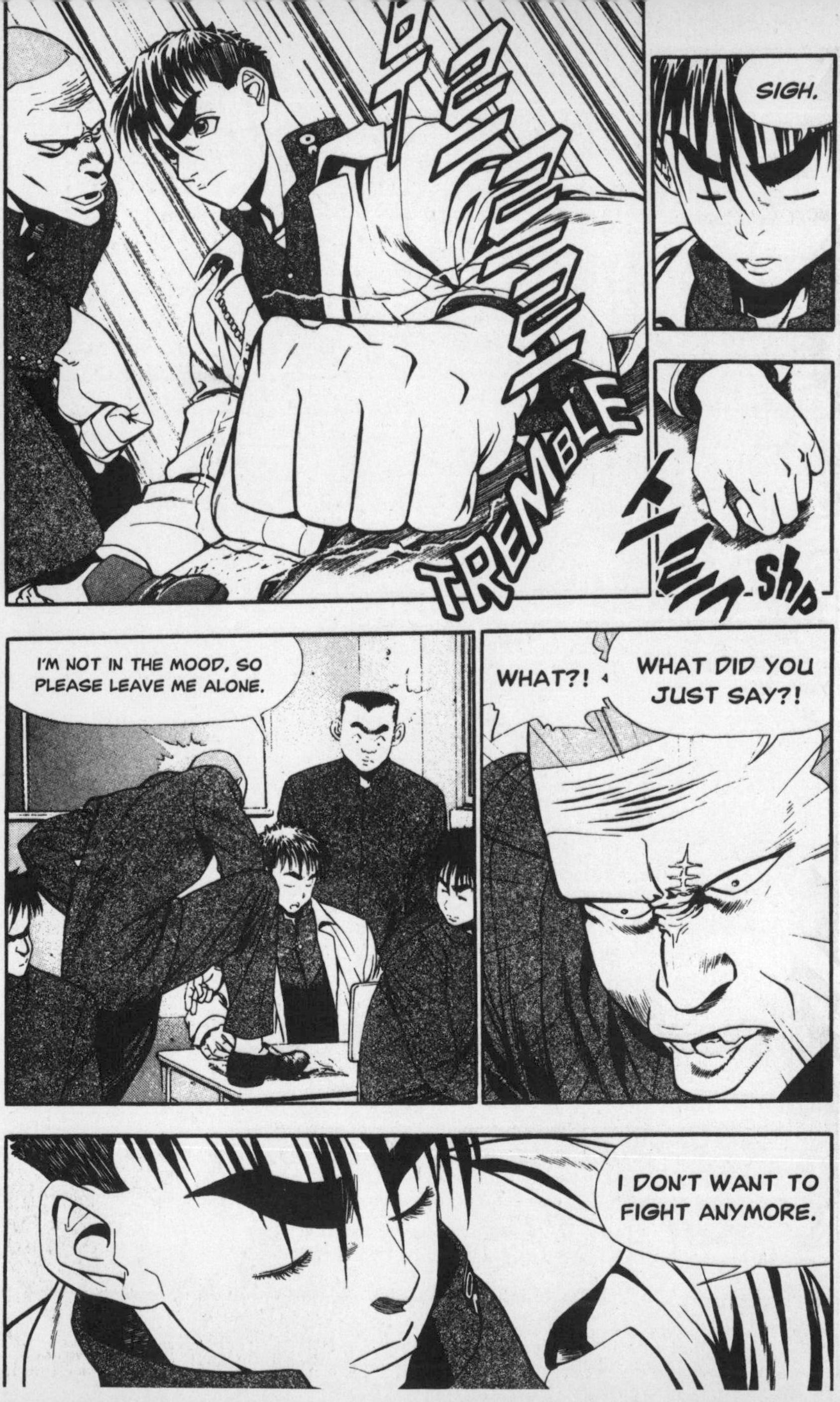
TREMBLE
SIGH.
shp
I'M NOT IN THE MOOD, SO PLEASE LEAVE ME ALONE.
WHAT?!
WHAT DID YOU JUST SAY?!
I DON'T WANT TO FIGHT ANYMORE.

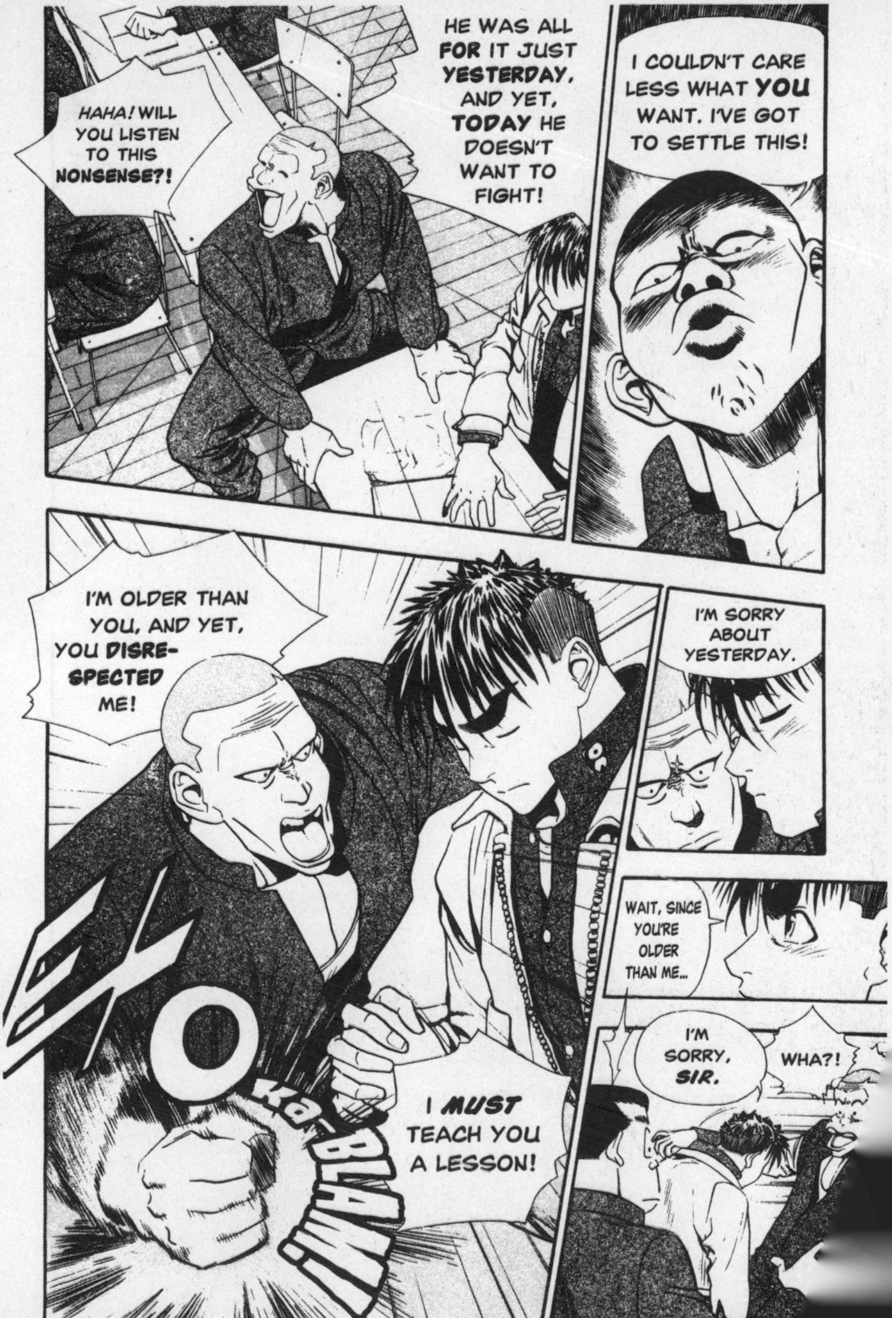
HAHA! WILL YOU LISTEN TO THIS NONSENSE?!
HE WAS ALL FOR IT JUST YESTERDAY, AND YET, TODAY HE DOESN'T WANT TO FIGHT!
I COULDN'T CARE LESS WHAT YOU WANT. I'VE GOT TO SETTLE THIS!
I'M OLDER THAN YOU, AND YET, YOU DISRE-SPECTED ME!
I MUST TEACH YOU A LESSON!
KO-BLAM!
I'M SORRY ABOUT YESTERDAY.
WAIT, SINCE YOU'RE OLDER THAN ME...
I'M SORRY, SIR.
WHA?!

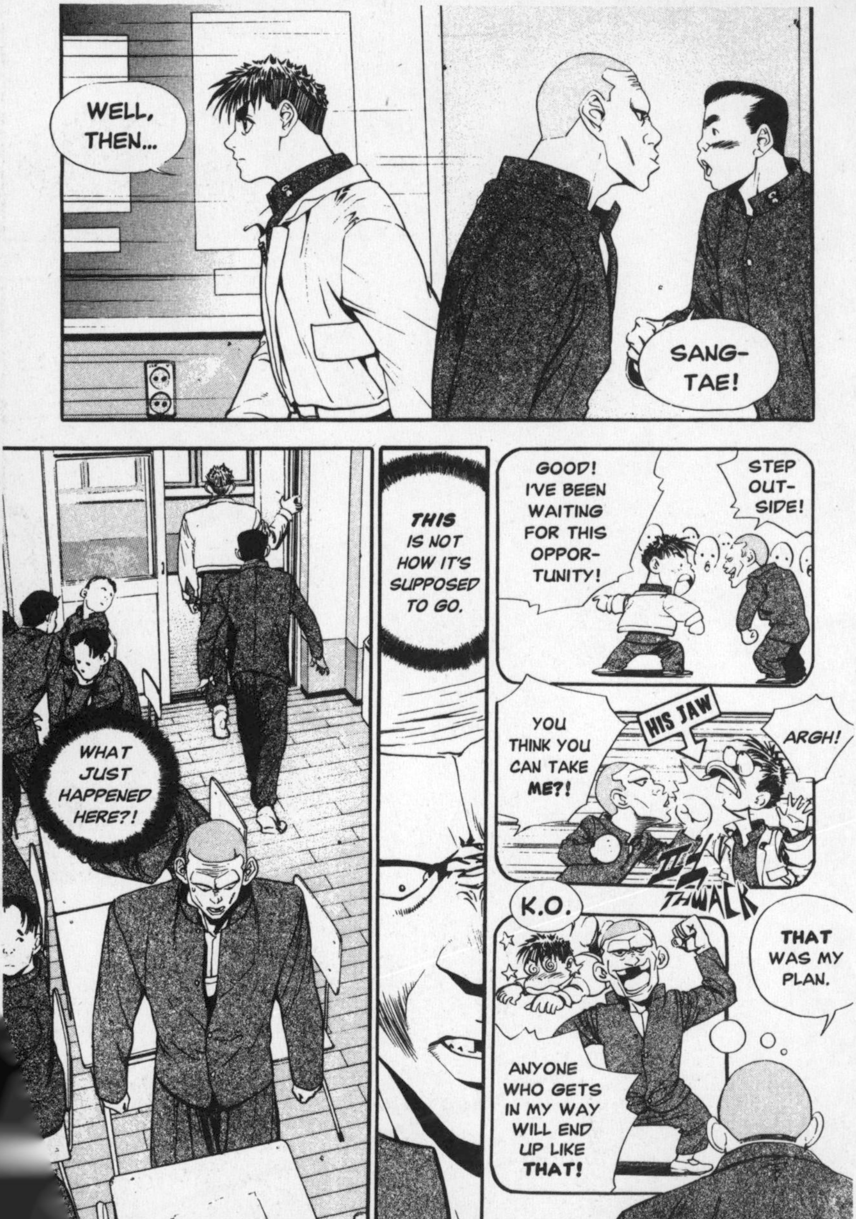

WELL, THEN...
SANG-TAE!
WHAT JUST HAPPENED HERE?!
THIS IS NOT HOW IT'S SUPPOSED TO GO.
GOOD! I'VE BEEN WAITING FOR THIS OPPORTUNITY!
STEP OUTSIDE!
YOU THINK YOU CAN TAKE ME?!
HIS JAW
ARGH!
THWACK
K.O.
THAT WAS MY PLAN.
ANYONE WHO GETS IN MY WAY WILL END UP LIKE THAT!

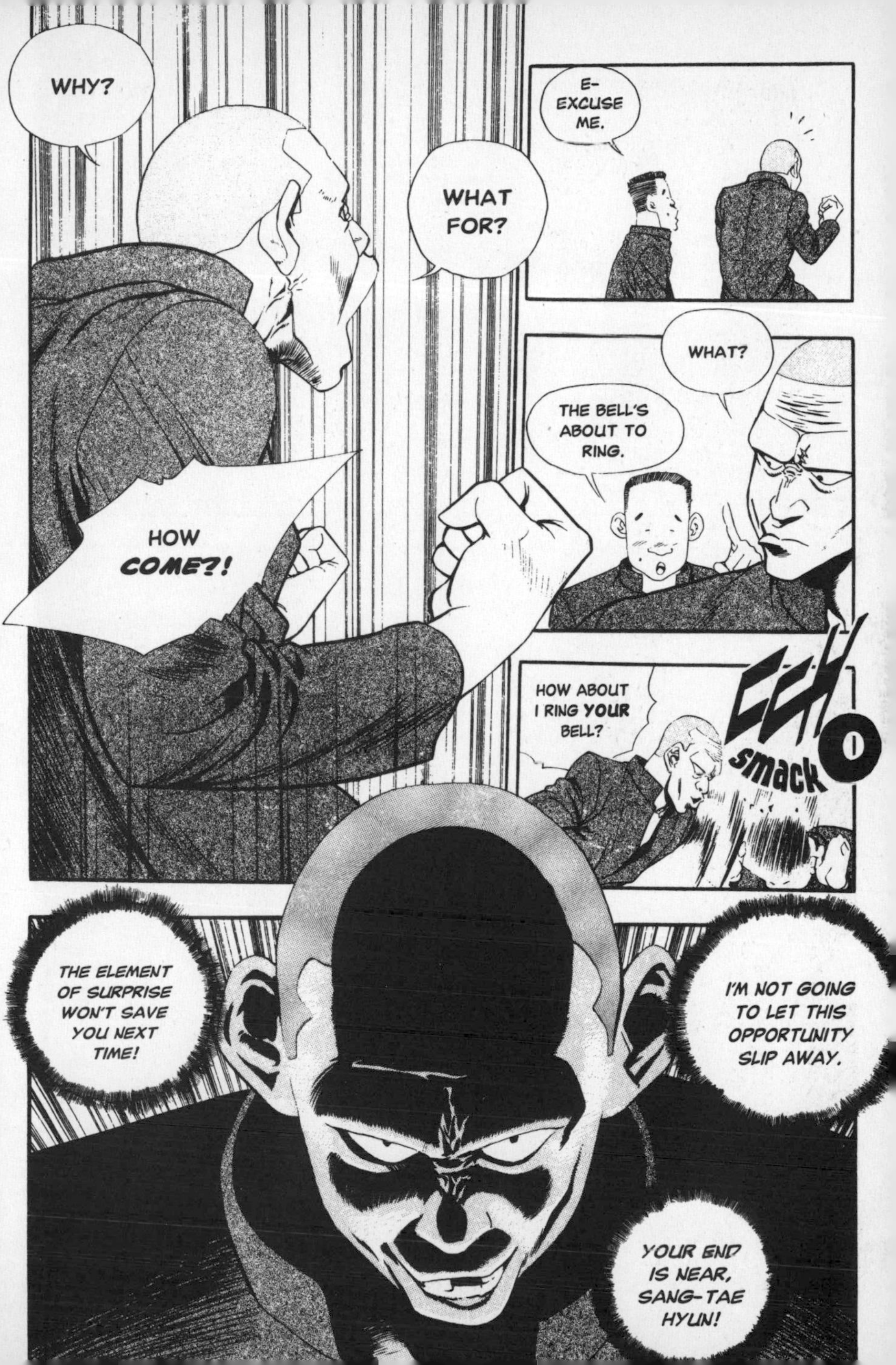
WHY?
WHAT FOR?
HOW COME?!
E-EXCUSE ME.
WHAT?
THE BELL'S ABOUT TO RING.
HOW ABOUT I RING YOUR BELL?
smack
THE ELEMENT OF SURPRISE WON'T SAVE YOU NEXT TIME!
I'M NOT GOING TO LET THIS OPPORTUNITY SLIP AWAY.
YOUR END IS NEAR, SANG-TAE HYUN!

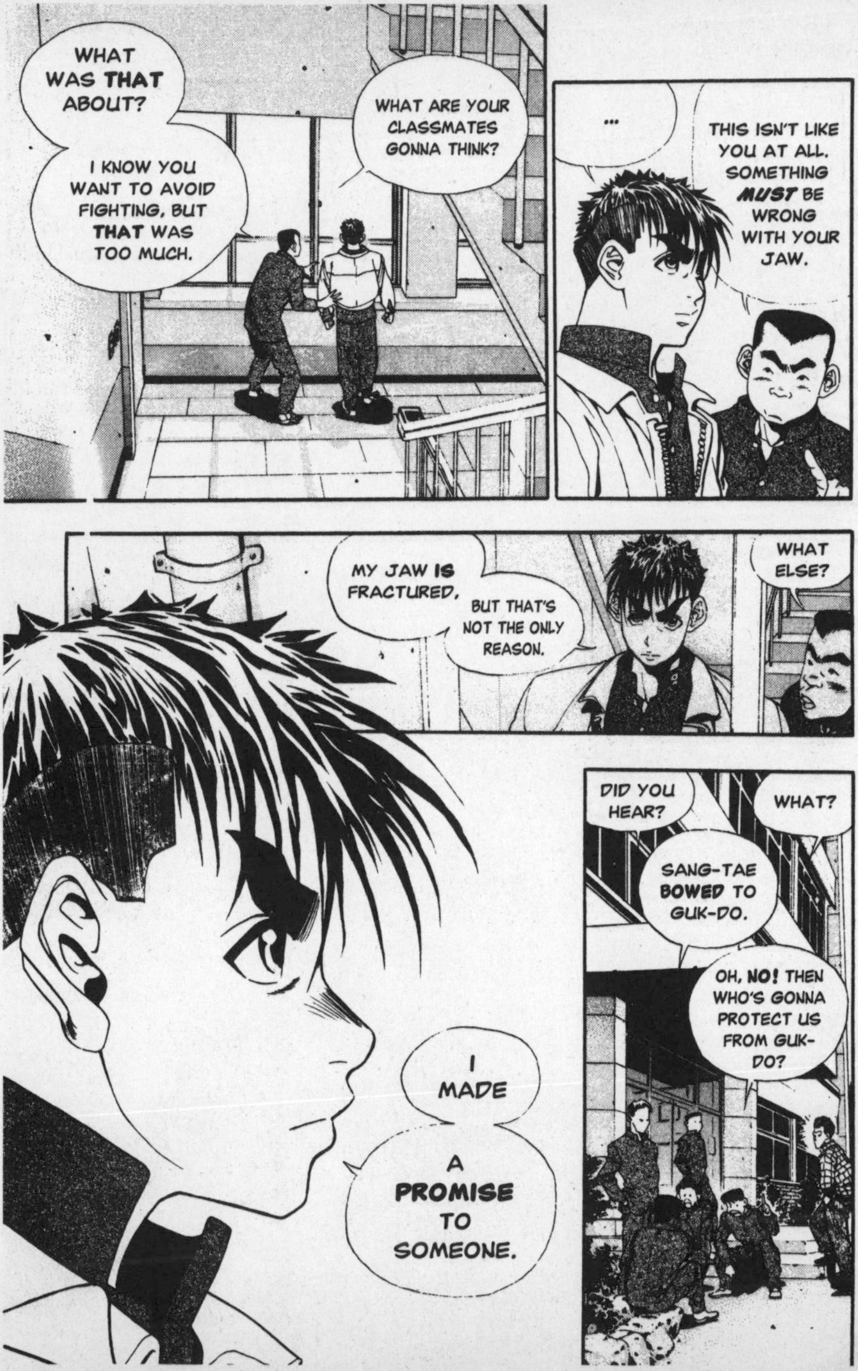
WHAT WAS THAT ABOUT?
I KNOW YOU WANT TO AVOID FIGHTING, BUT THAT WAS TOO MUCH.
WHAT ARE YOUR CLASSMATES GONNA THINK?
...
THIS ISN'T LIKE YOU AT ALL. SOMETHING MUST BE WRONG WITH YOUR JAW.
MY JAW IS FRACTURED,
BUT THAT'S NOT THE ONLY REASON.
WHAT ELSE?
I MADE
A PROMISE TO SOMEONE.
DID YOU HEAR?
WHAT?
SANG-TAE BOWED TO GUK-DO.
OH, NO! THEN WHO'S GONNA PROTECT US FROM GUK-DO?

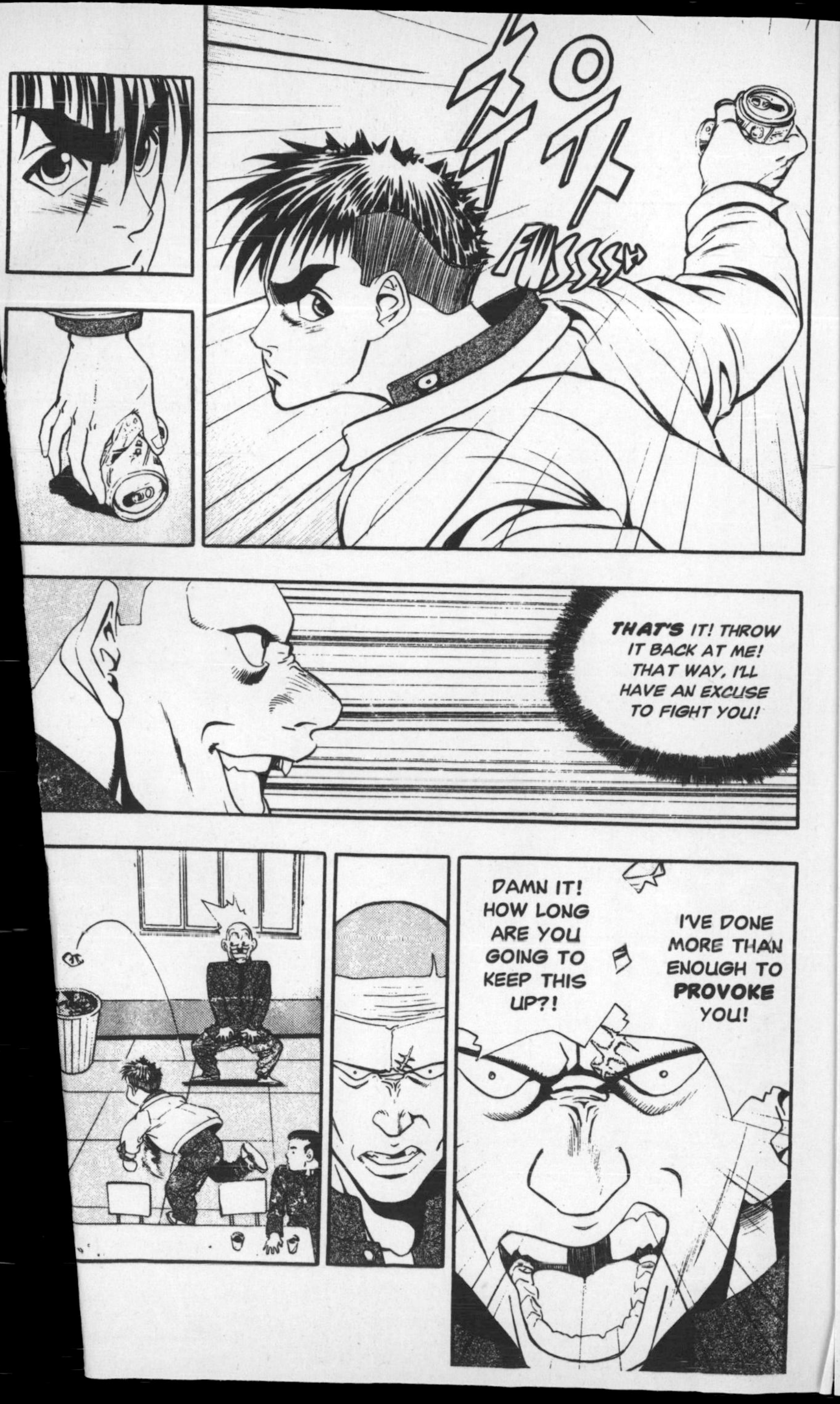
FWSSSH
THAT'S IT! THROW IT BACK AT ME! THAT WAY, I'LL HAVE AN EXCUSE TO FIGHT YOU!
DAMN IT! HOW LONG ARE YOU GOING TO KEEP THIS UP?!
I'VE DONE MORE THAN ENOUGH TO PROVOKE YOU!

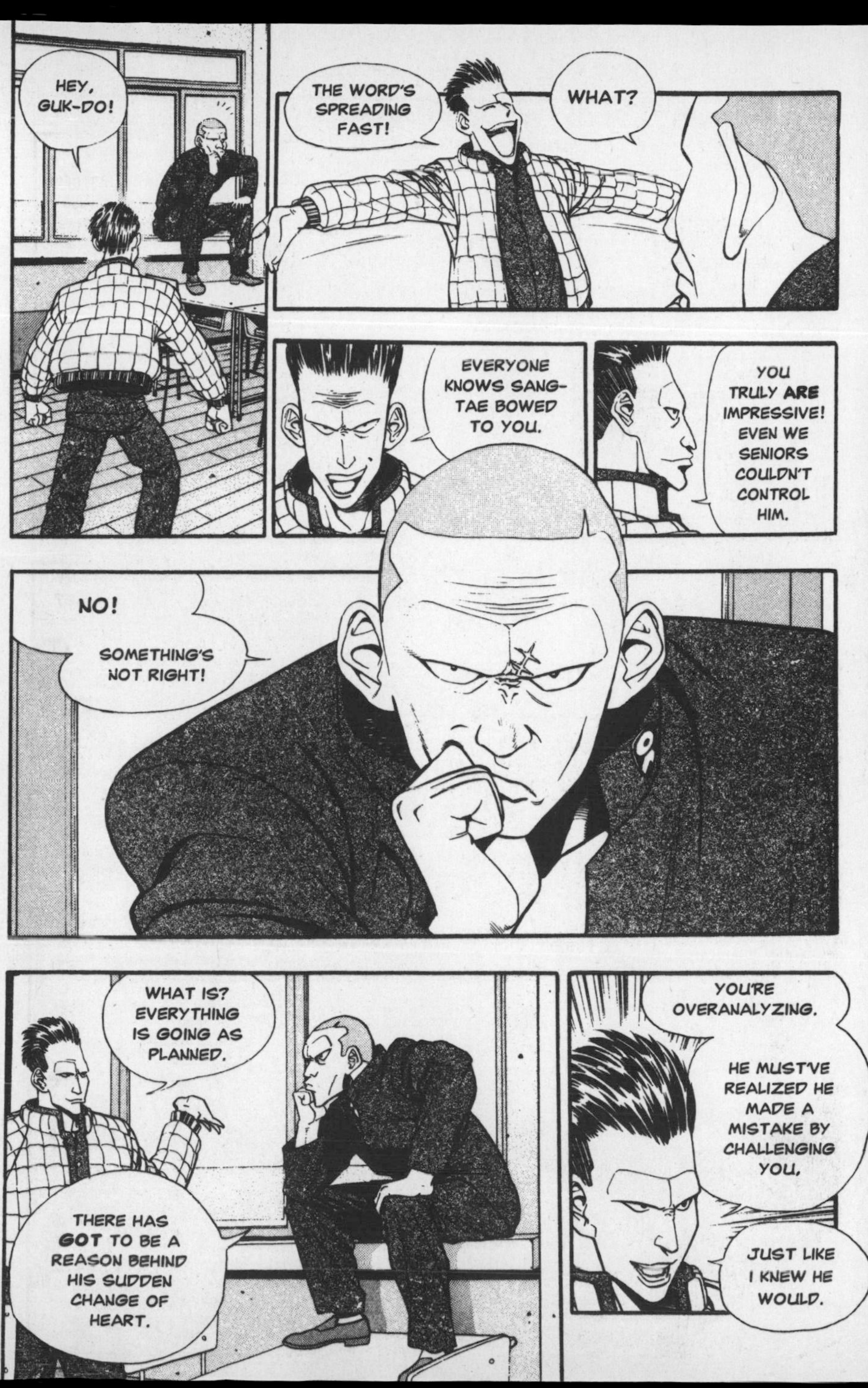
HEY, GUK-DO!
THE WORD'S SPREADING FAST!
WHAT?
EVERYONE KNOWS SANG-TAE BOWED TO YOU.
YOU TRULY ARE IMPRESSIVE! EVEN WE SENIORS COULDN'T CONTROL HIM.
NO!
SOMETHING'S NOT RIGHT!
WHAT IS? EVERYTHING IS GOING AS PLANNED.
THERE HAS GOT TO BE A REASON BEHIND HIS SUDDEN CHANGE OF HEART.
YOU'RE OVERANALYZING.
HE MUST'VE REALIZED HE MADE A MISTAKE BY CHALLENGING YOU,
JUST LIKE I KNEW HE WOULD.

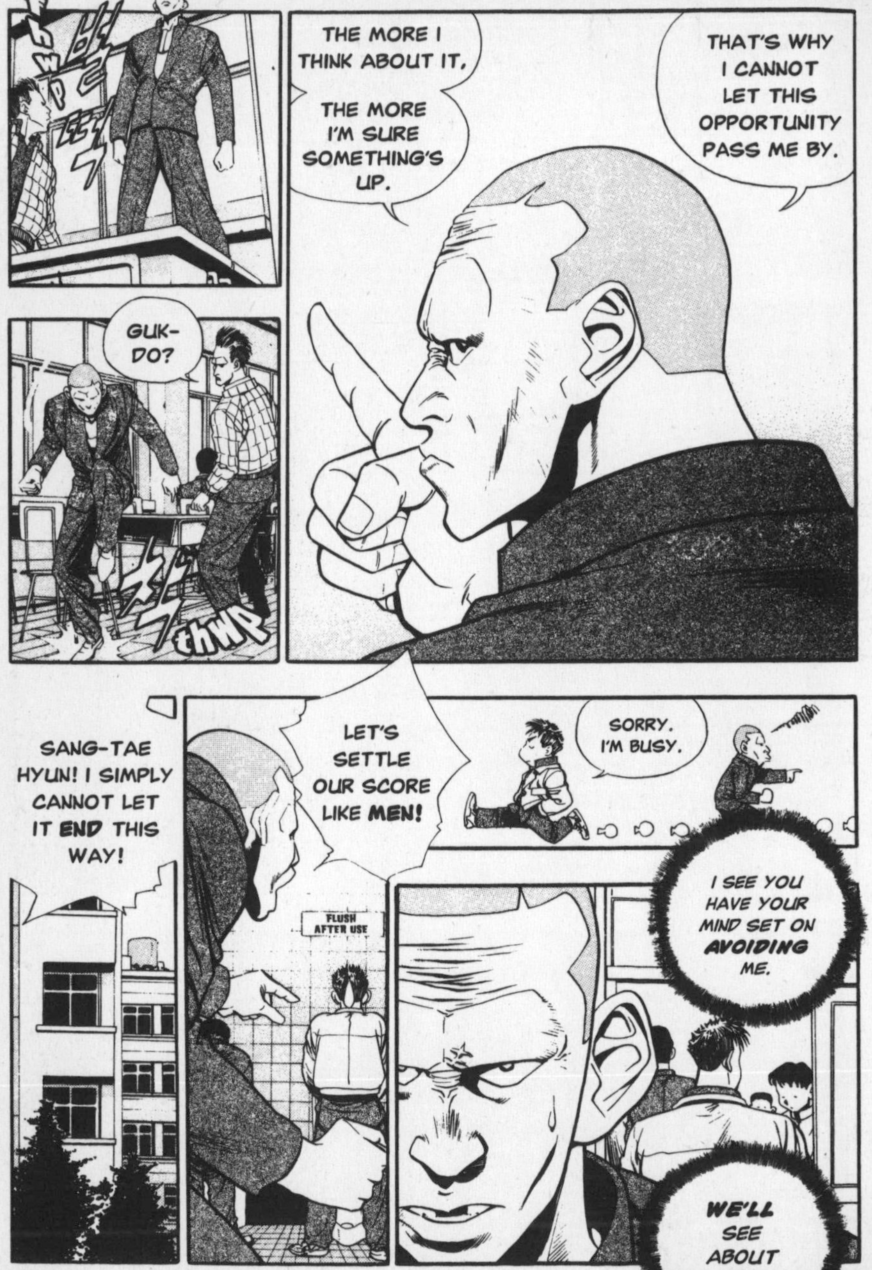
thwp
THE MORE I THINK ABOUT IT,
THE MORE I'M SURE SOMETHING'S UP.
THAT'S WHY I CANNOT LET THIS OPPORTUNITY PASS ME BY.
GUK-DO?
thWP
SANG-TAE HYUN! I SIMPLY CANNOT LET IT END THIS WAY!
LET'S SETTLE OUR SCORE LIKE MEN!
SORRY. I'M BUSY.
FLUSH AFTER USE
I SEE YOU HAVE YOUR MIND SET ON AVOIDING ME.
WE'LL SEE ABOUT THAT.

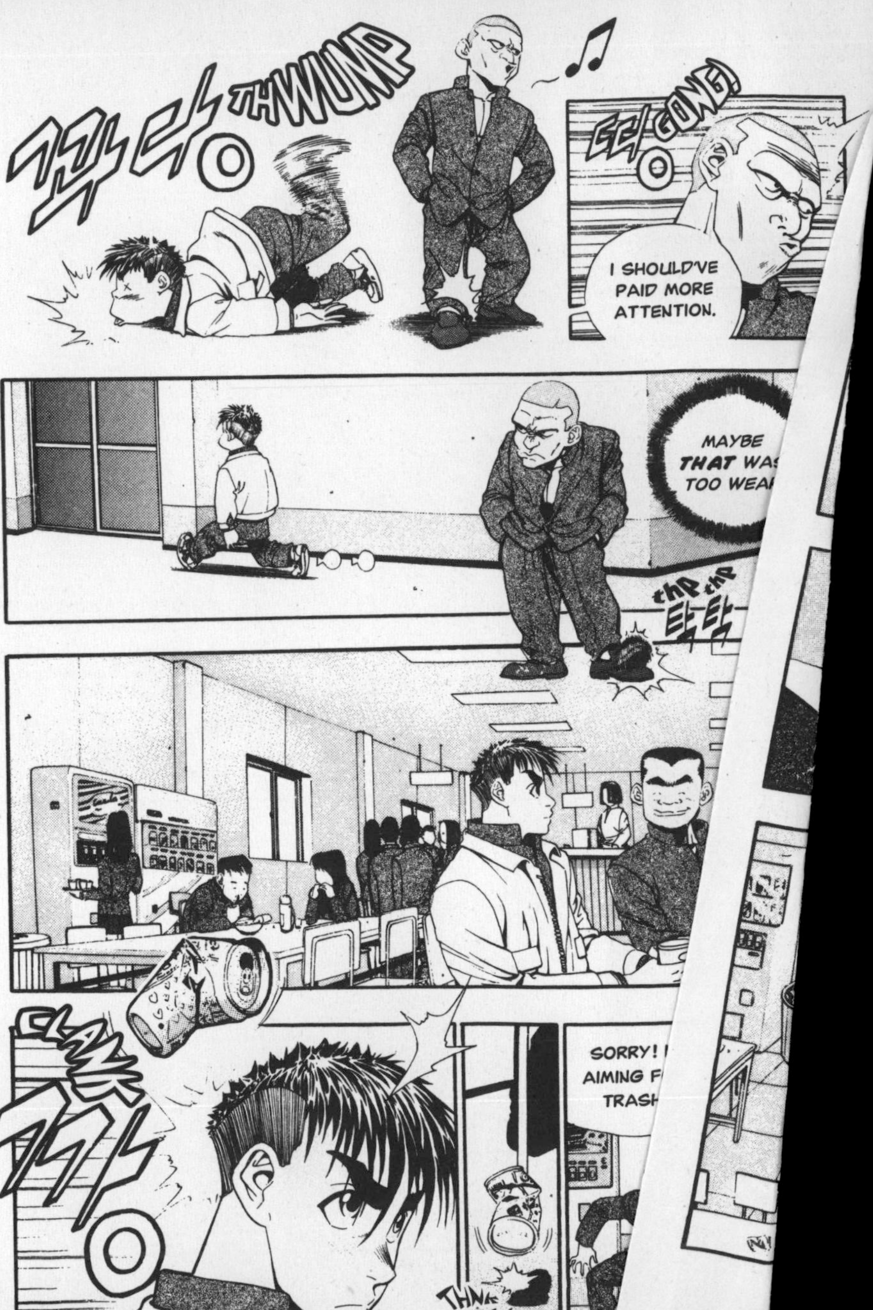
THWUMP
GONG!
I SHOULD'VE PAID MORE ATTENTION.
MAYBE THAT WAS TOO WEA
thp thp
CLANK
SORRY!
AIMING
TRASH
THNK

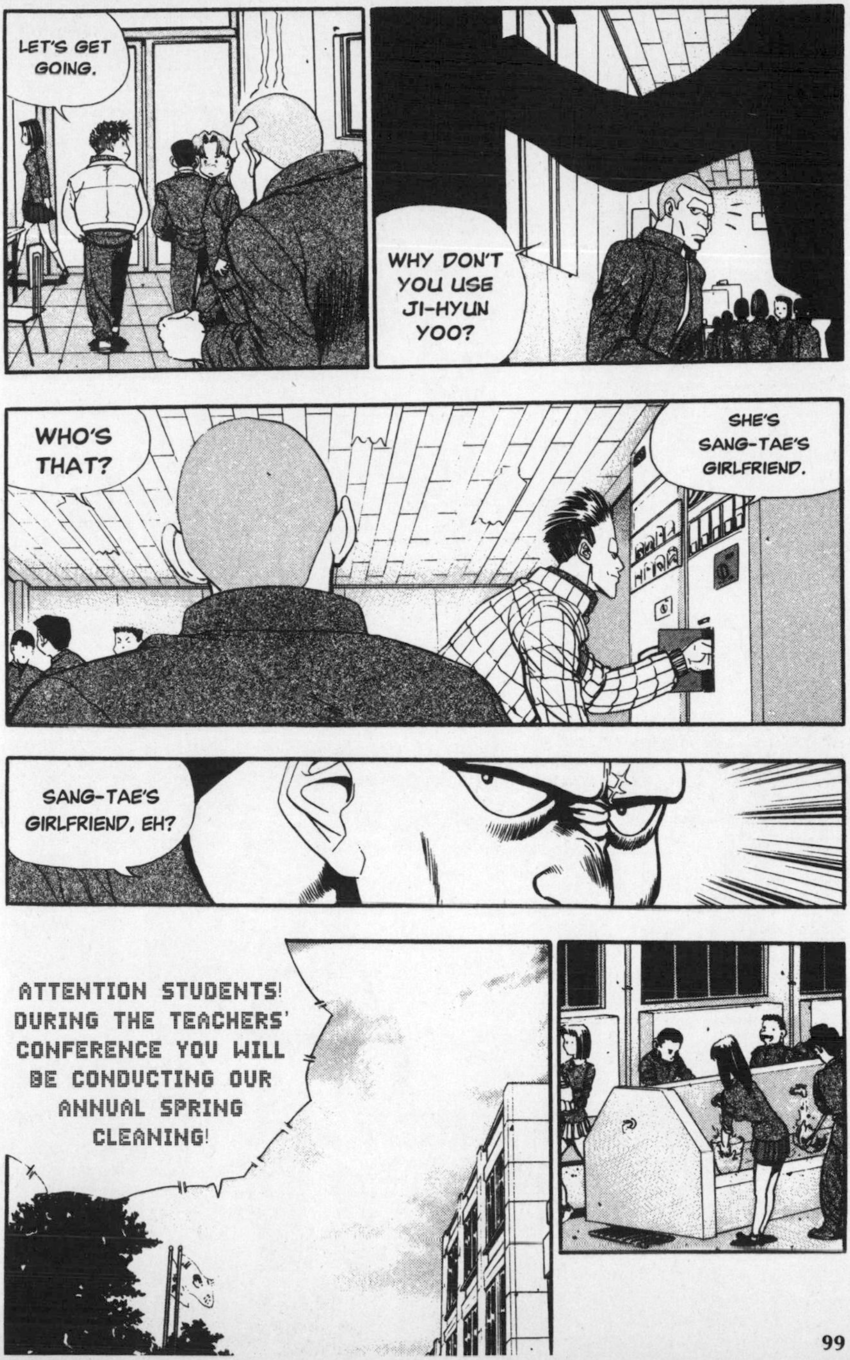
LET'S GET GOING.
WHY DON'T YOU USE JI-HYUN YOO?
WHO'S THAT?
SHE'S SANG-TAE'S GIRLFRIEND.
SANG-TAE'S GIRLFRIEND, EH?
ATTENTION STUDENTS! DURING THE TEACHERS' CONFERENCE YOU WILL BE CONDUCTING OUR ANNUAL SPRING CLEANING!

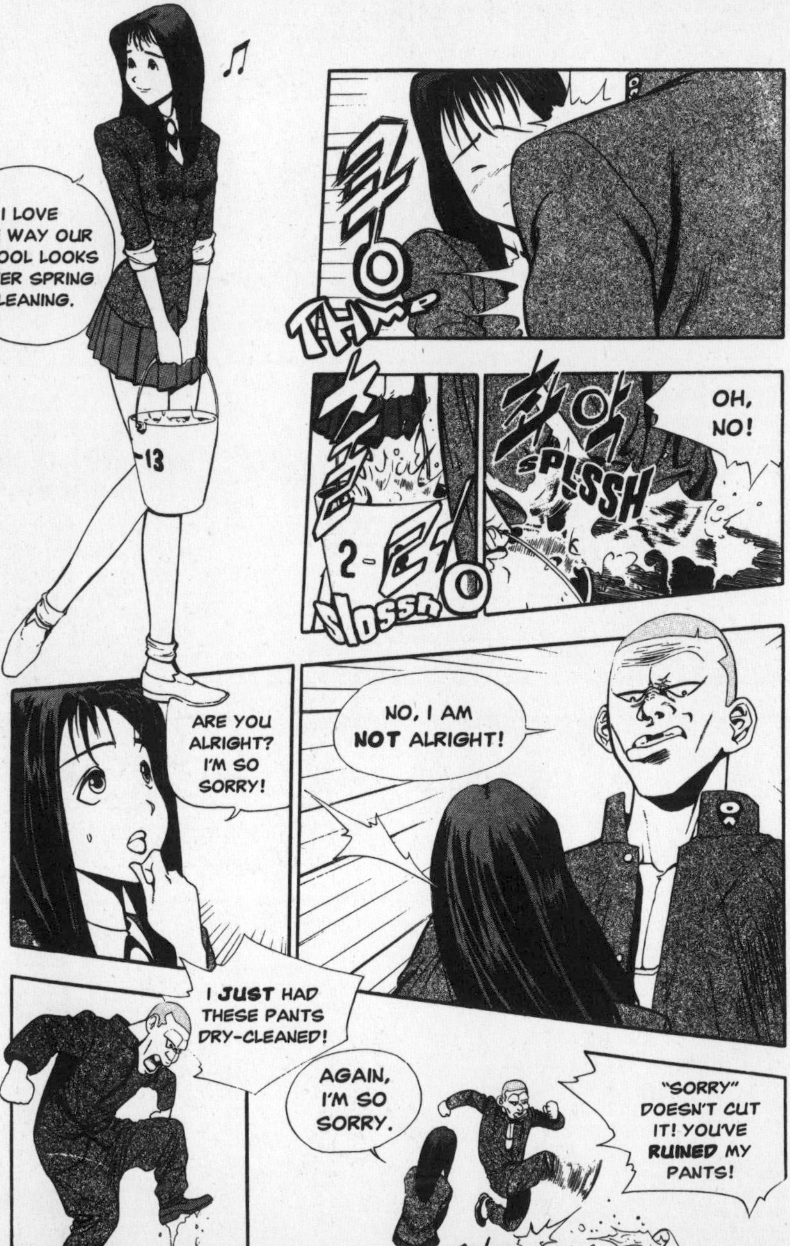
I LOVE THE WAY OUR SCHOOL LOOKS AFTER SPRING CLEANING.
THMP
SLOSSH
SPLSSH
OH, NO!
ARE YOU ALRIGHT? I'M SO SORRY!
NO, I AM **NOT** ALRIGHT!
I **JUST** HAD THESE PANTS DRY-CLEANED!
AGAIN, I'M SO SORRY.
"SORRY" DOESN'T CUT IT! YOU'VE **RUINED** MY PANTS!
KLANK

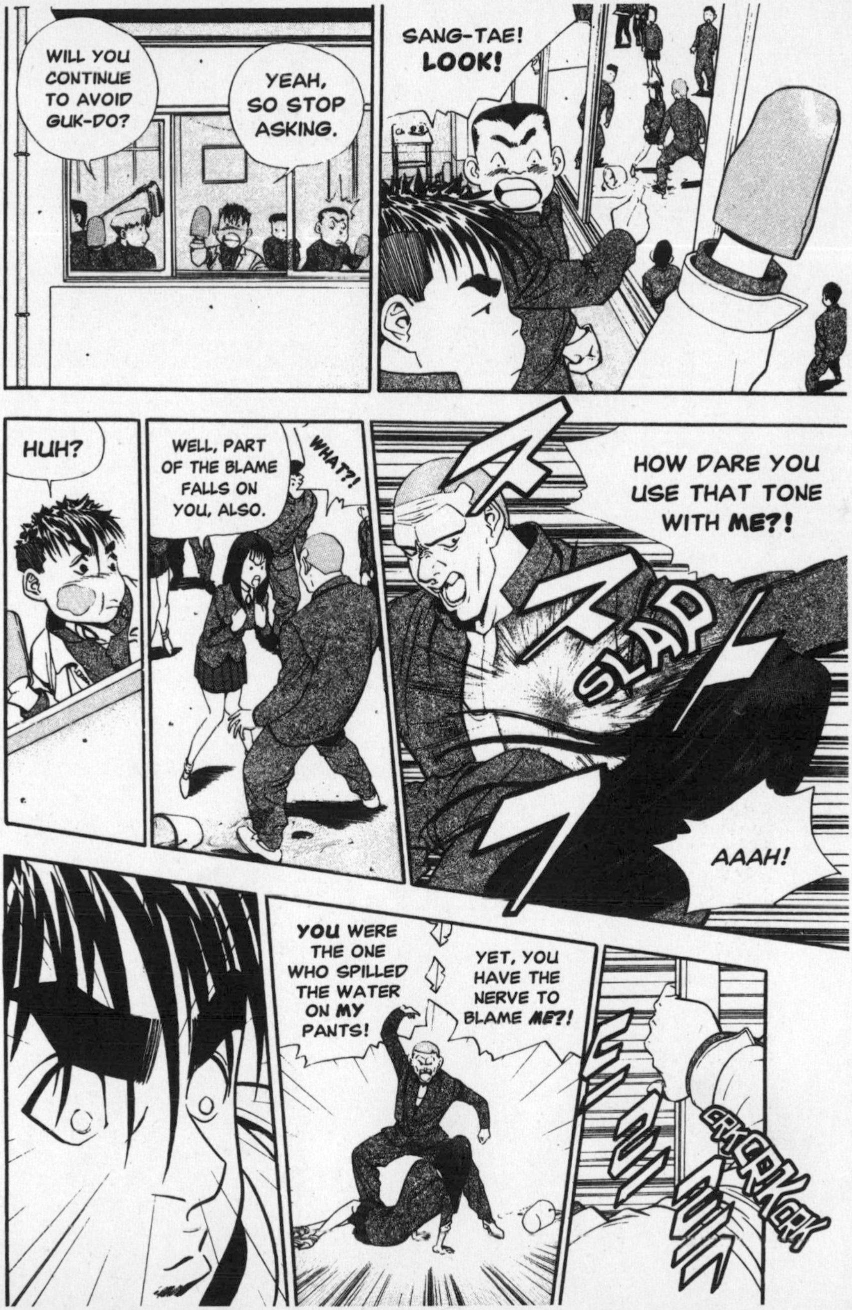
WILL YOU CONTINUE TO AVOID GUK-DO?
YEAH, SO STOP ASKING.
SANG-TAE! LOOK!
HUH?
WELL, PART OF THE BLAME FALLS ON YOU, ALSO.
WHAT?!
HOW DARE YOU USE THAT TONE WITH ME?!
SLAP
AAAH!
YOU WERE THE ONE WHO SPILLED THE WATER ON MY PANTS!
YET, YOU HAVE THE NERVE TO BLAME ME?!
CRK CRK CRK

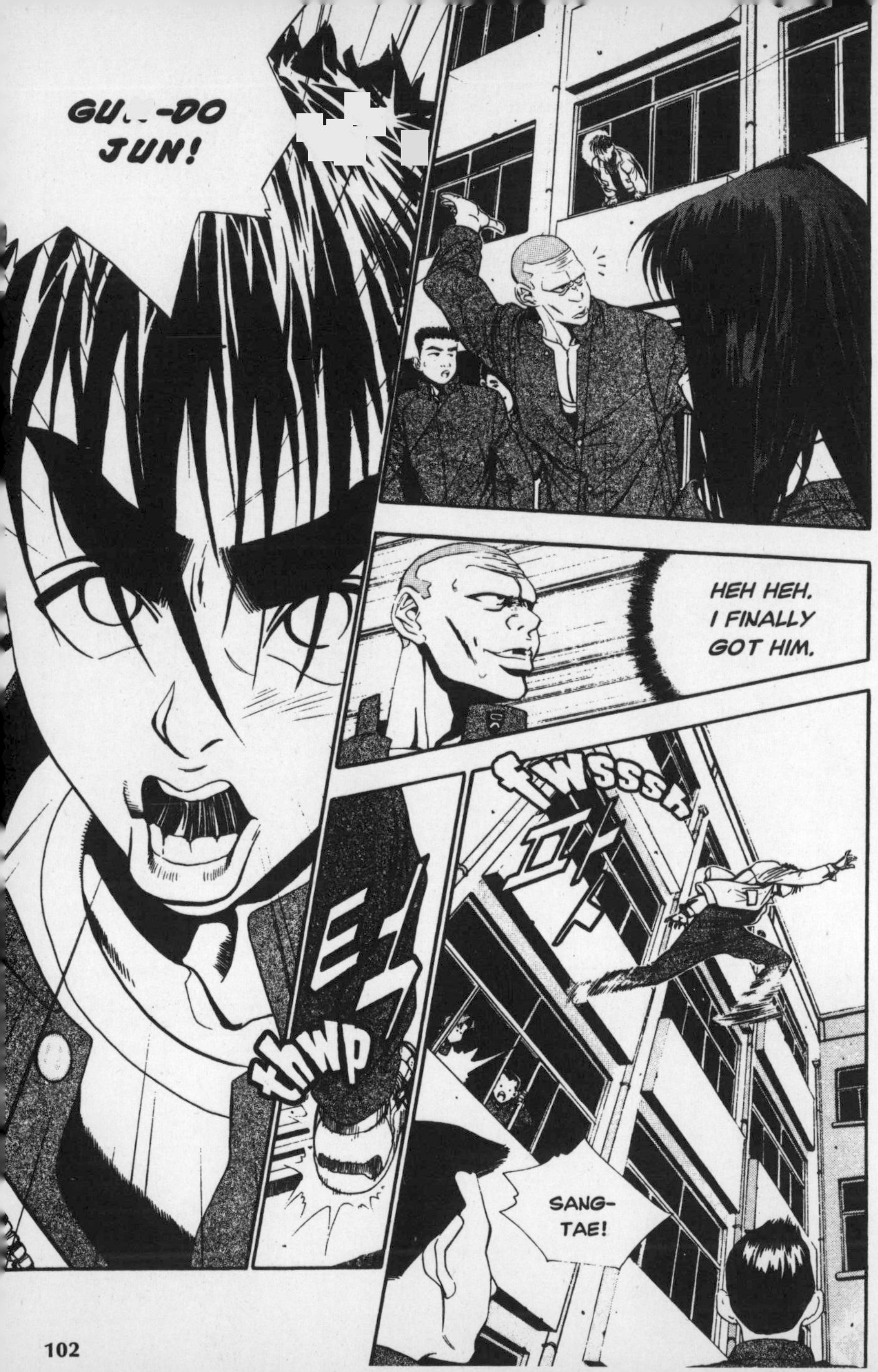
GU -DO
JUN!
HEH HEH.
I FINALLY
GOT HIM.
fwsssh
thwp
SANG-
TAE!

TO PROTECT THE
ONES THAT YOU LOVE.

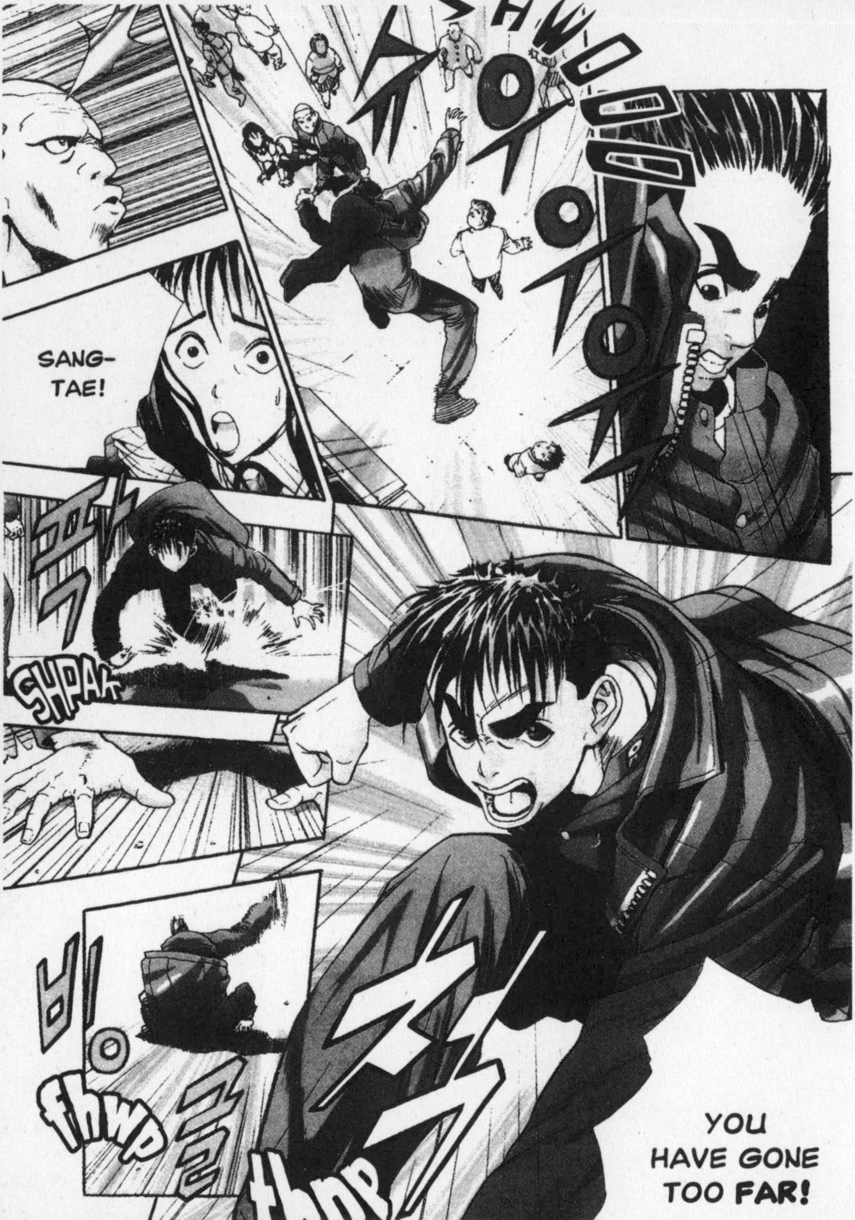
SHWOOO
SANG-TAE!
SHPAK
fhwp
thpp
YOU HAVE GONE TOO FAR!

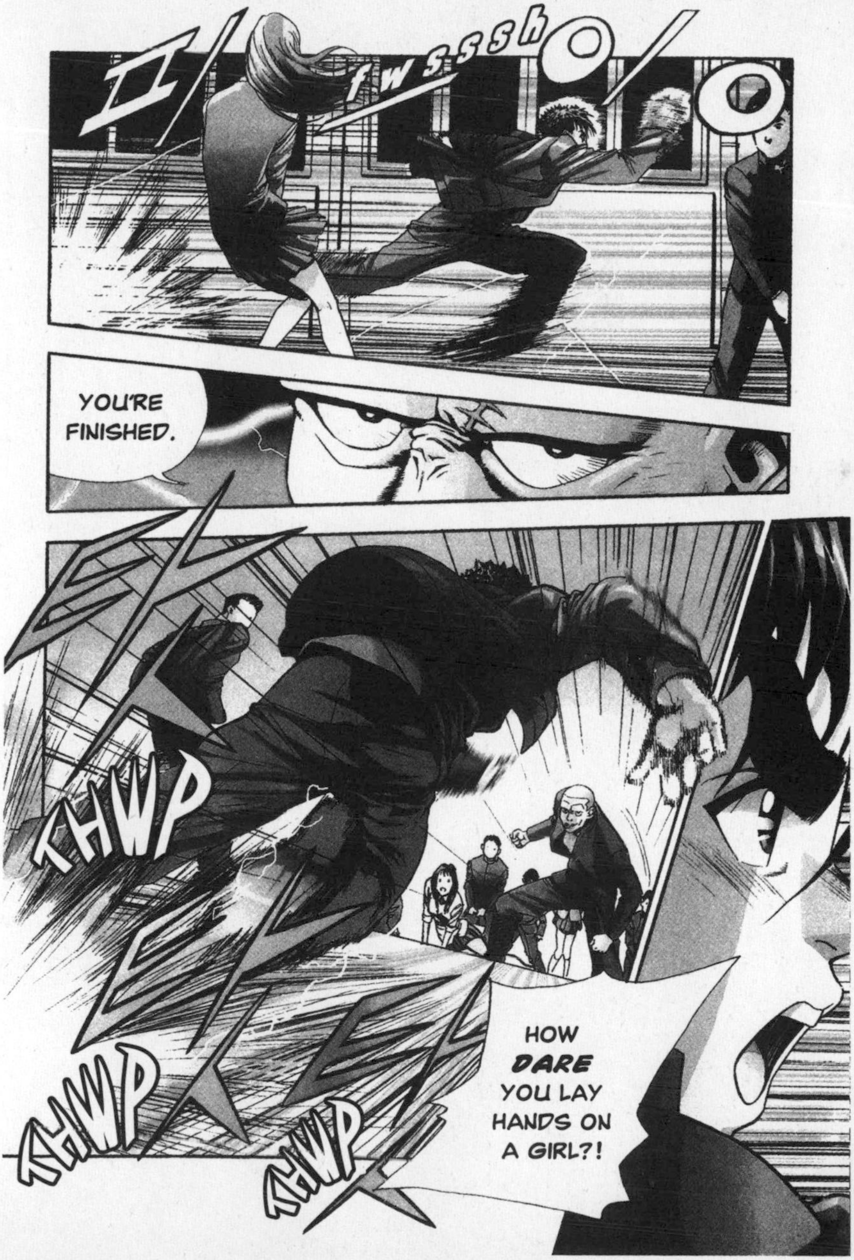
fwssshO/O
YOU'RE FINISHED.
THWP
HOW DARE YOU LAY HANDS ON A GIRL?!
THWP
THWP

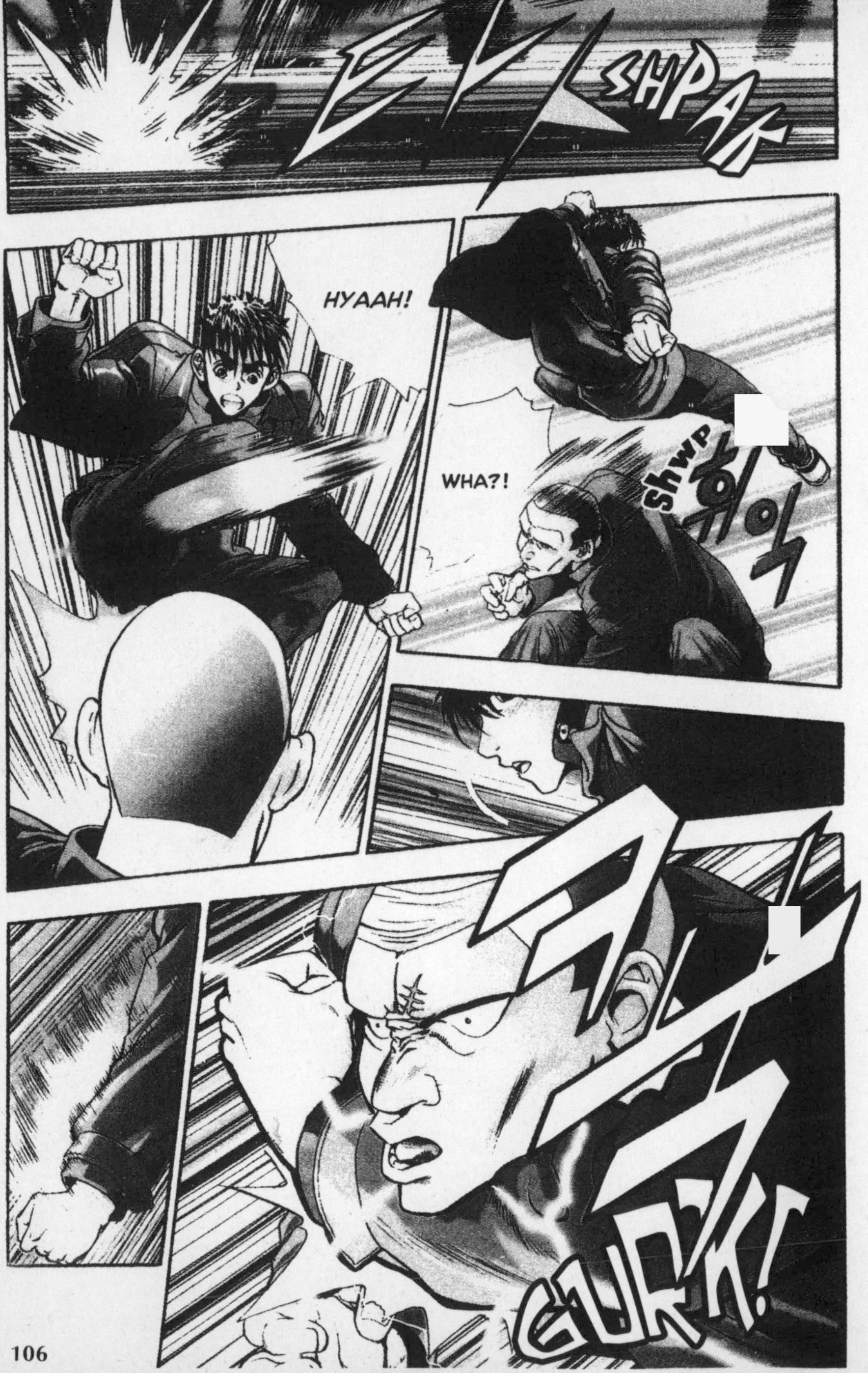
SHPAK
HYAAH!
WHA?!
shwp
GURK!

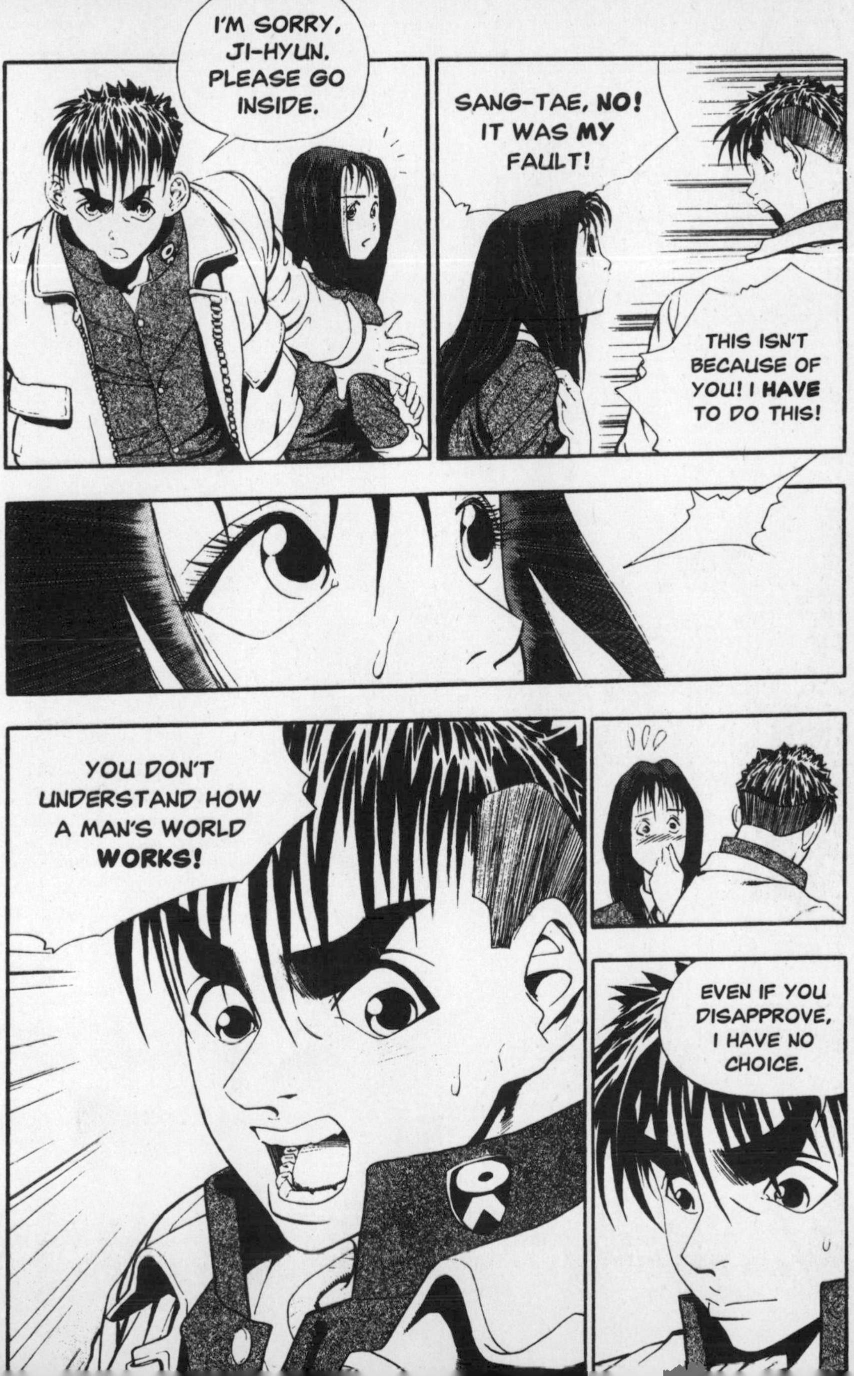
I'M SORRY, JI-HYUN. PLEASE GO INSIDE.
SANG-TAE, NO! IT WAS MY FAULT!
THIS ISN'T BECAUSE OF YOU! I HAVE TO DO THIS!
YOU DON'T UNDERSTAND HOW A MAN'S WORLD WORKS!
EVEN IF YOU DISAPPROVE, I HAVE NO CHOICE.

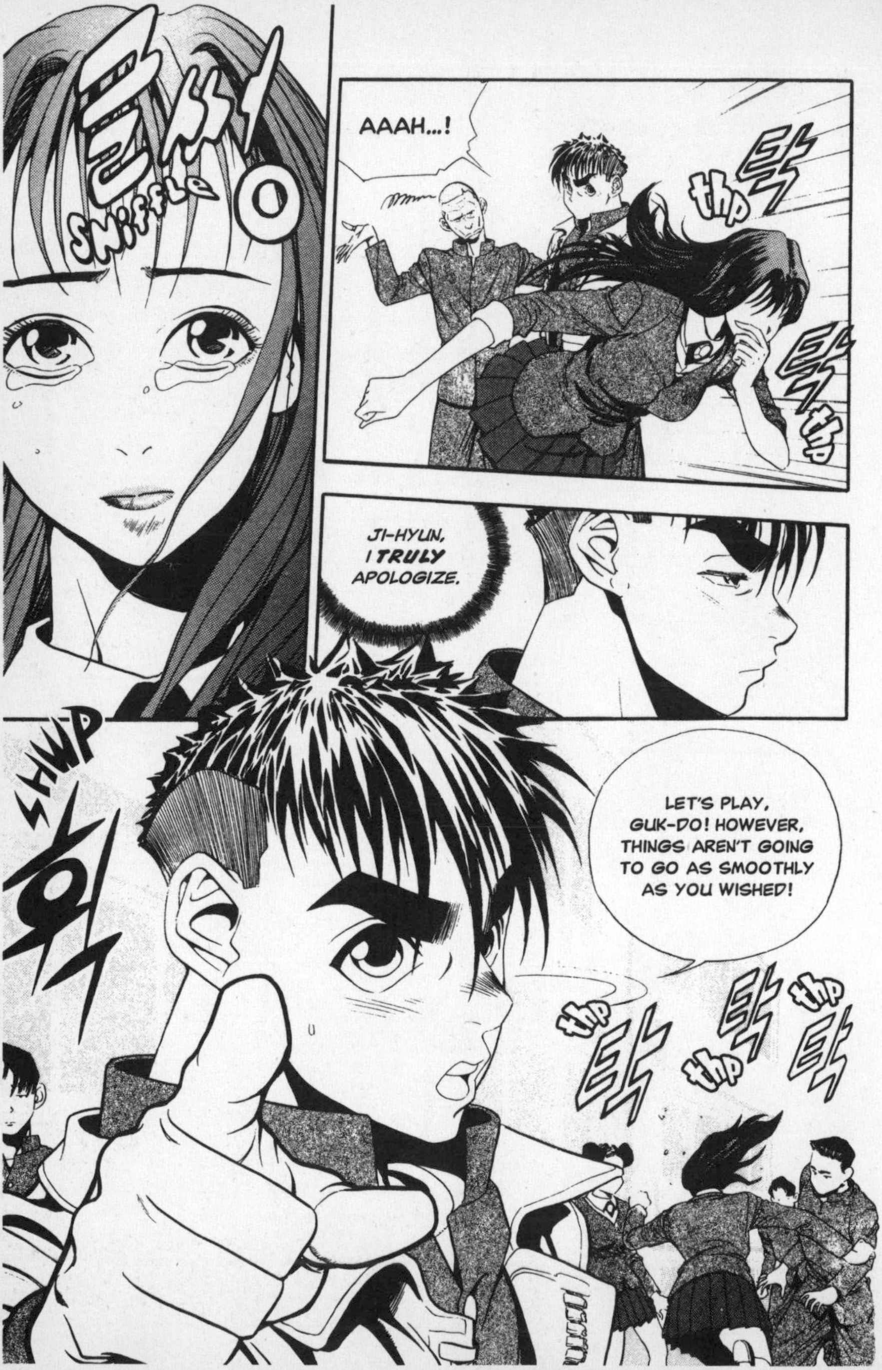
SNIFFLE
AAAH...!
thp
thp
JI-HYUN, I TRULY APOLOGIZE.
SHWP
LET'S PLAY, GUK-DO! HOWEVER, THINGS AREN'T GOING TO GO AS SMOOTHLY AS YOU WISHED!
thp
thp
thp

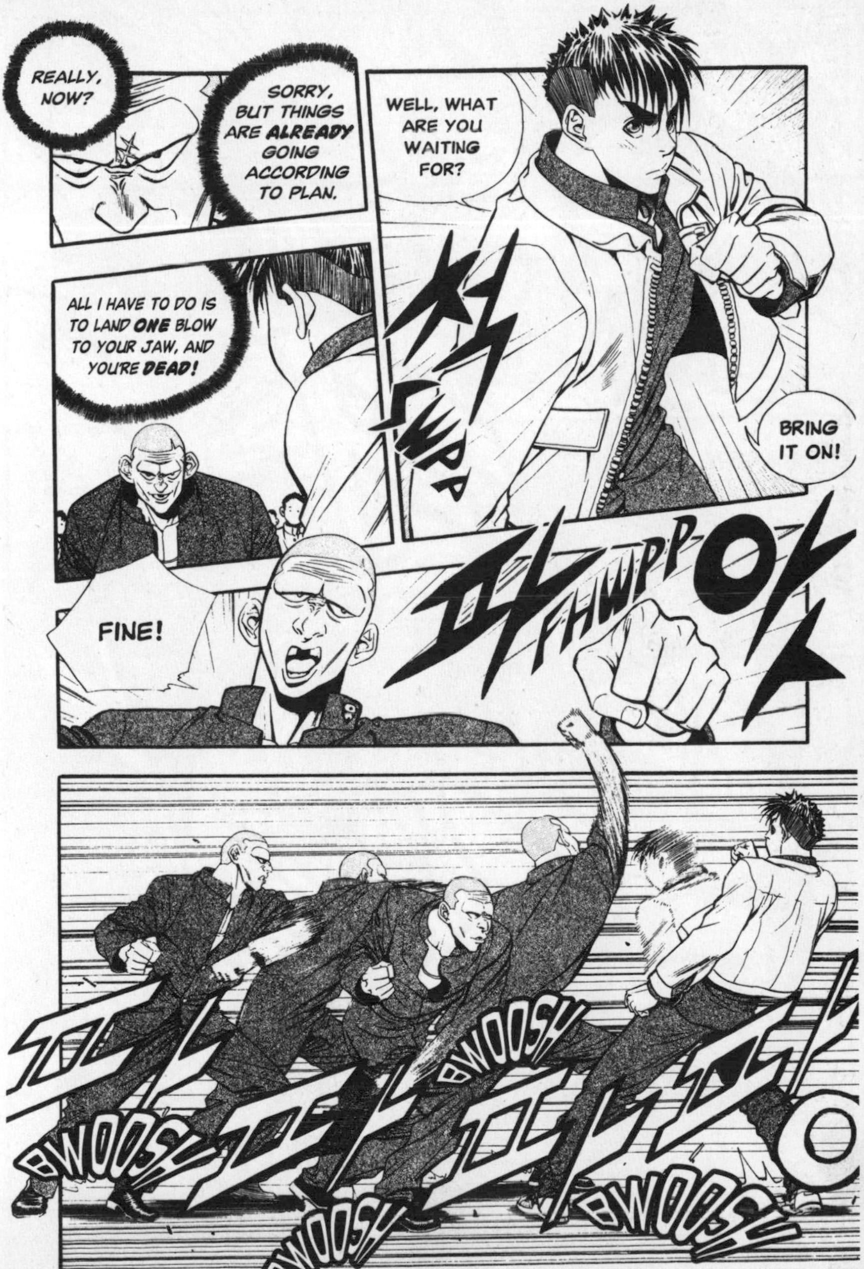
REALLY, NOW?
SORRY, BUT THINGS ARE **ALREADY** GOING ACCORDING TO PLAN.
WELL, WHAT ARE YOU WAITING FOR?
ALL I HAVE TO DO IS TO LAND **ONE** BLOW TO YOUR JAW, AND YOU'RE **DEAD**!
SWPP
BRING IT ON!
FINE!
FHWPP
BWOOSH
BWOOSH
BWOOSH
BWOOSH

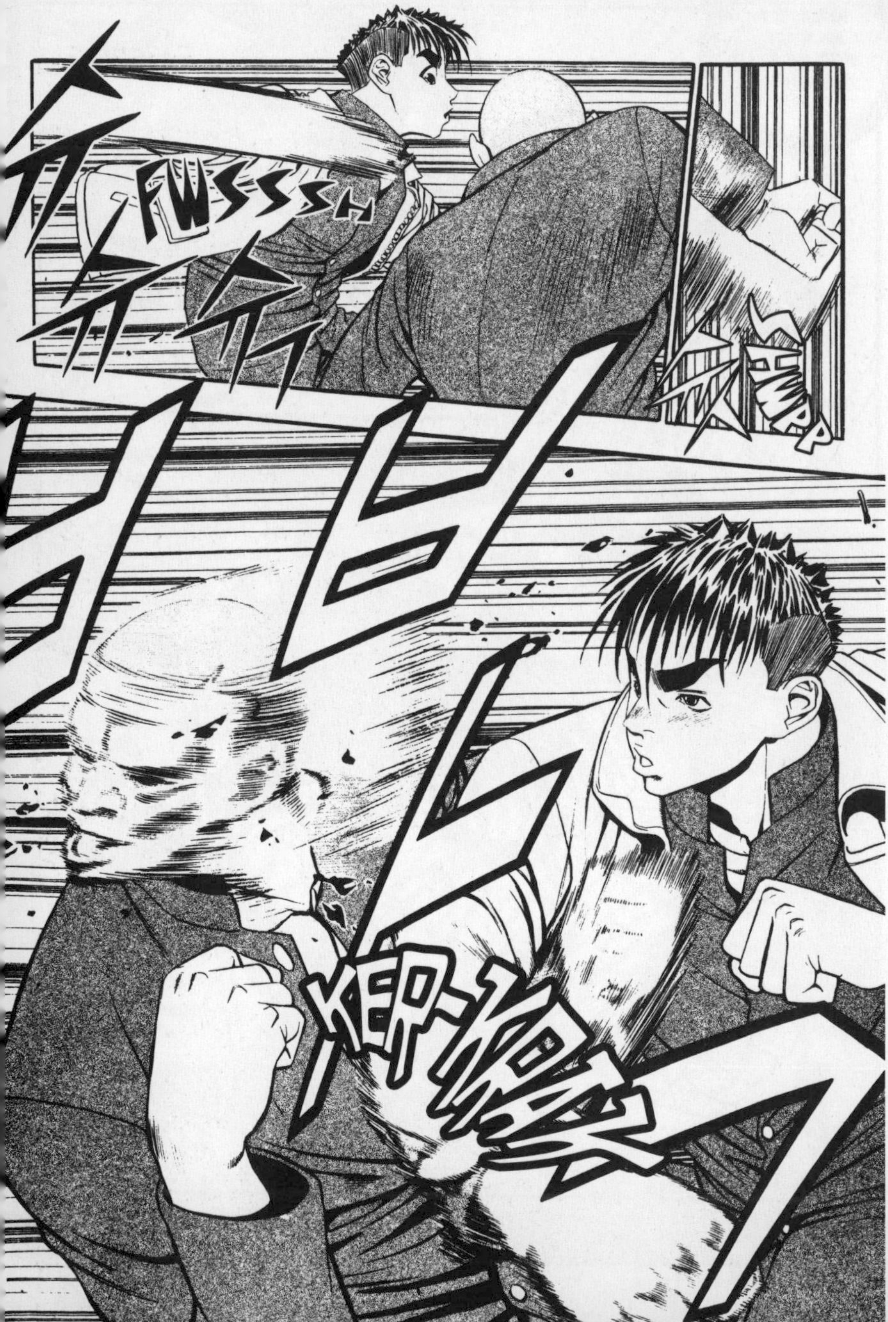

FWSSSH
HWPP
KER-WOOM

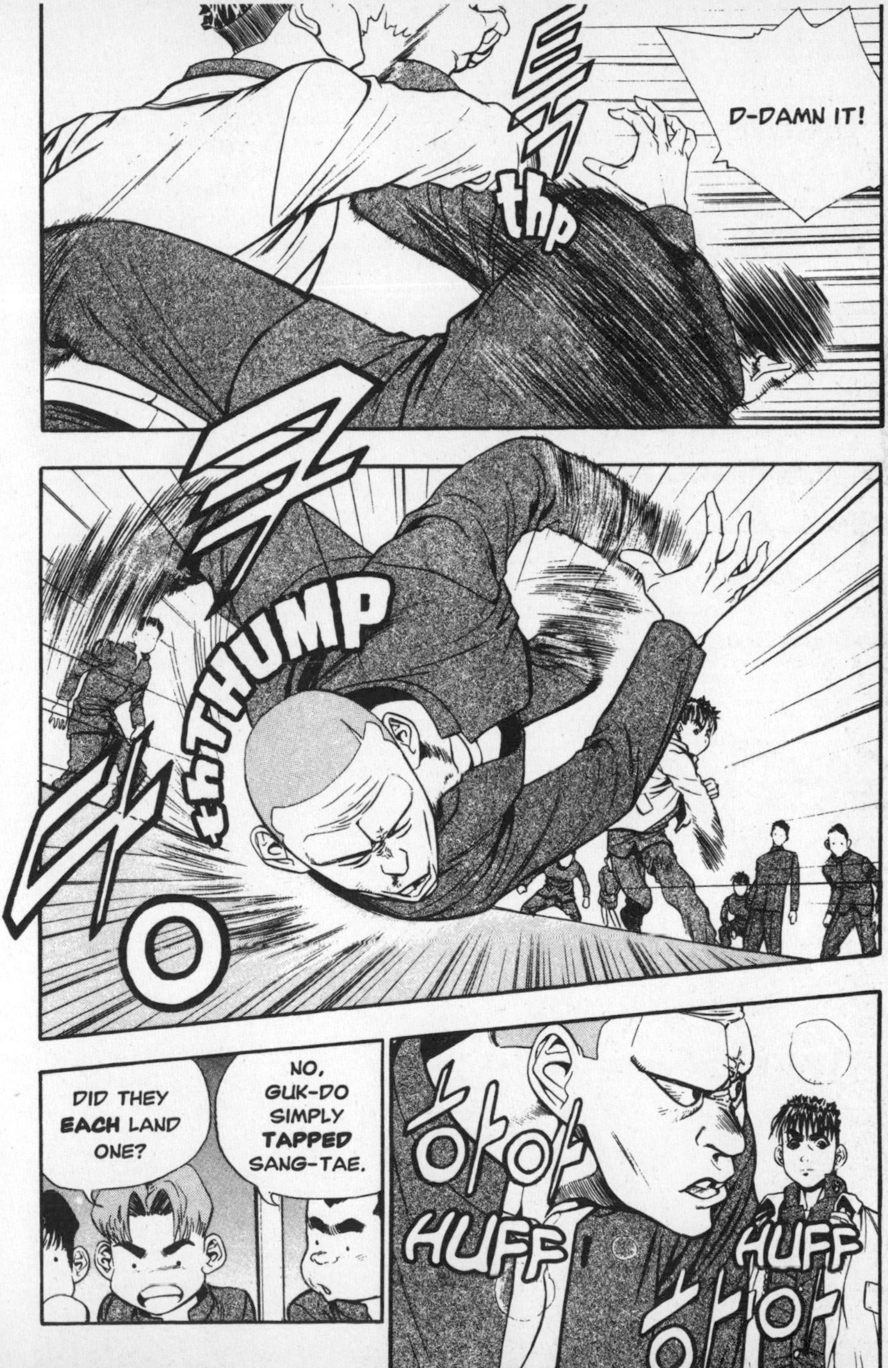
D-DAMN IT!
thp
thTHUMP
DID THEY EACH LAND ONE?
NO, GUK-DO SIMPLY TAPPED SANG-TAE.
HUFF
HUFF

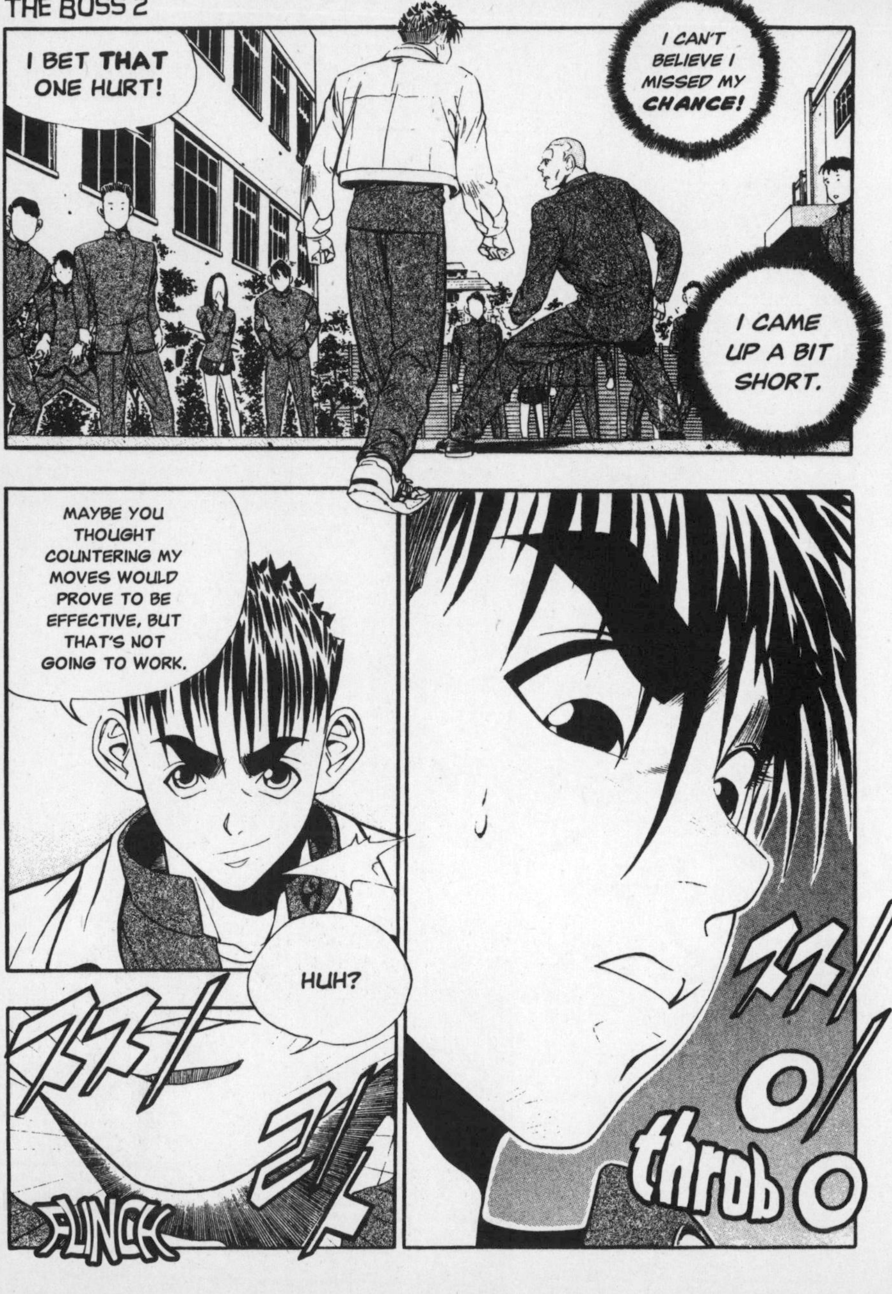
I BET THAT ONE HURT!
I CAN'T BELIEVE I MISSED MY CHANCE!
I CAME UP A BIT SHORT.
MAYBE YOU THOUGHT COUNTERING MY MOVES WOULD PROVE TO BE EFFECTIVE, BUT THAT'S NOT GOING TO WORK.
HUH?
FLINCH
throb

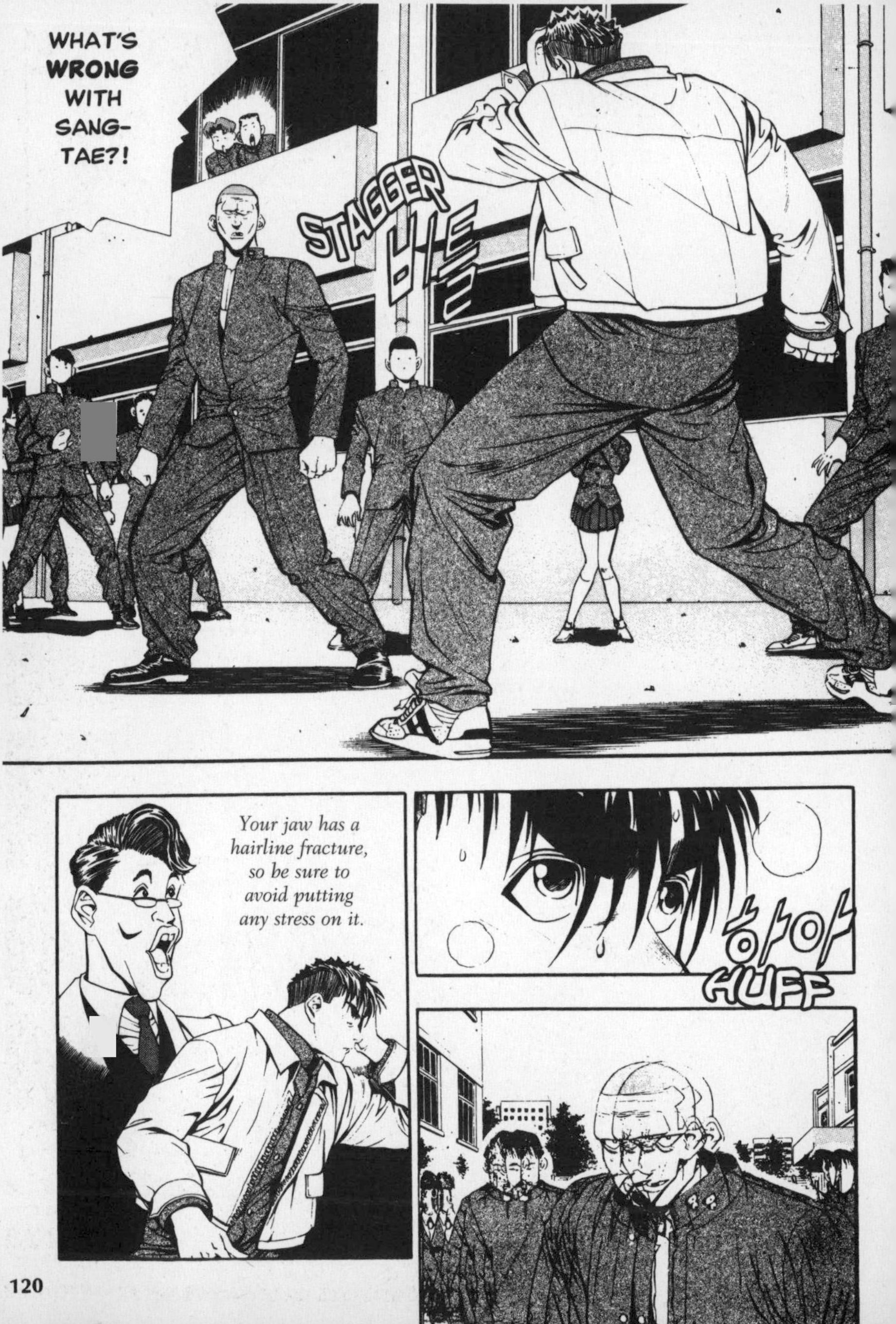
WHAT'S WRONG WITH SANG-TAE?!
STAGGER
비틀
Your jaw has a hairline fracture, so be sure to avoid putting any stress on it.
하아
HUFF

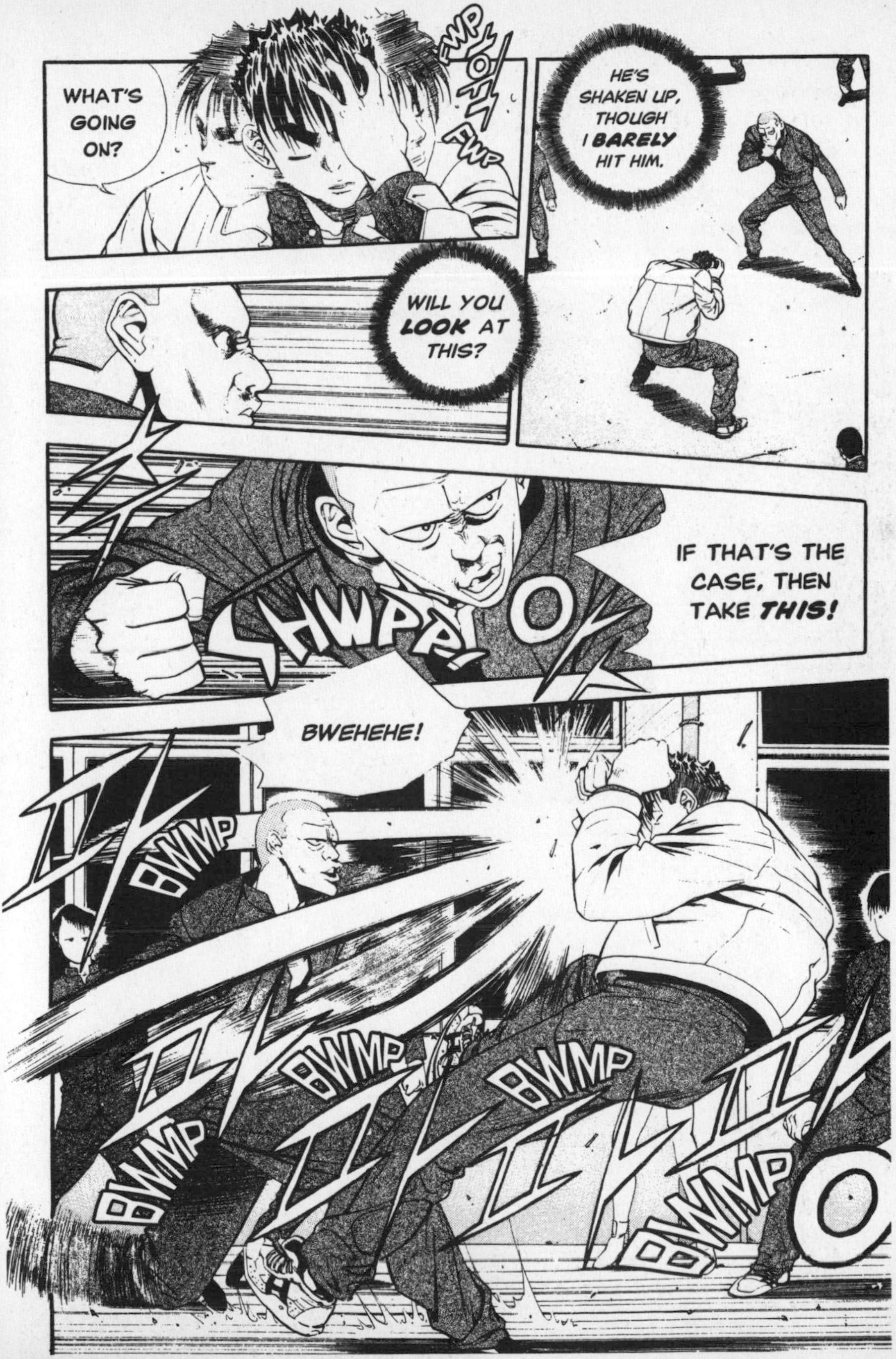
FWP
FWP
WHAT'S GOING ON?
HE'S SHAKEN UP, THOUGH I BARELY HIT HIM.
WILL YOU LOOK AT THIS?
IF THAT'S THE CASE, THEN TAKE THIS!
SHWPP
BWEHEHE!
BWMP
BWMP
BWMP
BWMP
BWMP

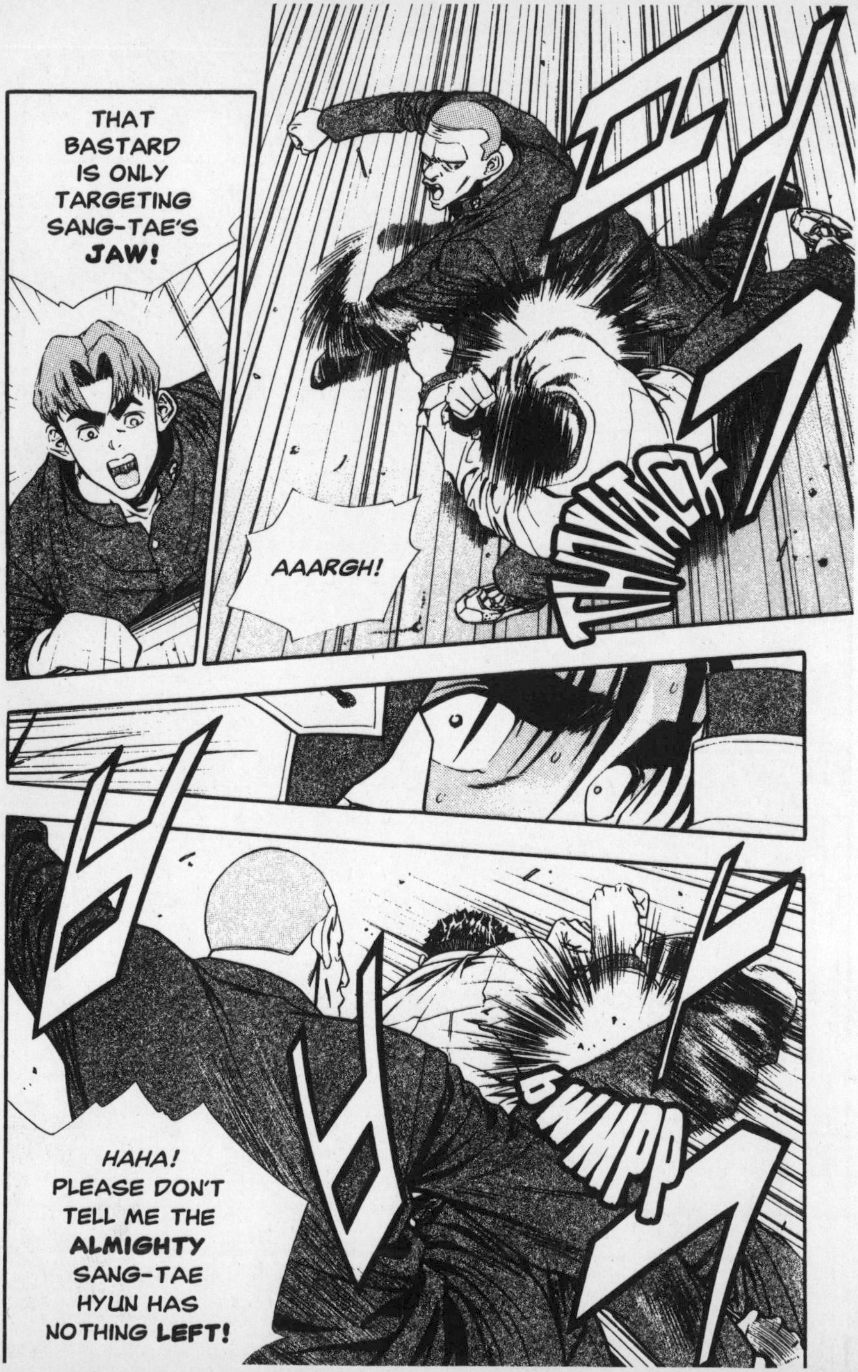
THAT BASTARD IS ONLY TARGETING SANG-TAE'S **JAW!**
AAARGH!
THWACK
HAHA! PLEASE DON'T TELL ME THE **ALMIGHTY** SANG-TAE HYUN HAS NOTHING **LEFT!**
BWMPP

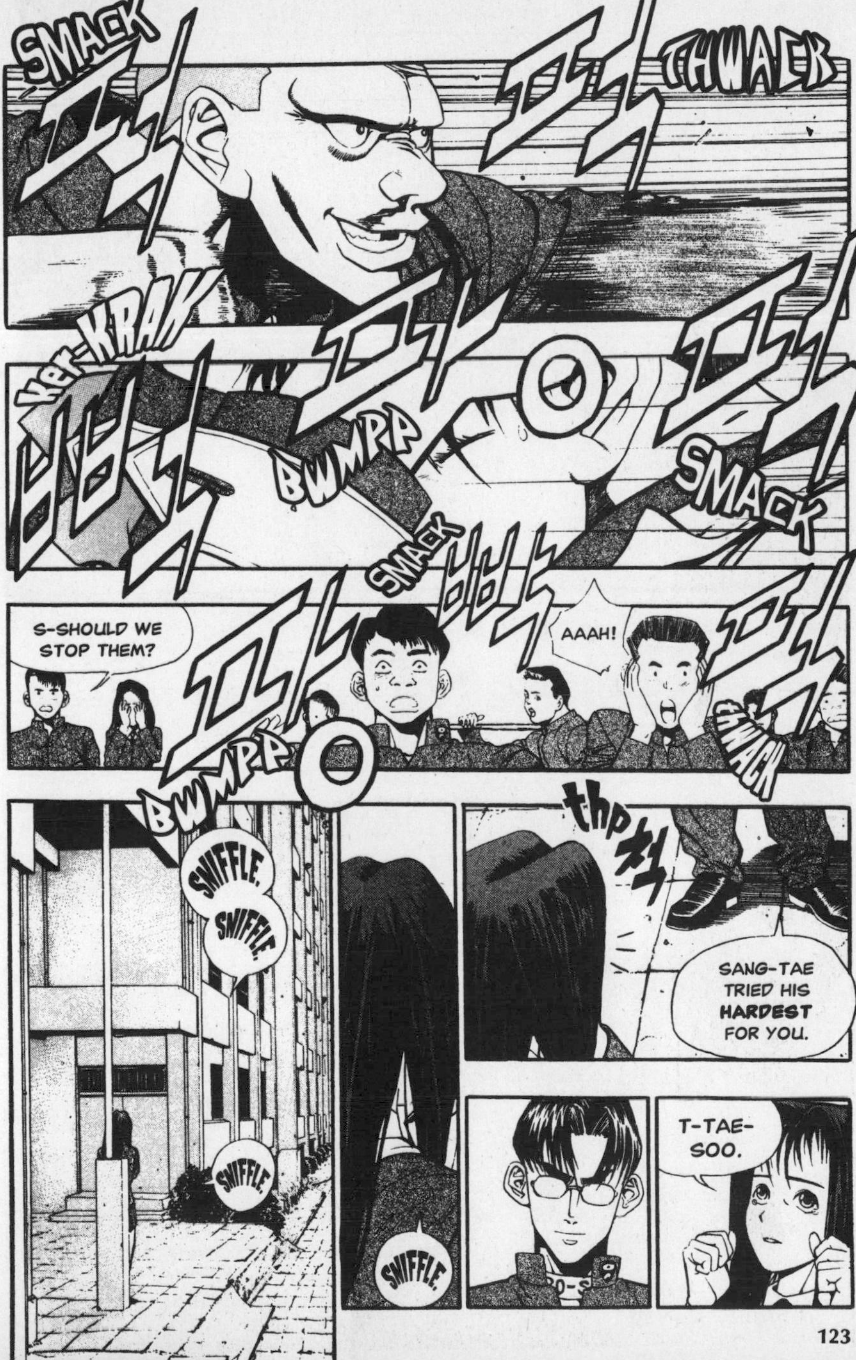

SMACK
THWACK
ker-KRAK
SMACK
S-SHOULD WE STOP THEM?
AAAH!
thp
SNIFFLE.
SNIFFLE.
SNIFFLE.
SNIFFLE.
SANG-TAE TRIED HIS **HARDEST** FOR YOU.
T-TAE-SOO.

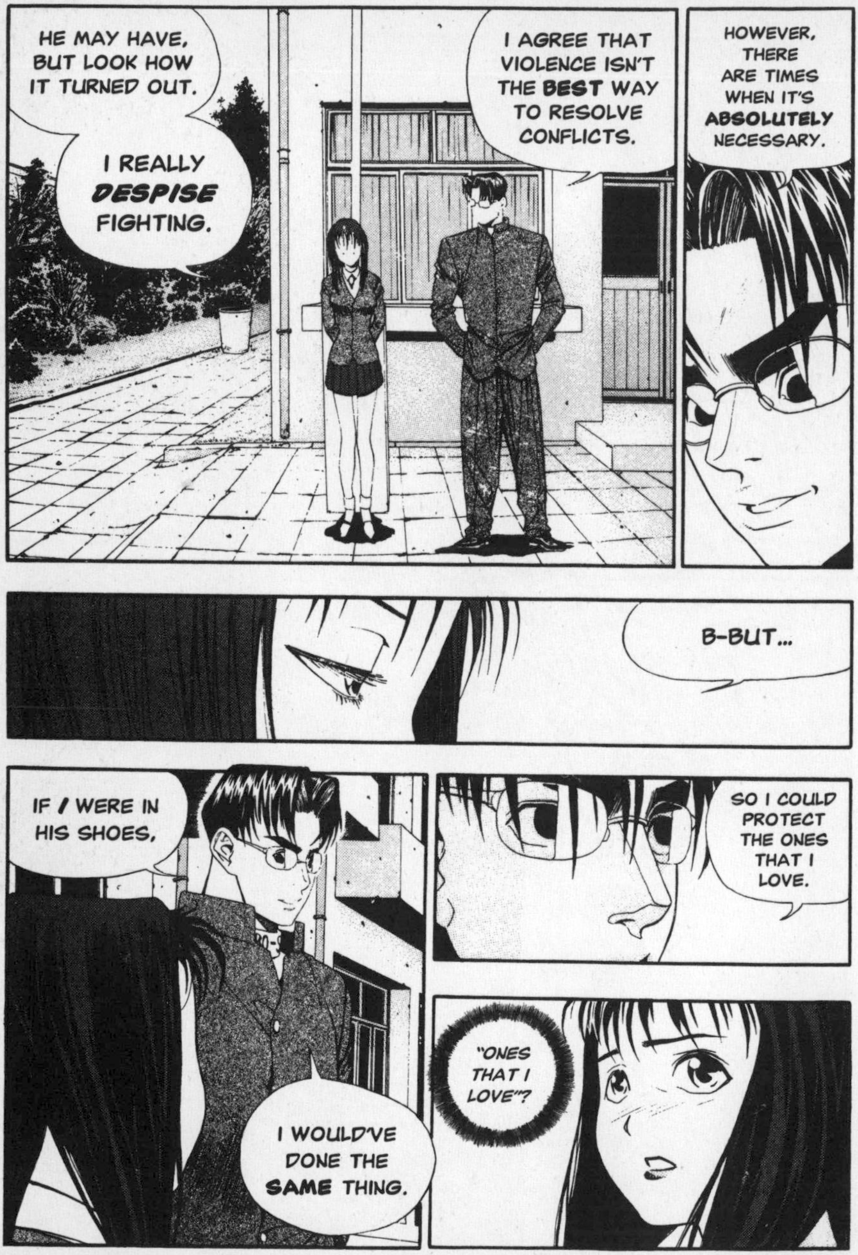
HE MAY HAVE, BUT LOOK HOW IT TURNED OUT.
I REALLY DESPISE FIGHTING.
I AGREE THAT VIOLENCE ISN'T THE BEST WAY TO RESOLVE CONFLICTS.
HOWEVER, THERE ARE TIMES WHEN IT'S ABSOLUTELY NECESSARY.
B-BUT...
IF I WERE IN HIS SHOES,
I WOULD'VE DONE THE SAME THING.
SO I COULD PROTECT THE ONES THAT I LOVE.
"ONES THAT I LOVE"?

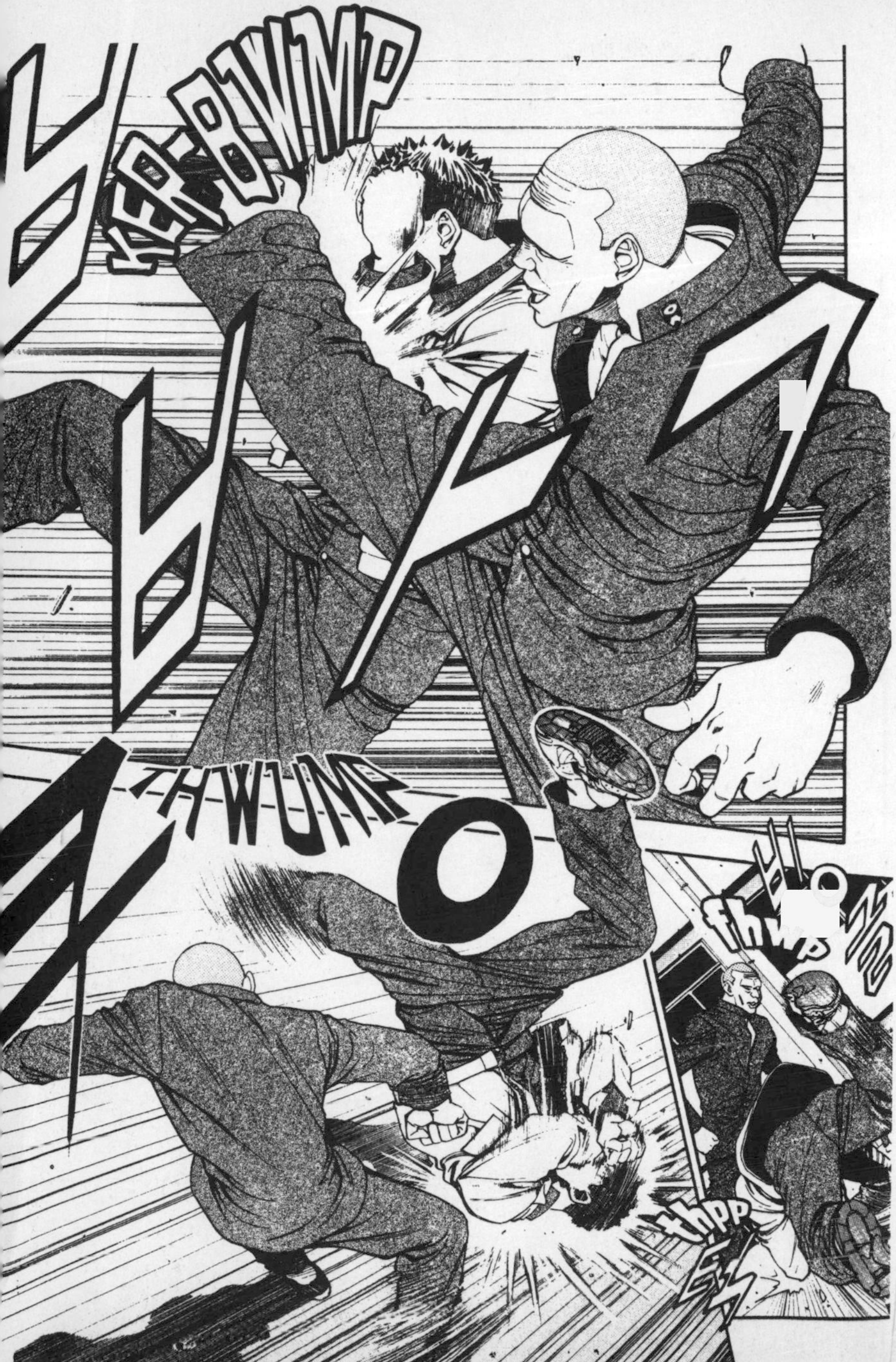
KER-BWUMP
THWUMP
fhwmp
thpp

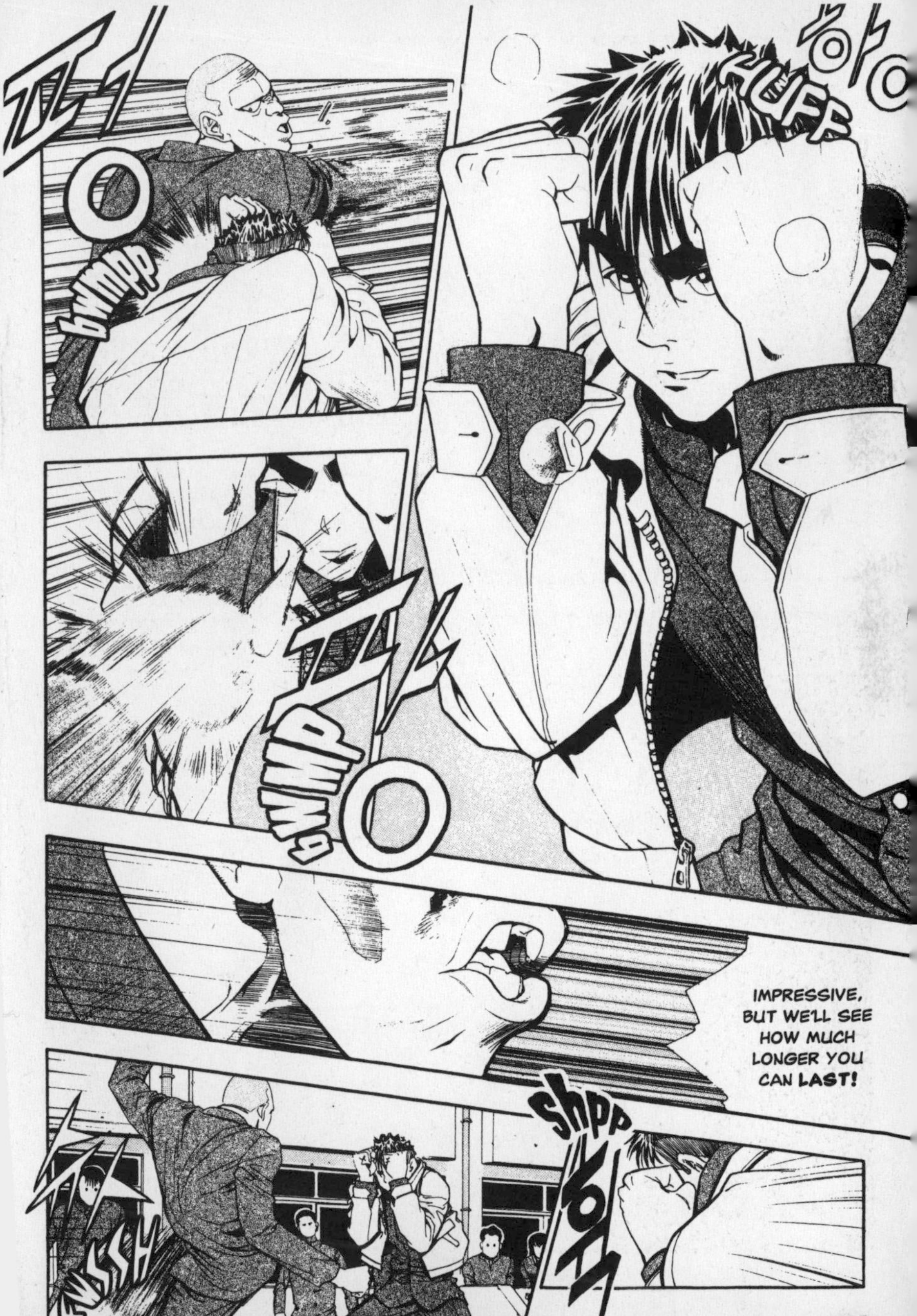
HUFF
bwmpp
bwmp
shpp
IMPRESSIVE, BUT WE'LL SEE HOW MUCH LONGER YOU CAN LAST!

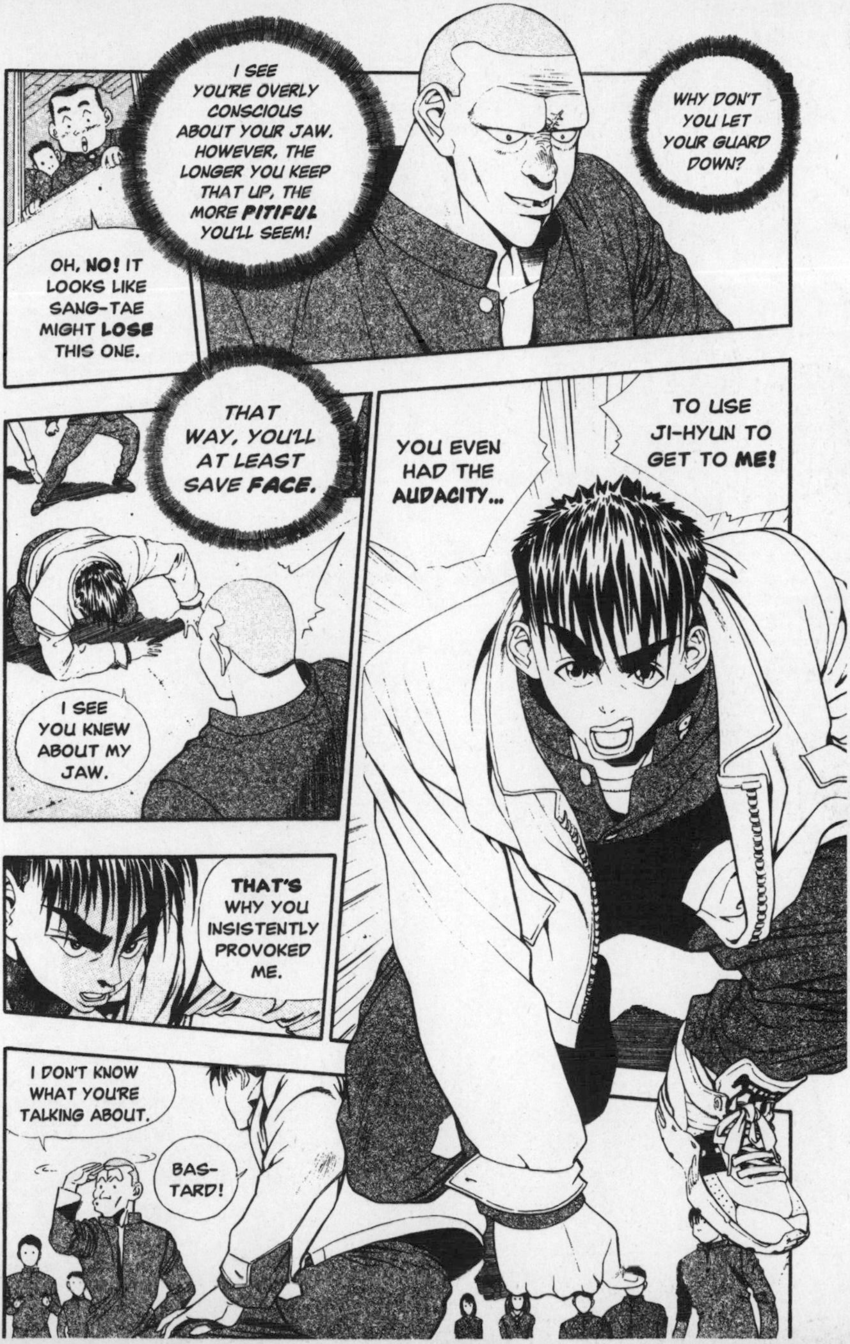

I SEE YOU'RE OVERLY CONSCIOUS ABOUT YOUR JAW. HOWEVER, THE LONGER YOU KEEP THAT UP, THE MORE PITIFUL YOU'LL SEEM!
WHY DON'T YOU LET YOUR GUARD DOWN?
OH, NO! IT LOOKS LIKE SANG-TAE MIGHT LOSE THIS ONE.
THAT WAY, YOU'LL AT LEAST SAVE FACE.
I SEE YOU KNEW ABOUT MY JAW.
THAT'S WHY YOU INSISTENTLY PROVOKED ME.
TO USE JI-HYUN TO GET TO ME!
YOU EVEN HAD THE AUDACITY...
I DON'T KNOW WHAT YOU'RE TALKING ABOUT.
BAS-TARD!

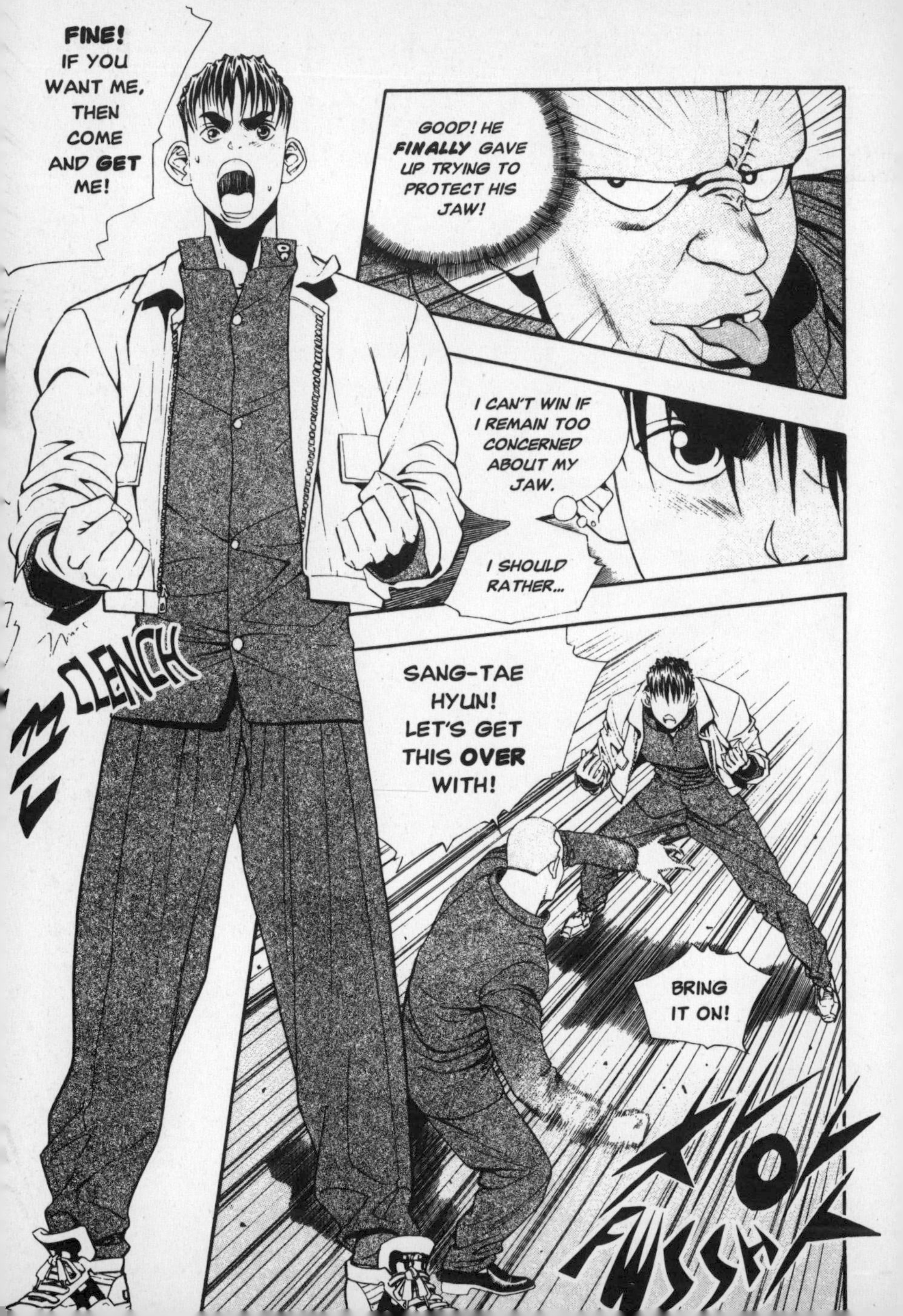
FINE! IF YOU WANT ME, THEN COME AND GET ME!
GOOD! HE FINALLY GAVE UP TRYING TO PROTECT HIS JAW!
I CAN'T WIN IF I REMAIN TOO CONCERNED ABOUT MY JAW.
I SHOULD RATHER...
CLENCH
SANG-TAE HYUN! LET'S GET THIS OVER WITH!
BRING IT ON!
FWSSSH

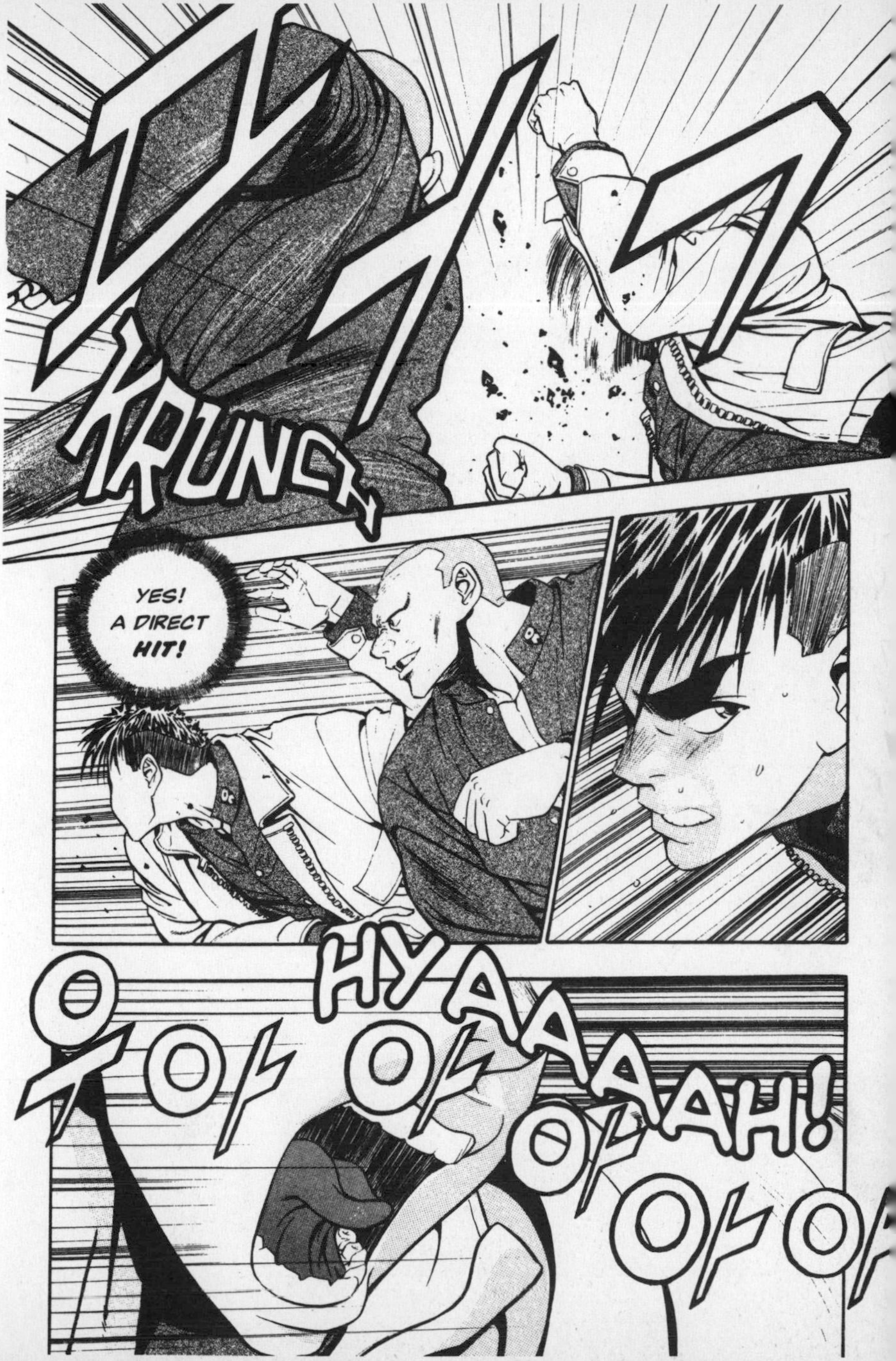
KRUNCH
YES! A DIRECT HIT!
HYAAAAAH!

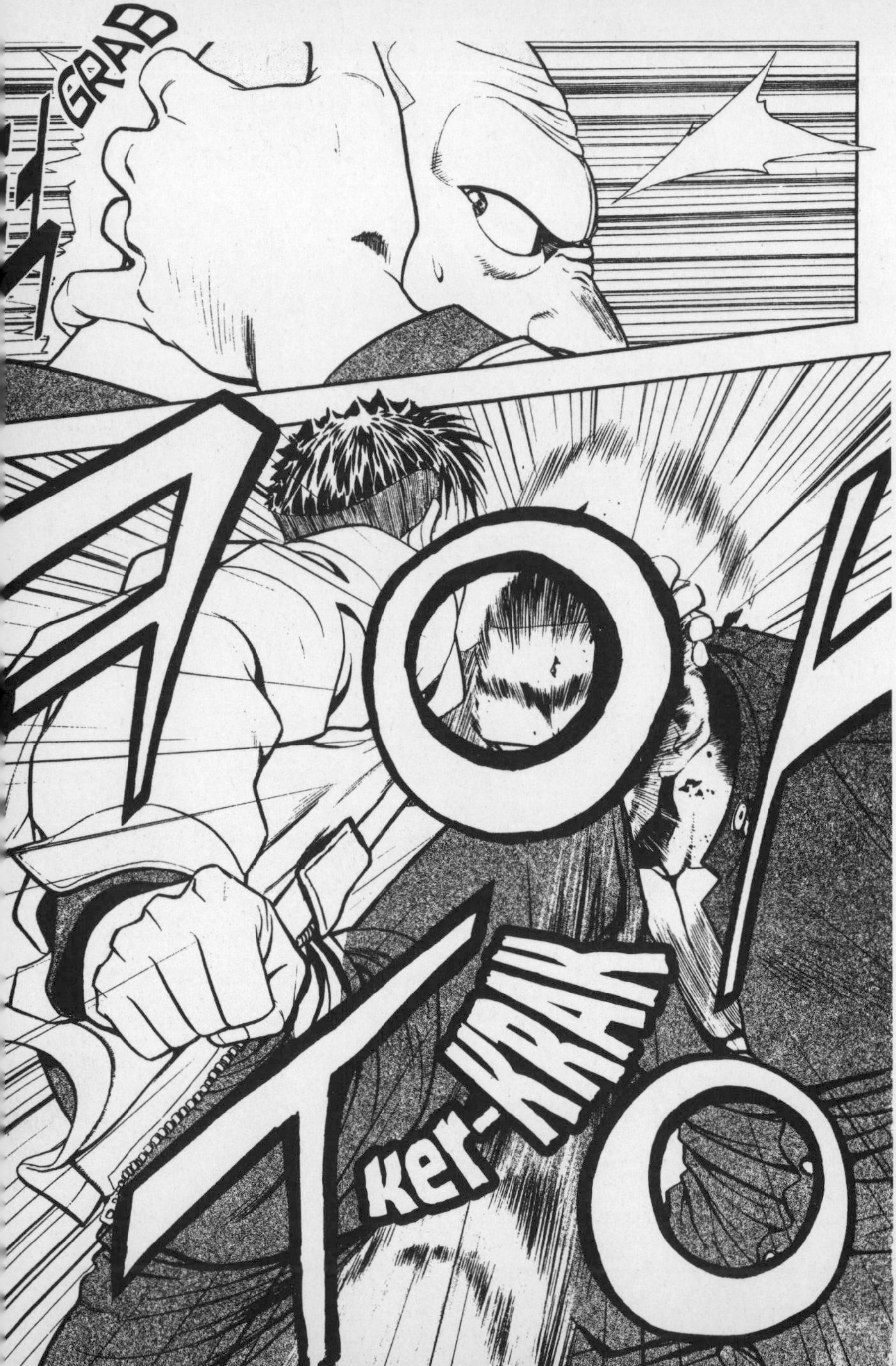
GRAB
Ker-KRAK

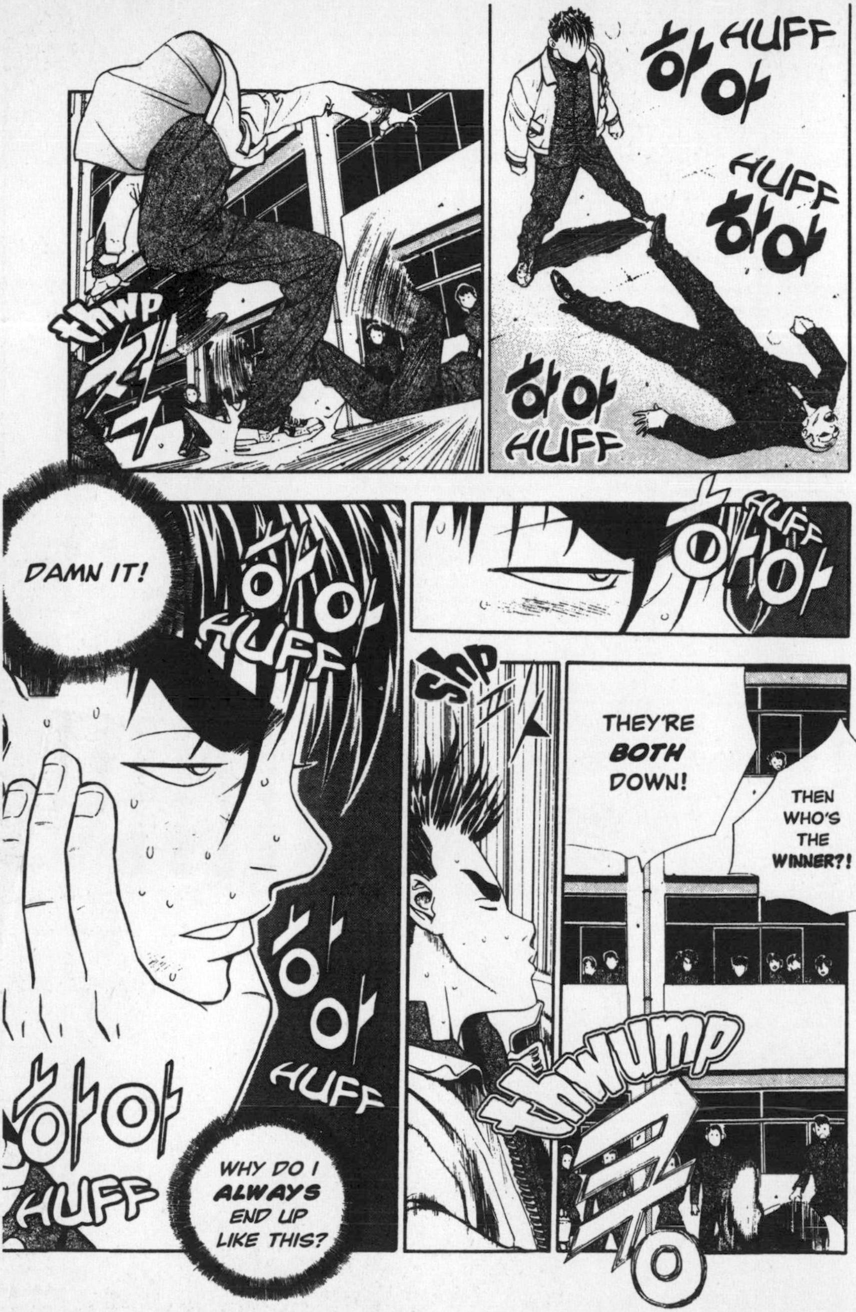
thwp
하아 HUFF
HUFF 하아
하아 HUFF
DAMN IT!
하아 HUFF
하아 HUFF
하아 HUFF
WHY DO I ALWAYS END UP LIKE THIS?
하아 HUFF
THEY'RE BOTH DOWN!
THEN WHO'S THE WINNER?!
thwump

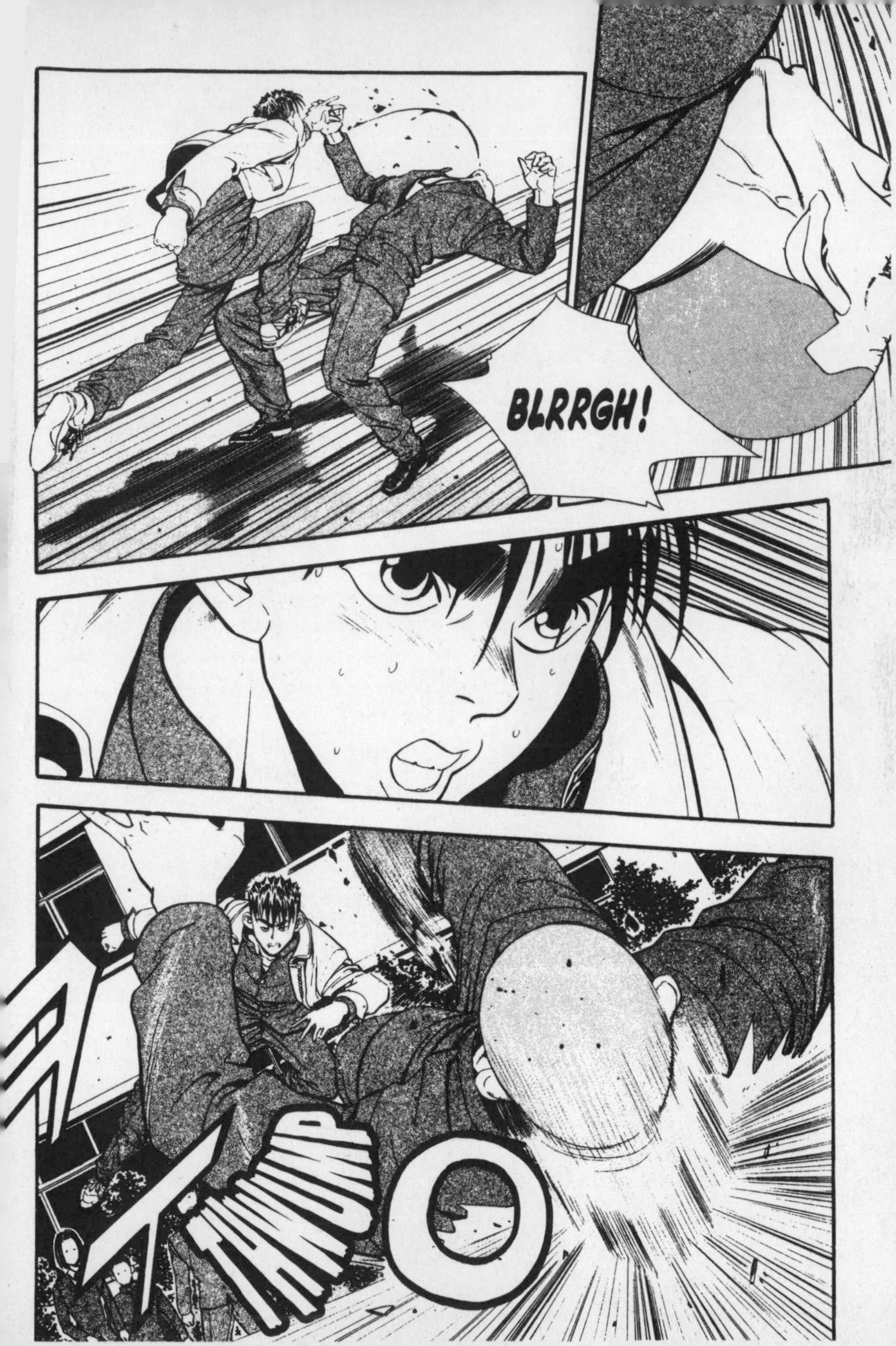
BLRRGH!
THUMP

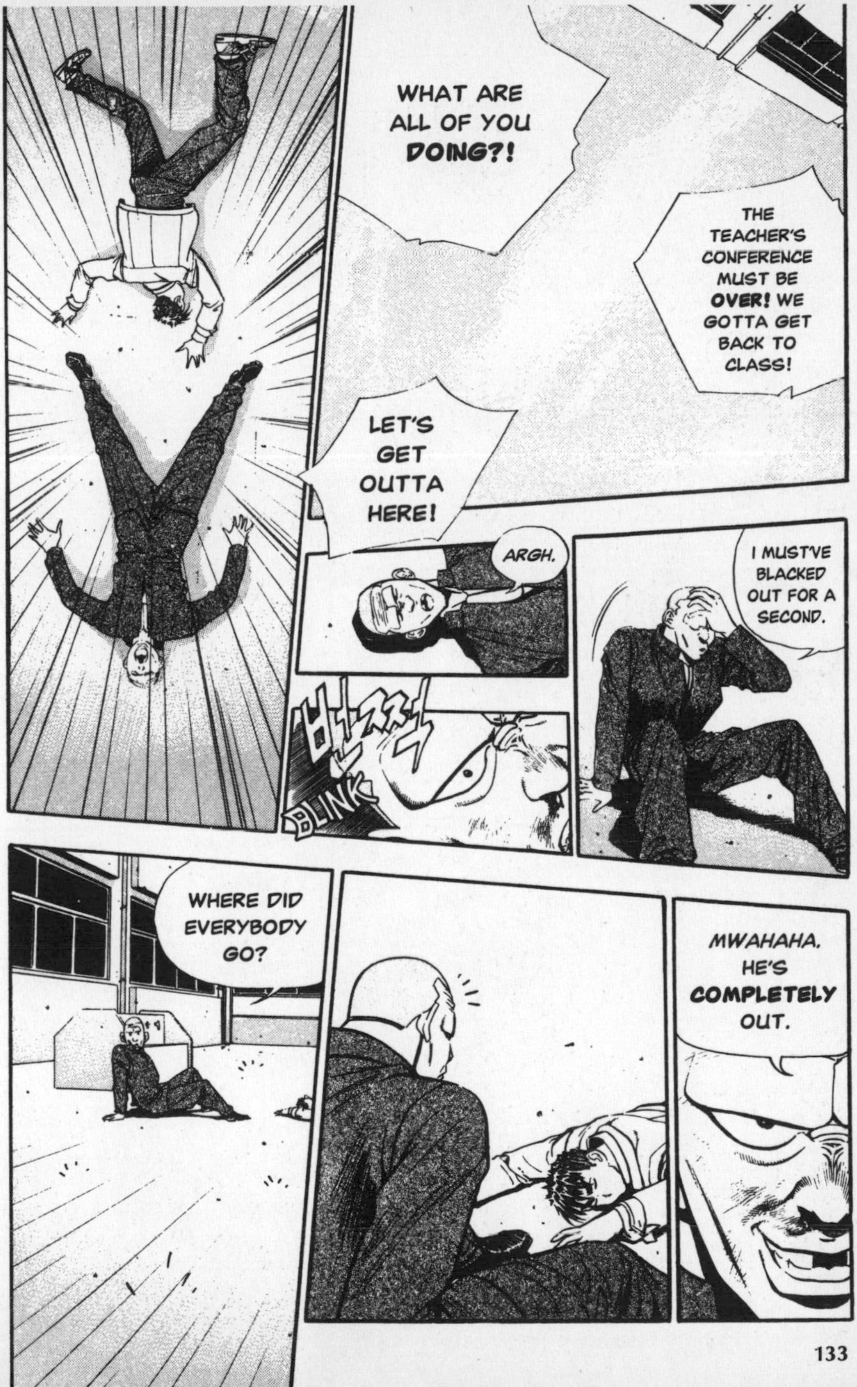
WHAT ARE ALL OF YOU DOING?!
THE TEACHER'S CONFERENCE MUST BE OVER! WE GOTTA GET BACK TO CLASS!
LET'S GET OUTTA HERE!
ARGH.
BLINK
I MUST'VE BLACKED OUT FOR A SECOND.
WHERE DID EVERYBODY GO?
MWAHAHA. HE'S COMPLETELY OUT.

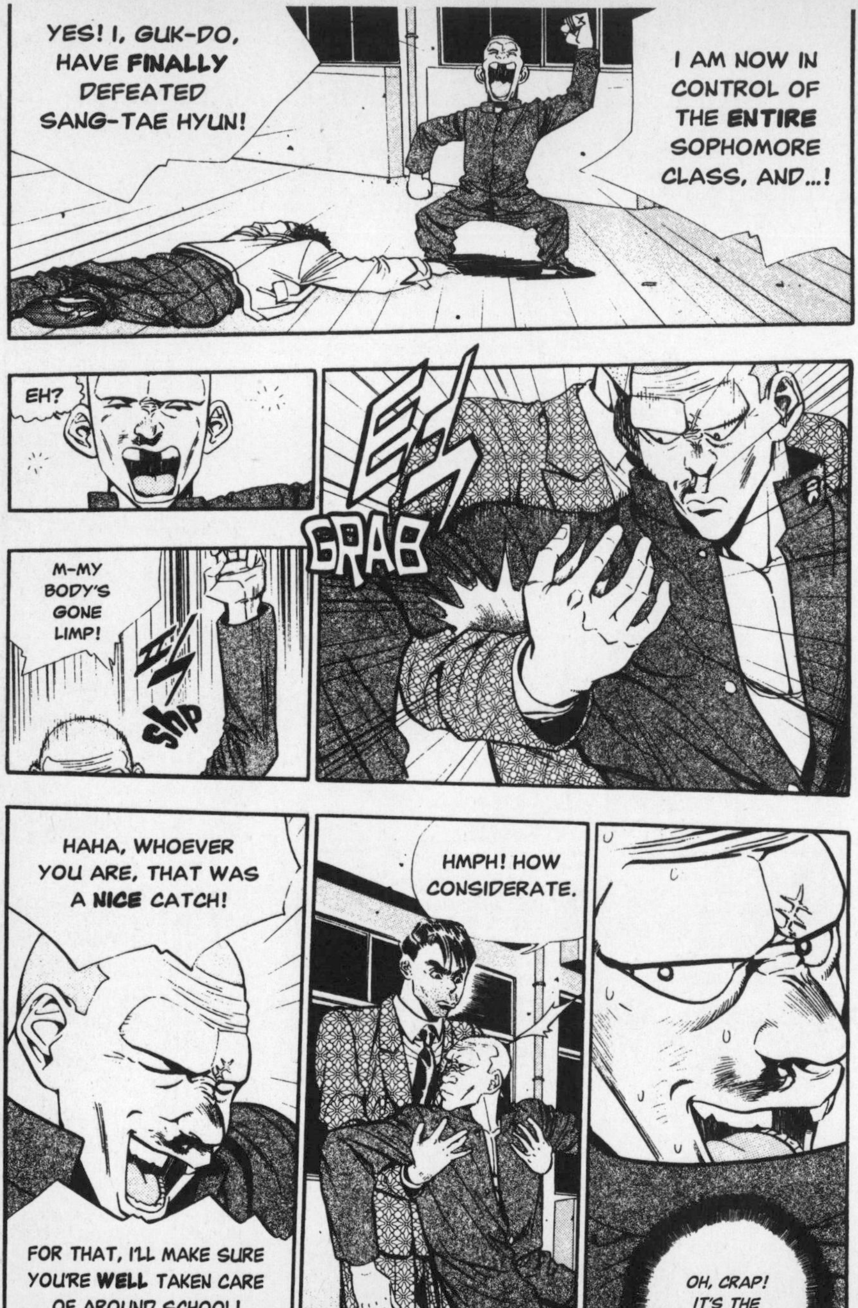
YES! I, GUK-DO, HAVE FINALLY DEFEATED SANG-TAE HYUN!
I AM NOW IN CONTROL OF THE ENTIRE SOPHOMORE CLASS, AND...!
EH?
GRAB
M-MY BODY'S GONE LIMP!
slip
HAHA, WHOEVER YOU ARE, THAT WAS A NICE CATCH!
FOR THAT, I'LL MAKE SURE YOU'RE WELL TAKEN CARE OF AROUND SCHOOL!
HMPH! HOW CONSIDERATE.
OH, CRAP! IT'S THE DISCIPLINARIAN!

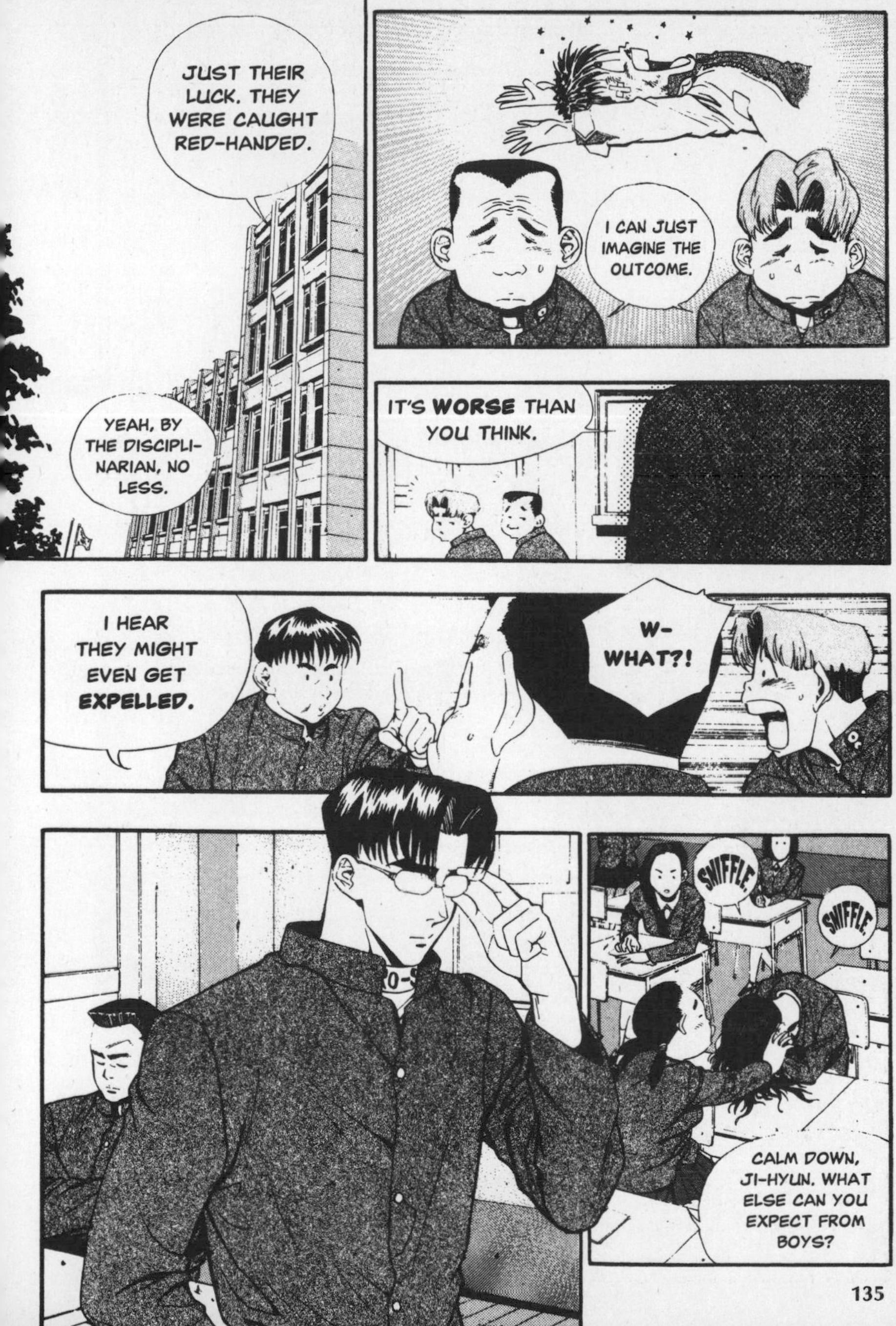
JUST THEIR LUCK. THEY WERE CAUGHT RED-HANDED.
YEAH, BY THE DISCIPLINARIAN, NO LESS.
I CAN JUST IMAGINE THE OUTCOME.
IT'S **WORSE** THAN YOU THINK.
I HEAR THEY MIGHT EVEN GET **EXPELLED**.
W- WHAT?!
SNIFFLE.
SNIFFLE.
CALM DOWN, JI-HYUN. WHAT ELSE CAN YOU EXPECT FROM BOYS?

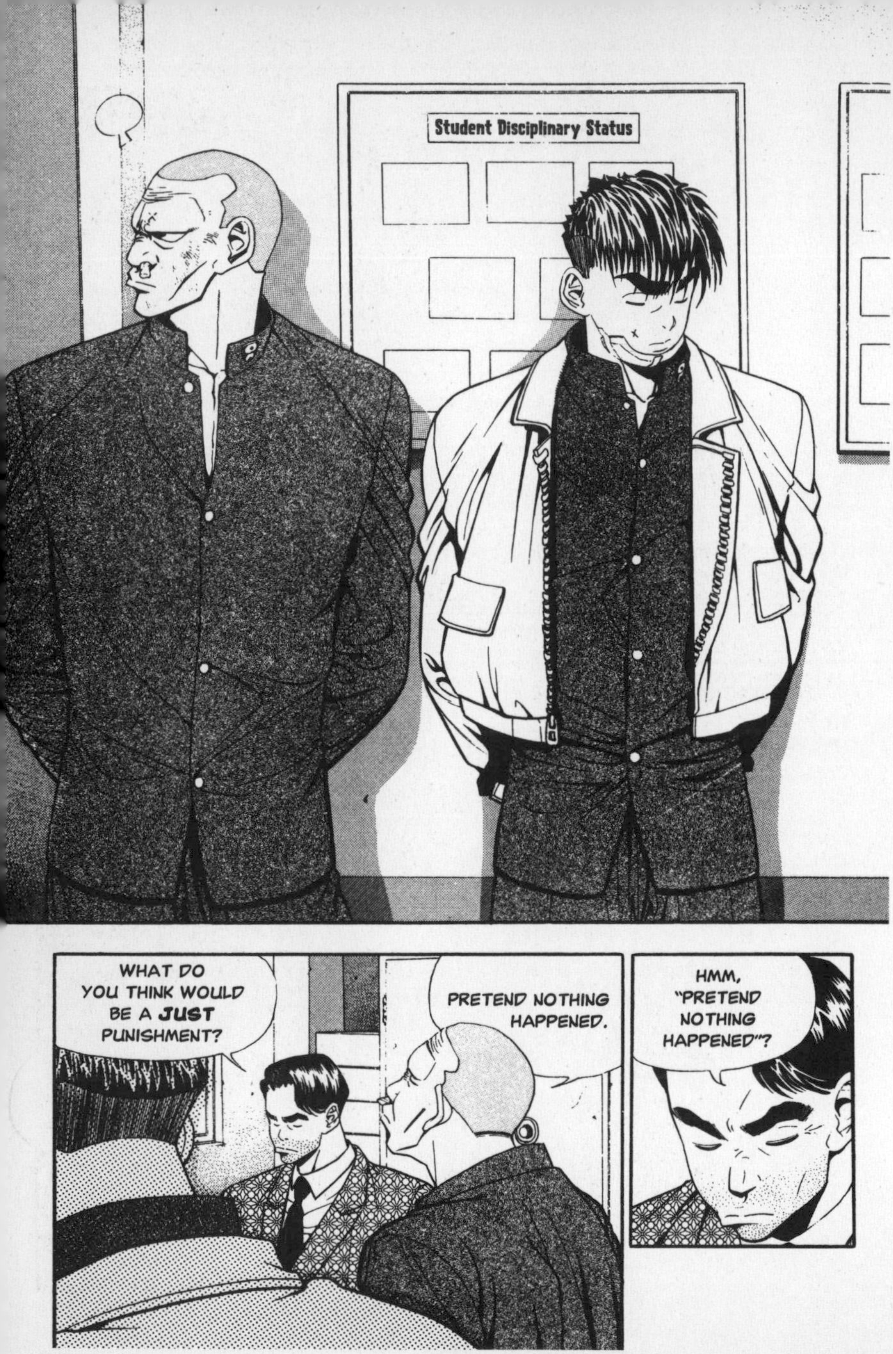
Student Disciplinary Status
WHAT DO YOU THINK WOULD BE A **JUST** PUNISHMENT?
PRETEND NOTHING HAPPENED.
HMM, "PRETEND NOTHING HAPPENED"?

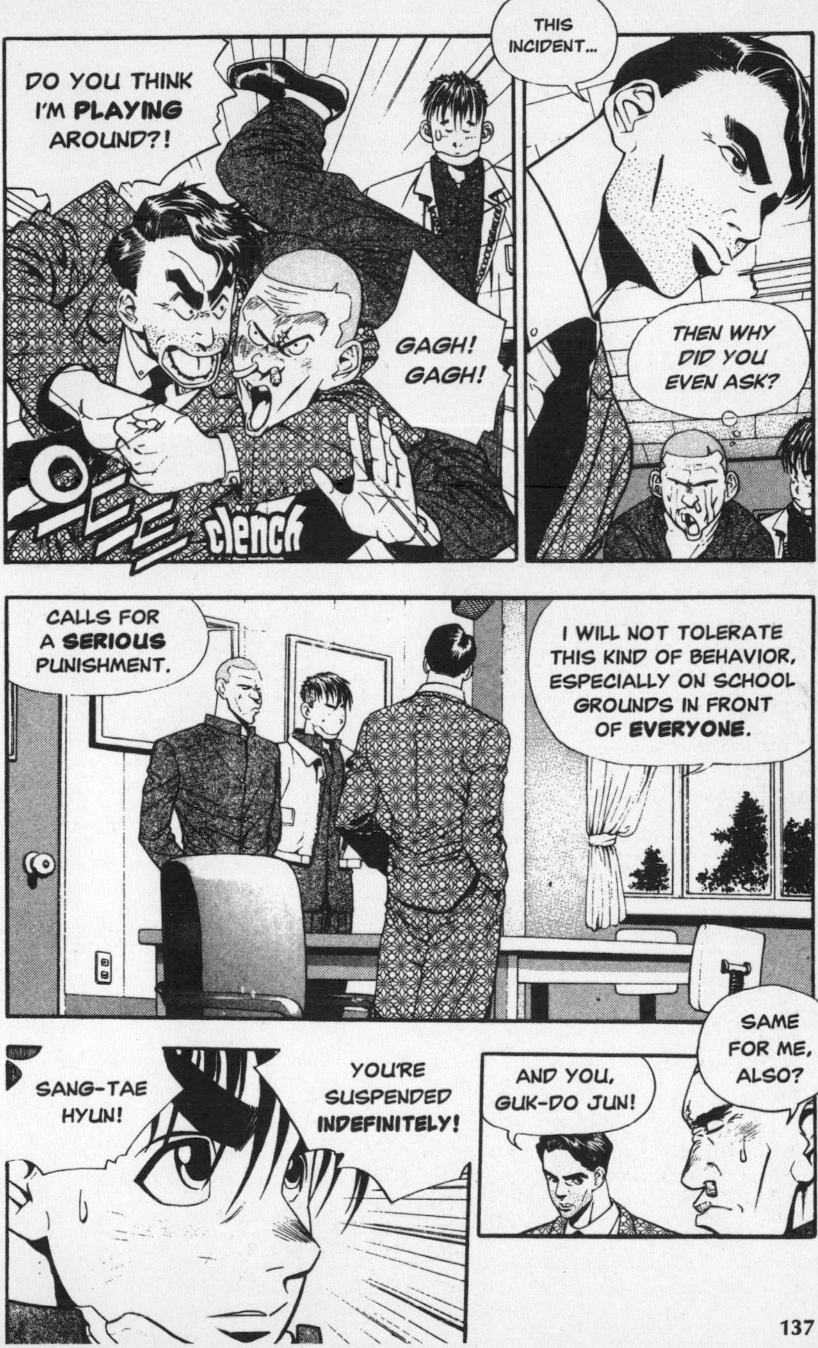
DO YOU THINK I'M PLAYING AROUND?!
THIS INCIDENT...
GAGH! GAGH!
clench
THEN WHY DID YOU EVEN ASK?
CALLS FOR A SERIOUS PUNISHMENT.
I WILL NOT TOLERATE THIS KIND OF BEHAVIOR, ESPECIALLY ON SCHOOL GROUNDS IN FRONT OF EVERYONE.
SANG-TAE HYUN!
YOU'RE SUSPENDED INDEFINITELY!
AND YOU, GUK-DO JUN!
SAME FOR ME, ALSO?

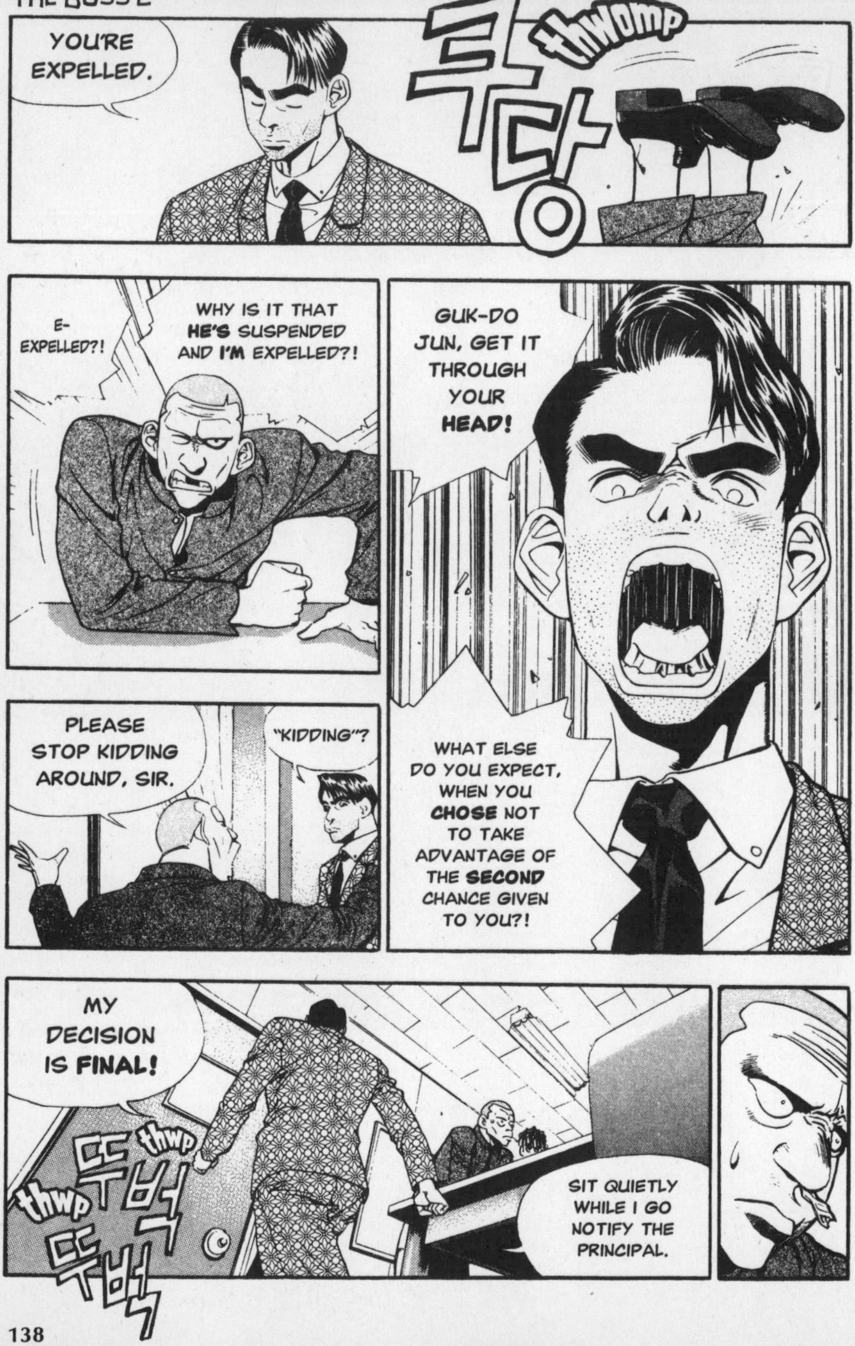
YOU'RE EXPELLED.
thwomp
쿠당
E- EXPELLED?!
WHY IS IT THAT **HE'S** SUSPENDED AND **I'M** EXPELLED?!
GUK-DO JUN, GET IT THROUGH YOUR **HEAD!**
PLEASE STOP KIDDING AROUND, SIR.
"KIDDING"?
WHAT ELSE DO YOU EXPECT, WHEN YOU **CHOSE** NOT TO TAKE ADVANTAGE OF THE **SECOND** CHANCE GIVEN TO YOU?!
MY DECISION IS **FINAL!**
thwp
뚜벅
thwp
뚜벅
SIT QUIETLY WHILE I GO NOTIFY THE PRINCIPAL.

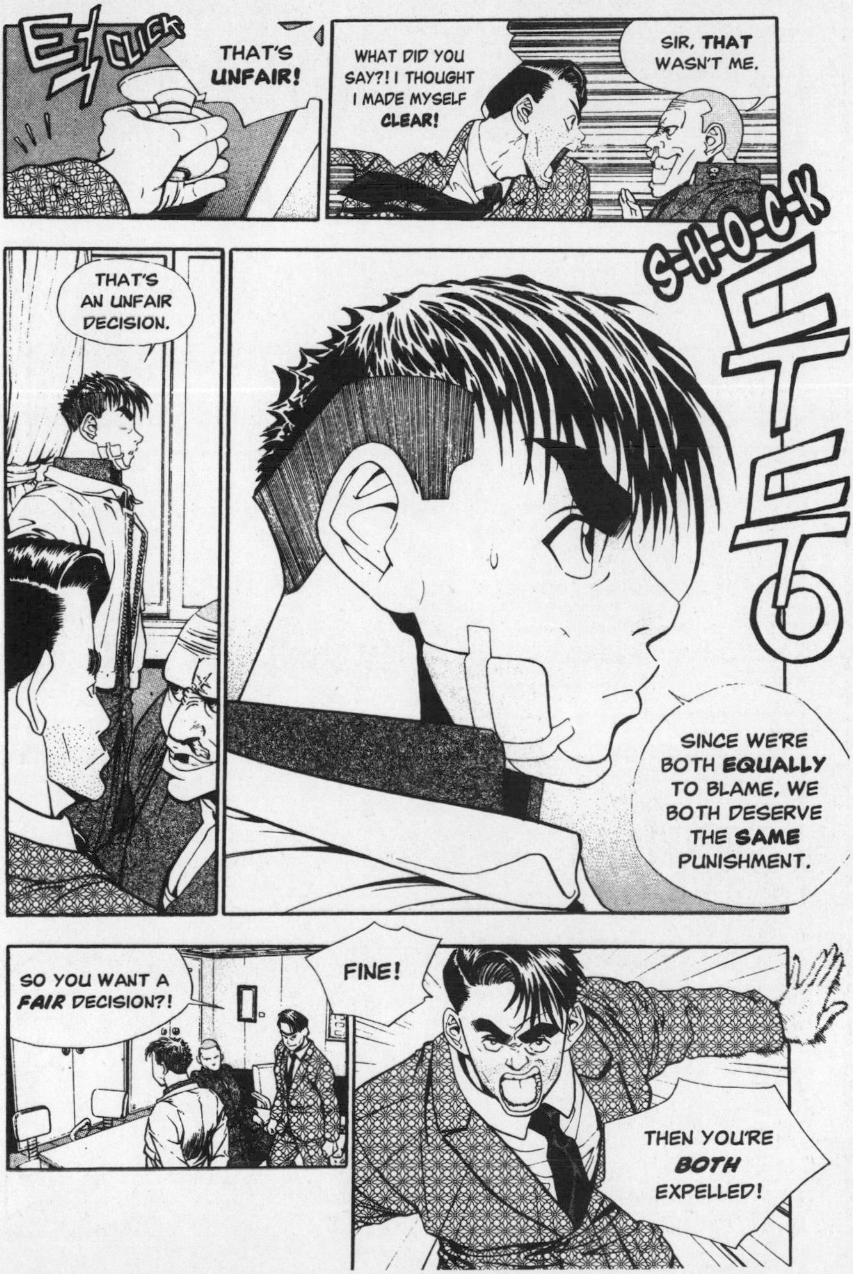
CLICK
THAT'S UNFAIR!
WHAT DID YOU SAY?! I THOUGHT I MADE MYSELF CLEAR!
SIR, THAT WASN'T ME.
S-H-O-C-K
THAT'S AN UNFAIR DECISION.
SINCE WE'RE BOTH EQUALLY TO BLAME, WE BOTH DESERVE THE SAME PUNISHMENT.
SO YOU WANT A FAIR DECISION?!
FINE!
THEN YOU'RE BOTH EXPELLED!

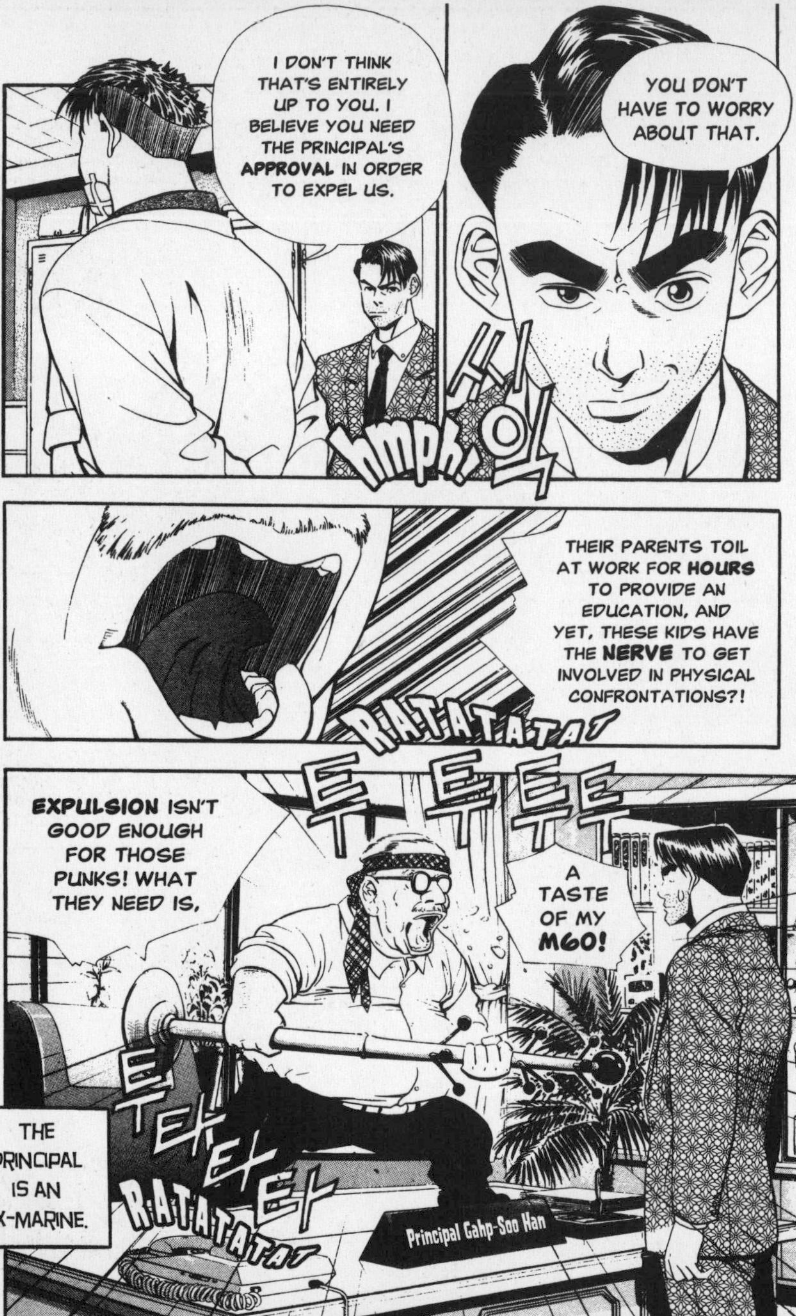
I DON'T THINK THAT'S ENTIRELY UP TO YOU. I BELIEVE YOU NEED THE PRINCIPAL'S **APPROVAL** IN ORDER TO EXPEL US.
YOU DON'T HAVE TO WORRY ABOUT THAT.
hmph!
THEIR PARENTS TOIL AT WORK FOR **HOURS** TO PROVIDE AN EDUCATION, AND YET, THESE KIDS HAVE THE **NERVE** TO GET INVOLVED IN PHYSICAL CONFRONTATIONS?!
RATATATATAT
EXPULSION ISN'T GOOD ENOUGH FOR THOSE PUNKS! WHAT THEY NEED IS,
A TASTE OF MY **M60!**
THE PRINCIPAL IS AN EX-MARINE.
RATATATATAT
Principal Gahp-Soo Han

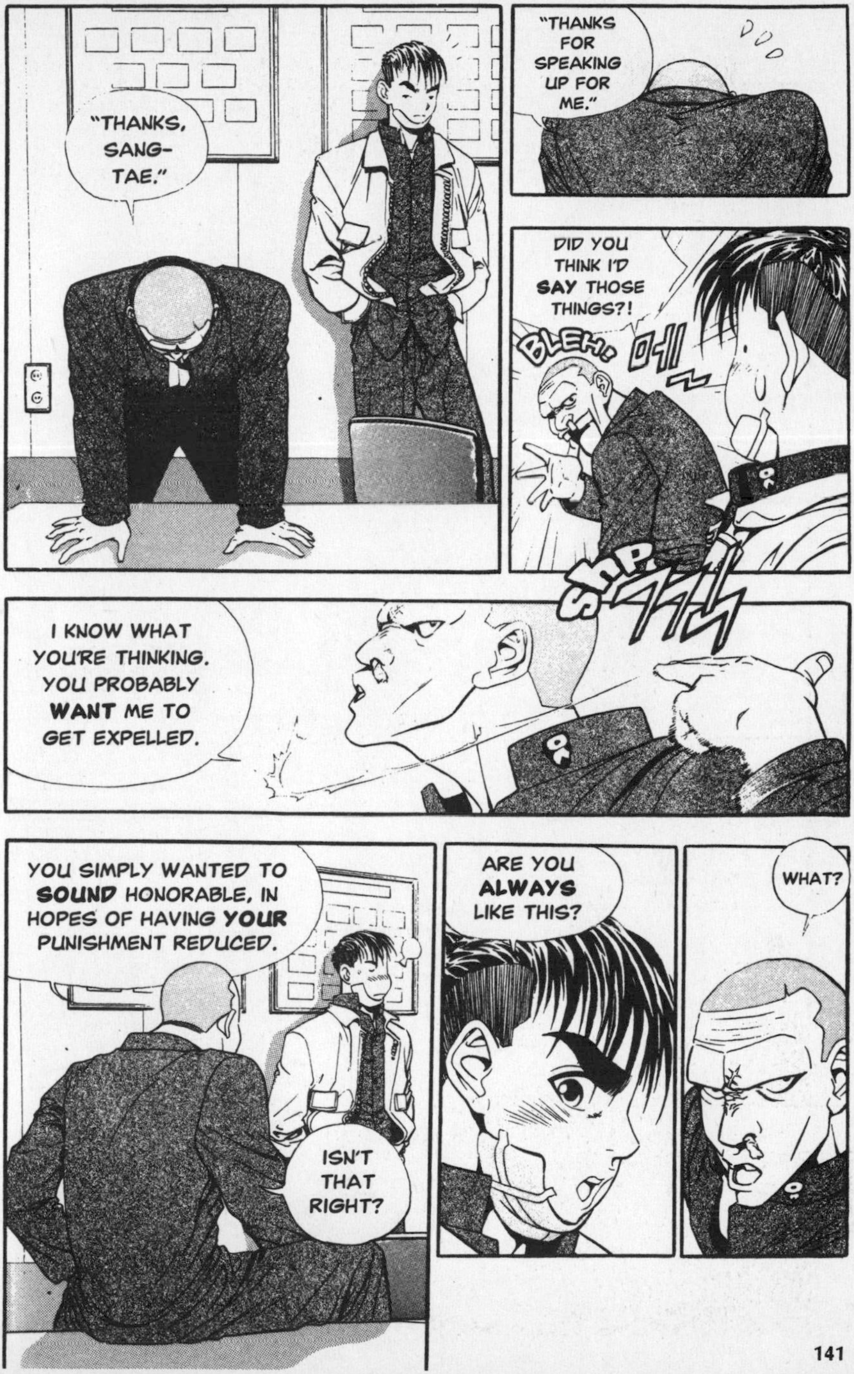
"THANKS, SANG-TAE."
"THANKS FOR SPEAKING UP FOR ME."
DID YOU THINK I'D SAY THOSE THINGS?!
BLEH!
메~
SHP
I KNOW WHAT YOU'RE THINKING. YOU PROBABLY WANT ME TO GET EXPELLED.
YOU SIMPLY WANTED TO SOUND HONORABLE, IN HOPES OF HAVING YOUR PUNISHMENT REDUCED.
ISN'T THAT RIGHT?
ARE YOU ALWAYS LIKE THIS?
WHAT?

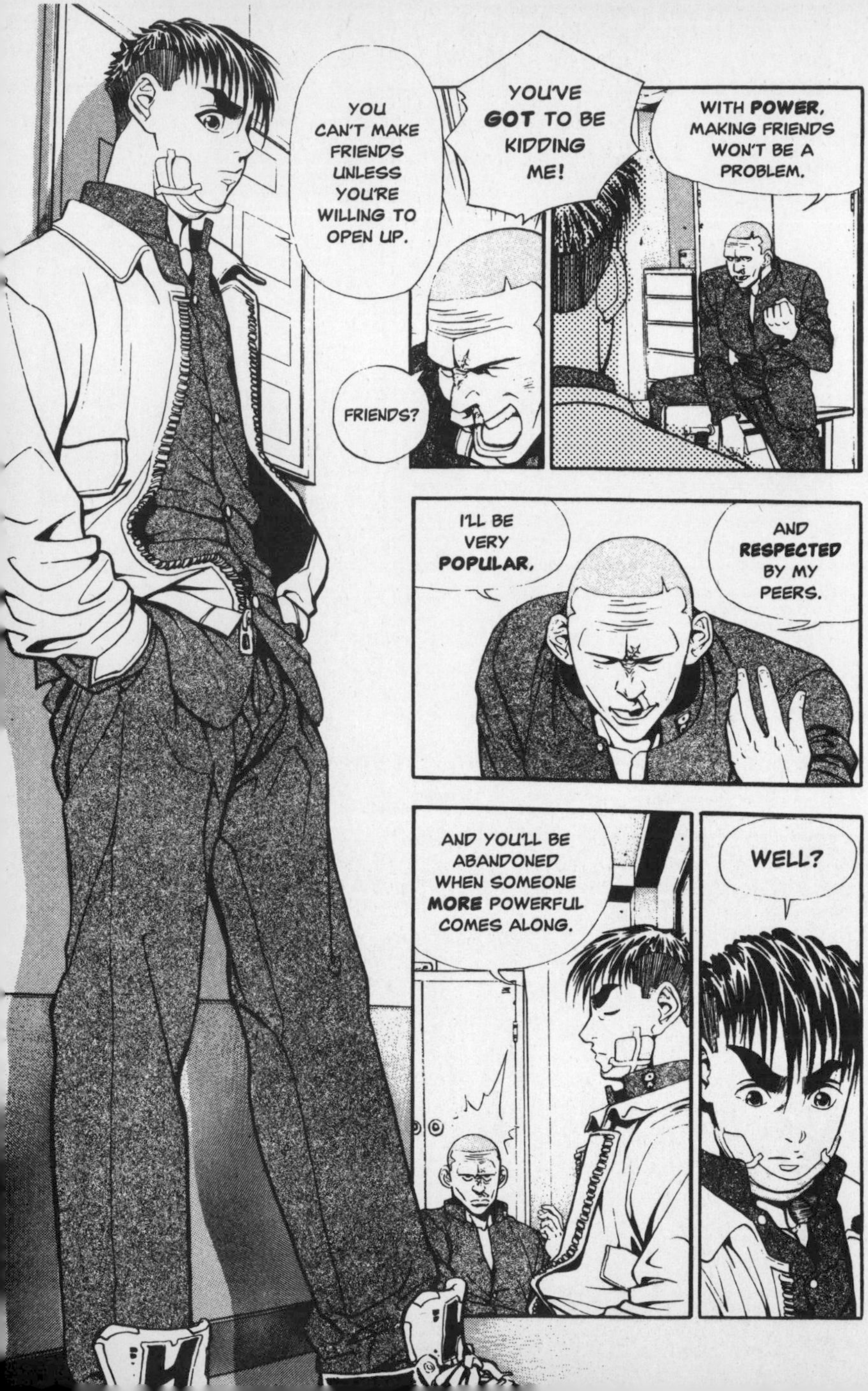
YOU CAN'T MAKE FRIENDS UNLESS YOU'RE WILLING TO OPEN UP.
FRIENDS?
YOU'VE GOT TO BE KIDDING ME!
WITH POWER, MAKING FRIENDS WON'T BE A PROBLEM.
I'LL BE VERY POPULAR,
AND RESPECTED BY MY PEERS.
AND YOU'LL BE ABANDONED WHEN SOMEONE MORE POWERFUL COMES ALONG.
WELL?

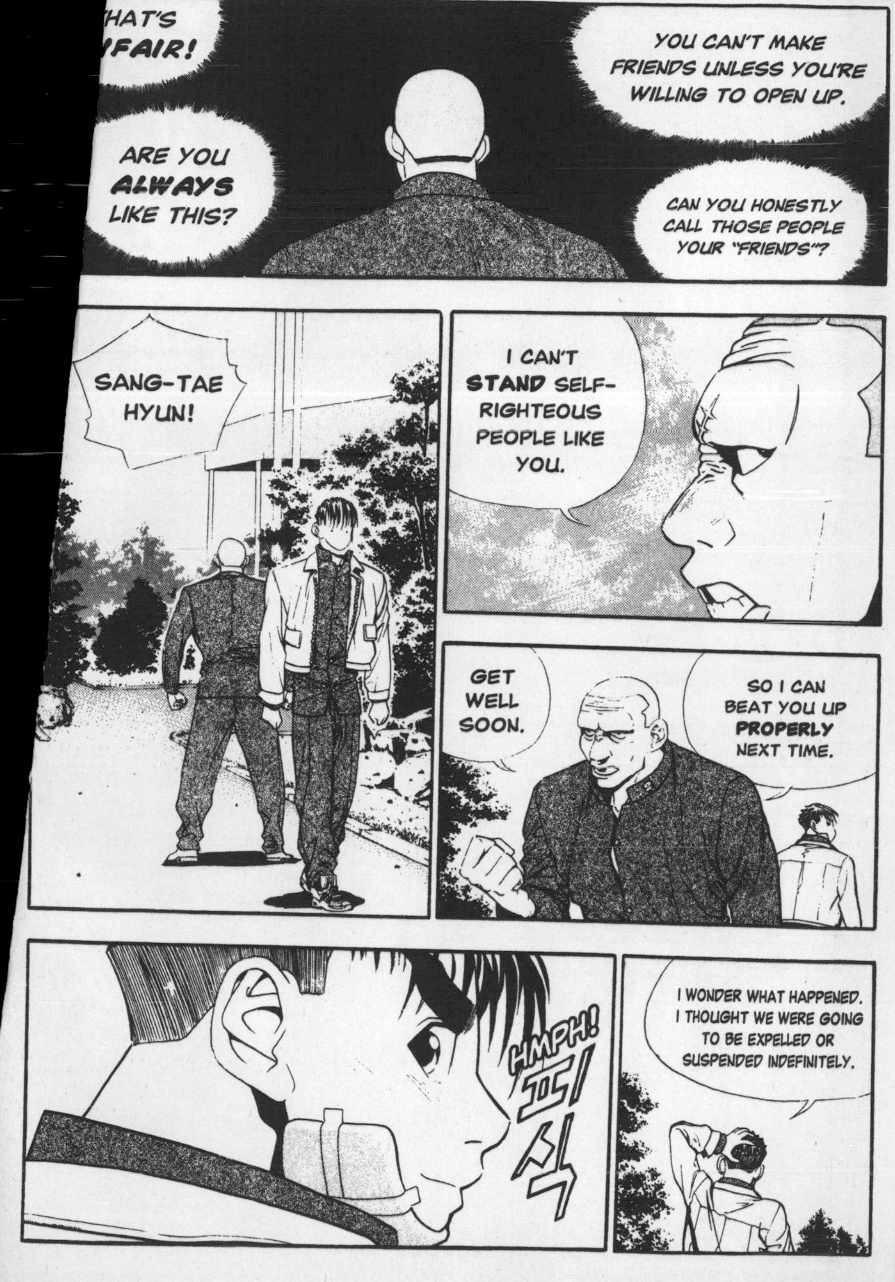
HAT'S
FAIR!
YOU CAN'T MAKE FRIENDS UNLESS YOU'RE WILLING TO OPEN UP.
ARE YOU ALWAYS LIKE THIS?
CAN YOU HONESTLY CALL THOSE PEOPLE YOUR "FRIENDS"?
SANG-TAE HYUN!
I CAN'T STAND SELF-RIGHTEOUS PEOPLE LIKE YOU.
GET WELL SOON.
SO I CAN BEAT YOU UP PROPERLY NEXT TIME.
HMPH!
I WONDER WHAT HAPPENED. I THOUGHT WE WERE GOING TO BE EXPELLED OR SUSPENDED INDEFINITELY.

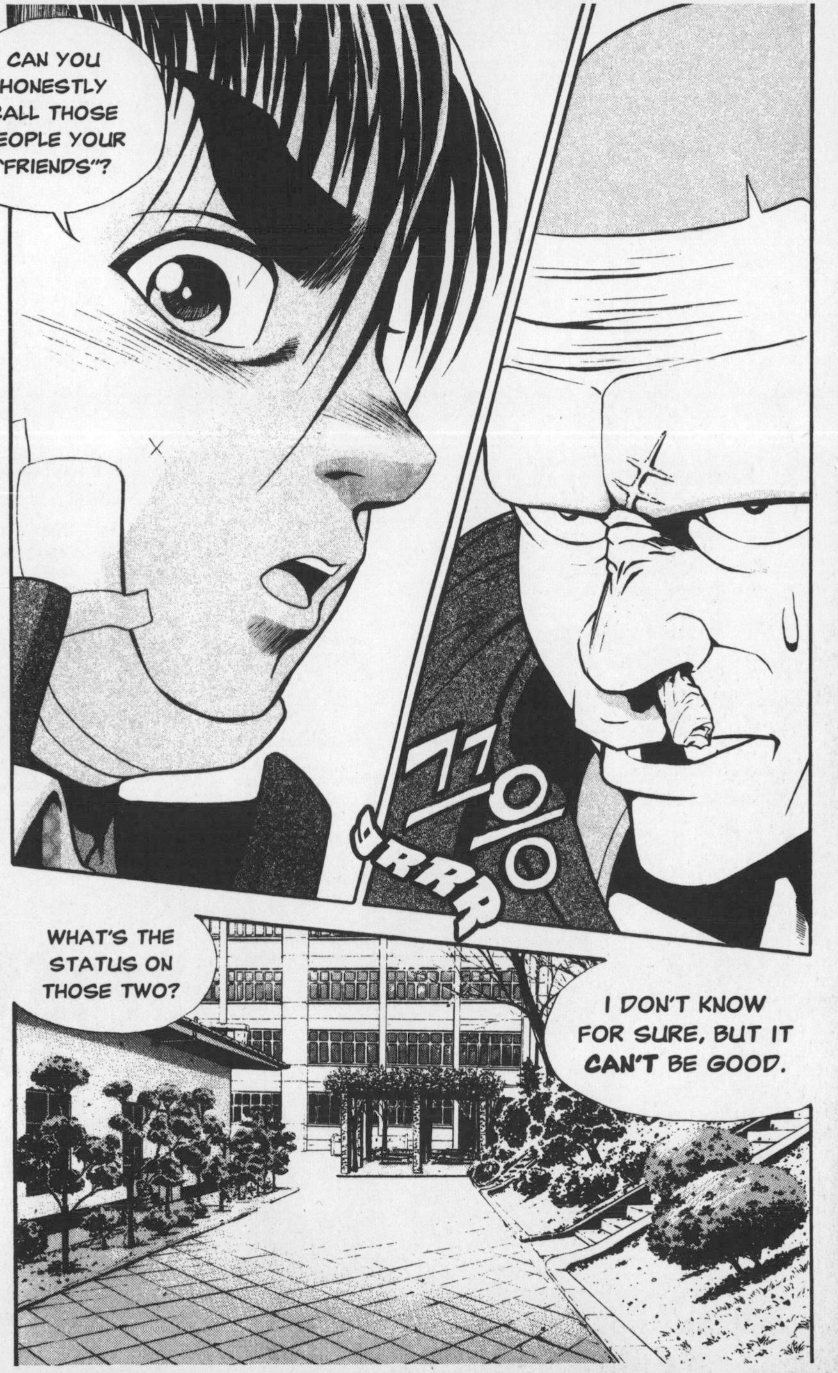
CAN YOU HONESTLY CALL THOSE PEOPLE YOUR "FRIENDS"?
GRRRR
WHAT'S THE STATUS ON THOSE TWO?
I DON'T KNOW FOR SURE, BUT IT CAN'T BE GOOD.

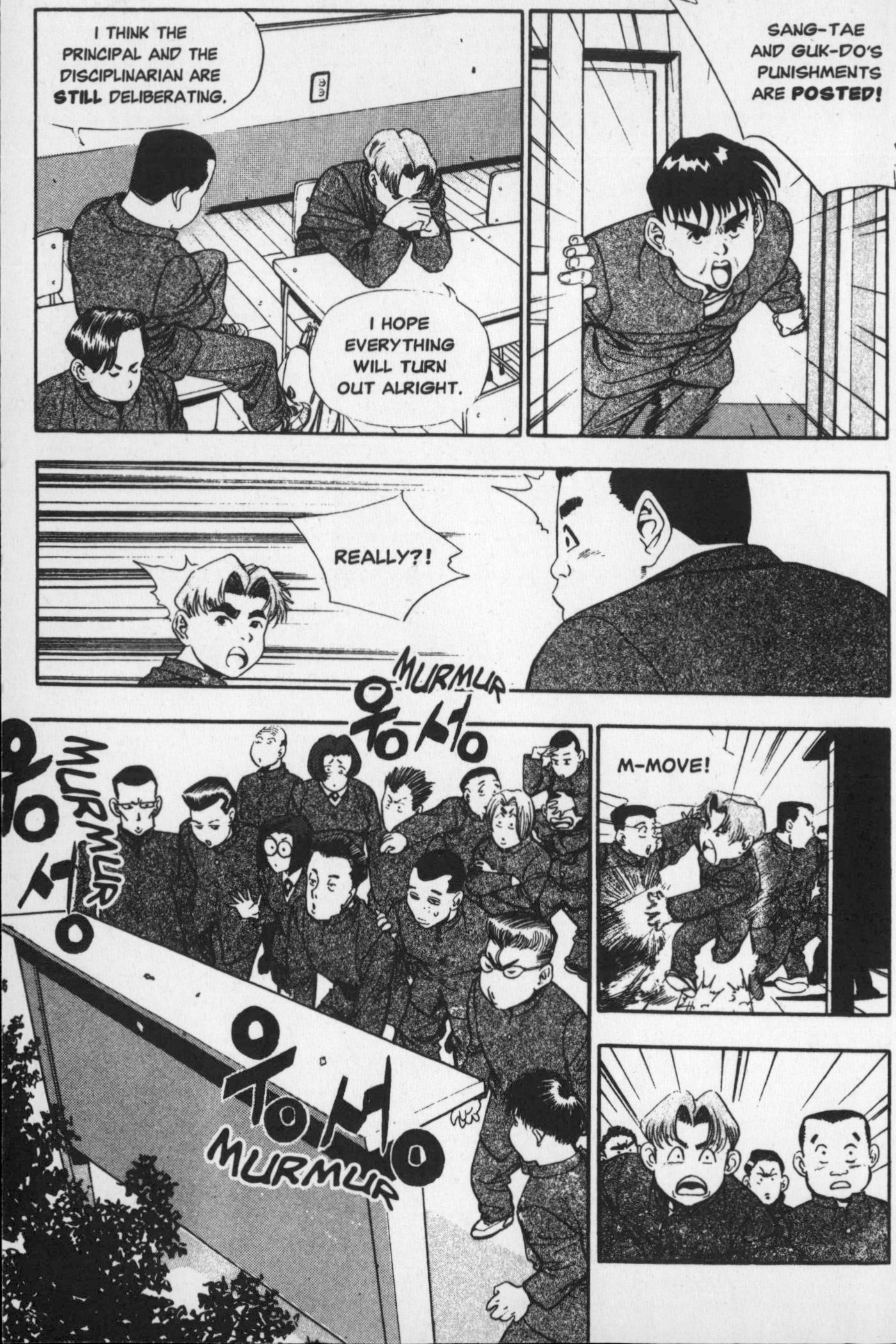

I THINK THE PRINCIPAL AND THE DISCIPLINARIAN ARE STILL DELIBERATING.
I HOPE EVERYTHING WILL TURN OUT ALRIGHT.
SANG-TAE AND GUK-DO'S PUNISHMENTS ARE POSTED!
REALLY?!
MURMUR
MURMUR
MURMUR
M-MOVE!

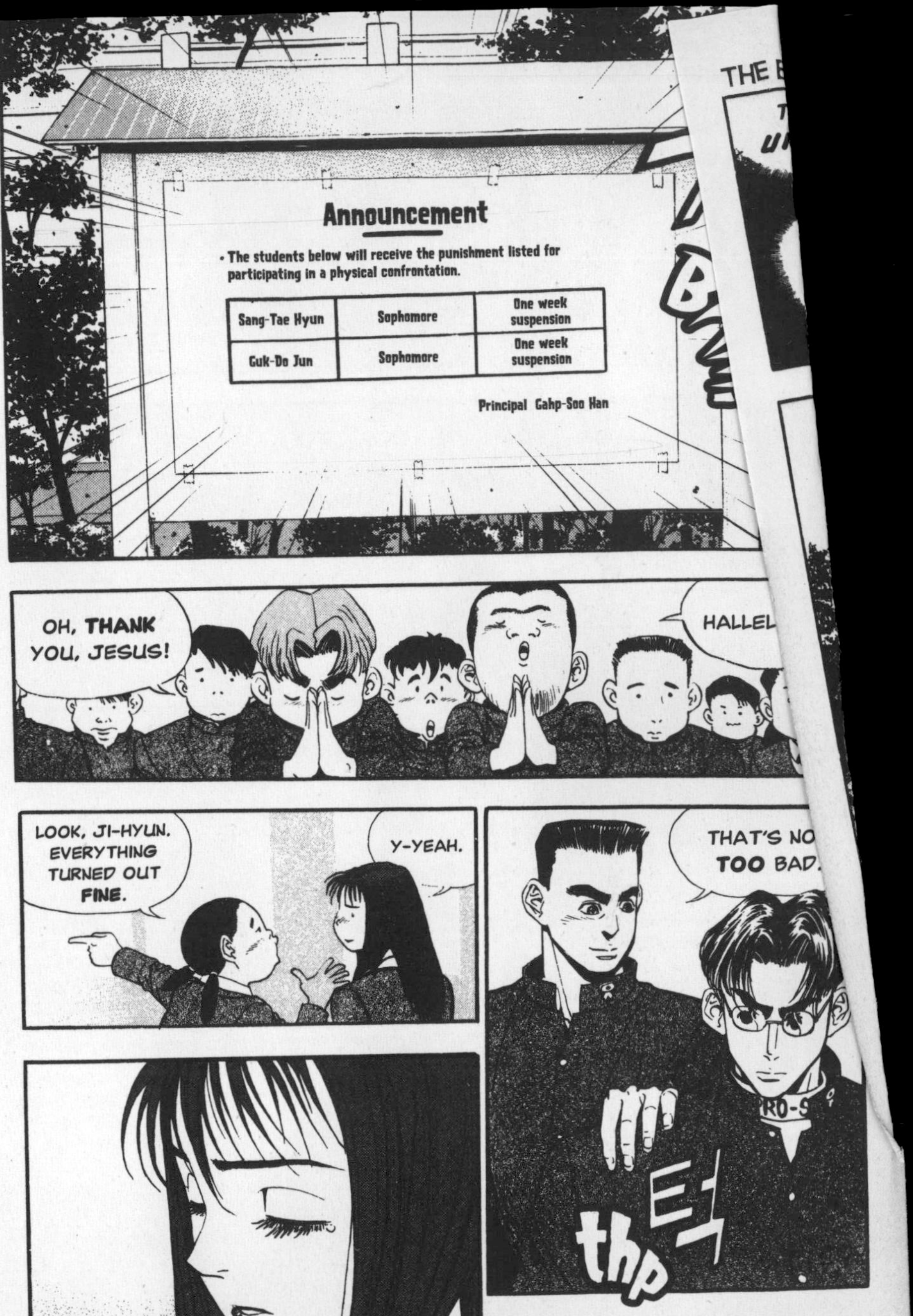

Announcement
• The students below will receive the punishment listed for participating in a physical confrontation.
Sang-Tae Hyun | Sophomore | One week suspension
Guk-Do Jun | Sophomore | One week suspension
Principal Gahp-Soo Han
OH, THANK YOU, JESUS!
HALLEL
LOOK, JI-HYUN. EVERYTHING TURNED OUT FINE.
Y-YEAH.
THAT'S NO TOO BAD.
thp
턱

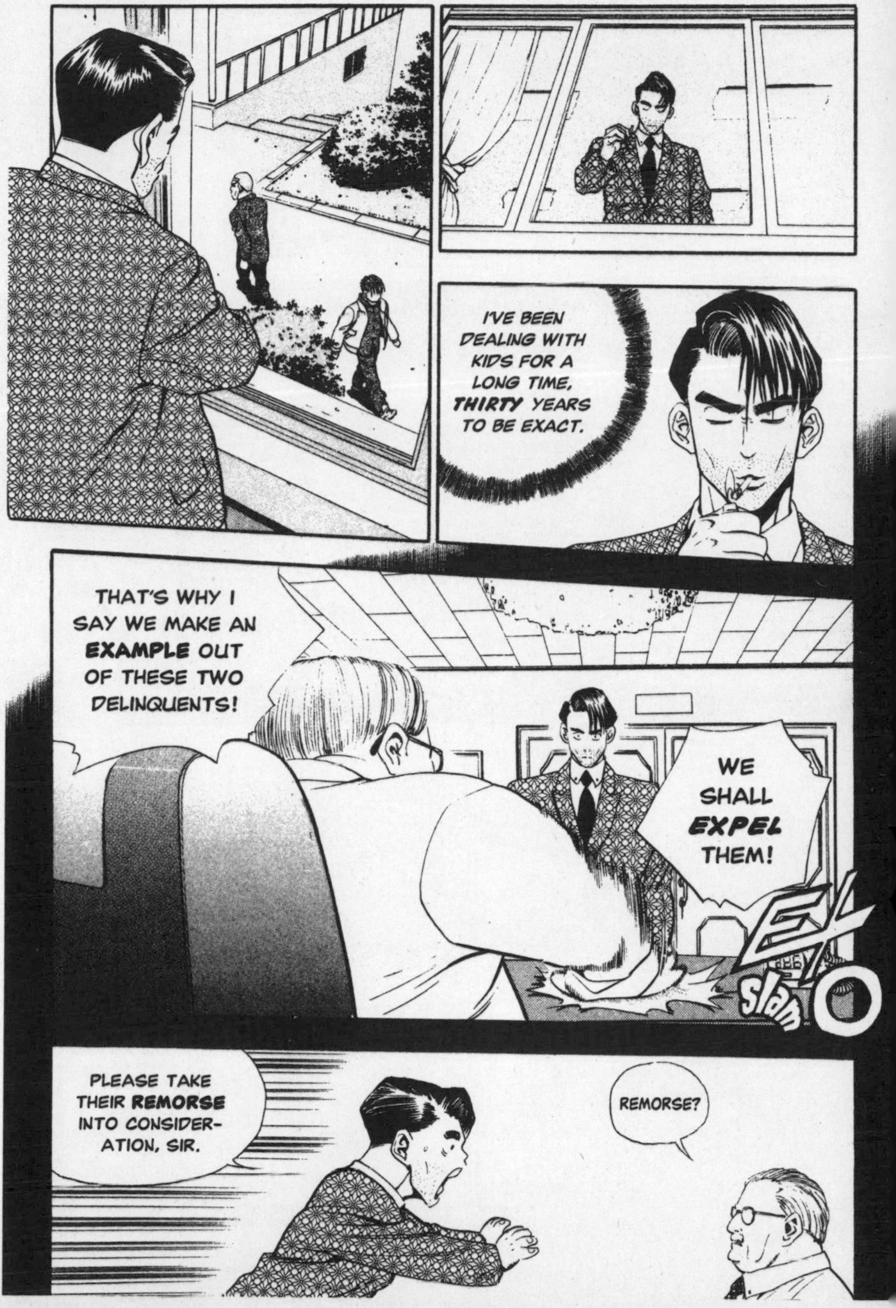
I'VE BEEN DEALING WITH KIDS FOR A LONG TIME, THIRTY YEARS TO BE EXACT.
THAT'S WHY I SAY WE MAKE AN EXAMPLE OUT OF THESE TWO DELINQUENTS!
WE SHALL EXPEL THEM!
slam
PLEASE TAKE THEIR REMORSE INTO CONSIDER-ATION, SIR.
REMORSE?

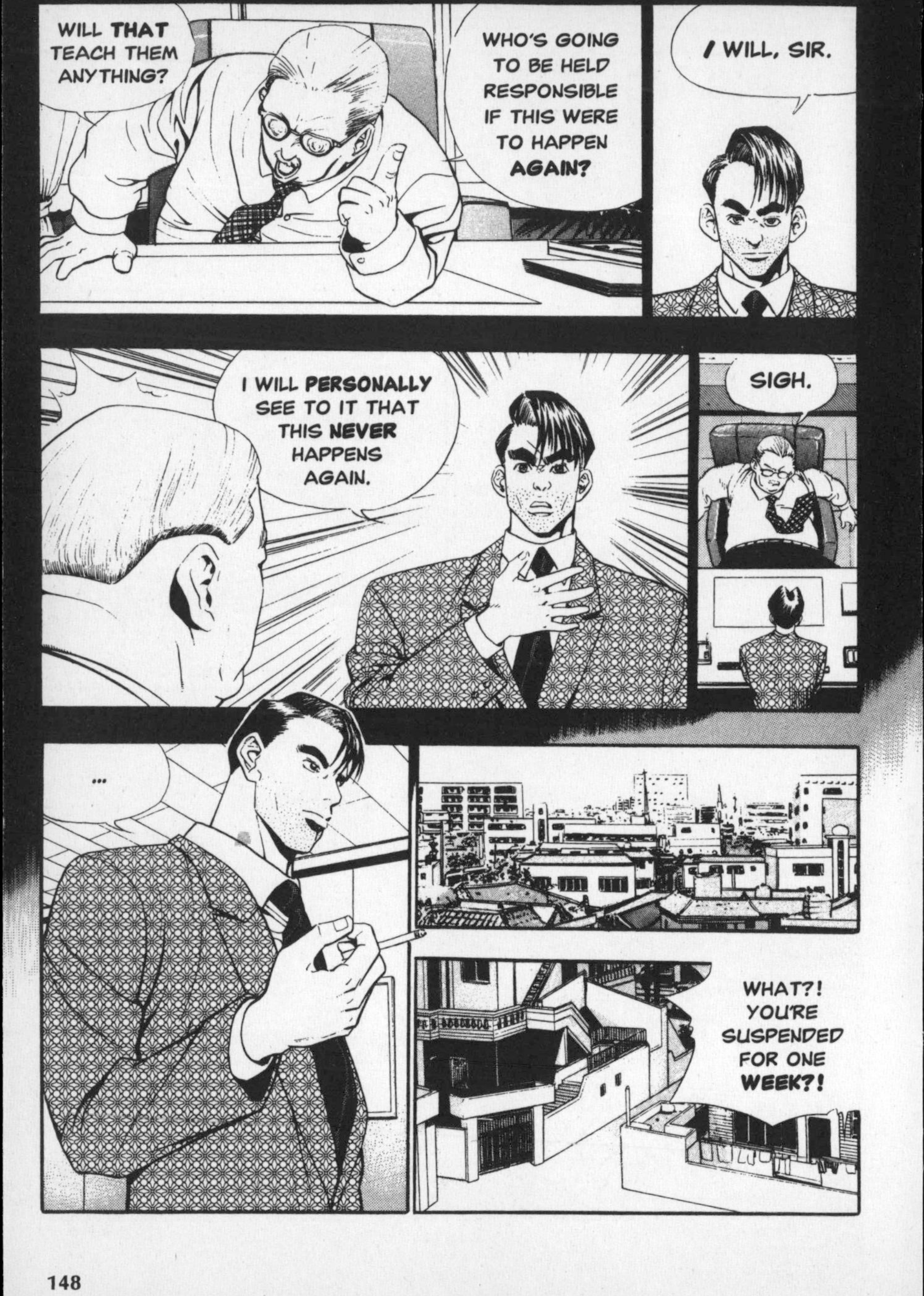
WILL THAT TEACH THEM ANYTHING?
WHO'S GOING TO BE HELD RESPONSIBLE IF THIS WERE TO HAPPEN AGAIN?
I WILL, SIR.
I WILL PERSONALLY SEE TO IT THAT THIS NEVER HAPPENS AGAIN.
SIGH.
...
WHAT?! YOU'RE SUSPENDED FOR ONE WEEK?!

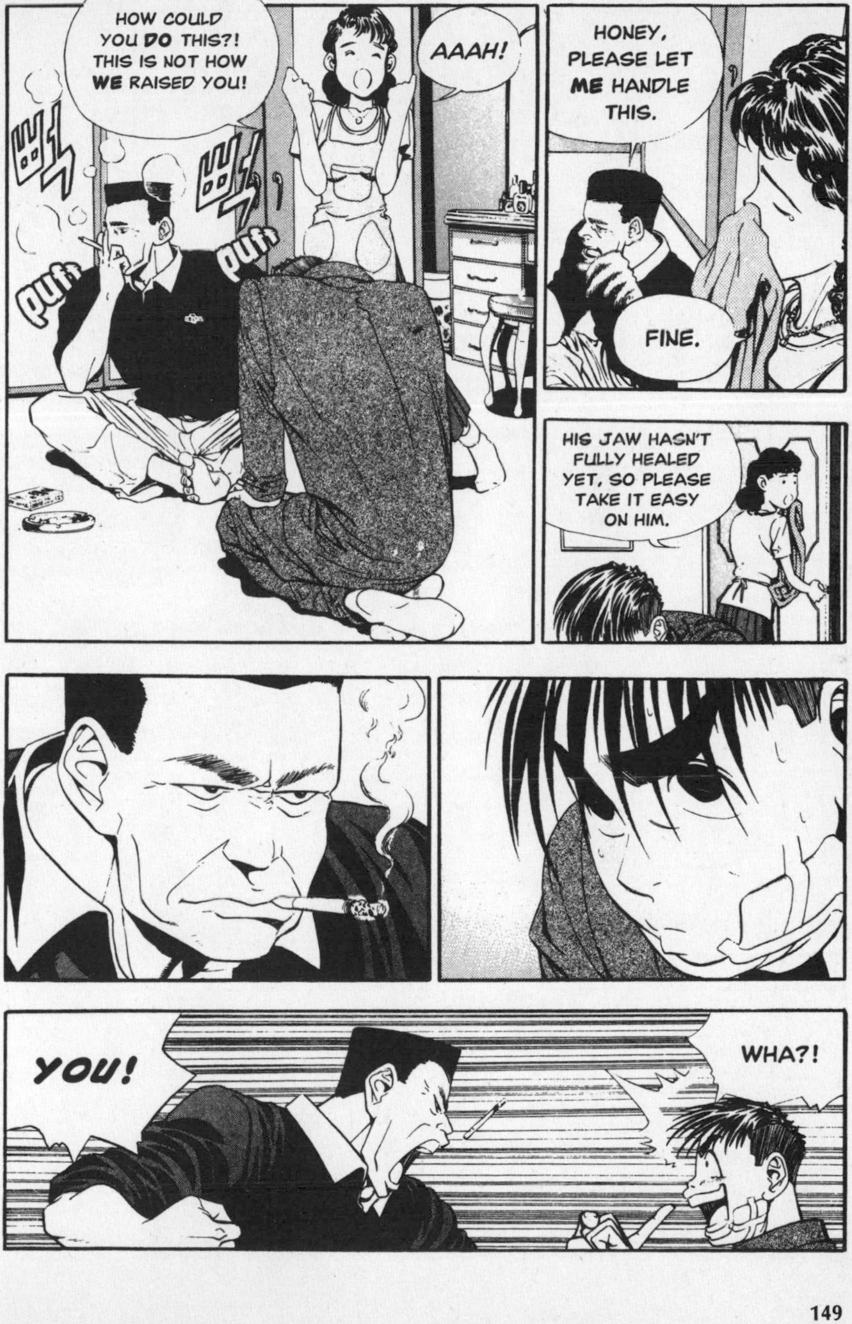
HOW COULD YOU DO THIS?! THIS IS NOT HOW WE RAISED YOU!
AAAH!
뻑
뻑
puff
puff
HONEY, PLEASE LET ME HANDLE THIS.
FINE.
HIS JAW HASN'T FULLY HEALED YET, SO PLEASE TAKE IT EASY ON HIM.
YOU!
WHA?!

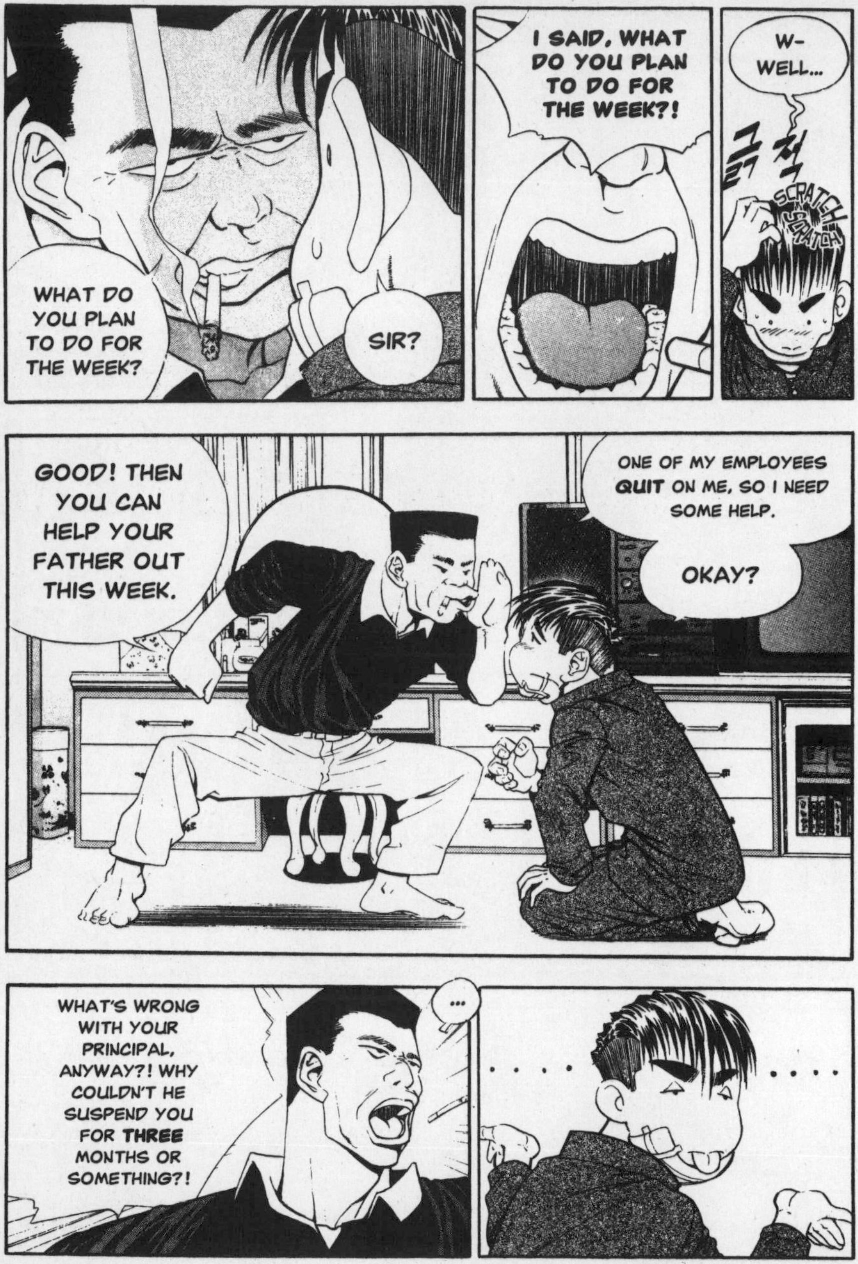
WHAT DO YOU PLAN TO DO FOR THE WEEK?
SIR?
I SAID, WHAT DO YOU PLAN TO DO FOR THE WEEK?!
W- WELL...
SCRATCH SCRATCH
GOOD! THEN YOU CAN HELP YOUR FATHER OUT THIS WEEK.
ONE OF MY EMPLOYEES QUIT ON ME, SO I NEED SOME HELP.
OKAY?
WHAT'S WRONG WITH YOUR PRINCIPAL, ANYWAY?! WHY COULDN'T HE SUSPEND YOU FOR THREE MONTHS OR SOMETHING?!
...
. . . .
. . . .

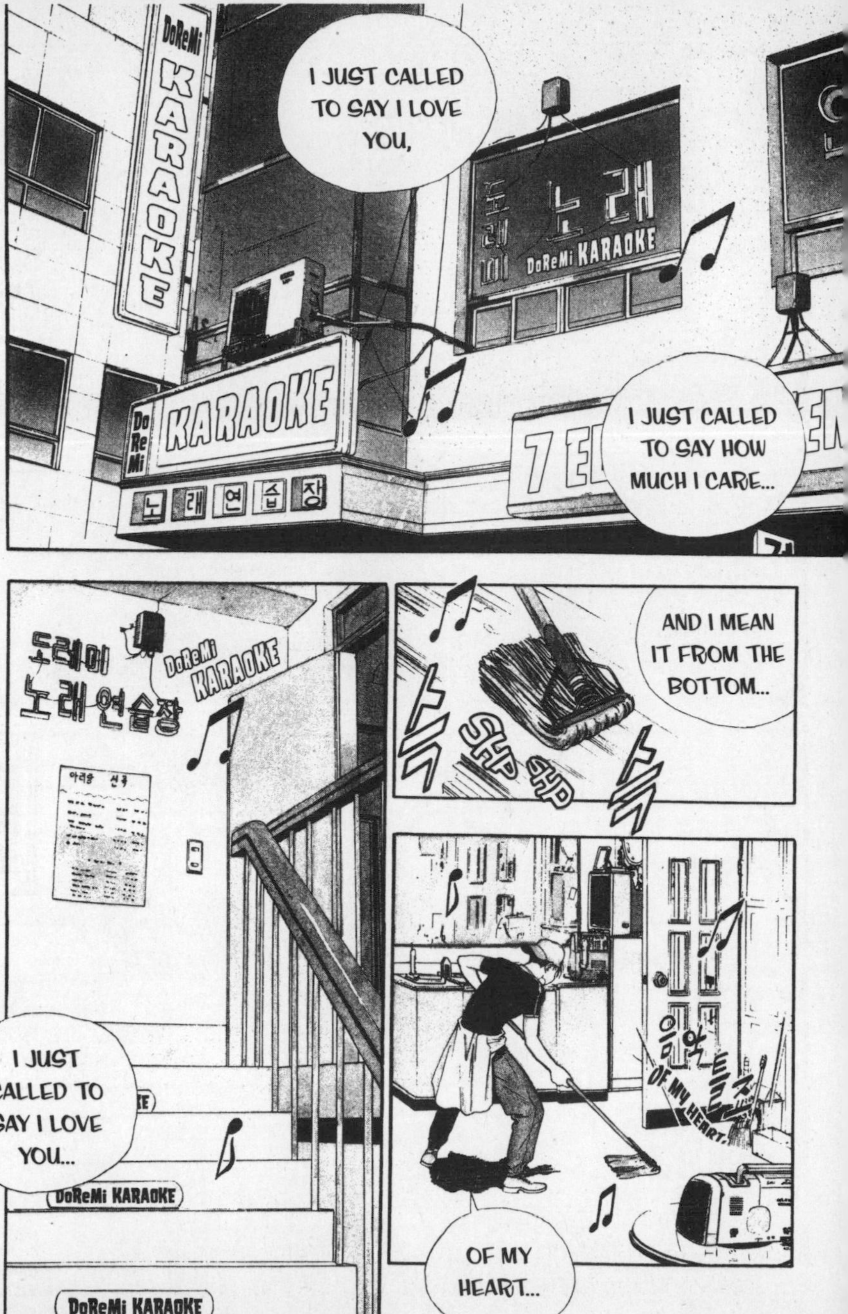
DoReMi KARAOKE
I JUST CALLED TO SAY I LOVE YOU,
도레미 노래
DoReMi KARAOKE
DoReMi KARAOKE
노래연습장
I JUST CALLED TO SAY HOW MUCH I CARE...
도레미 노래연습장
DoReMi KARAOKE
AND I MEAN IT FROM THE BOTTOM...
SHP SHP
I JUST CALLED TO SAY I LOVE YOU...
DoReMi KARAOKE
DoReMi KARAOKE
OF MY HEART,
OF MY HEART...

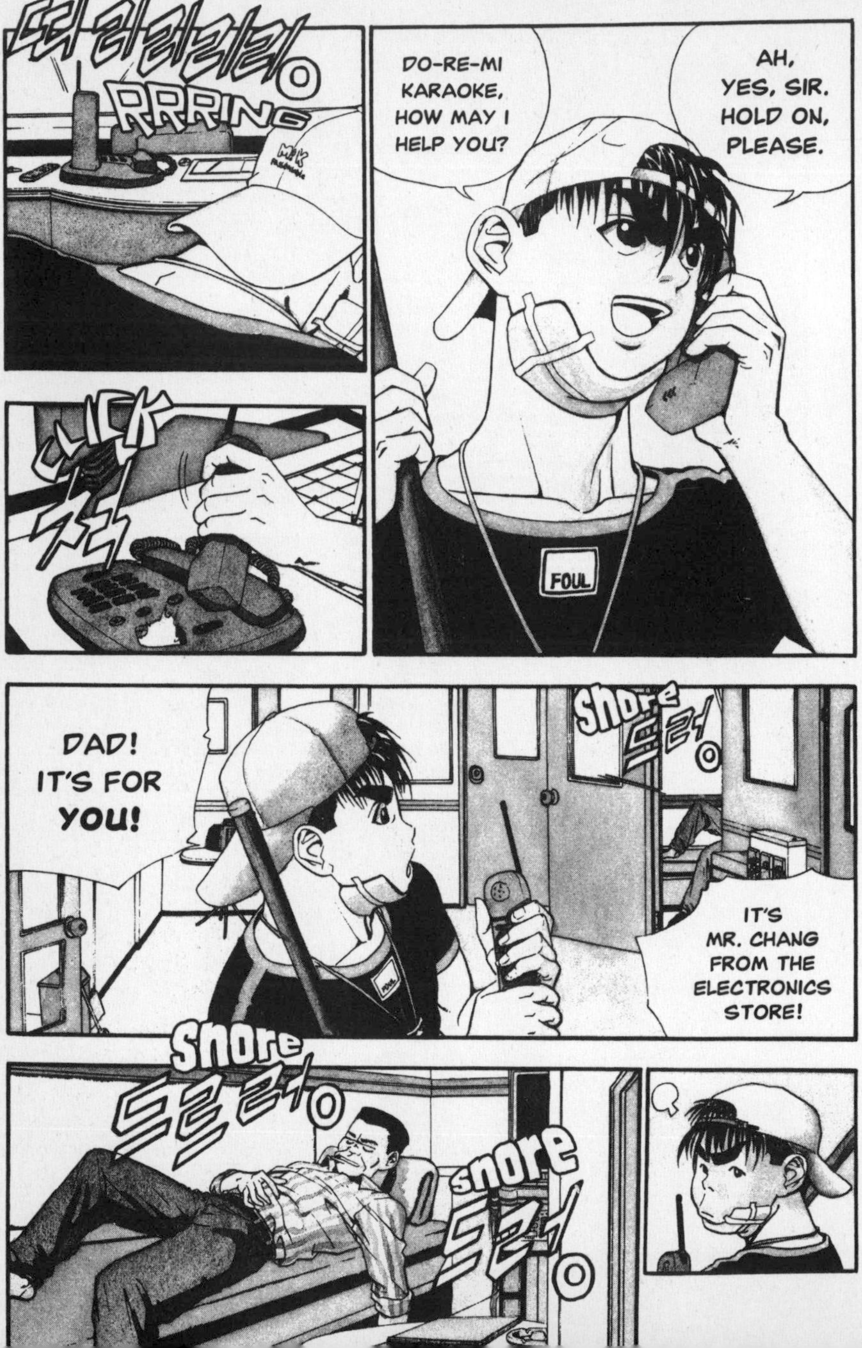
RRRING
CLICK
DO-RE-MI KARAOKE, HOW MAY I HELP YOU?
AH, YES, SIR. HOLD ON, PLEASE.
FOUL
DAD! IT'S FOR YOU!
snore
IT'S MR. CHANG FROM THE ELECTRONICS STORE!
snore
snore

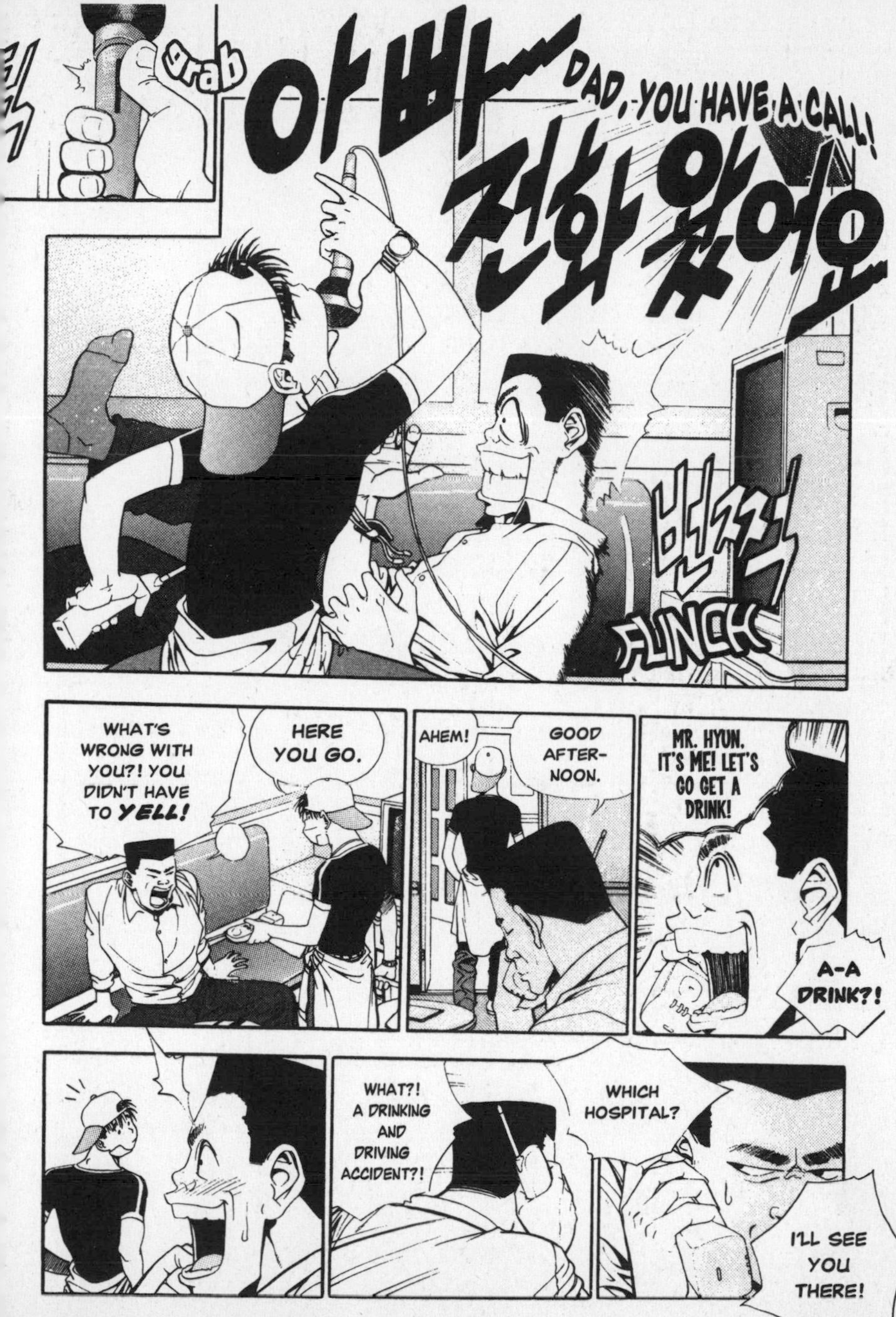
grab
아빠~ 전화 왔어요
DAD, YOU HAVE A CALL!
번쩍
FLINCH
WHAT'S WRONG WITH YOU?! YOU DIDN'T HAVE TO YELL!
HERE YOU GO.
AHEM!
GOOD AFTER-NOON.
MR. HYUN, IT'S ME! LET'S GO GET A DRINK!
A-A DRINK?!
WHAT?! A DRINKING AND DRIVING ACCIDENT?!
WHICH HOSPITAL?
I'LL SEE YOU THERE!

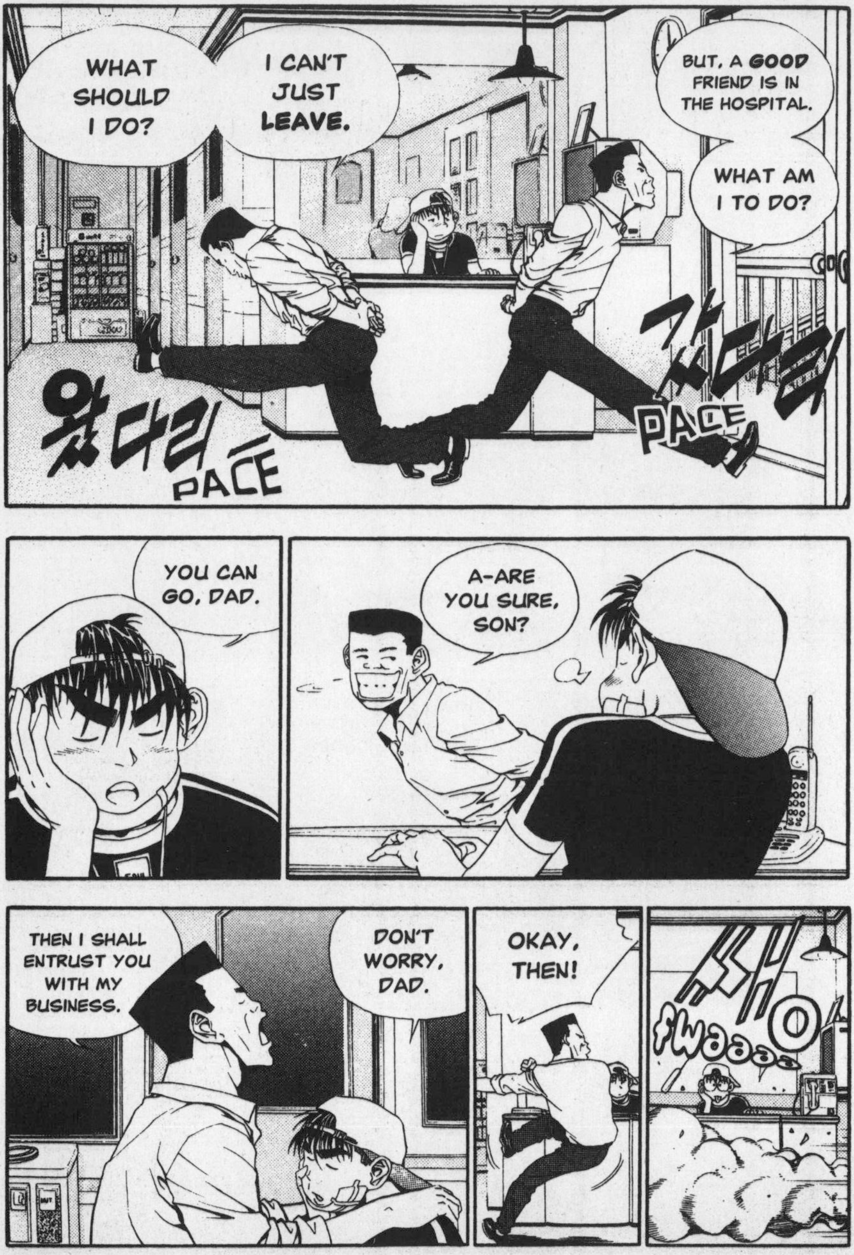
WHAT SHOULD I DO?
I CAN'T JUST LEAVE.
BUT, A GOOD FRIEND IS IN THE HOSPITAL.
WHAT AM I TO DO?
왔다리
PACE
갔다리
PACE
YOU CAN GO, DAD.
A-ARE YOU SURE, SON?
THEN I SHALL ENTRUST YOU WITH MY BUSINESS.
DON'T WORRY, DAD.
OKAY, THEN!
SHO
fwaaaaa

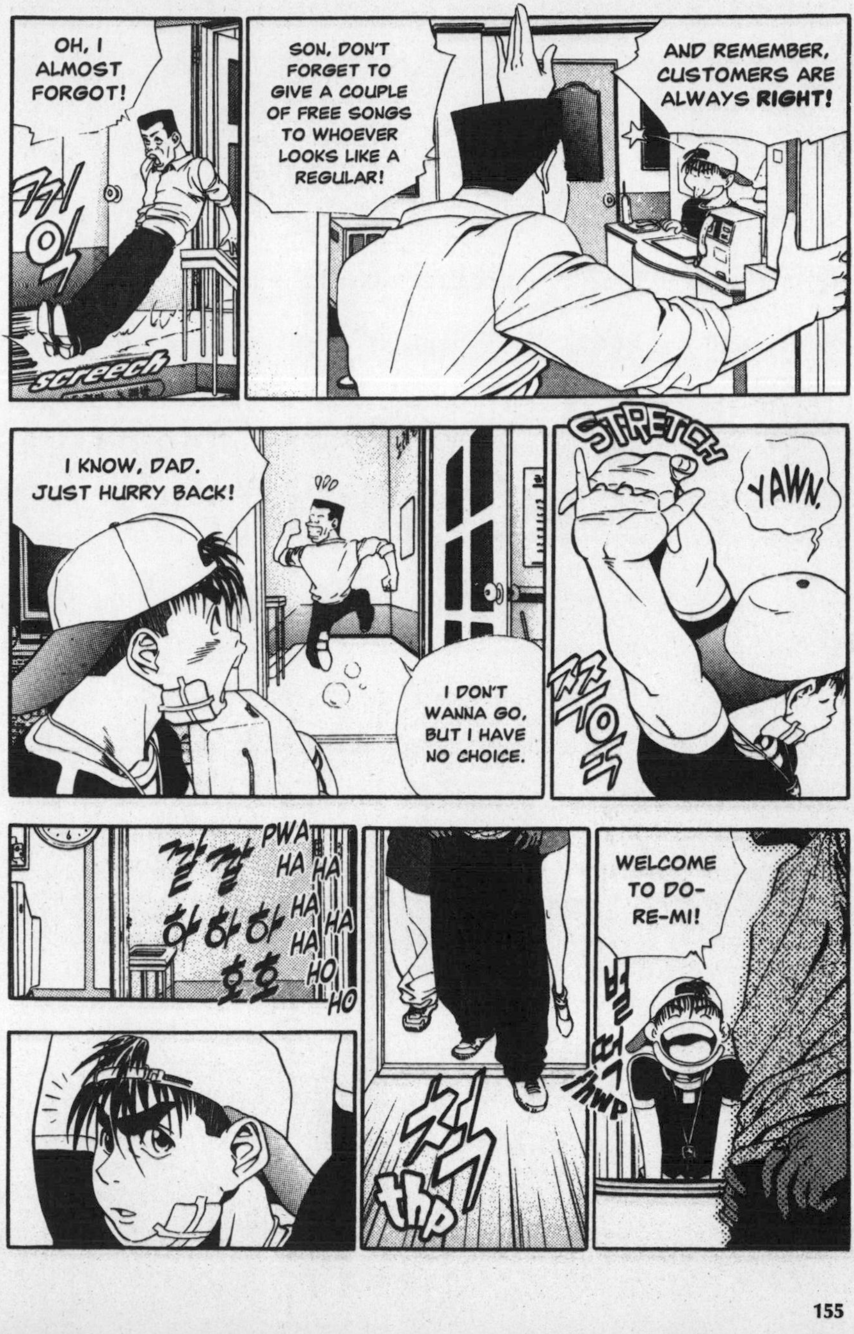
OH, I ALMOST FORGOT!
screech
SON, DON'T FORGET TO GIVE A COUPLE OF FREE SONGS TO WHOEVER LOOKS LIKE A REGULAR!
AND REMEMBER, CUSTOMERS ARE ALWAYS RIGHT!
I KNOW, DAD. JUST HURRY BACK!
I DON'T WANNA GO, BUT I HAVE NO CHOICE.
STRETCH
YAWN.
깔깔 하하하 호호
PWA HA HA HA HA HA HO HO
thp
WELCOME TO DO-RE-MI!
벌떡
thwp

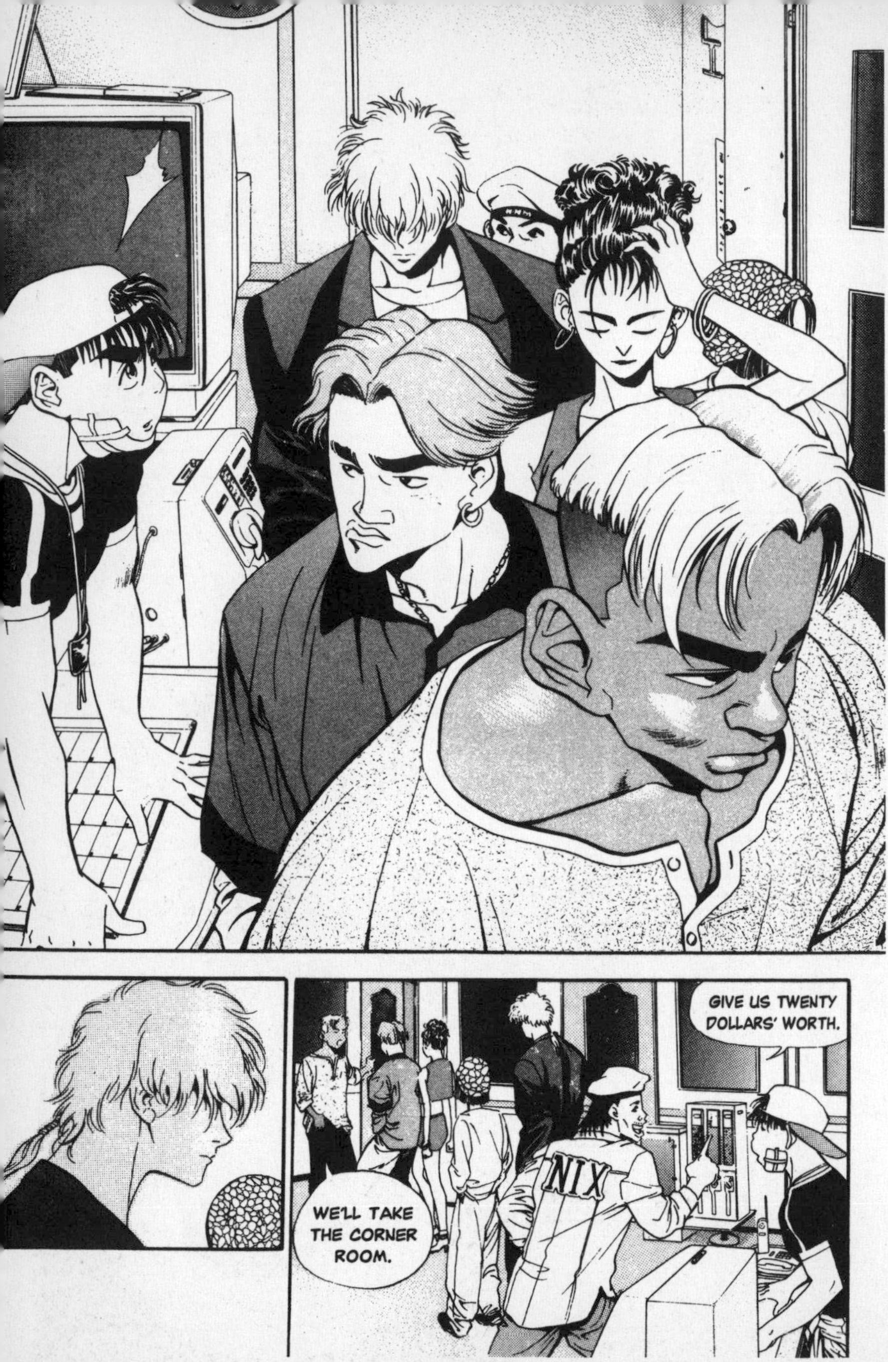
GIVE US TWENTY DOLLARS' WORTH.
WE'LL TAKE THE CORNER ROOM.

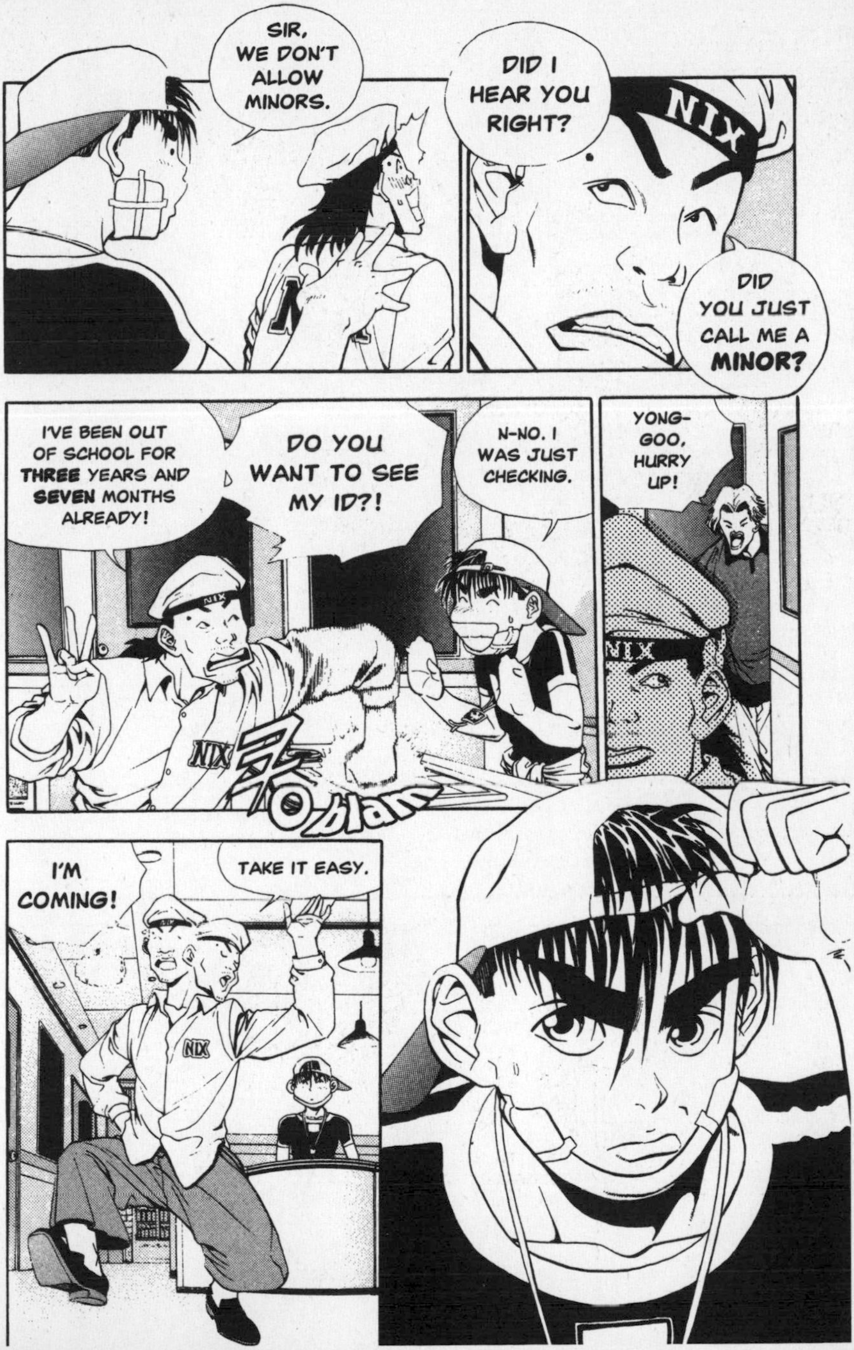
SIR, WE DON'T ALLOW MINORS.
DID I HEAR YOU RIGHT?
DID YOU JUST CALL ME A MINOR?
I'VE BEEN OUT OF SCHOOL FOR THREE YEARS AND SEVEN MONTHS ALREADY!
DO YOU WANT TO SEE MY ID?!
N-NO. I WAS JUST CHECKING.
YONG-GOO, HURRY UP!
blam
I'M COMING!
TAKE IT EASY.

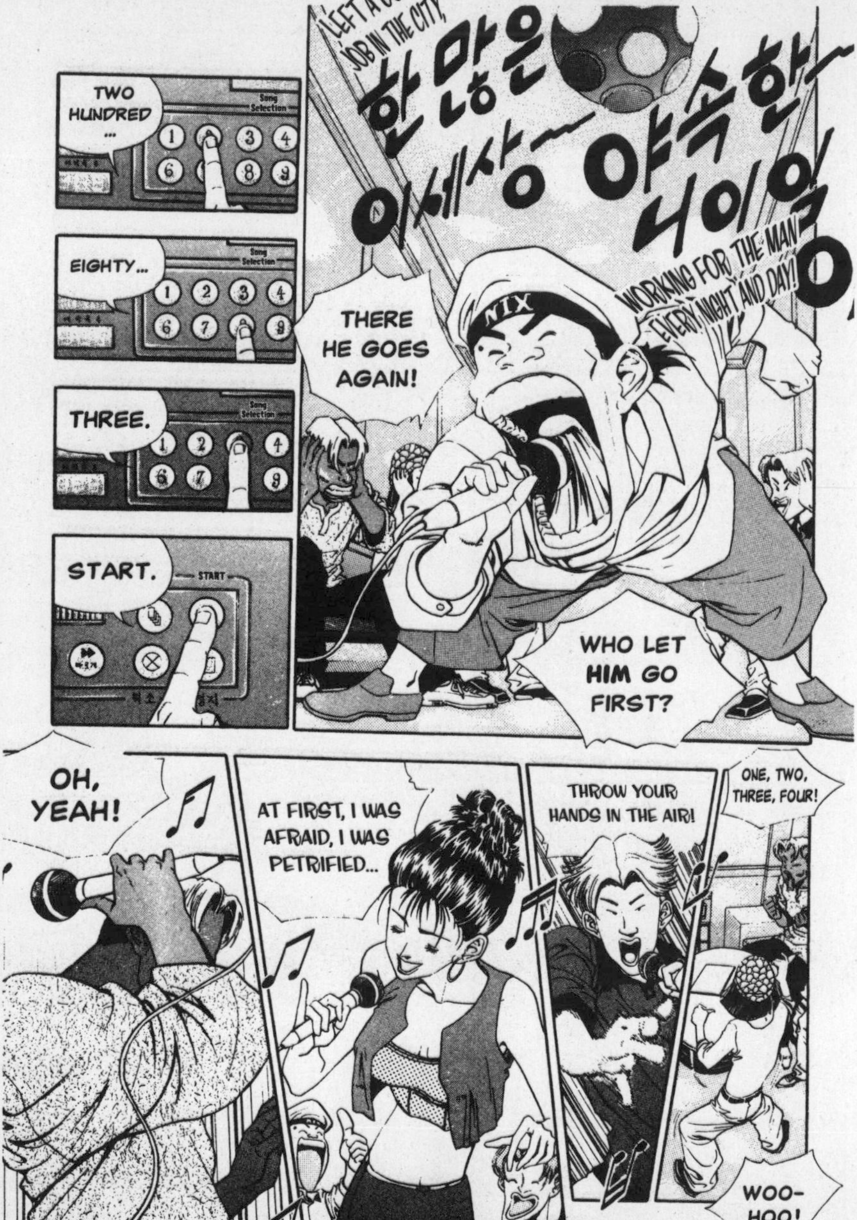

TWO HUNDRED ...
Song Selection
EIGHTY...
Song Selection
THREE.
Song Selection
START.
START
LEFT A GOOD JOB IN THE CITY,
한 많은 이세상~ 야속한~ 너이얼~
WORKING FOR THE MAN EVERY NIGHT AND DAY!
THERE HE GOES AGAIN!
WHO LET HIM GO FIRST?
OH, YEAH!
AT FIRST, I WAS AFRAID, I WAS PETRIFIED...
THROW YOUR HANDS IN THE AIR!
ONE, TWO, THREE, FOUR!
WOO-HOO!

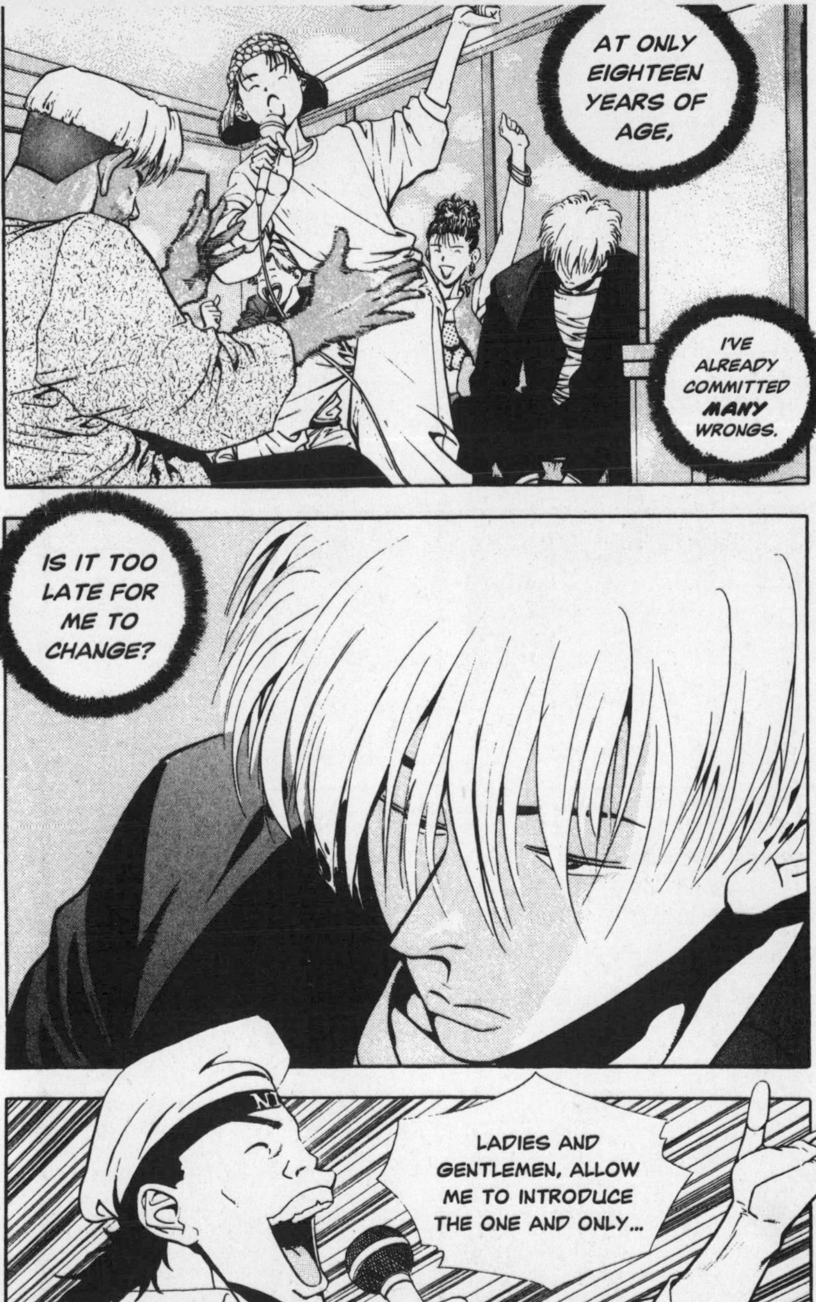
AT ONLY EIGHTEEN YEARS OF AGE,
I'VE ALREADY COMMITTED MANY WRONGS.
IS IT TOO LATE FOR ME TO CHANGE?
LADIES AND GENTLEMEN, ALLOW ME TO INTRODUCE THE ONE AND ONLY...

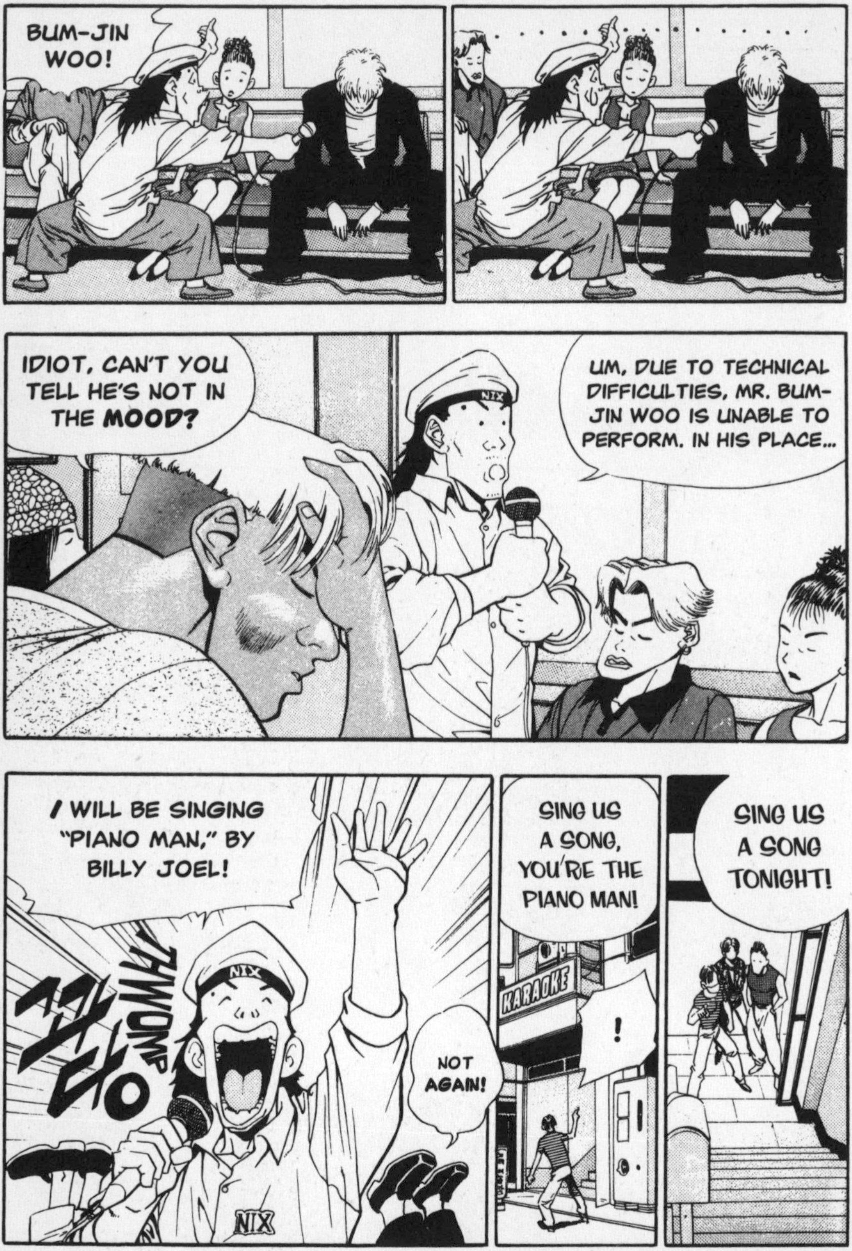
BUM-JIN WOO!
IDIOT, CAN'T YOU TELL HE'S NOT IN THE **MOOD?**
UM, DUE TO TECHNICAL DIFFICULTIES, MR. BUM-JIN WOO IS UNABLE TO PERFORM. IN HIS PLACE...
I WILL BE SINGING "PIANO MAN," BY BILLY JOEL!
THWOMP
NOT AGAIN!
SING US A SONG, YOU'RE THE PIANO MAN!
KARAOKE
!
SING US A SONG TONIGHT!

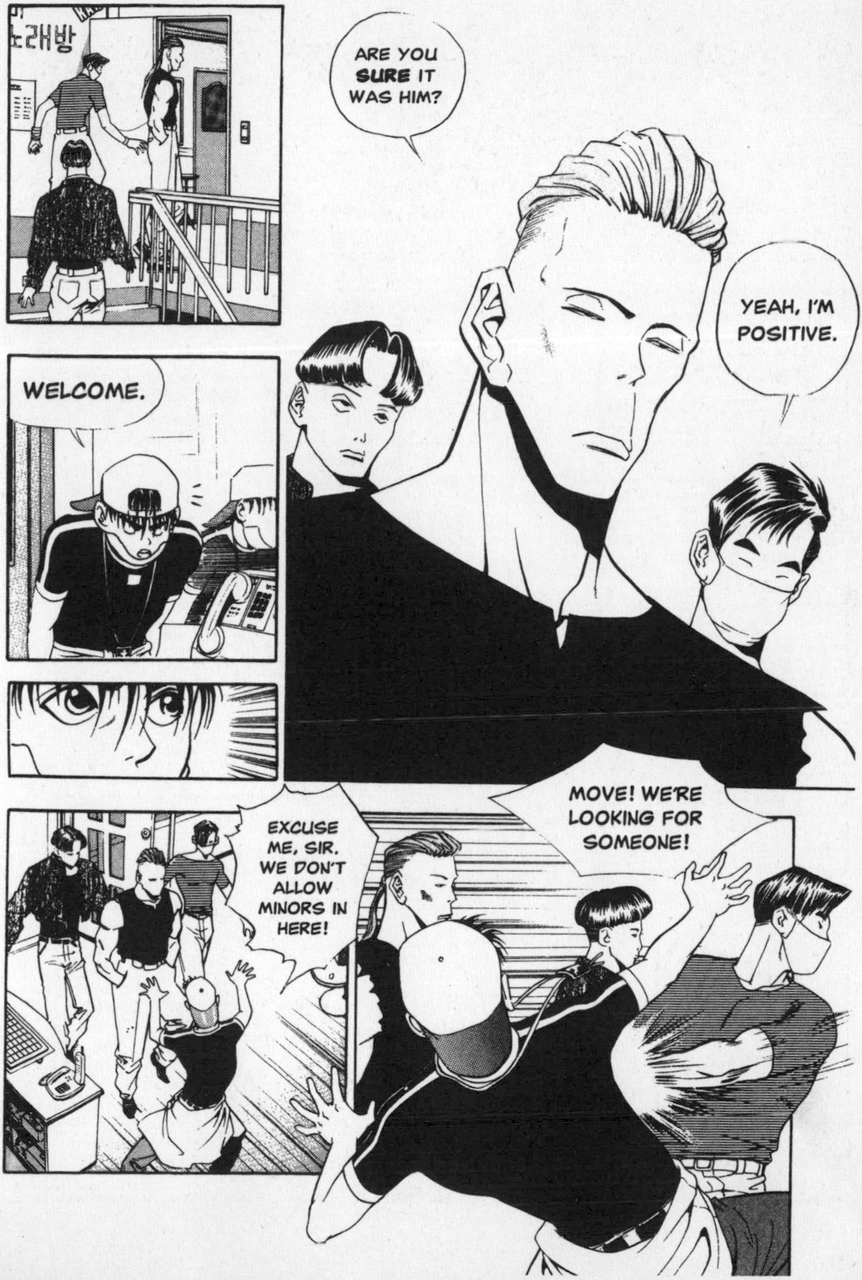
노래방
ARE YOU SURE IT WAS HIM?
YEAH, I'M POSITIVE.
WELCOME.
EXCUSE ME, SIR. WE DON'T ALLOW MINORS IN HERE!
MOVE! WE'RE LOOKING FOR SOMEONE!

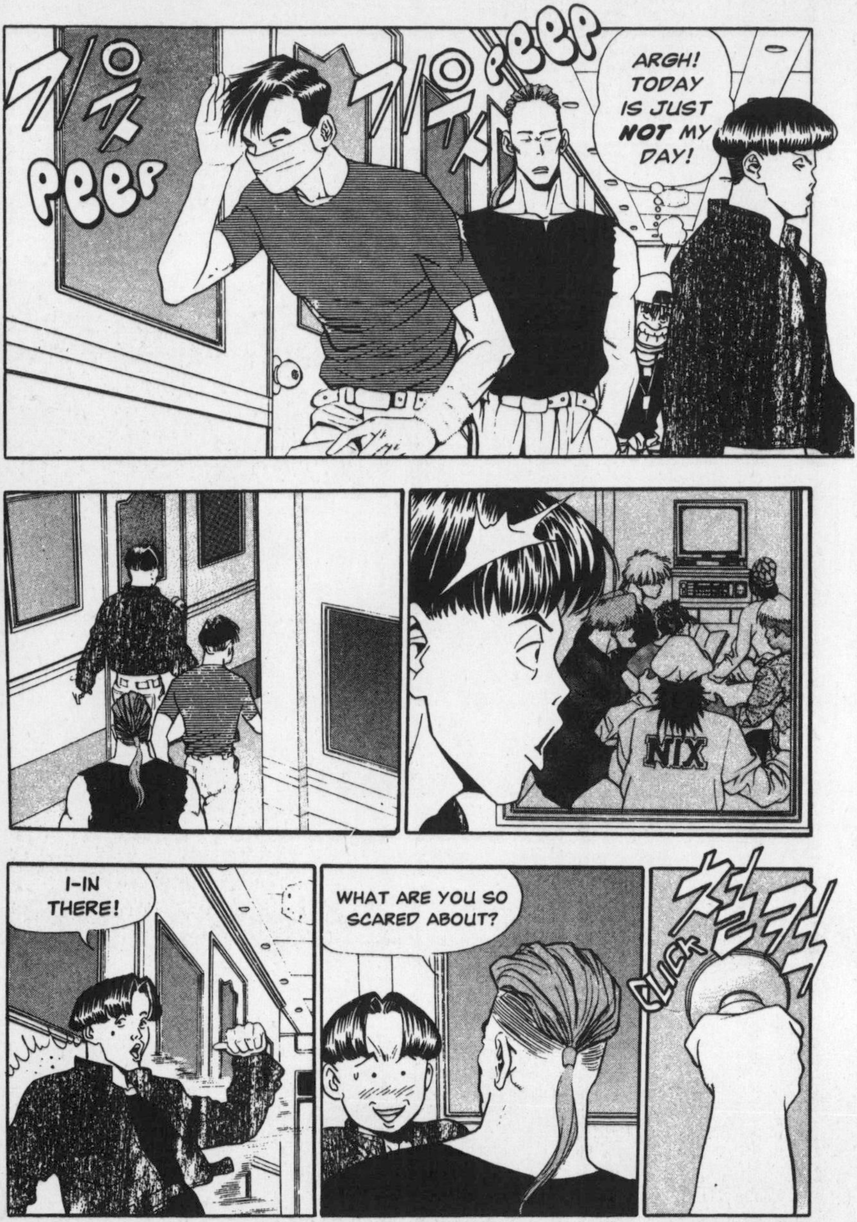
peep
peep
ARGH! TODAY IS JUST **NOT** MY DAY!
NIX
I-IN THERE!
WHAT ARE YOU SO SCARED ABOUT?
CLICK

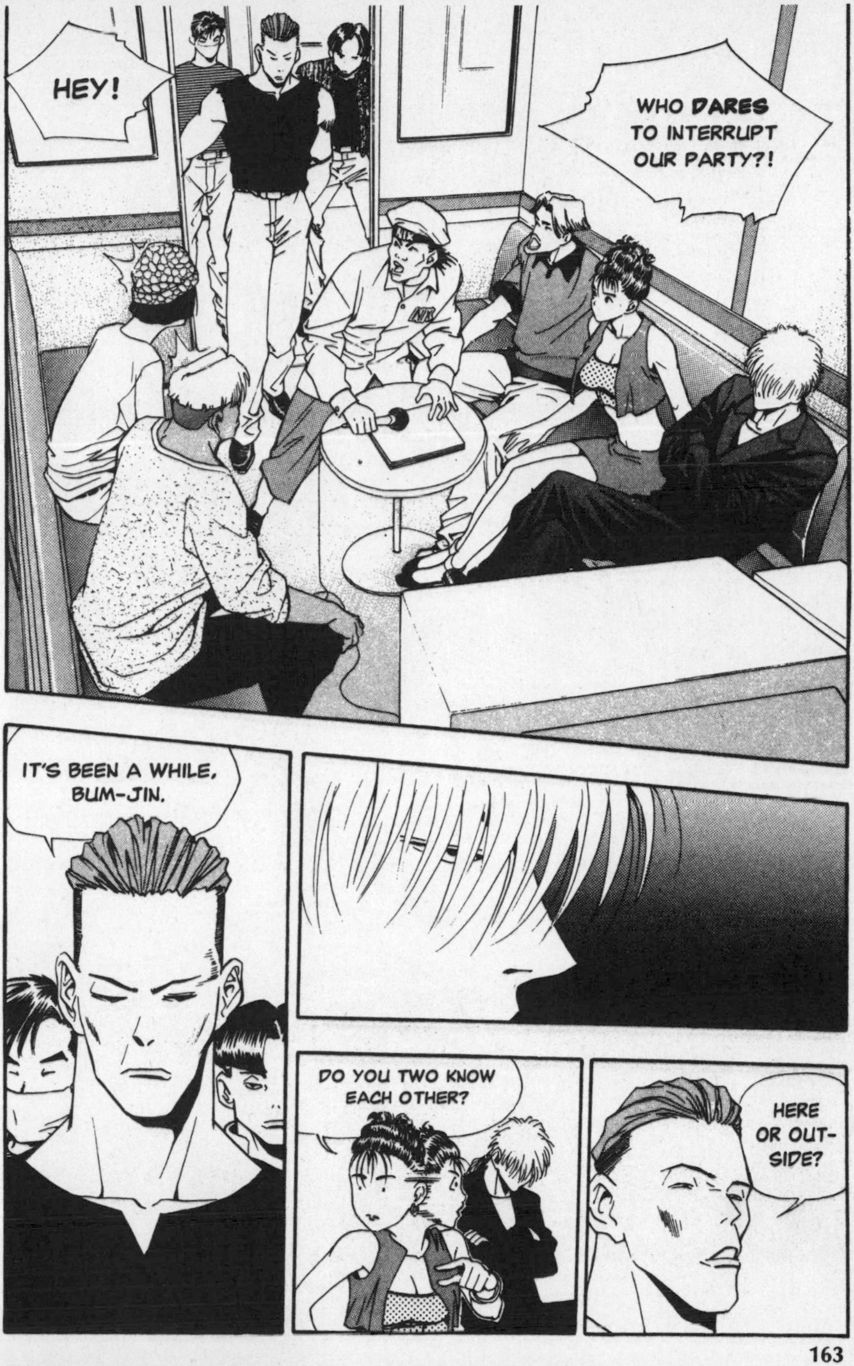
HEY!
WHO DARES TO INTERRUPT OUR PARTY?!
IT'S BEEN A WHILE, BUM-JIN.
DO YOU TWO KNOW EACH OTHER?
HERE OR OUT-SIDE?

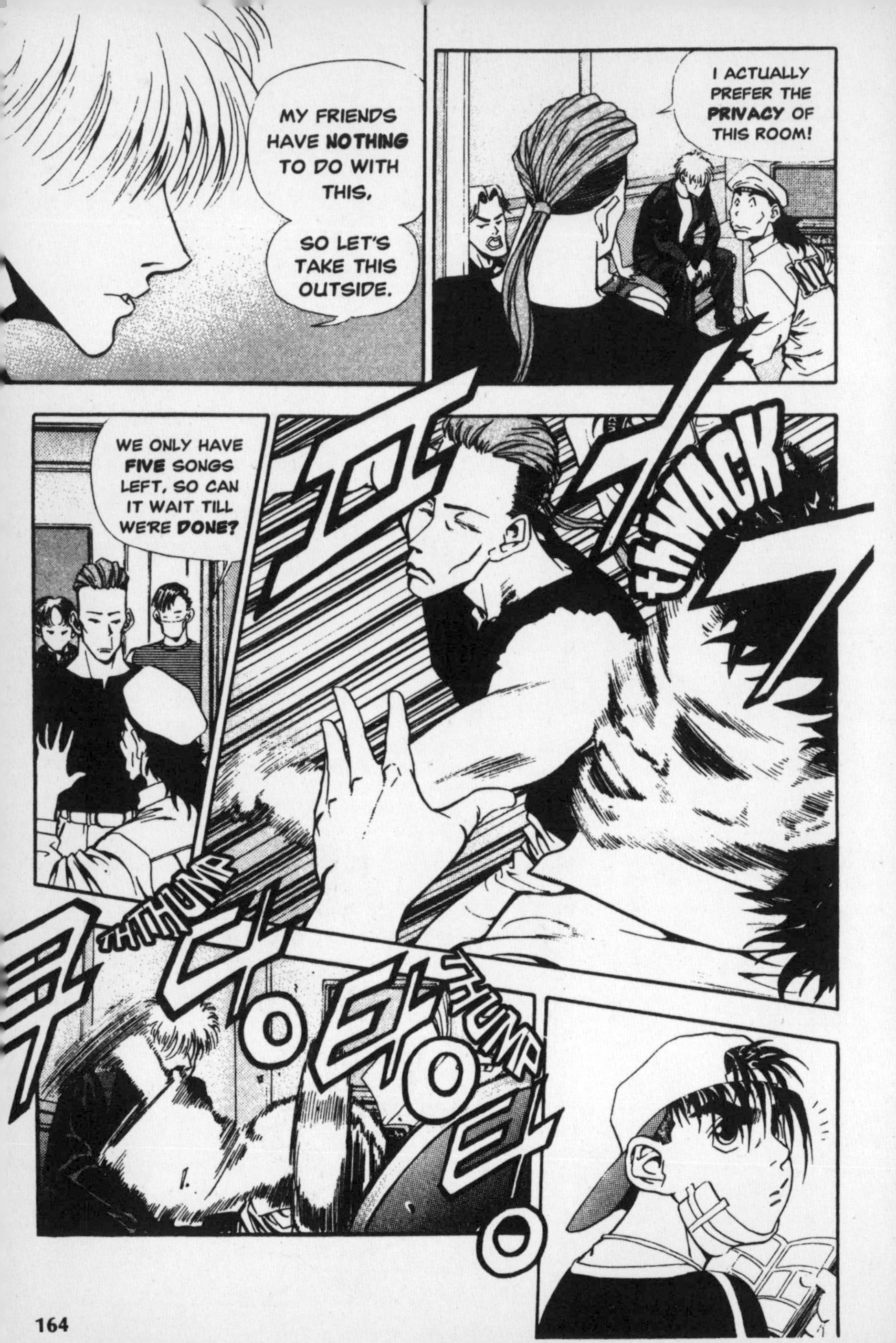
MY FRIENDS HAVE NOTHING TO DO WITH THIS,
SO LET'S TAKE THIS OUTSIDE.
I ACTUALLY PREFER THE PRIVACY OF THIS ROOM!
WE ONLY HAVE FIVE SONGS LEFT, SO CAN IT WAIT TILL WE'RE DONE?
SWACK
THTHTHUMP
THUMP

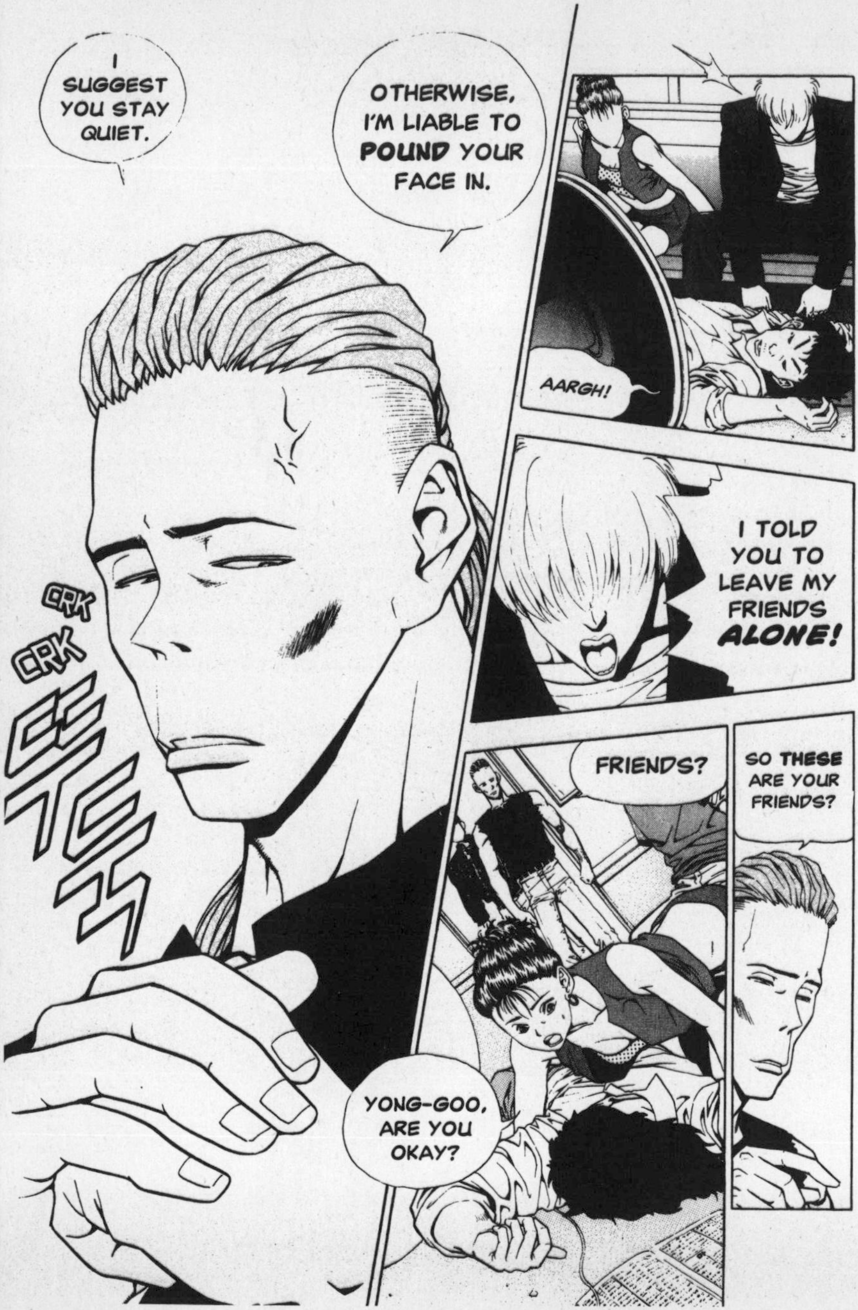
I SUGGEST YOU STAY QUIET.
OTHERWISE, I'M LIABLE TO POUND YOUR FACE IN.
CRK
CRK
AARGH!
I TOLD YOU TO LEAVE MY FRIENDS ALONE!
SO THESE ARE YOUR FRIENDS?
FRIENDS?
YONG-GOO, ARE YOU OKAY?

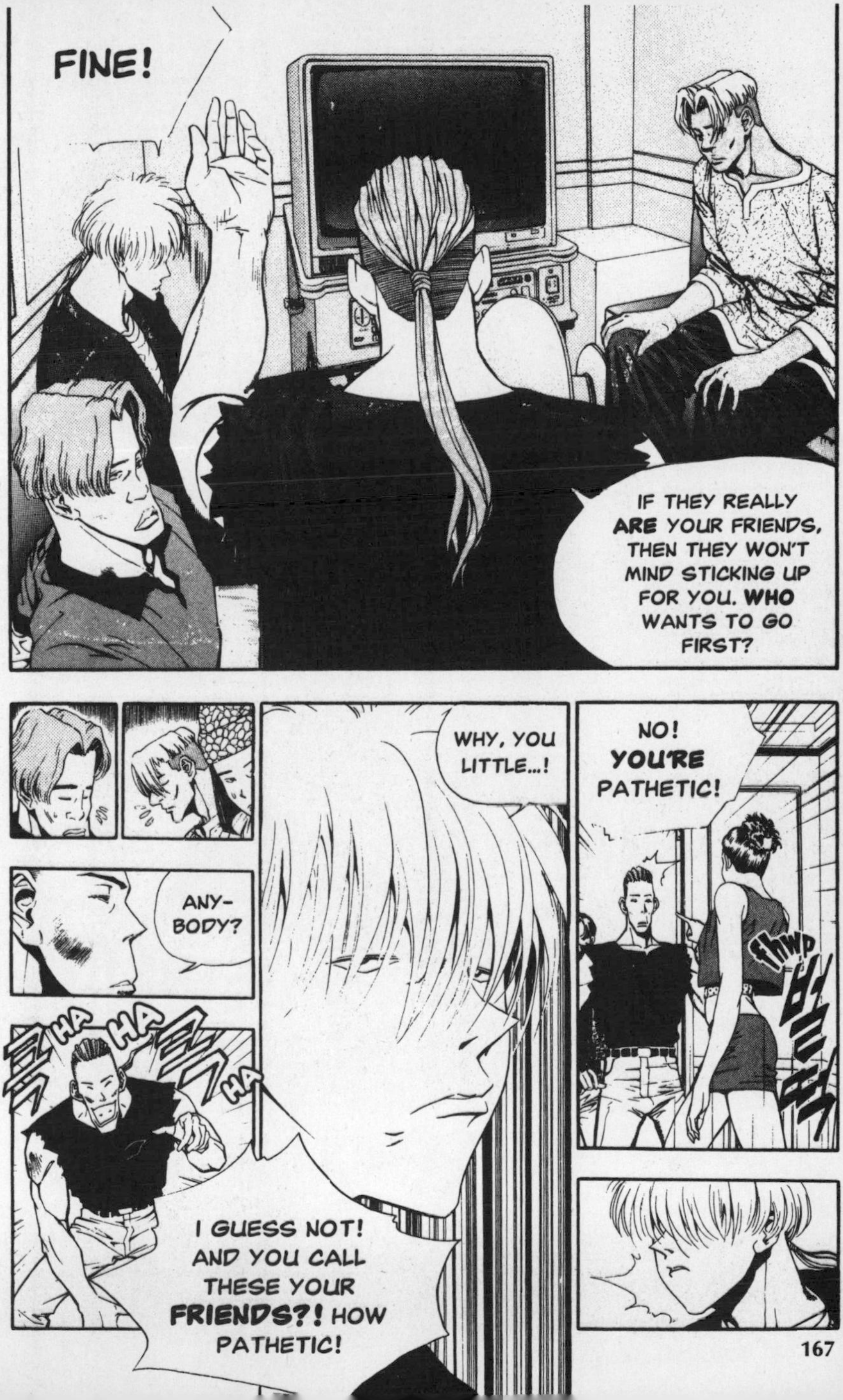
FINE!
IF THEY REALLY ARE YOUR FRIENDS, THEN THEY WON'T MIND STICKING UP FOR YOU. WHO WANTS TO GO FIRST?
ANY-BODY?
HA HA HA HA
I GUESS NOT! AND YOU CALL THESE YOUR FRIENDS?! HOW PATHETIC!
WHY, YOU LITTLE...!
NO! YOU'RE PATHETIC!
thwp

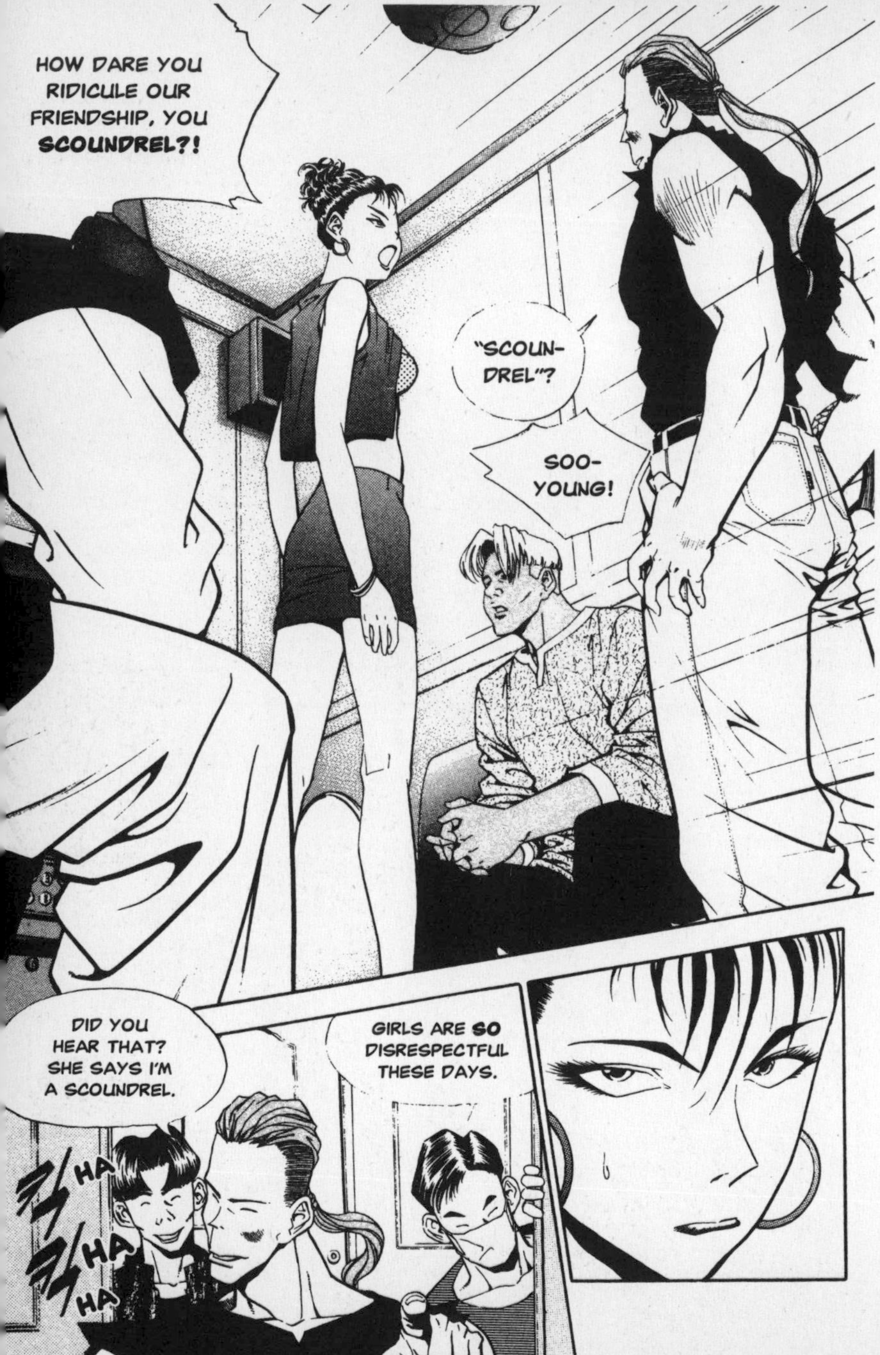
HOW DARE YOU RIDICULE OUR FRIENDSHIP, YOU **SCOUNDREL?!**
"SCOUN-DREL"?
SOO-YOUNG!
DID YOU HEAR THAT? SHE SAYS I'M A SCOUNDREL.
HA HA HA
GIRLS ARE **SO** DISRESPECTFUL THESE DAYS.

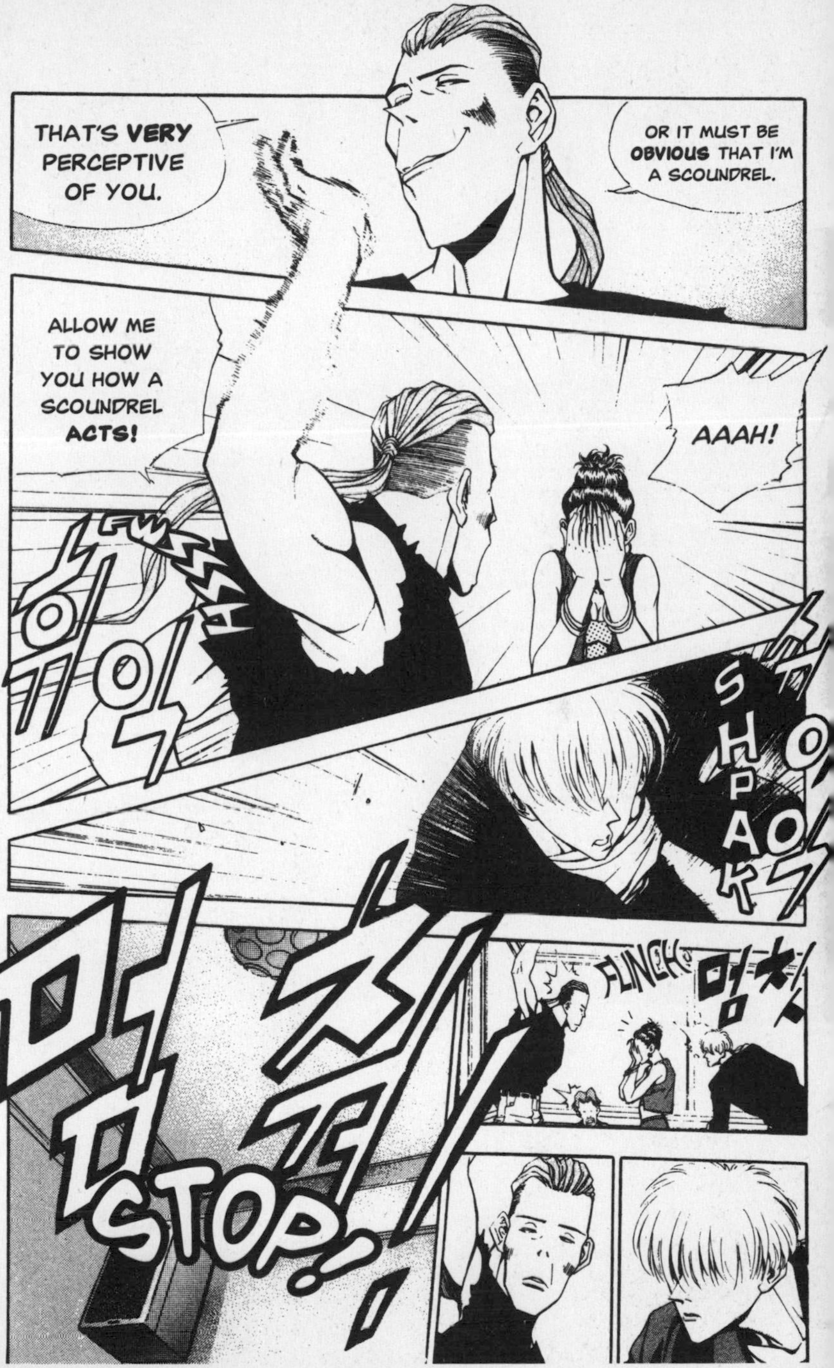
THAT'S **VERY** PERCEPTIVE OF YOU.
OR IT MUST BE **OBVIOUS** THAT I'M A SCOUNDREL.
ALLOW ME TO SHOW YOU HOW A SCOUNDREL **ACTS!**
AAAH!
SHPAK
FLINCH
STOP!

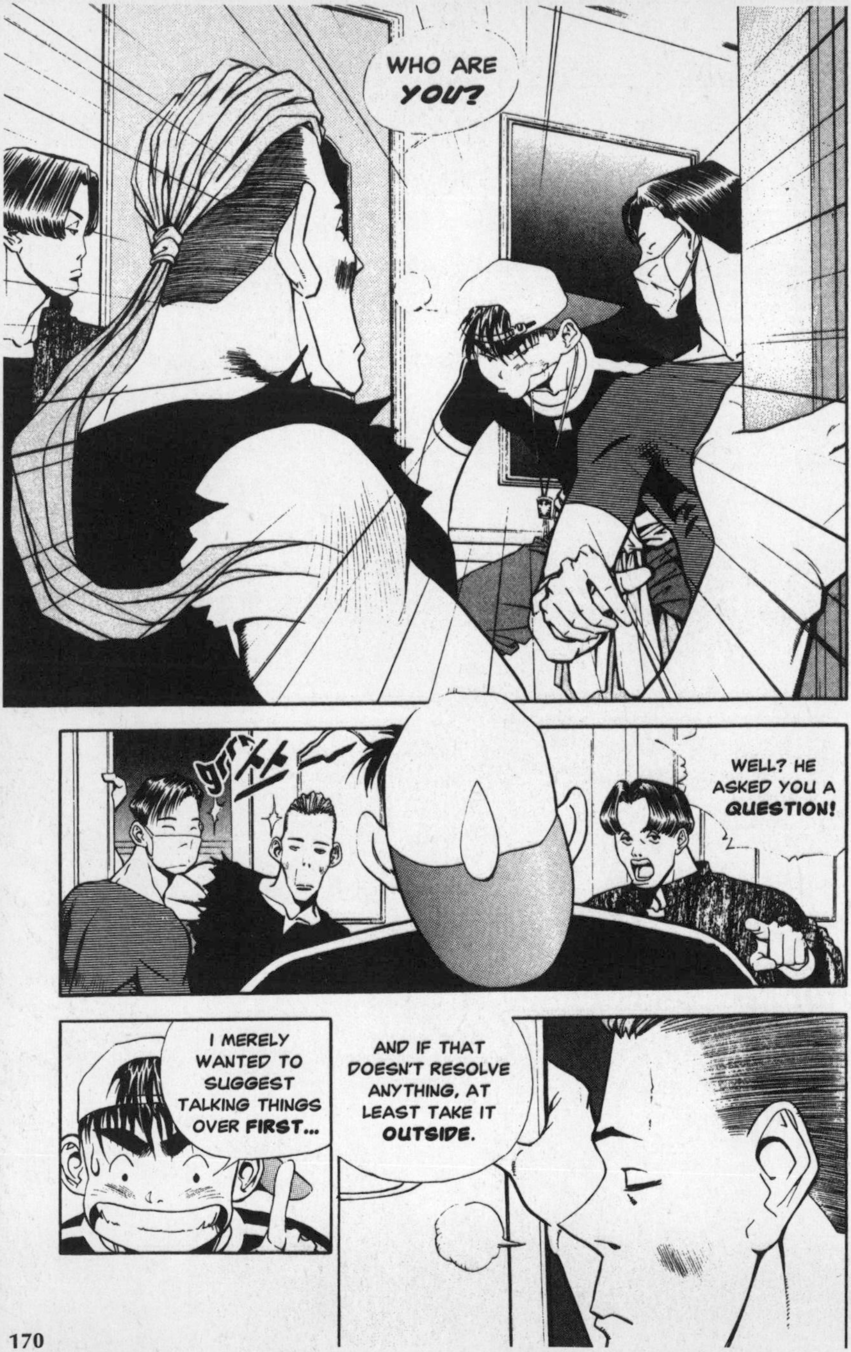
WHO ARE YOU?
grrr
WELL? HE ASKED YOU A QUESTION!
I MERELY WANTED TO SUGGEST TALKING THINGS OVER FIRST...
AND IF THAT DOESN'T RESOLVE ANYTHING, AT LEAST TAKE IT OUTSIDE.

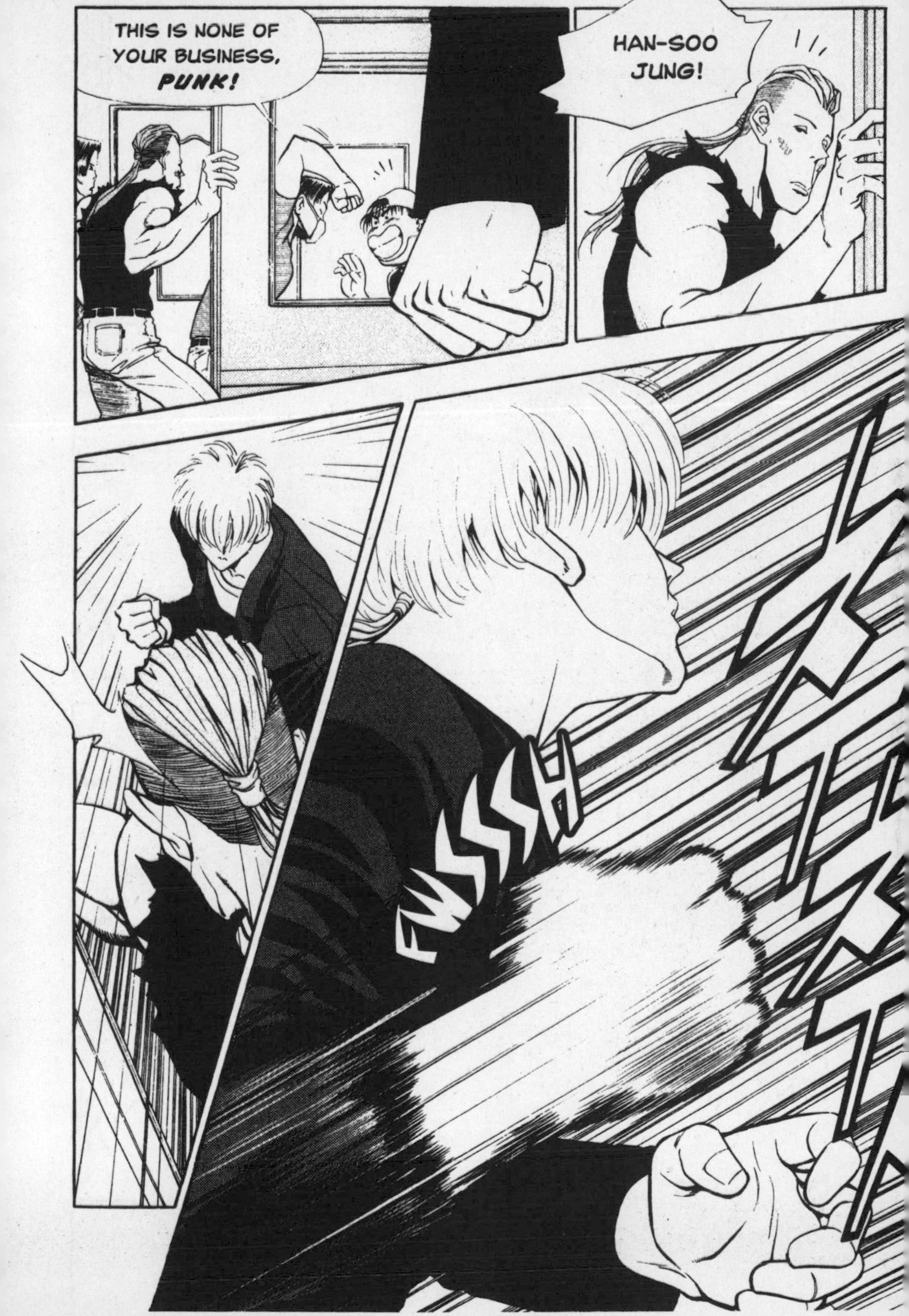
THIS IS NONE OF YOUR BUSINESS, *PUNK!*
HAN-SOO JUNG!
FWSSSH

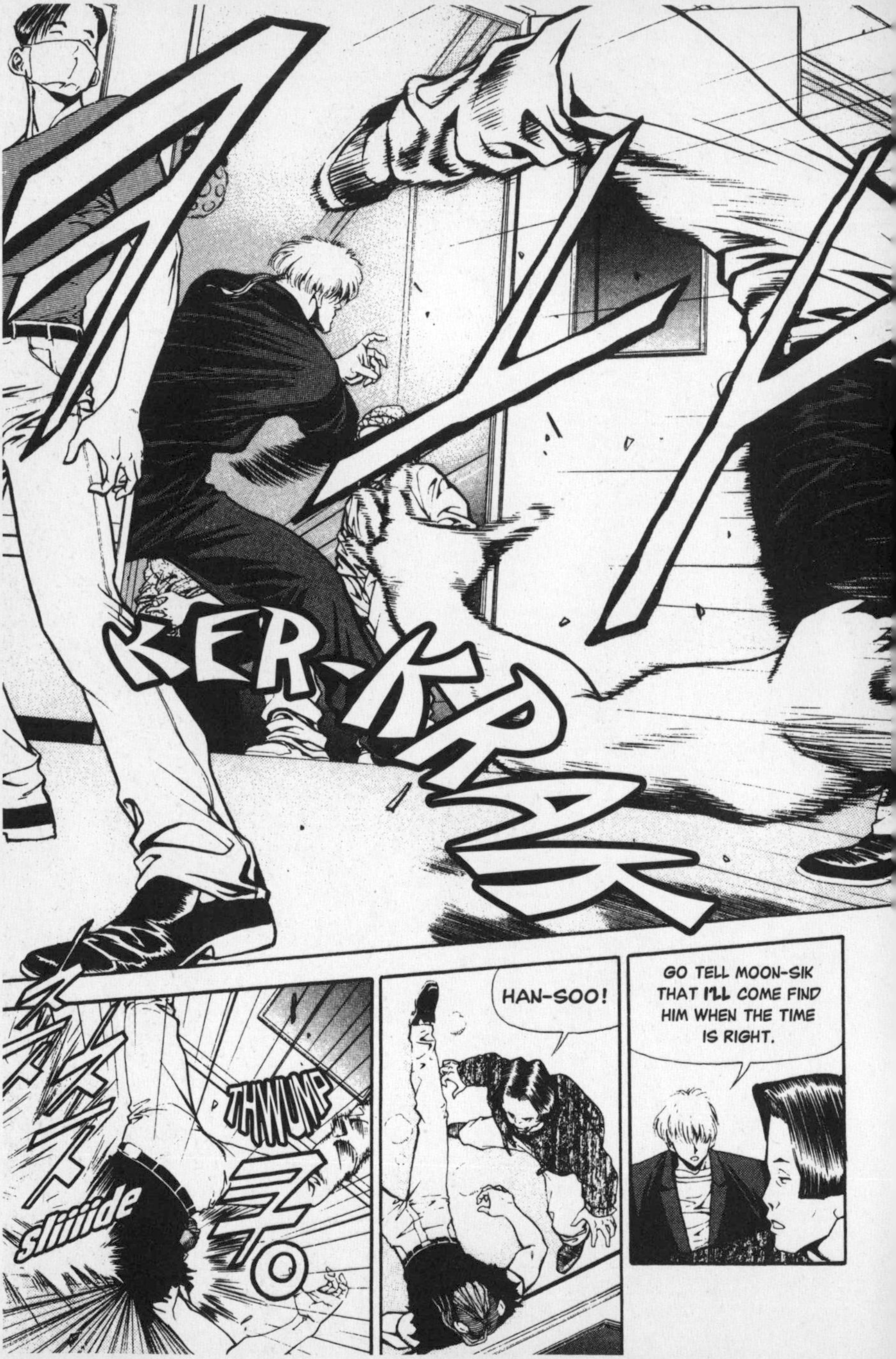
KER-KRAK
shiiiide
THWUMP
HAN-SOO!
GO TELL MOON-SIK THAT I'LL COME FIND HIM WHEN THE TIME IS RIGHT.

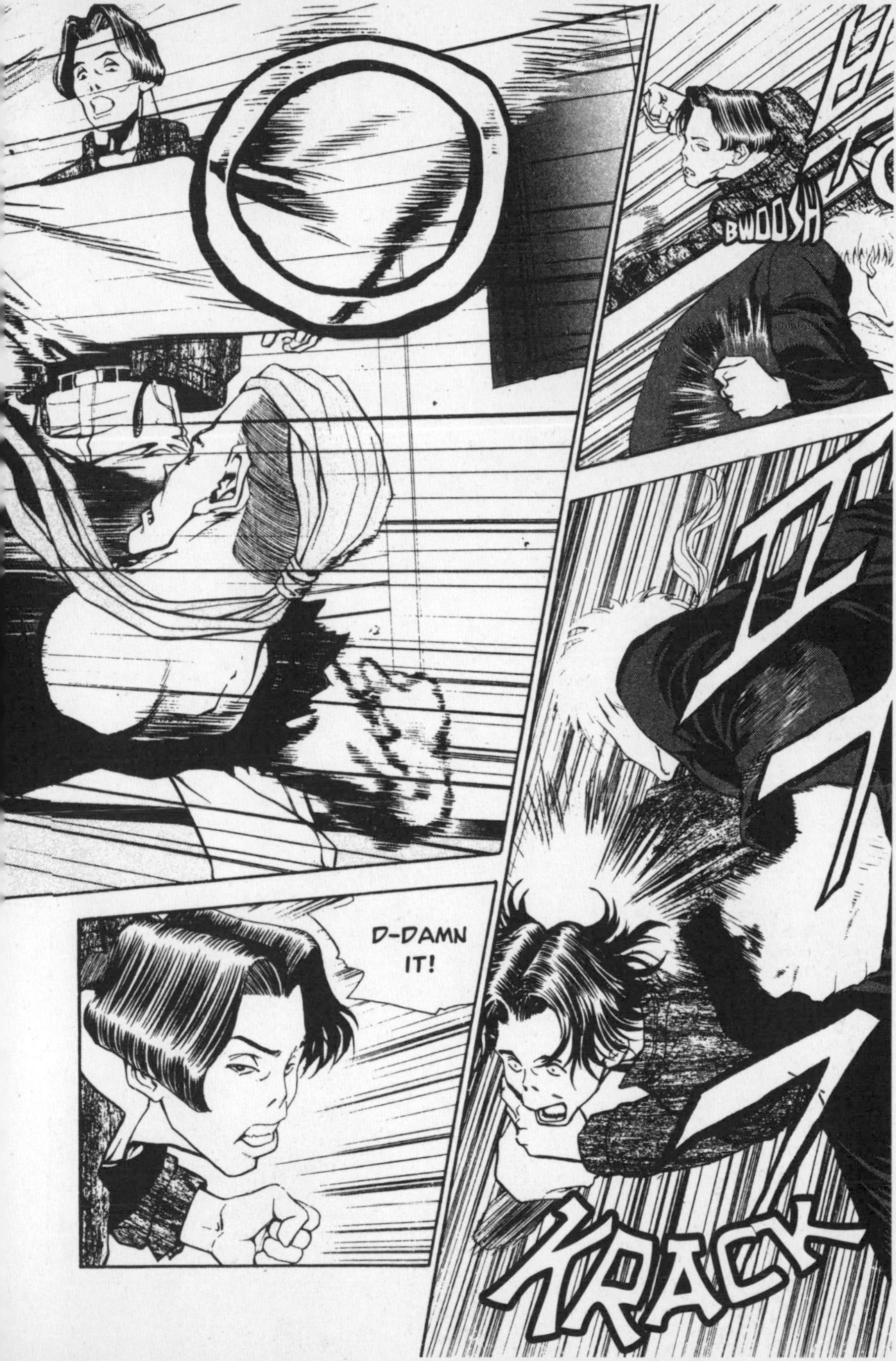
BWOOSH
D-DAMN IT!
KRACK

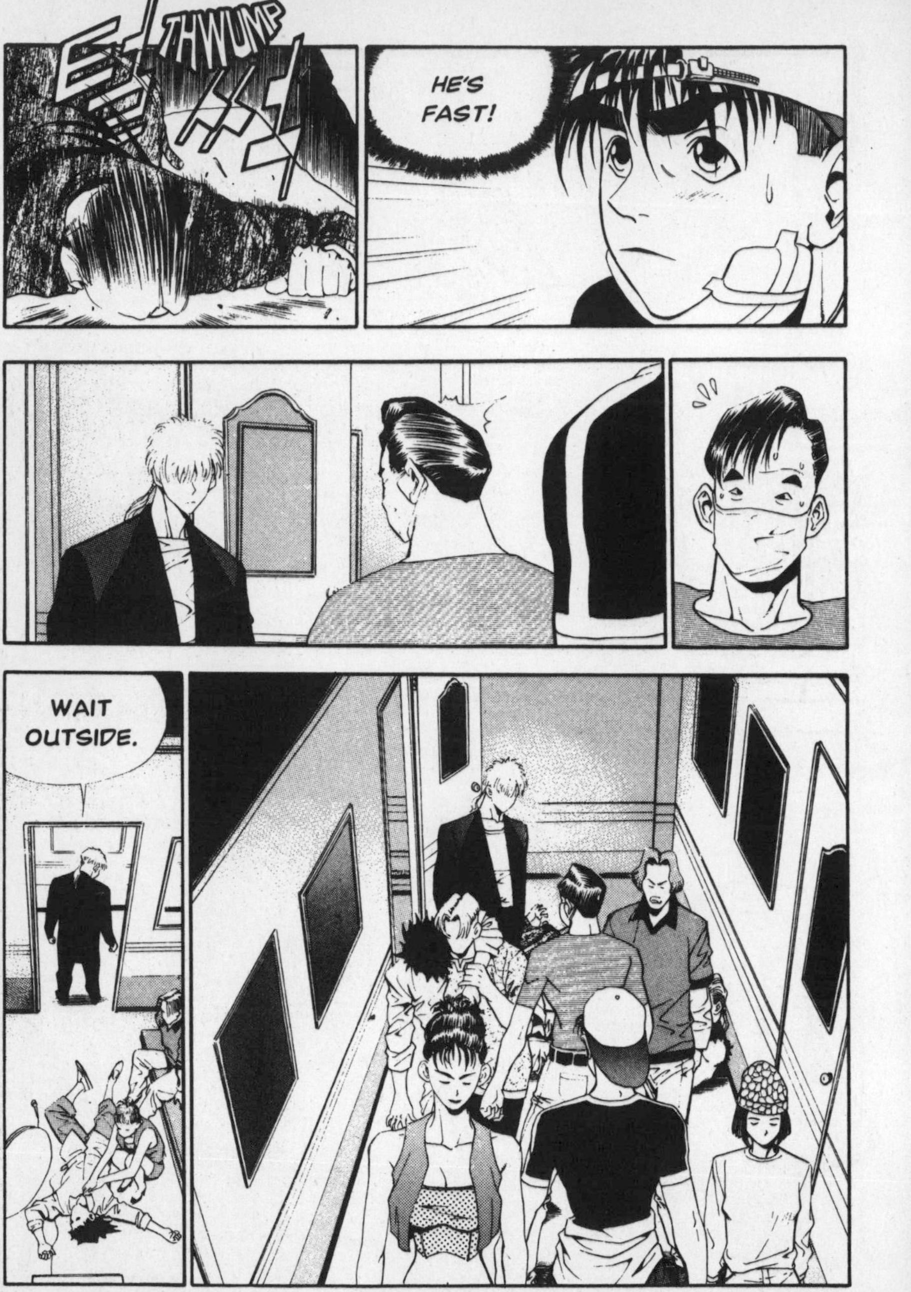
THWUMP
HE'S FAST!
WAIT OUTSIDE.

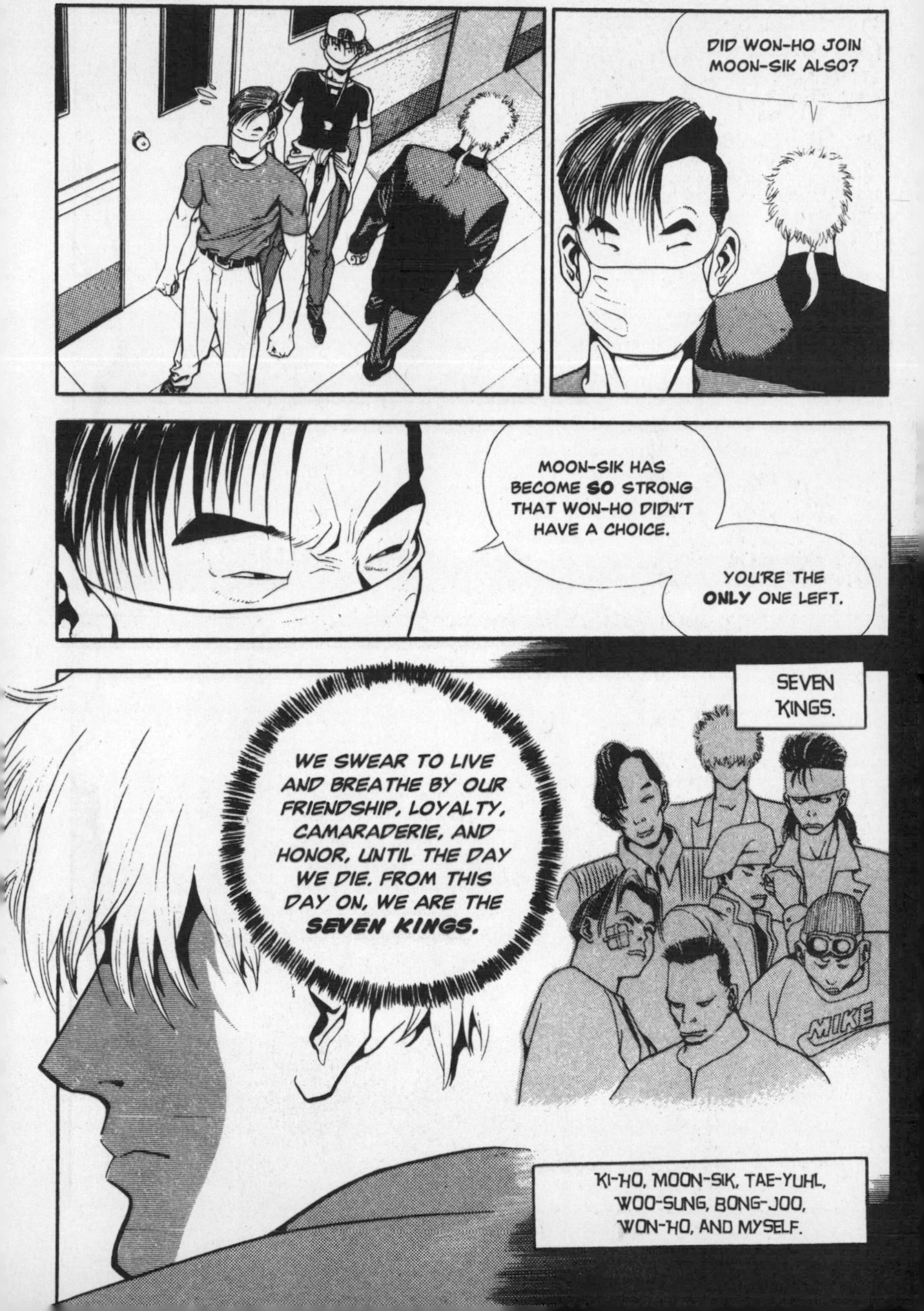
DID WON-HO JOIN MOON-SIK ALSO?
MOON-SIK HAS BECOME SO STRONG THAT WON-HO DIDN'T HAVE A CHOICE.
YOU'RE THE ONLY ONE LEFT.
SEVEN KINGS.
WE SWEAR TO LIVE AND BREATHE BY OUR FRIENDSHIP, LOYALTY, CAMARADERIE, AND HONOR, UNTIL THE DAY WE DIE. FROM THIS DAY ON, WE ARE THE SEVEN KINGS.
KI-HO, MOON-SIK, TAE-YUHL, WOO-SUNG, BONG-JOO, WON-HO, AND MYSELF.

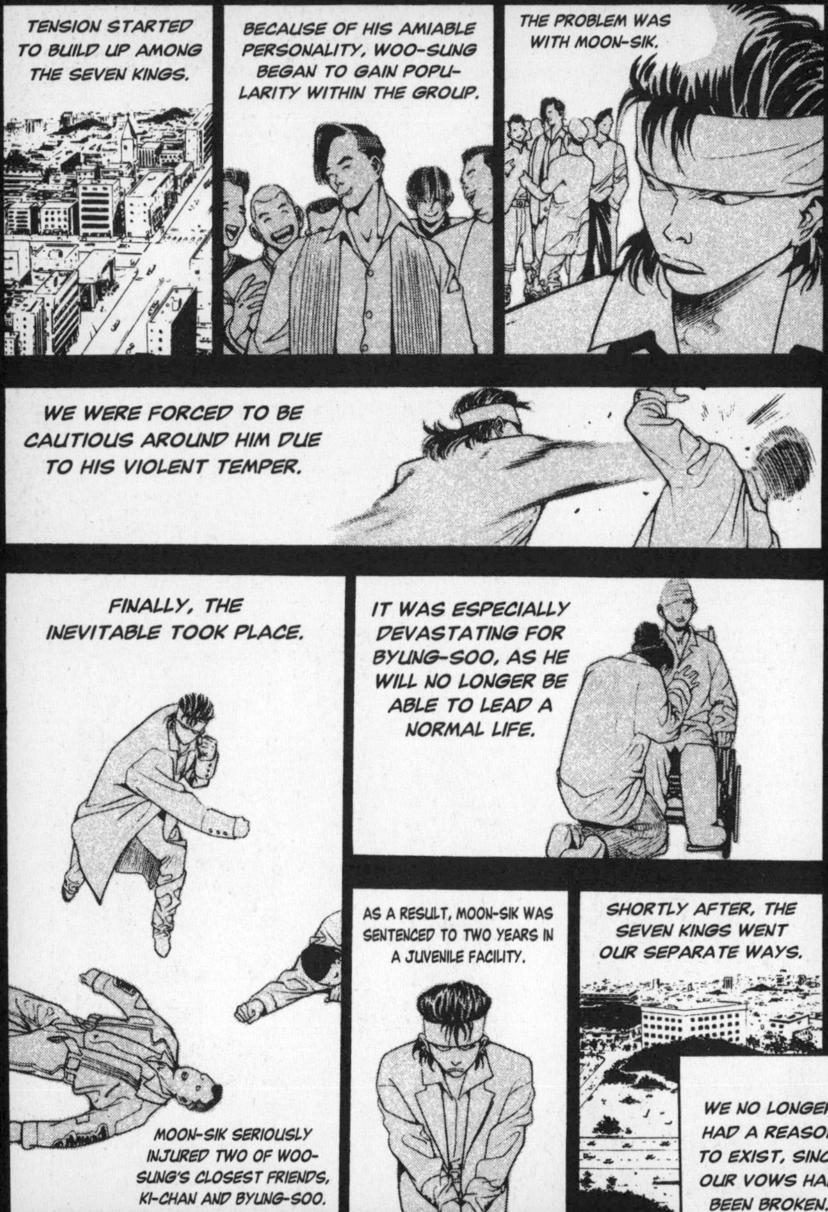
TENSION STARTED TO BUILD UP AMONG THE SEVEN KINGS.
BECAUSE OF HIS AMIABLE PERSONALITY, WOO-SUNG BEGAN TO GAIN POPULARITY WITHIN THE GROUP.
THE PROBLEM WAS WITH MOON-SIK.
WE WERE FORCED TO BE CAUTIOUS AROUND HIM DUE TO HIS VIOLENT TEMPER.
FINALLY, THE INEVITABLE TOOK PLACE.
MOON-SIK SERIOUSLY INJURED TWO OF WOO-SUNG'S CLOSEST FRIENDS, KI-CHAN AND BYUNG-SOO.
IT WAS ESPECIALLY DEVASTATING FOR BYUNG-SOO, AS HE WILL NO LONGER BE ABLE TO LEAD A NORMAL LIFE.
AS A RESULT, MOON-SIK WAS SENTENCED TO TWO YEARS IN A JUVENILE FACILITY.
SHORTLY AFTER, THE SEVEN KINGS WENT OUR SEPARATE WAYS.
WE NO LONGER HAD A REASON TO EXIST, SINCE OUR VOWS HAD BEEN BROKEN.

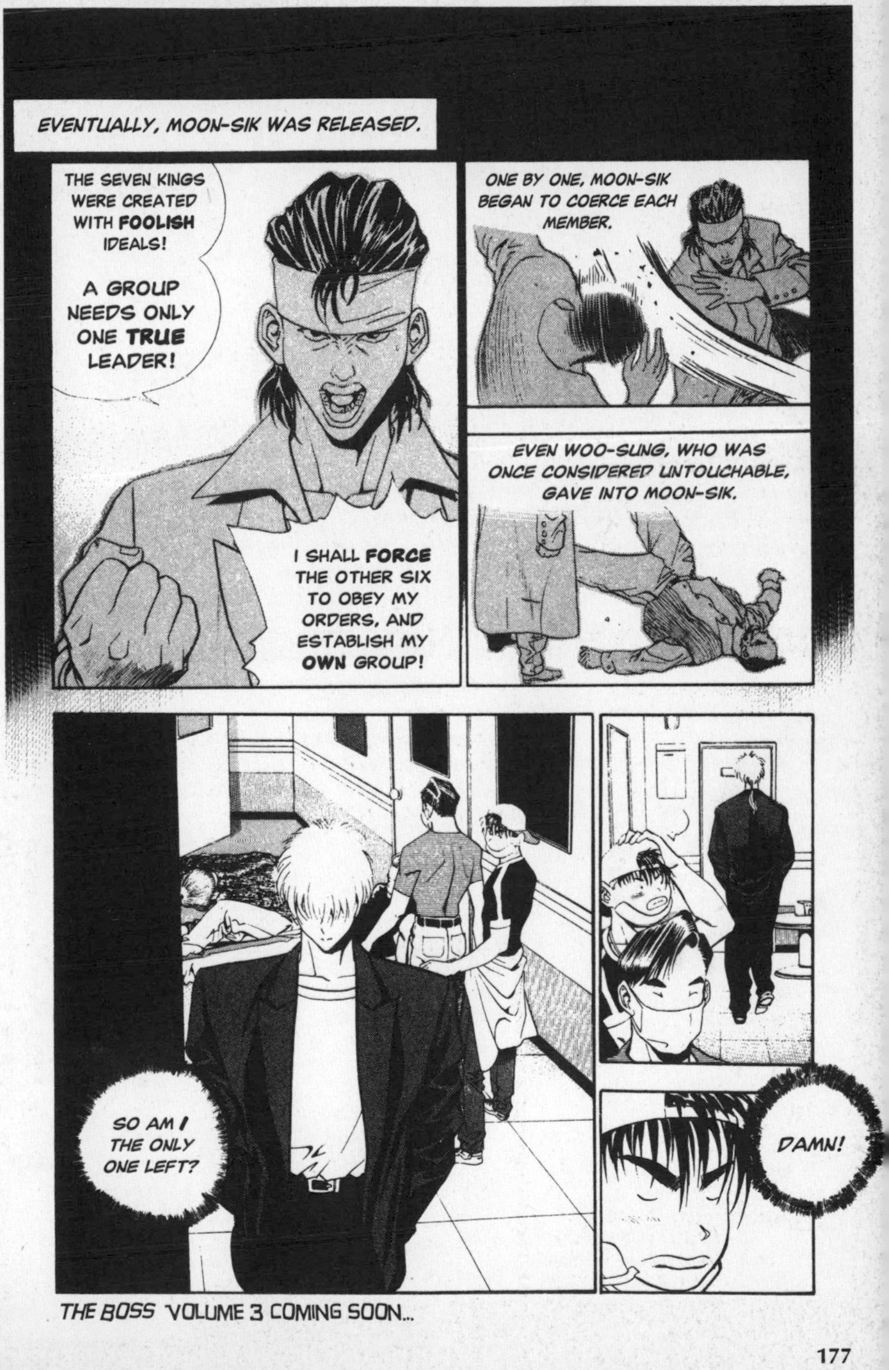
EVENTUALLY, MOON-SIK WAS RELEASED.
THE SEVEN KINGS WERE CREATED WITH FOOLISH IDEALS!
A GROUP NEEDS ONLY ONE TRUE LEADER!
I SHALL FORCE THE OTHER SIX TO OBEY MY ORDERS, AND ESTABLISH MY OWN GROUP!
ONE BY ONE, MOON-SIK BEGAN TO COERCE EACH MEMBER.
EVEN WOO-SUNG, WHO WAS ONCE CONSIDERED UNTOUCHABLE, GAVE INTO MOON-SIK.
SO AM I THE ONLY ONE LEFT?
DAMN!

THE BOSS VOLUME 3 COMING SOON...

The Boss Vol. 02

PG. 18 **Homerooms**
All Korean middle and high school students are individually assigned homeroom classes. Contrary to the traditional American public school system, the teachers move around from homeroom to homeroom according to their respective subjects and schedules, not students.

PG. 41 **2 – 3**
The 2 indicates it's a sophomore class, while the 3 is the actual class number. Most Korean public schools have numerous classes for each level to compensate for the large number of students enrolling each year.

PG. 68 **The disciplinarian**
All Korean middle schools and high schools appoint teachers to ensure discipline amongst students. Often, corporal punishment is employed to achieve said purpose.

PG. 99 **Annual spring cleaning**
As another means to instill discipline and responsibility among students, Korean public school systems require *students* to maintain clean facilities.

THE ADVENTURE CONTINUES IN

THE BOSS 3

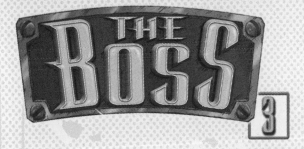

Sometimes, the better part of valor…is to not give up the good fight! Sang-Tae's attempts to thwart Guk-Do landed both a suspension, but it's all the worse for Sang-Tae—Ji-Hyun wanted him to keep his righteously indignant fists in his pockets or else! Sang-Tae has doled out a lot of pro-active justice, but he's also taken a lot of abuse—and now he's got some time to think about things while temporarily barred from attending classes. But when an attempt to revive an old gang involves an acquaintance who doesn't want any part of it, will the pain in Sang-Tae's bruises fuel his fists of fury? Find out who gets beaten to a pulp in ***The Boss***, Volume 3!

COMING IN SEPTEMBER 2004 FROM ADV MANGA!

ADV Manga™

www.adv-manga.com

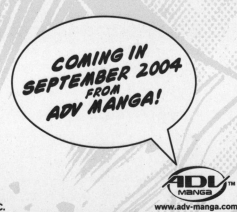

EDITOR'S PICKS

IF YOU LIKED *THE BOSS* VOLUME 2, THEN YOU'LL LOVE THESE!

PICK 1

QUANTUM MISTAKE

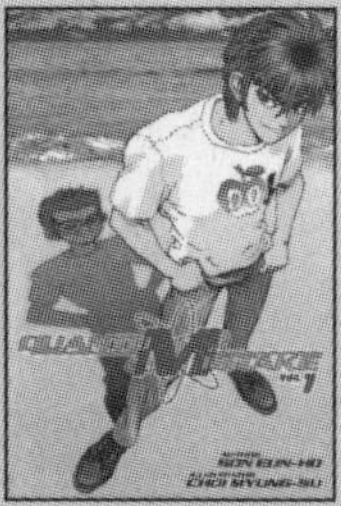

SON EUN-HO
CHOI MYUNG-SU

Too-Ji and Woo-Soo have swapped…their bodies! After becoming the subjects of a mad scientist's experiment with her latest invention—the quantum teleporter—their bodies are switched, leaving only their minds and spirits intact. Woo-Soo, who was once a model student, must face the life of Too-Ji, a teenage menace. He is now the enemy of many, but will his kinder, gentler demeanor help him? Or will survival dictate that he become the hardened fighter that matches his new exterior? Find out when you follow the tale of *Quantum Mistake*!

PICK 2

LOUIE THE RUNE SOLDIER

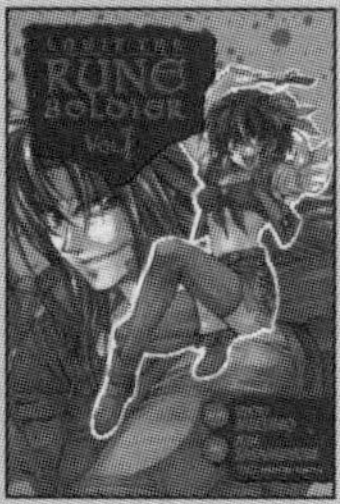

RUNE SOLDIER

Louie is a careless sorcerer who has tossed aside his studies for the all-important booze, babes and brawls, only to tarnish an important family legacy. But all that will change when this womanizing flunky is chosen to lead a group of gorgeous female adventurers on a journey of sorcery, swordplay and some good ol' fistfights. His new bevy of babes are none to excited about their chosen guide, but when faced with showdown after bone-breaking showdown, Louie could ultimately prove himself to be the right man for the job. From street fights to sorcery spells, Louie tries to get a handle on the whole hero thing, and busts a few heads along the way!

PICK 3

GADIROK

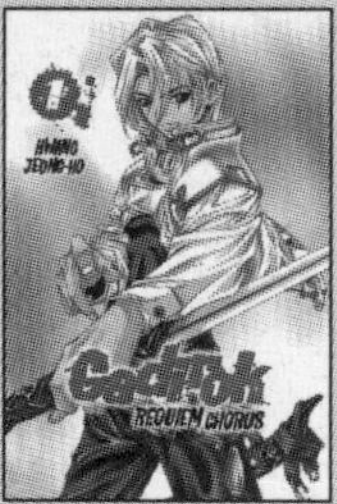

01
HWANG JEONG-HO
Gadirok
REQUIEM CHORUS

Violence and death plague the countryside, and the greed of one man has led to many fallen lands. General Hae-Mo-Soo has taken control of most territories in the region, and the only hope for a shackled population lies within the strength of a Prince, whose tumultuous past has left him clouded and confused. With the help of his dear friend Gat, Prince Chi-Woo must first escape the severe melancholy that plagues him, and then fight his way along the arduous path to reclaim his rightful place on the throne.

CHECK'EM OUT TODAY!

ADV Manga™

www.adv-manga.com

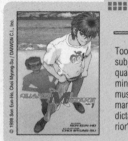

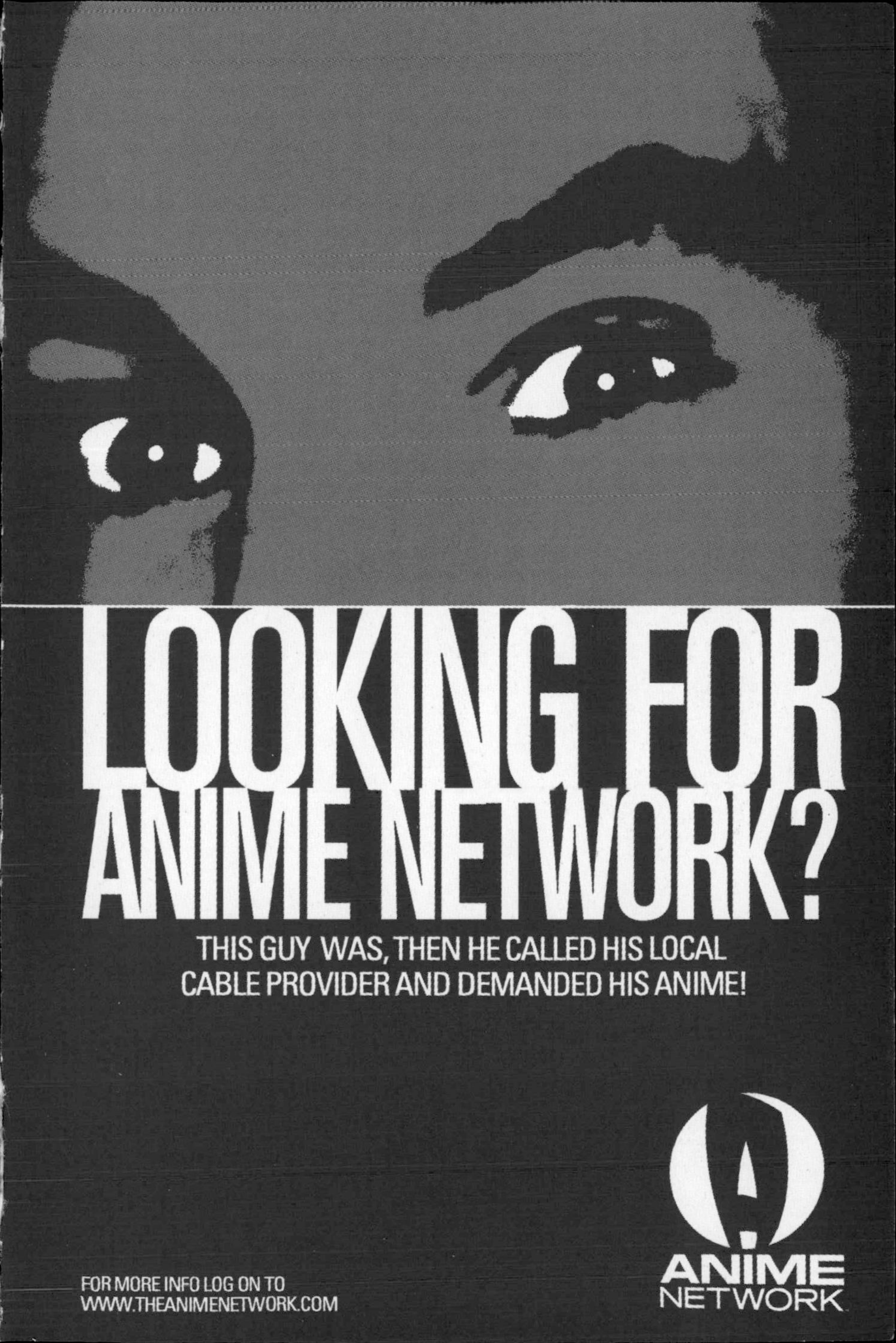
LOOKING FOR ANIME NETWORK?
THIS GUY WAS, THEN HE CALLED HIS LOCAL CABLE PROVIDER AND DEMANDED HIS ANIME!
FOR MORE INFO LOG ON TO WWW.THEANIMENETWORK.COM
ANIME NETWORK

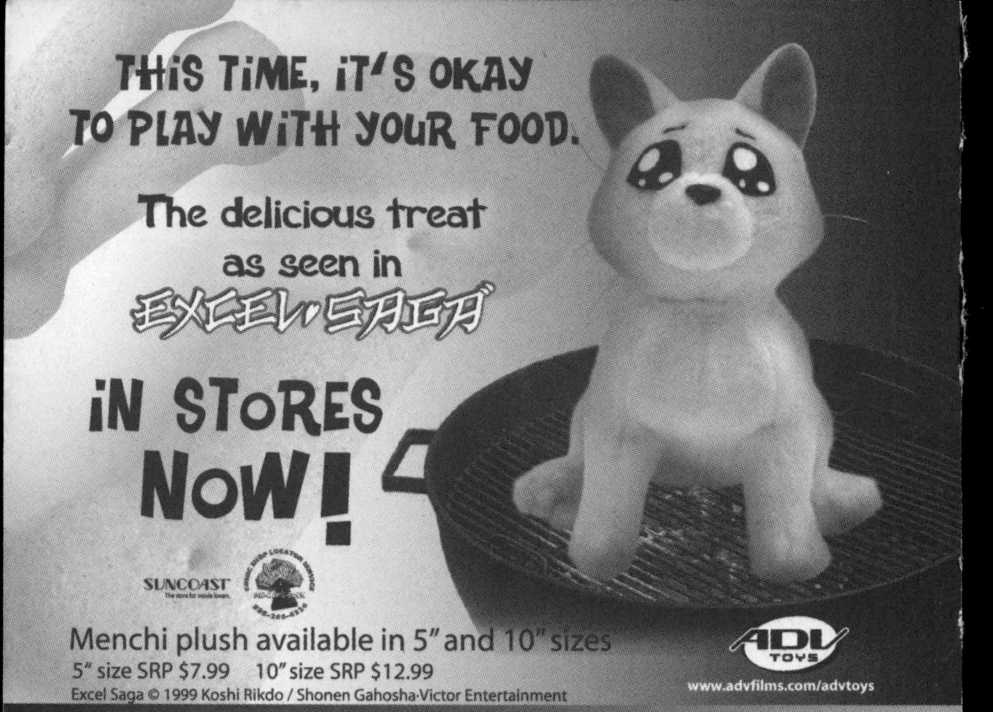
THIS TIME, IT'S OKAY TO PLAY WITH YOUR FOOD.
The delicious treat as seen in
EXCEL SAGA
IN STORES NOW!
SUNCOAST
Menchi plush available in 5" and 10" sizes
5" size SRP $7.99 10" size SRP $12.99
Excel Saga © 1999 Koshi Rikdo / Shonen Gahosha·Victor Entertainment
ADV TOYS
www.advfilms.com/advtoys

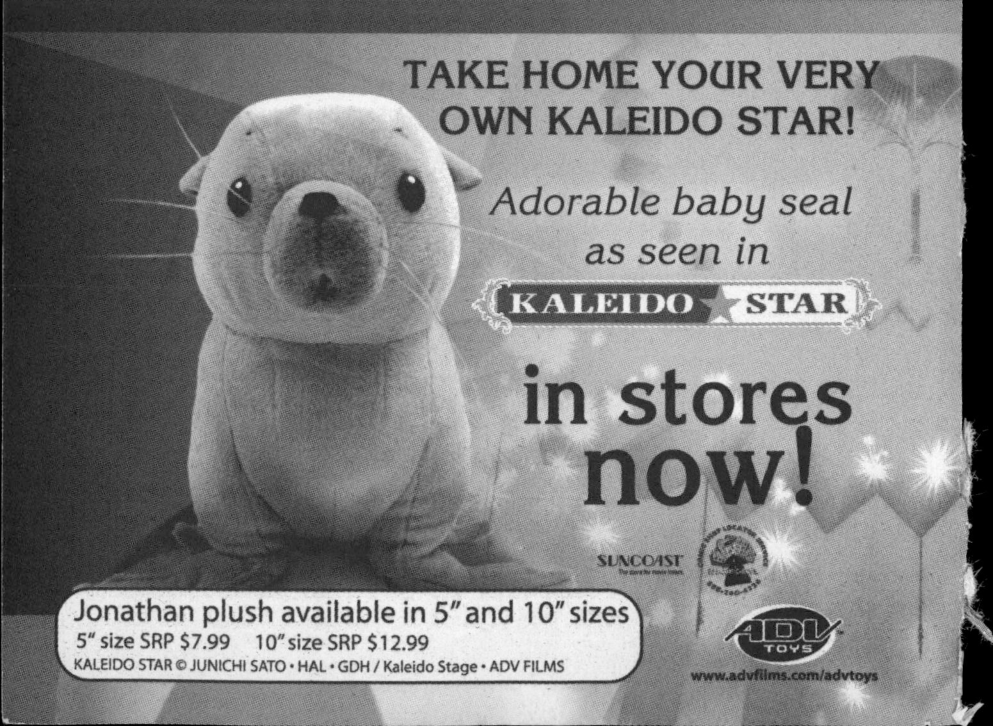
TAKE HOME YOUR VERY OWN KALEIDO STAR!
Adorable baby seal as seen in
KALEIDO STAR
in stores now!
SUNCOAST
Jonathan plush available in 5" and 10" sizes
5" size SRP $7.99 10" size SRP $12.99
KALEIDO STAR © JUNICHI SATO • HAL • GDH / Kaleido Stage • ADV FILMS
ADV TOYS
www.advfilms.com/advtoys

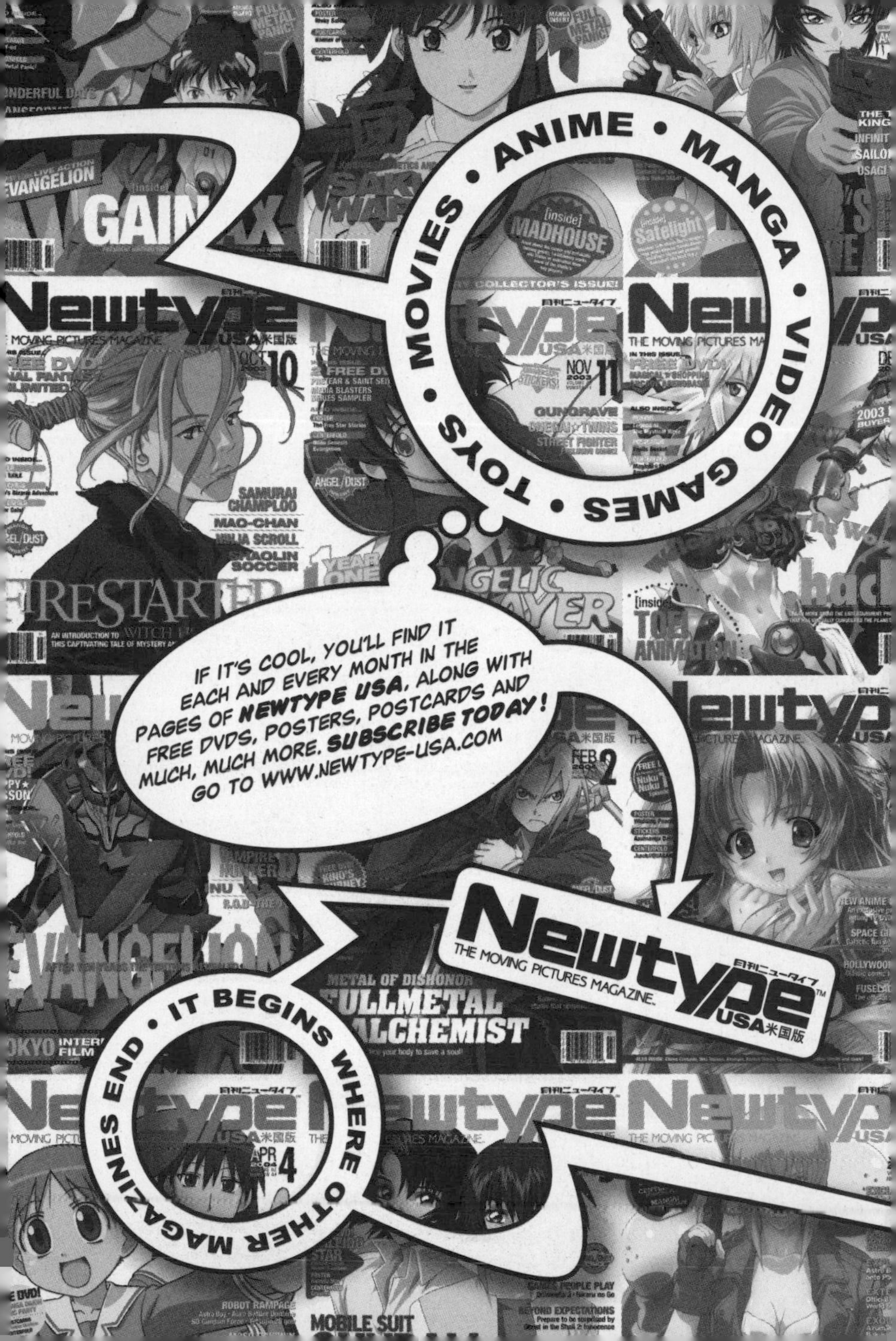
ANIME • MANGA • VIDEO GAMES • TOYS • MOVIES •
IF IT'S COOL, YOU'LL FIND IT EACH AND EVERY MONTH IN THE PAGES OF NEWTYPE USA, ALONG WITH FREE DVDS, POSTERS, POSTCARDS AND MUCH, MUCH MORE. SUBSCRIBE TODAY! GO TO WWW.NEWTYPE-USA.COM
月刊ニュータイプ
Newtype™
THE MOVING PICTURES MAGAZINE.
USA 米国版
IT BEGINS WHERE OTHER MAGAZINES END •

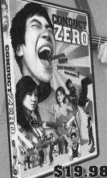

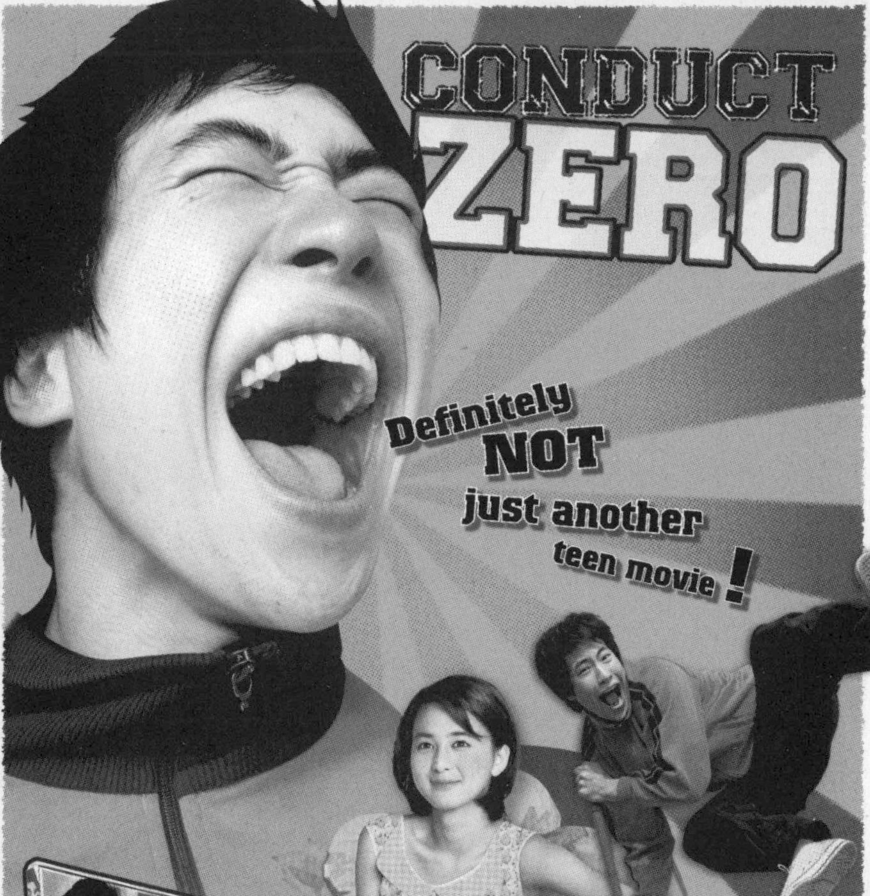
CONDUCT ZERO
Definitely NOT just another teen movie!
$19.98 SRP
Don't miss the hormonal hilarity!
DVD on sale August 2004.
ADV FILMS
www.advfilms.com